Poking God's Eye

A Theological & Historical View of Anti-Semitism
Based on the Blessings and Curses
of Genesis 12:3

Other Works by the Author

*Discovering the Mystery
of the Unity of God*

The Tri-Unity of God Is Jewish

*God in Eclipse:
God Has Not Always Been Silent*

*God in Eclipse
Russian Translation*

*Israel's Only Hope:
The New Covenant*

Poking God's Eye

A Theological & Historical View of Anti-Semitism

Based on the Blessings and Curses

of Genesis 12:3

JOHN B. METZGER

Poking God's Eye: A Theological & Historical View of Anti-Semitism Based on the Blessings and Curses of Genesis 12:3
John B. Metzger, author, *www.PromisesToIsrael.org*
Published by www.JHousePublishing.com under the Purple Raiment label, "Love Letters," Keller, TX
© 2018
First Printing, Second Edition
ISBN: 978-0-9912151-9-5

(First Edition: ISBN: 978-0-9912151-4-0, © 2016)

REL006210	RELIGION / Biblical Studies / Old Testament	
REL006090	RELIGION / Biblical Criticism & Interpretation / Old Testament	
PHI022000	PHILOSOPHY / Religious	

All rights reserved. No part of this publication may be reproduced or transmitted in any form or by any means without written permission of the publisher.

Scripture in this book has been quoted from the King James Version (Public Domain), with modernization of the language by the author.

Cover design: Jesse Gonzales
Editor: Joni Prinjinski
Paperback: Acid-free paper
Printed in the USA

Purple Raiment
Love Letters

What Others Are Saying About *Poking God's Eye*...

Anti-Semitism is at the root a theological problem that has perniciously manifested itself throughout Christian history – a fact of which most Christians are entirely ignorant. Perhaps for that reason, anti-Semitism has seen a resurgence in the modern Church, especially in a popular revival of a Reformed Theology that promotes anti-Zionism, Christian Palestinianism, and Replacement theology. For this reason, this book by John Metzger could not be more timely and necessary. It is a clarion call to become educated in the biblical cause and solution to anti-Semitism in all its forms and to honor the God of Israel. God has always kept His covenant with National Israel and measures the Gentile nations with respect to their attitude and actions to the Jewish People.

Randall Price, Ph.D.
Executive Director, Center for Judaic Studies, Liberty University

In this spirited book, John B. Metzger demonstrates that even though modern Israel has not come to belief in their promised Messiah, and certainly has not always responded appropriately toward Arabs and Christians, this does not negate the promises of God to His people, Israel. The Old Testament Scriptures, in unmistakable terms, indicate that God will turn His people back to Him at the end of days. Metzger carefully examines the language of promise and covenant as it relates to the teaching of Scripture. In so doing he demonstrates how the theological errors of Replacement, Amillennial, and Covenant Theologies have in part been responsible for the rise of modern anti-Semitic sentiments within much of Christendom.

Metzger challenges the modern claims of those who disavow Israel, God's promises, and the right to the Land that God gave them, as being built on inaccuracies. He then offers an abundance of biblical passages that support the claims that underlie the belief that God will continue to embrace the Jewish people for His name's sake. He will fulfill His commitment to Abraham, Isaac, and Jacob, and to His son David. This book needs to be read thoroughly if the reader is inclined to reject a future for national Israel.

H. Wayne House, M.A., Th.D., J.D.
Distinguished Research Professor of Theology, Law, and Culture
Faith Evangelical College and Seminary

Dedication

IN HONOR OF

Rev. Marlin Savidge

I would like to dedicate this book to my brother in Christ who is also my brother-in-law. Marlin Savidge has been an example of a man of integrity and godly character since the time of his salvation at a Gospel meeting led by Bob and Arden Lancaster at the Stonington Baptist Church in Sunbury, PA, in May 1935. He was 11 years old at the time. Today, Marlin is approaching his 93rd year of life, having been a believer in Christ for 82 of those 93 years as the first run of this book is being printed.

Coming to Faith turned Marlin's life around as a young ruffian to begin his journey of new life in Christ in every area of his life. His family all became believers, and they would travel around the Sunbury, PA, area holding evangelistic meetings with him and his four other brothers playing instruments and his two older sisters playing the piano and all singing together. His father would give the messages. Because of the testimony of the Savidge family, many people were blessed spiritually, and many came to Faith.

Marlin lived for Christ in his high school days and walked with the Lord while serving our nation in the Navy during World War II on an aircraft carrier. After the war, he married Grace Drumheller, who remained his companion for 65 years. Married after the war, he went to Wheaton College and later to Grace Theological Seminary. He founded a church in Indianapolis, IN, and pastored several others. The last one that I remember was Allentown Baptist Church in Camp Springs, MD. He also served as the Dean of Men and Dean of Students at Washington Bible College from 1971-1975, impacting the lives of many students. In all this, Marlin's goal in life was to be like Christ in all things, never compromising, but always serving his Lord and living a life of integrity and godly character.

During all those years, Marlin also became a great biblical counselor using Scripture as his sole source of authority in helping many people who came to him for spiritual help. Beyond all that, after retiring from the pastorate, he did not retire from working and continued to serve his Lord in his teaching ministry wherever he lived. In his 80s, he also served as an interim pastor in another church in Indiana.

Marlin has been a model of Christ and a person worth modeling one's life after. Though not perfect, as he would be quick to point out, it was his desire to walk with Christ. Today in his 90s, he is still teaching people and sharing the Gospel that so changed his life for eternity.

In writing this book, it is my desire that, as the hallmark of my life, I would model the same integrity and godly character as I speak the truth, which is not always very popular. Thank you, Marlin, for your godly example and godly life as a tribute to the finished work of Christ on the cross and His saving grace.

Acknowledgments

I would like to acknowledge the work of a couple that I have never had the opportunity of meeting: Brock and Bodie Thoene. Yet their writings have had a profound impact on my life. It was their writings, historical fiction on the Jewish people, that began to turn my head and then my heart to Jewish people. Theologically, I was already there; but at first my heart was not in tune. Their books opened up a door that I have walked through as God began to place within me a love for God's people Israel.

I had first read their *Zion Covenant Series* dealing with the plight of Jewish people in Europe in the 1930s, just before World War II. Then it was on to *Twilight of Courage*, which continued to deal with the plight of Jewish people between the Nazi attacks on Poland in September of 1939 and the attack on France in May of 1940. Finally, I read the *Zion Chronicles Series* dealing with the year before Israel's becoming a State in May of 1948. In this book, the Thoenes chronicled the struggles of the Jewish people, caught between the animosity of the British on one side and the hatred of the Palestinian Muslims on the other.

It has now been over 20 years since I began reading these three books. The LORD used the Thoenes with their hearts and love for Jewish people to change the course of my life and give me a love of Jewish people. It was through Brock and Bodie Thoene that God would lead me to Ariel Ministries and Dr. Arnold Fruchtenbaum, who would confirm and biblically establish me as a lover of Israel.

I personally recommend this series of books to be read by every Christian (www.ThoeneBooks.com), as Christians and church denominations today are losing their way and abandoning the people that God chose to be the instrument to reveal Himself to us and provide salvation through His Son Jesus Christ.

Preface

Of the many Bible verses that deal with the subject of God's heart for Israel, I will focus on two: Genesis 12:3 and Zechariah 2:8.

> Genesis 12:3: *I will bless them that bless you and curse him that curses you.*

> Zechariah 2:8: *...for he that touches you touches the apple (pupil) of His eye.*

This first verse is a promise to Gentiles, all the nations of the world, on what we can expect from God based on our treatment of the Jewish people and the nation of Israel. It is a verse to ponder long and hard. What kinds of blessings and curses has God reserved for us based on how we treat the Jewish people whom He loves?

The second verse is an ominous statement of warning to all who would stand actively or passively against Israel, whom He calls the "apple of His eye," expressing His devotion, affection, and protectiveness towards Israel and the Jewish people.

These two verses are connected, and their commonality is God's promised reaction to the ways that the world treats the Jewish people. The warnings and promises are directed to Gentiles, meaning individuals and nations in the world who are not Jewish. God's blessings and cursings for the Gentiles form a very serious subject that few consider or even desire to understand. As we shall see, the reason that this part of God's Word is often ignored is based on our human biases, which have been set by a long line of errors, human agendas, and human weaknesses.

Europe with its Christian heritage of persecuting the Jewish people is now running on nothing more than exhaust fumes of their once-upon-a-time faith. Europe in its past and present has been increasingly poking their collective finger into God's **eye**.

Unfortunately, even believing, true Christians are poking their collective finger in the very **eye** of their own Redeemer! Theologically, the majority of Christians in Europe as well as the U.S.A. hold a negative position about the very existence of the State of Israel. Yes, even America may be in the process of turning its back on Israel.

In Scripture, the **eye** is often used figuratively to indicate understanding or ignorance on the part of people. We use the following phrases that point out the concept of the figurative use of the word *eye* as it is used commonly by people today:

When we understand something we say "Oh, I **see** now."

When someone does not plan the future we say he was "**short-sighted**."

When we ignore something in front of us, we say, "He turned a blind **eye**."

When we disapprove of something we say, "We take a dim **view** of it."

When we take leadership over a project, we say that we took "**oversight**" of it.

When we speak of a hurricane meteorologically, we refer to the "**eye** of the storm."

When we thread the needle, we call it the "**eye** of the needle."

When we speak to someone face-to-face, we say we do so "**eyeball-to-eyeball**."

So we do have a common understanding of the use of the term **eye** even as God uses the term figuratively about His firstborn (Exodus 4:22), Israel. Yet we have Christians who are intent on taking the splinter out of their brother's **eye**, when they themselves have a wooden plank in their own **eye** (Matthew 7:3).

In this book we want to deal with anti-Semitism by two groups of people: on the one hand, unbelieving secularists and humanists; and on the other hand, religionists and believers who are members of the Church who want to refer to themselves erroneously as the "Israel of God." Jeremiah and Isaiah said of Israel that they have **eyes**, but they are blind; and with their mind, they do not discern (Jeremiah 5:21; Isaiah 44:8). Many Christians today have **eyes** but do not discern the heart of God to national, physical, and ethnic Israel. Instead, they lift themselves up unbiblically as the "Israel of

God." Nevertheless, God clearly reveals His heart for Israel throughout Scripture.

Studying God's Word concerning the **eye** should lead us to examine our own **eyes** to see if we are rightly dividing the Word of Truth. Are we accurate, or are believers parsing the Word of God to fit man's bias against God's clear statements? Discovering what the Bible has to say on the subject should lead us to be rightly related to the heart of God as He relates to His firstborn, Israel.

Unbelievers, atheists, agnostics and scoffers are antagonistic toward God (Isaiah 43:8; 42:20); they simply are living in complete darkness. With their **eyes** they practice idolatry, and today that is far more than bowing prostrate before an idol (Ezekiel 18:12); it is heart failure. Adultery is far more than a physical act; it is heart failure, first leading to viewing pornographic materials (Matthew 5:28) before the act is physically committed. Covetousness is a result of heart failure, and it is the name of the game in America. We want what everyone else has and, therefore, lack contentment (Genesis 13:10). *Their* **eyes** *are full of pride* (Isaiah 5:21).

Perhaps our common expression, "The **eyes** are the windows of the soul," is more accurate than we think, for we betray the sin of our hearts by our **eyes** as we look after sinful things. As a child's song has it, "Oh be careful little **eyes**, what you see." While unbelievers are blind toward God and use their **eyes** in sinful ways, believers look toward God as the source of their life (Psalm 25:15; 121:1; 141:8).

Indeed, it is God who brought us out of darkness and into His light so that we can see (Acts 26:18). The **eyes** show the attitude of the heart, whether or not it is inclined toward the Lord. When we understand that we have nothing to offer God (Romans 3:10-18), we can learn to be humble as God proves us and tests us in our walk with Him. God sees the attitude of our hearts in how we handle the written Word of God as He so clearly presented it from a Jewish perspective.

So as we study the Word of Life, let us understand the words of David as he clearly understood his position before His God: *Keep me as the apple of Your* **eye**, *hide me under the shadow of Your wings* (Psalm 17:8). Perhaps we may understand the prophetic snapshot of Israel's future story from Moses in Deuteronomy 32:10, which states:

> *He found him in a desert land, and in the waste howling wilderness; He lead him about, He instructed him, He kept him as the apple of His* **eye**.

Now Israel did not keep the Law of Moses and rebelled against God, going against Proverbs 7:2 which states, *Keep My commandments, and live; and My law as the apple of your* **eye**. The children of Israel were under the Mosaic Law; we as Christians are not. We are under the Law of Messiah. However, there is an application we can take from that passage that is applicable to all of us: For His Word is to be the apple of *our* **eyes**. That means applying God's Word to our hearts without reinterpreting it, applying it as God, Himself, gave it. **To Israel, the Law was the focus of showing their Faith and trust in their God, even as to the true believer in Christ (Messiah), the Law of Messiah is the focus of showing our Faith and trust in our Lord.**

Some believers will be humbled as they will bow before the LORD in that Day as they come to realize too late that Israel is Israel and the Church is the Church. The application is clear to us as it was given specifically to Israel by Isaiah:

> *The lofty looks of man shall be humbled, and the haughtiness of man shall be bowed down, and the LORD alone shall be exalted in that day* (Isaiah 2:11).

In returning to Zechariah 2:8, Israel, not the Church, is the apple of God's **eye**. By ignoring this distinction, the Church is exercising *vanity of vanities* in their attempt to usurp from Israel what only belongs to Israel by God's decree. When Zechariah states that to touch Israel is to touch the apple or pupil of God's **eye,** that is a negative experience. Humanly we will always protect our eyes from any foreign objects that get close and will bat them away.

Most translations of Zechariah 2:8 use the words as quoted above, but there is a dimension that is missed that three other translations capture:

> *The LORD of heavenly forces proclaims (after His glory sent Me) concerning the nations plundering you* [Israel]: **Those who strike you strike the pupil of My eye**. (Common English Bible)

> *For this is what the LORD of the Heavenly armies says: In pursuit of glory I was sent to the nations who plundered you, because* **whoever injures you injures the pupil of My eye**. (International Standard Version)

> *The LORD of Glory has sent Me against the nations that* **oppressed you,** for **he who harms you sticks his finger in Jehovah's eye**! (Living Bible)

These verses capture the intent of the LORD's statement for Israel and against anyone or any nation that curses Israel. They are attacking the very **eye** of God. They strike with intent to injure the **eye** of God – ISRAEL.

In the book of Joel where the LORD, through Joel, speaks of a future time in the life of physical, national, ethnic Israel when He judges the nations in the Valley of Jehoshaphat, he states the following:

> *I will also gather all nations, and will bring them down into the valley of Jehoshaphat, and will plead with them there for My people and for My heritage Israel, whom they have scattered among the nations, and parted My Land* (Joel 3:2).

Yes, physical, national, ethnic Israel is the Prophet's reference, not a spiritual Israel that some assume by inserting the Church unbiblically as many do. The timing of Joel 3:2 is the same as the words of Jesus in Matthew 25:31-46. We are in the Last Days now. We see that the Jewish people have returned to the Land of Israel in unbelief (Ezekiel 37). We know from Scripture that at the middle of the Tribulation period, Antichrist will set in motion Holocaust II, and the present government of Israel will collapse. Yet Israel's fall will be short lived, for the Antichrist and his armies will be destroyed by Yeshua Ha-Mashiach.[1] God clearly references in Joel 3:2 the enemies of Israel *parting of My Land*. There may be a Two-State plan by the world to make a Palestinian Nation, but God is going to judge the nations, including the United States, for their anti-Semitism. I invite you to read the following verses which summarize the content of this book:

> *⁶ For you* [the children of Israel] *are a holy people unto the LORD your God: the LORD your God has chosen you to be a special people unto Himself, above all people that are*

---

[1] *Yeshua* is the Hebrew name for Jesus.

upon the face of the earth. ⁷ The LORD did not set His love upon you, nor choose you, because you were more in number than any people; for you were the fewest of all people. ⁸ But because the LORD loved you, and because He would keep the oath which He had sworn unto your fathers [Abraham, Isaac and Jacob], *has the LORD brought you out with a mighty hand, and redeemed you out of the house of bondmen, from the hand of Pharaoh king of Egypt.* (Deuteronomy 7:6-8)

For he that touches you [the children of Israel] *touches the apple* [pupil] *of His eye.* (Zechariah 2:8b)

Behold, I have graven you [Israel] *upon the palms of My hands; your walls are continually before Me.* (Isaiah 49:16)

I challenge you to search through the Scriptures with me to see what God has said about Israel – His **eye** – and His future plans for the Land and His beloved people. He calls Israel His **eye,** whom He has not forgotten or cast aside. I pray that your discernment will be gloriously enlightened so that you might see with your own inner **eye** His heart of love for His people Israel.

Matthew 13:12:

For whosoever hath, to him shall be given, and he shall have more abundance: but whosoever hath not, from him shall be taken away even that he hath.

This verse speaks of the results of attaining discernment, which comes from reading the Word of God. Those who pay attention will gain understanding, but those who do not will lose any little discernment that they had. It pays to read God's Word and pursue discernment!

Mark 4:23-25:

²³ If any man has ears to hear, let him hear.

²⁴ And he said unto them, Take heed what you hear: with what measure you mete [measure out], *it shall be measured to you: and unto you that hear shall more be given.*

²⁵ For he that has, to him shall be given: and he that has not, from him shall be taken even that which he has.

Those who hear God's Word will gain in discernment. The more they hear, the more discernment they will receive. Interesting to note, *behold* means to "take in, pay attention to, and learn from," relating to the **eye**. It is more than physical sight or even insight; it is inspired sight. In the same way, having an **ear** to hear relates to taking something in and intelligently reflecting on and conforming to it. The biblical word for hear is closely related to the Hebrew word obey, and in both cases, the indication is that hearing and obeying result in a response of intelligent conformance in the listener or observer. This act of conforming to God's Word changes our perception and ability to respond to God in a positive way!

John B. Metzger

Table of Contents

Dedication vii
Acknowledgments ix
Preface xi

PART 1 How Theological Error Promotes Anti-Semitism

Introduction 1
Chapter 1   Why Is there a Need for this Book? 9
   Clarity Regarding Jesus' (Yeshua's) Ministry 10
   Recognition of God's Faithfulness towards His People Israel 11
Chapter 2   Understanding Replacement and Amillennial Theologies 21
   The First Century 22
   The Second Century 24
      Justin Martyr (100-165 A.D.) 26
      Melito of Sardis (120-185 A.D.) 26
      Ignatius, the Bishop of Antioch of Syria (Died in Rome around 110 A.D.) 27
      The Epistle of Barnabas 27
      Irenaeus, Bishop of Lyon (Lugdunum in Gaul, or Lyon, France) after 177 A.D. 27
      Hippolytus of Rome (170-235 A.D.) 27
   The Third Century 28
      Tertullian (155-240 A.D.) 29
      Origen (185-254 A.D.) 29
      Diannisian 30
      Bishop Thasciua Caecilius Cyprianus of North Africa (200-258 A.D.) 31

    Hippolytus (170-235 A.D.) 31
    A Comparison of the Literal and Allegorical Methods................... 32
  The Fourth Century 34
    Constantine, Emperor of Rome (272-337 A.D.).............................. 35
    Jerome (345-420 A.D.) 35
    Emperor Theodosius (reigned from 379-395 A.D.)......................... 35
    Hilary of Potieres (Pictavium, Gaul) (310-367 A.D.)...................... 35
    Ambrose Bishop of Milan (340-397 A.D.) 36
    Gregory of Nyssa (331-396 A.D.) 36
    John Chrysostom (347-407 A.D.) 36
    Augustine the Bishop of Hippo (354-430 A.D.) in North Africa 39
  The Death of the Jewish Church 42
    Council of Caesarea: 196 A.D. 42
    Council of Nicaea: 325 A.D.. 43
    Council of Antioch: 341 A.D. 43
    The Third and Fourth Centuries.. 43
  The On-Going Effects of Replacement Theology................................ 43
  Suggested Readings on History of Church Anti-Semitism 47

Chapter 3 Errors of Covenant Theology 49
  Is the Background of God's Word Greek or Jewish?.......................... 49
  What Are the Disconnects of Covenant and Replacement
    Theology? 50
    Covenant Theology, a Newcomer.. 51
  How Does Dispensational Theology Differ from Covenant
    Theology?... 55
  What Differences Does It Make – God's Covenants or Man's
    Ideas about Grace? 58

Chapter 4 What Is Dispensationalism? 71
  A History of Dispensationalism 71
  The Jewish Background of the Scriptures.. 75
  The Facets of Dispensations 76
  Progressive Dispensationalism... 80
  Summary of Dispensationalism 86

Chapter 5 Israel: Violent Perpetrator or Defender of Their Country?........89
   Eighteen Facts about Israel..91
   Is Israel the Problem? 98
Chapter 6 The Character of God – His Integrity 107
   Blessings and Cursings...110
   The Covenants 111
      Land Covenant 115
      Davidic Covenant 116
      New Covenant 116
Chapter 7 Who Has Ownership of the Land?.....................................117
   The Land Covenant 117
      Genesis 12:1-3, 7...117
      Genesis 13:14-17...118
      More Confirmations: Genesis 17, Genesis 22:15-18, and
        Genesis 26:3-4 118
      Reconfirmation of the Land Covenant to Abraham and His
        Descendants 118
      David L. Cooper's Principle of Applying Literal
        Interpretation to the Bible 119
      The Land Covenant in Leviticus and Deuteronomy......................120
   Eight Points Moses Makes About Israel (Deuteronomy 30:1-10)....125
   Promises for Israel's Restoration..127
   God's Judgment vs. His Unconditional Covenant with Israel..........129
   The Value of Language 131
      Ezekiel and the Land Covenant...132
      The Land Covenant in Joel..135
      The Land Covenant in Other Prophetic Passages........................136

PART 2 The Abrahamic Covenant: How We Bless or Curse God

Chapter 8 The Residual Effects of the Blessings and Curses of the
    Abrahamic Covenant 141
   Introduction 141

    Blessings and Curses of God (Genesis 12:1-3) 141
    Regarding Gentiles and the Abrahamic Covenant 143
    The Fourth "I Will" of God Regarding Abraham 146
    How We Bless or Curse God 148

Chapter 9   The Outworking of the Abrahamic Covenant Individually 151
    King of Egypt – Cursing 151
    Abimelech – Cursing, Part 1 152
    Abimelech – Cursing, Part 2 153
    Laban – Blessing/Cursing 153
    Joseph – Blessing 154
    Hebrew Midwives – Blessing 155
    Rahab – Blessing 155
    Balaam – Cursing 156
    Jezebel – Cursing 157
    Woman of Zarephath – Blessing 159
    Athaliah – Cursing 160
    Naaman – Blessing 161
    Haman – Cursing 162
    Presidents Under Darius 163
    Summary Points 164

Chapter 10   The Outworking of the Abrahamic Covenant Nationally 167
    Egypt – Cursing 167
    Amalekites – Cursing 169
    Midian – Cursing 170
    Kenites/Rechabites – Cursing/Blessing 171
    Edom – Cursing 173
    Moab – Cursing 176
    Ammon – Cursing 178
    Damascus – Cursing 180
    Philistines – Cursing 181
    Tyre – Cursing 184
    Sidon – Cursing 185
    Assyria – Cursing 186
    Babylon – Cursing 189

Chapter 11 The Outworking of the Abrahamic Covenant During the Inter-Testament Period 197
    King Seleucus IV of Syria – Cursing 197
    Summary Points 199

Chapter 12 The Outworking of the Abrahamic Covenant in the New Testament 201
    Centurion of Capernaum – Blessing 201
    Syro-Phoenician Woman – Blessing 202
    Centurion Cornelius – Blessing 203
    Alexander the Coppersmith – Cursing 203
    Summary Points 204

Chapter 13 The Outworking of the Abrahamic Covenant in Post-Biblical History 205
    The Church of Rome – Cursing 205
    The Church through History 211
    Europe – Cursings and a Blessing 213
        Spain – Cursing 214
        England – Blessing/Cursing 216
        Germany – Cursing 218
        France – Cursing 220
        Portugal – Cursing 221
        Summary of European Nations 222
    Russia – Cursing 222
    Muslim States – Cursing 224
    Summary Points 226

Chapter 14 The Outworking of the Abrahamic Covenant in Prophecy 229
    United States of America – Blessings and ??? 229
    Islam and Russia – Cursing 236
    The Apostate Church – Cursing 238
    Armageddon – Cursing 239
    Egypt – Cursing 240
    Summary Points of Current Nations 241

Chapter 15 Summary of Curses 243

Chapter 16   The Outworking of the Abrahamic Covenant in Missions.. 251

    Romans 1:16 253
    Three Examples of the "Great Omission"....................................... 258
    God's Foundation – His Truth Stands.. 273
        God's Word Is Truth!... 274
        How Does Error Start?... 274
        Three Waves of Anti-Semitic Theology 274
        Dispensational Theology: Going Back to God's Word 275
        The Accuracy, Certainty, and Continuity of God's Blessings and Cursings 276
        Are We Condemned for Past Wrongs? 277
    Conclusion 278

Appendix One   Palestinian Liberation Theology (PLT) 281

Appendix Two   Biblical References to the Abrahamic Covenant in Scripture 295

    The Old Testament (116) 295
    The New Testament (73).. 308

Appendix Three   References to the Land of Israel Belonging to God and Israel 315

    The Torah – The Law – The Books of Moses (106)....................... 316
    The Prophets (125).. 328
    The Writings – (21)... 340

Appendix Four A Failure of the Reformation....................................... 343

    Scriptural Interpretation in the Early Church 343
    The Triumph of Spiritualization.. 344
    The Return to Literal Interpretation 347
    Consistent Literal Interpretation 351

Appendix Five   Answer Key to Quiz on Pages 4-6 353

List of Tables and Figures

Figure 1. Comparison of Literal vs. Allegorical Interpretation (Genesis 25:23) 32

Figure 2. The Relationship of the Dispensations & Covenants of the Bible 56

Table 1. Replacement Theology's Bias in Bible Headings 68

Table 2. God's Eight Covenants 113

Table 3. Interrelationship of Abrahamic Covenant with Land, Davidic, and New Covenants..115

Table 4. Ezekiel 16: Israel's Relationship to God Described.....................129

Table 5. Summary of God's National Blessings and Cursings 194

PART 1
How Theological Error Promotes Anti-Semitism

Introduction

Today the world is coming apart at the seams, and Israel is hanging in the balance because the nations are poking God's **eye**! Israel remains a nation only by *His outstretched Arm, The Arm of the LORD*. The Arm of the LORD is the authority and power behind the present State of Israel, and Israel at this point in their history does not recognize it. It will be *The Arm of the LORD* (Isaiah 53:1) that will bring salvation (Isaiah 52:10) and regeneration (Jeremiah 31:31) to Israel (Isaiah 59:16), for Israel cannot heal itself (Isaiah 59:12-13; Deuteronomy 30:6). The Prophet Hosea records in his book in 6:1-2 the healing that the LORD will give them;

> *He hath torn* [us – Jewish people], *and He will heal us, He hath smitten* [us] *and He will bind us up. After two days will He revive us; in the third day He will raise us up, and we shall live in His sight.*

Only the LORD can heal and deliver Israel; there is no religion, theology, individual, philosophy, political party, or government that can heal Israel or this broken planet for that matter. Only God can do that!

What is the key to the healing and salvation of Israel and the world? Through whom will that salvation be accomplished? What is the instrument of that healing? The answer begins to unfold in Genesis 3:15,[2] and continues in 12:3 with the Abrahamic Covenant where God promised Abraham that anyone who blesses Abraham or his descendants, the Jewish people, He will bless. At the same time, God will curse anyone who curses or even dares to treat Abraham or his descendants lightly. God also promises that *all the families of the earth will be blessed* through Abraham. That is the theme and focus of this, His book, the Bible.

We have the tendency as fallen, sinful human beings to view "old" things as becoming less significant over time. Well, it has been 4,000 years since the LORD spoke those words to Abraham in Genesis 12:1-3. Have they

---

[2] Genesis 3:15 is the beginning of the promises of salvation being provided to humanity. God will focus in on one man, one family, one son, and one people – called Israel – as progressive revelation is opened to the reader of Scripture.

become unimportant or obsolete in the meantime? It is not so surprising that many Gentiles (non-Jewish people) in general have lost sight of what God's Word, the Bible, says about Israel. Their eyes have been clouded over. More surprising is that many believers in Christ specifically have lost sight of God's promises to Israel, or have outright rejected them, both in their hearts and minds. Yes, the world and even most Christians view the Abrahamic Covenant as unimportant and irrelevant. They are unaware of the strength and importance of God's yet unfulfilled promises to Abraham, which are beginning to play out before our **eyes**. We can see and understand if we are willing to look to His Word for enlightenment.

How did God's promises to Israel become sidelined in current times among God's beloved, believing Church? The story has many dark and disappointing chapters that reflect poorly on the hearts of "Christians" throughout the ages, such as the Crusades of the Middle Ages, the vicious mob-led pogroms, and the Holocaust. In a more subtle way, theological error has continued to creep into the Church body. Subtle, false teachings have created several popular brands of theology that twist the Scriptures to meet faulty human expectations. Among these brands are Replacement, Amillennial, and Covenant Theologies, and each is led by strong personalities who believe God has given up on the Jewish people.

Remember as it relates to the Church, there are two biblical perspectives. First, a large percentage of the Church population has been Christianized but are not true believers. Second, there are true believers that make up a much smaller element of the visible Church. One may conclude that those most likely to hold a literal interpretation of the Bible, meaning conservative and fundamental believers in the Church, would uniformly "get" the meaning of God's promises and prophecies regarding Israel; but, sadly, that has largely not been the case.

The focus of this book will be on one aspect of God's Word: the Abrahamic Covenant. From God's perspective, the theme of the Bible is His love for His chosen people, Israel. He chose them to bear a message of salvation using a long line of Jewish poets, prophets, and writers, from Genesis to Revelation. He carefully reveals His redemption theme for the Jewish people. As part of the mystery of His salvation plan, He reveals that Gentiles (those other than Jewish people), also can receive the blessing of salvation: forgiveness of sins, regeneration, and indwelling of the Holy Spirit. However, the Jewish writers of both Testaments all knew and looked forward to God's salvation of the Jewish people in the End Times, along with many Gentiles.

To get started, let's take a look again at God's covenant as He declared it in Genesis 12:1-3. Specifically, notice the four "I will's" of God:

> *¹ Now the LORD had said unto Abram, get you out of your country, and from your kindred, and from your father's house, unto a land that* **I will** *show you. ² And* **I will** *make of you a great nation, and* **I will** *bless you, and make your name great; and you shall be a blessing: ³ And* **I will** *bless them that bless you, and curse him that curses you: and in you shall all families of the earth be blessed.*

What makes this promise or covenant to Abraham so significant is God's use of the unconditional words, *I will*. Behind the scenes, God controls the earth, and He will bring all things to His conclusion. He alone will be glorified, and that statement summarizes our belief in the complete sovereignty of God in all areas. The underlying theme in this book is to begin to understand the nature, essence, and character of God and His sovereignty over all things. We may have our own ideas about who He is and what His heart is like, but God has taken the time to reveal these things in His own Word if we have an ear to hear and an eye to see.

Before we deal with the blessings and curses of the Abrahamic Covenant, we must understand another promise of God that is interwoven within the Abrahamic Covenant; and that is God's promise to Israel of the Land. Because His Word is unbreakable, we must understand how closely related the Land is to the Jewish people. This is especially important because the blessings and curses of Genesis 12:3 apply to the Gentiles as to how we treat Israel in the Land or outside of the Land. This covenant has never been canceled or superseded. I cannot emphasize this enough, because anti-Semitism is emerging once again from the apostate church and humanist secularists, and now Evangelical Christians are losing sight of God's hand and heart.

All nations, religions, and unbiblical theological systems are in danger of cursing Israel to their own demise as they move away from God's message that was once held strongly among Christian believers a hundred years ago. God has judged, and is judging, and will judge all peoples and nations on the basis of how they have dealt with Israel.

Let us trace through the Scriptures the consequences that individuals and nations have received in fulfillment of God's promise to bless those who have blessed Abraham and the Jewish people and to curse those who have cursed Abraham and the Jewish people. The point to be made, and that God clearly makes, is that the blessing and curses of the Abrahamic Covenant apply to Gentile (non-Jewish) individuals and nations. It is just as active today, and will continue in the future, as on the day that it was given to Abraham 4,000 years ago.

I do not know how to be subtle or smooth; I only know how to state clearly the issue at hand, and here it is. The question that this book wants you to answer after a careful study of the biblical and historical evidence is this: Are you blessing Israel and the Jewish people, or are you cursing Israel and the Jewish people?

Please grasp the centrality of the Scriptures. The author is God, and His focus is on two primary things: Israel and Israel's Messiah. Take a short quiz to see if you understand the basic flow of Scripture as God gave it. Score five points for each correct answer. (The Answer Key is at the back on the book in Appendix Five.)

1. T - F   All of the writers of the Old and New Testaments were Jewish.

2. What is the context of the culture and customs of the Old Testament and most of the New Testament? _____

3. What is the main original language of the Old Testament? _____

4. What ethnic frame of reference did God use as He wrote the Scriptures through His 40 sub-authors? _____

5. What was Jesus' heritage? Circle the correct answer:

   a. Caucasian   b. Arab   c. Hebrew

6. To what people group did the Father send His Son Jesus for His earthly ministry? _____

7. During what religious holiday was Jesus crucified? _____

8. On what religious holiday did Jesus raise from the dead?
   _____

9. On what religious holiday did the Holy Spirit come and indwell believers? _____

10. To what ethnic people does the bulk of unfulfilled Scripture in the Old and New Testaments pertain?
    _____

11. Did God make covenants with the Church or Israel? (Circle correct answer.)

12. The theme in Scripture of the Promised Seed is given to what ethnic people? _____

13. What is the theme of the unfulfilled Scriptures?

    ___ a. How the Church will replace Jewish people.

    ___ b. God's plan to save and restore the Jewish people.

    ___ c. How man will turn the world into a Utopian state.

    ___ d. The glorious future of human theology.

14. Whom does the final chapter of history revolve around?
    _____

15. What is the common characteristic or trait of each of the saints listed in Hebrews 11? _____

16. What is the meaning of "one new man" in Ephesians 2:14-15? (Check one)

    ___ a. An individual who comes to Faith in Jesus, whether male or female

    ___ b. Adam

    ___ c. Jesus

    ___ d. The Body of Christ made up of both Jews and Gentiles

17. What are the differences between conditional and unconditional love? Check all that apply.

___ a. No difference; they are the same thing.

___ b. Unconditional love is given without regard to whether or not it is deserved.

___ c. Conditional love can be withdrawn if the loved one is found to be deficient.

___ d. Conditional love is based on a commitment that can change with circumstances.

___ e. Unconditional love is not canceled out by rejection or changing circumstances.

18. What is meant by an unconditional promise? Check all that apply.

___ a. No matter what happens, the promise will not be broken.

___ b. The promise will only be fulfilled if the other party first upholds certain conditions or requirements.

___ c. No matter what happens, the promise will eventually be fulfilled.

___ d. The promise can be legally broken if two witnesses confirm that the recipient is not worthy.

19. By what standard can men be saved in both Testaments? _____

20. If God could cancel His unconditional, future salvation plan for the Jews, might He also cancel His unconditional offer of salvation to those in the Church? _____

Again, the answer key is in Appendix Five on page 353. Score yourself to see if you have an aptitude or hunger to learn more about God's promises to the Jewish people and be part of His outreach of grace and mercy to them.

The proceeding questions are designed to see if you understand the heart of God for His people Israel. When God shows us His heart and shows us how to abide and connect with His heart, He has given us a clear choice. Are we working with God or against Him? If you bless Israel, you are actively blessing your Lord, the author of the Abrahamic Covenant, your Savior, who was born a Jew and walked the Land of Israel as a Jew. Do you deem Israel as the Covenant People of God to be blessed, or do you esteem Israel lightly? God has given us a clear choice.

Anyone who esteems Israel lightly or outright curses the Jewish people is also cursing the God of Israel who provided the salvation of the world based on the **Blood** of the New Covenant, the **Blood** of Messiah on the cross. Regarding those who are poking God in His **eye**, God does take notice and He does remember!

We can apply insight from God's Word as we look at the turmoil in the Middle East today. The Two-State plan that our government is pushing upon Israel is cursing God. The propaganda machine of Palestinian Christians and radical Islam does not recognize the right of Israel to exist. Both preach hatred towards the Jewish people and even reach far beyond their regional conflict to actively turn the hearts of believers away from Israel. Where do you stand? Are you blessing God or cursing God?

So many today have fallen into the cursed category through their ignorance of the Word of God, unbelief in the God of Israel, or because of a long history of anti-Semitic sentiments, whether they be Christian, Palestinian Christian, Muslim, religionist, humanist, or secularist. You may say, "Isn't that an extreme, radical statement?" Open your Bibles with me and look for yourself as we move though the Scriptures and investigate what God in His Word has to say about these issues.

Chapter 1
Why Is there a Need for this Book?

Increasingly, I see danger signs looming against the United States of America as a nation, as individuals or groups of people, whether they are Christians or not, attack and slander Israel. Israel currently is the target of hate speech. In the past it has been discriminated against in unimaginable ways: They have been kicked out of countries, walled up in ghettos, accused of unspeakable crimes that they never committed, been murdered and ravaged and even dehumanized for over 1,800 years of Replacement Theology.

Now, as a nation since 1948, Israel has finally gained the ability to defend herself. Yet the world makes Israel out to be oppressive because the world is ignorant of history, calling Israel an Apartheid state. The world has assembled themselves, encouraging individuals, businesses, and countries to boycott and disinvest in Israel's economy and actively support continued and expanded sanctions against Israel. This policy of **b**oycott, **d**ivestment and **s**anctions against Israel is known as BDS. All of this is instigated by a world that hates the Jewish people (Israel).

These anti-Jewish people are illiterate in the Scriptures or reinterpret the Scriptures to suit their own personal or theological biases. The world operates on a double, inconsistent standard of hatred of Israel, a hatred which comes from a satanic root. Satan opposes the chosen of God because they have been called to reveal His person and work of redemption to us.

Ultimately, Satan will be humiliated (1 Corinthians 6:3) and defeated (Revelation 20:10) by the Almighty hand of God![3] Evil towards Israel and the Jewish people comes from Lucifer, Satan, the Dragon as he continues to use unsuspecting naïve peoples and nations as his pawns to rid the world of Jewish people. As I said in the introduction of this book, Jewish people and Israel are only in existence today because of the *outstretched Arm of the*

---

[3] Arnold Fruchtenbaum, *The Six Abodes of Satan*: Manuscript #77 (San Antonio, TX: Ariel Ministries Press, 2005), 34.

LORD. He is their preserver, and He will fulfill all His covenants and promises to the Jewish people.

I will say that Israel is not always innocent in how they handle situations with Palestinian Muslims and Christians. Israel is currently an unregenerate people who do not walk in the ways of their God, the God of Israel. They have continually violated God's law given to them, and they have completely ignored their only hope of survival in this world: the New Covenant given by Moses, Jeremiah, and Ezekiel, not to exclude statements by Joel and Isaiah.

Clarity Regarding Jesus' (Yeshua's) Ministry

Because of a question by a rabbi friend, I do need to explain what the term *New Covenant* directly applies to. The New Covenant is a promise and not a book. It was first clearly stated in Jeremiah 31:31-34 and applies to God's people Israel. It is an unconditional covenant given directly to the Jewish people to provide for their regeneration and redemption. The New Testament shows the ministry of Yeshua (Jesus), who initiated the New Covenant by offering Himself as the sacrificial Lamb of God who satisfied the Law of Moses. His ministry was to the Jewish people. While many individuals believed and followed Him, there is yet to come a national day of repentance followed by a glorious restoration of the Jewish people, according to the New Covenant promises in the Tanakh (Jewish Scriptures).[4]

Most believers mistakenly apply the New Covenant to the Gentile Church, but it is and was a covenant with the Jewish people. The New Covenant is expressed and "unpacked" in the New Testament. As a result of the failure of the Jewish leaders to recognize the significance of Yeshua's sacrifice, God opened salvation to anyone through Faith, as the familiar verse, John 3:16 quotes Jesus (Yeshua), saying: *...whosoever believes in Him shall not perish but have everlasting life.* He later affirmed that in the Great Commission, in which He directed His followers to reach out to the Jewish people and beyond, to all the Gentile nations as well.

Ironically, at the beginning, Yeshua's Jewish followers were not convinced that Gentiles could be saved. Today, Gentile believers have

---

[4] Please see my book, *Israel's Only Hope: The New Covenant,* for a more complete look at what the Jewish Scriptures say about Jewish people and the New Covenant (published in Keller, TX, by JHousePublishing, Purple Raiment imprint, 2015).

forgotten that Yeshua's ministry focused on God's people Israel, the New Testament was written largely by and for Jewish believers, and Yeshua called His sacrifice the New Covenant in His blood for the remission of sin, referring back to the teachings of the Tanakh.

There is still only one way of salvation for all, and that is through Faith in Jesus (Yeshua); however, the concept is not new; it is part of God's outworking of His New Covenant promise to Israel. As we shall see, salvation to the Gentiles is part of God's overflow of spiritual blessings to His Jewish people. God fulfilled His very first promise to Abraham in Genesis 12:3 to bless all the families of the earth because of Abraham's Faith.

Recognition of God's Faithfulness towards His People Israel

Many Christians down through the ages have claimed that God is done with the Jews because of their disobedience. Nevertheless, Israel being at odds with God's perfect will does not minimize the unconditional, unilateral Abrahamic Covenant. God's promise to bless people who bless Israel and curse people who curse Israel still stands.

If you are a biblical student, you should realize from Scriptures that God judged many nations in biblical history because of their anti-Semitic attitudes and actions against Israel. He judged those who harmed Israel even as Israel was walking in rebellion against their God, even when they were violating the Law of Moses in every possible way and committing spiritual adultery against the LORD with idols as Hosea and other Prophets record.

Christian and Muslim Palestinians have been motivated today because of their active hatred and animosity against the Jewish people – Israel – to oppose the very existence of Israel. Israel has often reacted to their enemies as mere men, no different than other people who have reacted poorly at times of severe national stress when they have been tormented or attacked.

The year 2019 marks 100 years of terrorism that Israel has had to deal with. I would like to see how Americans would respond if we had to tolerate 100 years of terrorists murdering American citizens because of whom we are. In the last century, Israel has been repeatedly attacked militarily by Islamic nations and by radical Islamic terrorists. Now the ongoing propaganda war by Muslims and Palestinian Christians against Israel has begun taking hold among Evangelical Christians in America.

In the past, Evangelical Christians had been completely unified in their support for Israel; now Evangelical Christians attack Israel, instigated by Christian Palestinian Liberation Theology (PLT)[5] proponents who have an incorrect biblical understanding of God's Word and the place of Israel in the plan and purpose of God. Palestinian Christians have a theological bias called Replacement Theology, which goes back to the second century A.D. with the development of anti-Semitic teachings and rhetoric in the Church.

Replacement Theology from the early Church Fathers polluted the biblical understanding of God's purpose and plan for Israel over 18 centuries ago, and these false and misleading teachings remain an active ingredient in their "Kool-Aid"[6] mixture. Bible ignorance and the bias of self-deception turn those who embrace Replacement Theology against the State of Israel and Jewish people in general.

This book will be a balanced biblical document against the unbiblical behavior of deceived or rebellious Christians and Gentiles who, in general, over the centuries, have cursed and are cursing the people that God said are to be blessed.

Some of you may be saying that I have blind hatred toward the Palestinians and Muslims by what I have already written. My answer is a resounding NO! Please do not misinterpret biblical honesty as hatred. God instructs all believers in Jesus Christ to love all people, and I do! Being biblically honest with the text of Scripture is my goal.

Remember the Prophets of old; they were often brutally honest with Israel, BECAUSE the LORD God of Israel loved Israel and wanted His people to repent and turn back to Him. My prayer is that you will look at Israel as God looks at Israel and respond to them in truth and love with unquestioned love and support. Again that does not mean turning a blind eye to things that they do wrong.

---

[5] See Appendix One of this book, "Palestinian Liberation Theology (PLT)."
[6] The use of the figure of speech, *Kool-Aid,* is a reference to an American Christian cult headquartered in South America where error cost 900 people their lives. The cult leader, Jim Jones, convinced his followers to commit suicide by drinking the normally harmless beverage which had been laced with cyanide. "Drinking the Kool-Aid" now means to be deceived or forced into accepting destructive directions because of a general loss of common sense and discernment.

I have spoken about the Abrahamic Covenant of Genesis 12:1-3 and I need to provide briefly some details of what these three verses teach, so let us look at the passage again before we study it:

> *¹ Now the LORD had said unto Abram, Get you out of your country, and from your kindred, and from your father's house, unto a land that* **I will** *show you: ² And* **I will** *make of you a great nation, and* **I will** *bless you, and make your name great; and you shall be a blessing: ³ And* **I will** *bless them that bless you, and curse him that curses you: and in you shall all families of the earth be blessed.*

In these three verses we see four promises of God, four things He **will** do.

The first *I will* is that God will make of Abram a great nation, which involves descendants: seed. In Genesis 10, God references 70 nations that will come from the descendants of Shem, Ham, and Japheth. Now it will be 71 nations, to include this nation, later called Israel, that God raised up through Abraham. His desire was to use the Jewish people as His instrument to reveal Himself to the other 70 nations. So this nation from Abraham has a specific purpose which is spelled out further as you move through Scripture. This covenant with Abraham will make Israel indestructible; Israel cannot be destroyed (Jeremiah 31:35-37).

The second *I will* is God's promise to bless Abraham. The overwhelming usage of this Hebrew word simply means to bless, blessed, blesses.[7] This promise of God will include both material and spiritual blessings. This we will also see is passed on to the descendants of Abraham; God will uniquely bless Israel not because they are better or privileged, but simply because they were the chosen instrument for God to reveal Himself to the world. Israel, in contrast to any other ethnic people in the world, has been and is today to be blessed.

The third *I will* of God's promise is multifaceted. In this verse there are three aspects that need to be understood by us Gentiles because they relate directly to us and our treatment of Jewish people throughout history. Look at the three facets of this *I will* of God:

- *I will* bless them that bless you – Positive.

---

[7] Taken from the Hebrew word bless as charted out in the *Libronix* (Logos Software) word graph.

- *I will* curse him that curses you – Negative. The cursing is a continued thought from the blessing mentioned just before it.
- In you *shall all the families of the earth be blessed* – Positive.

Please notice that these three promises, two positive and one negative, relate to Gentiles and their treatment of Abraham, Isaac and Jacob and all their descendants. **First promise:** If you bless Israel, God will in turn bless you! However, if you choose to curse Israel, then the **second promise** will apply: God will curse you! **Promise three:** Whether others bless or curse Israel, ultimately all the families of the earth will be blessed in Messiah through the redemption provided in Him at the cross of Calvary.

The next statement is critical to understand with its implications for us Gentiles. An unconditional (covenant) pledge by God does not fade over the years, nor should it be neglected! However, in Christianity it has gotten old and has been greatly neglected by theologians and held in ignorance by Christians in general. As to the nations of the earth, it is ignored because they do not know what the Bible teaches concerning Israel, the Jewish people. I will throughout this book be dealing with the response of Gentiles to these *I will*'s of God in this verse as it relates to the Gentile blessings they have received because they blessed Israel or the curses they have received by cursing Israel.

In this paragraph I want to deal with some individual words and their meanings as they relate to the Abrahamic Covenant. Here are the words we need to understand:

- The meaning of the words *I will make*.
- The meaning of the word *bless*.
- The meaning of the word *curse*.

When God says *I will*, it simply means that God will do and accomplish His Word. It is not a suggestion; it is not God's desire, as is stated in the new Messianic Tree of Life version.

> *My heart's **desire** is to make you into a great nation, to bless you, to make your name great so that you may be a blessing.*

The words *I will make* in our Bibles are accurate; they are in the imperfect tense[8] in the Hebrew and clearly mean that God will do what He said; He is not just expressing His heart's desire. I have reviewed my lexicon and Hebrew dictionaries, and here are the meanings for *I will make:*

- The verb *asa* has the basic connotation of "do" or "make."[9]
- Brown, Driver & Briggs (BDB) interprets it as "to make, manufacture; to do" as noted in the Logos Software.

The next word used by God is the word to *bless,* and it carries the meaning of "to bless; to praise; blessed, filled with strength, full; praised, adored." Again Brown, Driver & Briggs (BDB) interprets it to mean "to kneel, bless," according to Logos Software. Other sources state:

- The act of declaring, or wishing, favor and goodness upon others. The blessing is not only the good effect of words; it also has the power to bring them to pass.[10]
- Bend the knee; also to give, grant, bring, invoke, say or share a blessing. Several [other] meanings occur, including "worship or praise," "bestow favor and goodness."[11]
- To bless means variously to worship or praise, to bestow goodness and favor, and to invoke such qualities upon another.[12]

Simply, if you bless and lift up Israel, God will in turn bless you. That is very straightforward, and it is clearly the intended meaning given by God.

The next word used by God is *curse,* and it carries the meaning of "to be small, insignificant, to declare cursed, accused, to belittle." The Hebrew word used here is *kalal* which means to treat lightly, to hold in contempt, to curse.[13] So to curse Abraham and his descendants means to treat them lightly,

---

[8] John Joseph Owens, *Analytical Key to the Old Testament: Genesis – Joshua* (Grand Rapids, MI: Baker Book House, 1989), 1:45.

[9] R. Laird Harris, Gleason L. Archer, Jr., and Bruce K. Waltke, *Theological Wordbook of the Old Testament* (Chicago, IL: Moody Press, 1981), 2:701.

[10] Ronald F. Youngblood, *The New Illustrated Bible Dictionary* (Nashville, TN: Thomas Nelson Publishing, 1995), 220.

[11] Geoffrey W. Bromiley, *The International Standard Bible Encyclopedia* (Grand Rapids, MI: Erdmann Publishing Co., 1979), 1:523.

[12] Logos Bible Software, *Erdmann Bible Dictionary – Bible Word Study – Bless.*

[13] Arnold Fruchtenbaum, *Ariel Bible Commentary: The Book of Genesis* (San Antonio, TX: Ariel Press, 2009), 242.

to count them as insignificant, to belittle, to hold in contempt, to curse them. It is further stated by another author: "to be light or slight" and thus "to treat someone with disdain," "to despise" or "to depreciate."[14] It is important to understand word usages in the Scripture. But that is not all for the word *curse* used by God to those who curse Israel; it is a stronger word for curse. It is the word *aor*, from the Hebrew root word *arah*, which means "to impose a barrier, to ban,"[15] which is simply expressed "to bind with a curse; to lay/be under a curse." *The Theological Dictionary of the Old Testament* states the following:

> Those nations who seek friendly relationships with Israel [Abraham and his descendants] are placed under a blessing, but those who are hostile to Israel by means of the curse formulas are placed under a curse.[16]

So God draws clear and precise meanings in His words. Israel is to be blessed if you want favor with God and His blessing. But if you are hostile to Israel by cursing those whom God has blessed, then God lays a curse upon you. People today who attack Israel for wrongs that they have done in their struggle for survival misunderstand the Word of God. As I go through the Scriptures with you, you will discover that God held the surrounding nations cursed, judging them even when Israel was at its lowest point morally, ethnically, and spiritually. There is no escape hatch for anyone to curse Israel and try to worm their way out of God's impending judgment for their cursing of Israel.

Finally, the third aspect of the promised blessing is that through Israel all the families of the earth will be blessed. Now that blessing will be unfolded to Gentiles in two ways; first we are blessed physically,[17] and we will be blessed spiritually because of the finished work of a Jewish Messiah on a Roman cross, because God laid on Him the curse of our sin (Genesis 3; Isaiah 53). Messiah took our place as our substitute. Based on that blessing, when Jew and Gentile place their Faith and trust in Jesus Christ the Jewish Messiah, we have imputed to us His righteousness; we are reconciled with

---

[14] T. Desmond Alexander and David W. Baker, *Dictionary of the Old Testament Pentateuch* (Downers Grove, IL: InterVarsity Press, 2003), 84.

[15] Fruchtenbaum, *Ariel Bible Commentary: The Book of Genesis*, 242.

[16] G. Johannes Botterweck and Helmer Ringgren, *Theological Dictionary of the Old Testament* (Grand Rapids, MI: Erdmann Publishing Co., 1974), 1:411.

[17] For one aspect of our physical blessing that we have received because of the Jewish people, see chapter 16 of this book, pages 255-258.

God, declared righteous, and set apart for holy use by God. What an amazing blessing we have through Abraham and the Seed that comes from him, the Jewish Messiah!

These teaching points from Genesis 12:1-3 must be understood to grasp the fullness of our salvation of which we are completely unworthy. Please study and contemplate the ramifications of the blessings and curses of the Abrahamic Covenant that echo off every page of Scripture from Genesis through the book of Revelation.

Now as we move into the next three chapters of this book, we want to get a background on the reasons why there have been so many negative words and actions (cursings) against Israel. It is a theological issue, motivated by unbiblical interpretation coming from the heart of Satan, who manipulates from behind the scenes.

In the next chapter (chapter 2), we will take a good look at the effects of Replacement Theology that dominated the early Church, and Amillennial Theology. Amillennial Theology was the next system of theology, developed by Saint Augustine for the Roman Catholic Church. After Replacement and Amillennial Theologies appeared, Covenant Theology developed in the seventeenth century (chapter 3). These theological systems have served as the theological push behind anti-Jewish and anti-Semitic words, actions, philosophies, and theologies ever since. Together, these three theological schools have instructed and turned people against the Jewish people and the present state of Israel. Chapter 4 will discuss Dispensational Theology, which emphasizes the importance of blessing Israel, recognizes the distinctions between Israel and the Church, and teaches on God's future plan for the Nation of Israel.

I regret to have to take the time and page space to do this, but if we do not, we will never grasp the damage that the first three forms of theology (Replacement, Amillennial, and Covenant Theologies) have contributed to the lack of interest by the Jewish people in Jesus Christ who is the Jewish Messiah.

These three theologies – Replacement, Amillennial, and Covenant – are actually trying to thwart the very future plans of the Father, the Son, and the Holy Spirit; these plans have been clearly recorded, but many have chosen to allegorize and spiritualize them away. These theological systems have also caused great harm for anyone endeavoring to understand Scripture. One rabbi has said, "Well, there are so many ways of interpreting the Scriptures." Many would agree with him. The Church and Rabbinic Judaism have moved away from the literal approach of interpreting the Bible to allegorizing or spiritualizing Scripture according to scholars' pre-set biases. Rabbis are saying everyone has an interpretation, so who is right?

If a person uses the literal approach to the Scriptures, he or she will not find the kind of "spiritual" diversity in interpretation that is now popular. An easy principle in Scripture asserts that God has given one, and only one, interpretation to His Word. While there can be many applications, God has intended only one interpretation.

Satan has used false interpretation of Scripture as a means to make the divide between the Jewish people and their Messiah much greater than it needs to be. Romans 11:11 states the following:

> *I say then, Have they* [the Jewish people] *stumbled that they should fall?* [NO] *God forbid: but rather through their fall* **salvation is come unto the Gentiles** *for* **to provoke them to jealousy**.

Much can be said about this verse; but look at the bolded words, and think it through as we move through these chapters. What these systems of theology have done in practice throughout history is beat up the Jewish people, committing unspeakable crimes that are not only unethical, but unbiblical, and many times completely satanic.

Now I already know that those who hold to those theological positions will bristle at what I am saying. I simply challenge them to follow along with me and study the subtle path blazed against Jewish people by allegorizing God's Word instead of taking it literally. They have brought great shame upon the name of Jesus.

You may say but they, the Jewish people, killed Christ and rejected Him, their own Messiah. You should be educated enough to understand what the Jewish Prophets and David prophesied, that it would happen that way! If the Jewish people had not rejected Him, He would not have been able to be the vicarious, substitutionary sacrifice for our sins and Jewish sins (Isaiah 52:13-53:12). You should know that without the rejection and death of Christ YOU are still lost in your sins and completely separated from God! I recommend a book called *In the Shame of Jesus*[18] that will give a clear, accurate history of

---

[18] William Heinrich, *In the Shame of Jesus: The Hidden Story of Church-Sponsored Anti-Semitism* (Keller, TX: JHousePublishing, 2016). This book can be purchased from John Metzger.

the Church and its erroneous theologies and actions that we must guard against.

I also know and understand the arguments that Jewish rabbis put forth as to why they would never want to accept a Christian Jesus as their Messiah, and their arguments are compelling and articulate. However, their arguments do not align with the words of Moses and the Prophets or the Apostles as recorded in the Bible.

I am not trying to make enemies; but if truth continues to be hidden by error, how will truth ever been known?

Chapter 2
Understanding Replacement and Amillennial Theologies

Three errant theologies are linked together in much of Christianity: (1) Replacement, (2) Amillennial, and (3) Covenant theologies. Each of these is coupled with the allegorical method of interpretation. They are triplets, and their DNA is linked.

The term Replacement Theology (RT) will be mentioned frequently throughout this book, so explaining and defining it is important. What we need to know about Replacement Theology (RT) is how it began or developed and the ramifications of that form of theology, specifically as it relates to Israel and the Jewish people. If you look it up in the dictionary, you will not find the term Replacement Theology. However, if we look up the words individually, we can grasp what Replacement Theology conveys. So the words *replacement* and *theology* are defined as follows:

> *Replacement* is the action or process of replacing, the state of being replaced.
>
> *Theology* is the study of religious faith, practice, and experience: the study of God and of God's relation to the world.
>
> *Theology* is listed as a systemic study of the Scriptures.[19]

RT is a systemic study of the Scriptures that **replaces** someone or something. Today those embracing RT will not necessarily refer to themselves as *replacement*. They will camouflage themselves by using other terminology. RT in its general meaning has taken something from the Scriptures and has **replaced** it with something else that is not related to the statement or thing that it replaces. The practice of theology that **replaces** something or someone that is not in the context changes the interpretation

---

[19] *Merriam-Webster's Collegiate Dictionary* (Merriam-Webster, Inc: Springfield, MA, 2003), 1056, 1296.

and understanding of the subject of the biblical text or passage that it replaces.

Before we look at what RT does, we need to know the history of what gave RT its birth. I will keep this as simplistic as possible. I want you to see the flow of history as the Church moved away from its Jewish roots to become completely anti-Jewish. While Faith in the Messiah began as a Jewish movement, it changed within the Gentile setting as the Church became more organized. How did this happen? Let us begin with an overview of the first four centuries of the Christian era.

Let me begin by giving a summary statement by James Showers, executive director of the Friends of Israel Gospel Ministry, as he correctly relates the core element of Replacement Theology at its beginning:

> Christianity has been at the forefront of Jewish persecution for much of the Church Age. The rise of Replacement Theology in the second and third centuries turned love and appreciation for the children of Jacob into hatred and rejection. As the Church began to believe it had superseded Israel, its disdain for Jewish people coalesced into Anti-Semitism and violence against them in the name of Christ – teaching them to be extremely cautious, if not fearful, of Christians.[20]

Let us now continue with following RT through the early centuries of the organized Church from the second through the fifth centuries. But first we will look at the biblical standard set by the Apostles in the first century.

The First Century

The Church was first centered in Jerusalem, and for a number of years it was completely Jewish. These early believers initially never had any intentions of separating from Judaism. However, Judaism separated itself from the early Jewish Christian Church. The Jewish Church believed that their Faith was the fulfillment of Scripture and not the enemy of their fathers – Abraham, Isaac, and Jacob – nor in any opposition to David or the Prophets. They believed that the rest of the Jewish nation would come to see that Jesus was the Messiah and come to embrace Him. However, that did not occur on a broad scale. So two things happened:

---

[20] James Showers, *Inside View: Israel* My Glory Magazine (Bellmawr, NJ: Friends of Israel Gospel Ministry, May-June, 2016), 5.

- Thousands of Jewish people did become believers in the Messiah Yeshua (Jesus). Estimates range as high as 25 percent of the Jewish people in the Land of Israel came to Faith.

- Persecution broke out, first within the Jewish community, and then by Rome. The majority of the Jewish community, led by the Sadducees and Pharisees and their religious body called the Sanhedrin, rejected the Messiah. The unbelieving Jewish people separated themselves from the Jewish believers in Messiah, especially after Rome's 70 A.D. destruction of the Temple in Jerusalem and after the crushing 135 A.D. Roman defeat of the remaining Jewish community that had revolted against Roman oppression.

In Acts 4:1-22, we see the first persecution initiated by the high priest, a Sadducee, the captain of the Temple and the Sadducees. The second persecution is reported in Acts 5:17-42, which, again, was initiated by the Sadducees and the High Priest who brought Peter and John before the Sanhedrin, the ruling religious body of the Jewish people. However, Luke in his historical account of the early Church refers to the fact that many of the priests who were Sadducees did embrace Yeshua as the Messiah of Israel and *were obedient to the faith* (Acts 6:7). The Sanhedrin was composed of about one-third Sadducees and two-thirds Pharisees. Then the third persecution broke out in Acts 7 against Steven, and this early persecution was principally done by the Pharisees. The fourth persecution broke out right after the death of Steven by the Pharisees and Saul (later, the Apostle Paul), who seemed to lead the charge against Jewish believers in Messiah so that the believers scattered (Acts 8:1) for their lives. Saul chased them to places like Damascus (Acts 9:1-2) to put them in chains and take them back to Jerusalem. Unbelieving Jews began to persecute the Jewish Church heavily.

So we see that the first persecutions in the Church involved Jews persecuting other Jews for religious reasons. This occurred even before the Gentiles ever became members of that body of Messiah. This persecution forced the early Jewish believers to scatter to other areas. There they began to preach the Gospel to other groups, such as the Samaritans in Acts 8. Later in Acts 10 the first Gentile believer in Messiah Yeshua was saved and entered the Church, which had been Jewish up to that point.

The Church, which started out as completely Jewish, became predominantly Gentile by the end of the first century, as at Antioch of Syria.

This was the sending Church of the Apostle Paul. The ultimate result of Paul's evangelism was that more and more Gentiles were being saved; but because of the ongoing Jewish rejection of Jesus [Yeshua][21] by the Jewish leaders, less and less Jews were being saved by the end of the first century. That resulted in the Church being overwhelmingly Gentile by the end of the first century.

Early on in the outreach of the Apostle Paul, the Gentiles that became believers were largely the *God fearers,* as they are referred to in the Acts of the Apostles, those who had been attending Jewish synagogues. These Gentile believers could understand the Jewish context of Scripture. But at the close of the first century, more and more Gentiles of pagan background became believers with no understanding or appreciation of the Jewishness of the Scriptures; and they flooded into the Church. This fact would set the tone of the Church for the centuries that followed.

The Second Century

During this century the Church spread to all the provinces of the Roman Empire, plus over into Mesopotamia. The new converts were largely Gentile and not Jewish. The spiritual background of these Gentiles was pagan worship of many gods. There were fewer and fewer Jewish people and God-fearers that Paul interacted with in his missionary journeys. Most came out of pagan backgrounds with no understanding of the Jewishness of their faith. Also add the dimension that Gentile believers without a Jewish perspective increasingly began to see the Jews as the murderers of Christ. Jewish believers in Christ who were not breaking with unsaved Jewish people were seen by Gentile believers as still trying to associate with those they considered to be murderers of Christ.

By the second century, the Church was full of former pagan Gentiles with no understanding of the Jewishness of their faith. As a result, Gentile believers began to turn against Jewish believers in Christ and viewed their teaching and association with unbelieving Jewish people as well as their retention of their Jewish culture as hypocrisy. Let us look at a few statements from the Church Fathers, who introduced anti-Jewish and anti-Semitic teaching into the heart and life of the Church during the rise of the Gentile era of the Church, on into today.

---

[21] Jesus Hebrew name is Yeshua.

What began with the early Church Fathers was the development of **replacement** rhetoric that made the Church out to be Israel. They rejected the Jewish people because in their minds, they held them responsible for the crucifixion of their Messiah, Jesus. Correct theology teaches that we all had a part in Messiah's death, because we all have sinned. We also know that Jesus forgave those who crucified Him as He hung, dying, on the cross. The Bible also teaches that God will never reject His covenant people, the Jews. However, the Gentiles had no understanding of the Jewish perspective, so this basic theological foundation was overlooked.

According to Gentile logic, if Jews had fallen away from their Messiah, who was left to receive the promises? To their reasoning, it must be that the promises to the Jewish people would now belong to the Gentile believers, and the promises to Israel would now belong to the Church.

Strong words have been used against the Jewish people by Christians, rooted in second-century and later teachings from the Church Fathers. Below is a sample of the anti-Semitic statements of the Church Fathers as they built the foundations for RT:

> The war of the Christian Church against the Jews began with the Church Fathers' relentless attacks on those Jews who stubbornly refused to accept Jesus as Messiah. "The unbridled utterances of bigotry and hate coming from the venerated Church Fathers of the early Christian Church raise some doubt as to both their sanity and their saintliness." … Despite their belief that Christ's death was necessary and predestined, they denounced the Jews as a "condemned race and hated of God."[22]

Because of the growing power of the Church, Christian theology and the Church Fathers were to become more and more obsessed with Jewish guilt. The following teachings of the Fathers were handed down throughout succeeding generations in Christendom. Let us start with Justin Martyr and some of his statements.

---

[22] Fred Gladstone Bratton, *The Crime of Christendom* (Boston: Beacon Press, 1969), 79.

Justin Martyr (100-165 A.D.)

"The Christians are the true Israeli race."[23]

"Tribulation was justly imposed on you for you have murdered the Just One."[24]

The Church Father Justin Martyr also claimed that the term, *the seed of Jacob*, in the Bible, when properly understood, now referred to the Gentile Christians, not to the Jews. This is a very important point because it signals the beginning of a shift in understanding of the early Church of biblical passages, especially relating to Israel. What Justin is saying is that now the Gentile Church **replaces** Israel. This teaching is the spiritualization of Genesis 25:23, a departure from its literal meaning. He taught that the Gentiles in the Church were now the true Israeli race;[25] and that the Gentile believers in Jesus were now the seed of Jacob, and the Jews were not the seed of Jacob. This is the beginning of **Replacement Theology**. So Replacement Theology actually began millennia ago and is not a recent development.

Melito of Sardis (120-185 A.D.)

Sardis was near the seven churches of Revelation in Asia Minor. Melito himself was born Jewish, and He became one of the first to accuse the Jewish people of murdering God – Deicide – when he wrote:

He who hung the earth is hanging; he who fixed the heavens has been fixed; he who fastened the universe has been fastened to a tree; the Sovereign has been insulted; God has been murdered, the King of Israel slain by an Israelite hand.[26]

---

[23] Bernhard Blumenkranz, *"Church Fathers" Encyclopedia Judaica*. CD ROM 1977.

[24] Jeffrey S. Siker, *Disinheriting the Jews: Abraham in Early Christian Controversy* (Louisville, KY: Westminster/John Knox Press, 1991), 169. (Dialogue 16.2-4, attributed to Trypho, potentially a fictional character used to generate dialogue.)

[25] Graham Harvey, *The True Israel: Uses of the Names Jew, Hebrew & Israel in Ancient Jewish & Early Christian Literature* (The Netherlands: E.J. Brill, 1996), 253.

[26] William Nicholls, *Christian Anti-Semitism: A History of Hate* (Jason Aronson Inc: Northvale, NJ, 1995), pp. 177-178.

Ignatius, the Bishop of Antioch of Syria
(Died in Rome around 110 A.D.)

Ignatius claimed in his epistle to the Philippians at the beginning of the second century that: "Satan fights along with the Jews to a denial of the cross," and that "if any one celebrates the Passover along with the Jews, or receives emblems of their feast, he is a partaker with those that killed the Lord and His apostles."[27] This man was the bishop of the same church that 50 years earlier was Paul's sending church. My, how things change! Ignatius had to "forget" that the Apostle Paul was a Jewish rabbi who celebrated the Jewish holidays and took the Gospel message to the Jews wherever he traveled.

The Epistle of Barnabas

The Epistle of Barnabas circulated about the same time as the Epistle of Ignatius, but claimed that the Jewish sacrifices were abolished, their fasts not acceptable to God, and that Christians – not Jews – were actually the heirs of God's Covenant with Abraham. To anyone who believed the Jewish people still had a future through the Covenant, the Epistle of Barnabas harshly stated:

> Take heed now to yourselves, and not to be like some adding largely to your sins, and saying, "The covenant is both theirs and ours." But they (the Jews) finally lost it.[28]

Irenaeus, Bishop of Lyon
(Lugdunum in Gaul, or Lyon, France) after 177 A.D.

Irenaeus declared that Jews were "disinherited from the grace of God" and "would never have hesitated to burn their own Jewish Scriptures."[29]

Hippolytus of Rome (170-235 A.D.)

In 200 A.D., Hippolytus wrote these words, revealing the rise of vitriolic rhetoric within the Church:

---

[27] *The Sacred Writings of Saint Ignatius:* "The Epistle of Ignatius to the Philippians: Farewells and Cautions," Chapter 15 (Altenmunster, Germany).
[28] William Cunningham, *A Dissertation of the Epistle of S. Barnabas* (London: England: Macmillan And Co,), 256.
[29] R. Kendall Soulen, *The God of Israel and Christian Theology* (Minneapolis, MN: Augsburg Fortress, 1996), 48.

> Hear my words, and give heed, you Jews. Many a time did you boast yourself that you did condemn Jesus of Nazareth to death.... Of what retribution does Jesus speak? Manifestly of the misery which has now got hold of you.[30]

The foundation had been laid by these early Church Fathers. According to them, the Jewish people were no longer God's chosen people. The Gentile Christian Church, instead, had inherited the covenant promises of God. The Church was then considered God's chosen people. To their thinking, the curses of the Bible had been bestowed on the Jews and all the blessings of the Bible to the Christians. Eventually, even Hitler would draw on this foundation, one of religious and theological anti-Semitism. While listening to human reason and embroiled in human passions as they attempted to organize and rule the early Church by their own authority, the Church Fathers turned away from God's own Words.

Rabbi A. James Rudin, who was ordained by the Hebrew Union College, says in his book, *Israel for Christians:*

> Some Christian theologians and Bible scholars have long taught that ancient Israel, the "Old Israel" of the "Old Covenant" has been replaced by the "New Israel" of the "New Covenant" – the Christian Church.... Not only has such Christian thinking rendered the Jews vulnerable to violent anti-Semitism, it has also negated any Jewish claim to the land of Israel because it maintains such claims have been emptied of all concrete meaning... This position has resulted in theological anti-Semitism on the part of some Christian leaders.[31]

Rabbi Rudin's words are correct. Fundamental and conservative believers need to understand he is merely confirming what has happened historically in the Church. Anti-Semitism crept in early and has remained within the Church, calling question towards God's Word.

The Third Century

The Church experienced tremendous growth as Rome declined. Many of the institutions of the Roman Empire that provided protection, security, and

---

[30] Alexander Roberts and James Donaldson, *The Ante-Nicene Fathers: Translations of the Writings of the Fathers down to A.D. 325* (New York, NY: Charles Scribner's, 1903), 219.

[31] James Rudin, *Israel For Christians* (Philadelphia, PA: Fortress Press, 1983), 125-126.

stability were now disintegrating. The Empire was plagued with internal strife and exterior wars and even civil wars within the empire. So more and more people were turning to the Church for their security. From a human viewpoint, this is one of the reasons why the Church was growing so quickly.

By the end of the third century [200s] the Church had become the most powerful institution in the Roman Empire after the State. The emperors persecuted the Church because they viewed it as a threat. Also, during this time, some conflicts arose between the Church and the Jews. Here are some additional statements made by some Church leaders:

Tertullian (155-240 A.D.)

Tertullian of Carthage in North Africa, in the **western branch** of the Church, wrote some very strong Anti-Semitic statements against the Jews.[32]

Meanwhile in the eastern branch of the Church, there was a very strong anti-Semitic spirit that was developing against the Jewish people. Christians were calling Jews "Christ killers." They also developed a very strong bias against anything Jewish. The Premillennial view of the Scriptures was believed by the early Jewish Church and Judaism for centuries. Because the Premillennial view of the Messiah setting up the earthly Messianic Kingdom was taught and believed by the Jews, the Church stigmatized Premillennial teaching as "**Jewish**" and therefore "**heretical.**" Thus, one irrational anti-Semitic sentiment spawned even more irrational thinking. As a result, Eastern Church leaders looked at Premillennialism as heretical, renouncing the literal, biblical teaching of the Second Coming of Jesus in the End Times.

Origen (185-254 A.D.)

Origen was a brilliant man who at the age of 18 was made the president of the Alexandrian School of Theology in Egypt. Origen opposed Premillennialism, calling it a Jewish dream. He developed a whole new way of interpreting the Scriptures called the *Allegorical Method of Interpretation*. This he inherited from Philo, who was born in Alexandria, Egypt (25 B.C.-50 A.D.).

Origen was a Hellenized Jewish philosopher who used philosophical allegory to attempt to fuse and harmonize Greek philosophy with Jewish philosophy. In this method, instead of giving the Scriptures a literal meaning, one can simply spiritualize them, making them mirror whatever meaning is

---

[32] William Nicholls, *Christian Anti-Semitism*, 181-187.

desired for the person's purpose. According to this approach, when the Bible says "Israel," it does not necessarily mean literally *Israel*, but could be interpreted as meaning *the Church*. The following quote expresses well the idea of allegorical interpretation:

> According to Origen, the understanding of Scripture is "the art of arts," and "the science." The words of the Scripture are its body, or the visible element, that hides its spirit, or its invisible element. The spirit is the treasure hidden in a field: hidden behind every word, every letter and even behind every iota used in the written Word of God. Thus **"everything in the Scripture is mystery."**[33] [Bolding my emphasis]

Are there mysteries in Scripture that are difficult to understand? Of course! Only as we grow spiritually in the LORD do we come to understand things that we did not see in a surface reading. But Origen is saying that everything in Scripture has a hidden meaning. Now when the Scriptures are not studied literally or from a Jewish perspective, our interpretation of what God has written ceases to have any validity or any spiritual reality. When we look for God's message – His intent – these so-called "mysteries" become a moot issue.

The teaching of mysteries is similar to the Agnostic heresies of ancient times, in which people believed that knowledge came from reflection, and that knowledge was hidden from most. In error, they proposed the belief that Jesus was a man who became God by gaining knowledge, which is a theme of many heresies through the centuries. The Bible teaches that the Gospel message is clear and open to all.

Diannisian

Diannisian, one of Origen's pupils, taught that allegorizing the Old Testament and the Prophets, in particular, was the only credible way of interpreting Scripture.

The danger of Allegorical Interpretation is that the interpreter becomes the sole authority of Scripture instead of God. Some continued statements by Origen as he echoed the growing hostility between the Church and Jewish people are the following:

---

[33] Article by St. Mark Coptic Church, Jersey City, NJ, "The School of Alexandria - Origen and the Holy Scriptures: Allegorism," Chapter 3 on www.CopticChurch.net on Origen, last accessed on 11/01/16.

> On account of their unbelief and other insults which they heaped upon Jesus, the Jews will not only suffer more than others in the judgment which is believed to impend over the world, but have even already endured such sufferings. For what nation is in exile from their own metropolis, and from the place sacred to the worship of their fathers, save the Jews alone? And the calamities they have suffered because they were a most wicked nation, which although guilty of many other sins, yet has been punished so severely for none as for those that were committed against our Jesus.[34]

Notice, in his statement there is truth; but his speech is derogatory. Origen's words were repeated by the Church Fathers to discredit Israel, raising negative attitudes, words, and actions against the Jewish people. Jesus was extremely clear that His body, the Church was to LOVE those who curse it and persecute it, not persecute them or beat them to death with anti-Jewish words, actions, and deeds, which is exactly what the Church has wound up doing for almost two millennia.

Bishop Thasciua Caecilius Cyprianus of North Africa (200-258 A.D.)

Cyprianus wrote a book called *The Three Books of Testimonies against the Jews*. Shortly we will look at what he and other Church Fathers did with Genesis 25:23 by applying Origen's method of allegorical interpretation.

Hippolytus (170-235 A.D.)

Justin Martyr along with Hippolytus was obsessed with the belief that the Jews were receiving and would continue to receive God's punishment for having murdered Jesus. Hippolytus wrote:

> Now then, incline thine ear to me and hear my words, and give heed, thou Jew. Many a time does thou boast thyself, in that thou didst condemn Jesus of Nazareth to death, and didst give him vinegar and gall to drink; and thou dost vaunt thyself because of this. Come, therefore, and let us consider together whether perchance thou dost boast unrighteously, O, Israel, and whether thou small portion of vinegar and gall has not brought down this fearful threatening upon

---

[34] Roberts and Donaldson, *The Ante-Nicene Fathers: Translations of the Writings of the Fathers down to 325 A.D.*, 433.

thee and whether this is not the cause of thy present condition involved in these myriad of troubles.[35]

Did the Prophets speak of such things? Yes, they did, but the hatred and animosity was not in their hearts. Yes, God would judge Israel in His wisdom and mercy; but God's wrath was never placed into the hands of the Church, the so-called Body of Messiah, to be used against the Jewish people.

By this time the Church Fathers had developed a non-literal method of interpretation of Scripture that would support their strong bias against Israel and Jewish people in general. This method of interpretation is called the Allegorical method of interpretation. Below I will give you a comparison or contrast between literal and allegorical methods of interpretation by illustrating the difference when applied to Genesis 25:23.

A Comparison of the Literal and Allegorical Methods

Let me share an example of applying allegorical interpretation to Scripture. "Because the Jews were here before the Christians, they are the 'older brother,'" and are therefore condemned to serve the younger brothers, the Christians. Jews will be subservient to the Christians and the Christians will be stronger than the Jews. Now, is that what the text of Genesis 25:23 (above) teaches? NO, it is the twisting of God's Holy Word to fit it into an unbiblical bias that promotes hatred and suppression of Jewish people, and not the loving of them in Christ.[36]

Genesis 25:23: *Esau would serve Jacob.*

Literal Method
Jacob's people would be stronger than Esau's people

Allegorical Method
Esau (the Jews) would serve Jacob (the Church or Christians)

Figure 1. Comparison of Literal vs. Allegorical Interpretation (Genesis 25:23)

---

[35] Hippolytus, *The Sacred Writings of Saint Hippolytus: Expository Treatise Against the Jews.*
[36] Dan Cohn-Sherbok, *Anti-Semitism* (England: The History Press, 2002), 38.

This is a complete radical departure from what God had intended for the Genesis passage to mean. This again is RT, the method of interpretation that is used by the greater portion of Christianity today. By this process, and to varying degrees, theologians through the ages have perverted the true literal meaning of Bible texts. Although this pattern has been used to insert references to the not-yet-existent Church into the Hebrew Scriptures whenever God addressed Israel, this was not the way Paul, Peter, or John interpreted passages that relate to Israel.

Unfortunately, the error of allegorical interpretation took root early on and has been followed by many Christian theologians dating back to the second century. Eventually it would contaminate all theology, but the first area of theology to fall to RT was Ecclesiology (the study of the Church), and the second was Eschatology (the study of future things).[37] Collectively, the early Church Fathers laid the foundation for the assumption that the Church superseded Israel by their development and application of RT and the allegorical interpretation method. Here is how one Baptist denomination has spoken of it:

> For example, Justin Martyr (100-165 A.D.), who defended Christianity against a Jewish enemy, claimed Christians "are the true Israeli race," and asserted that the biblical expression *the seed of Jacob*, when properly understood, now refers to the Christians, not the Jew. Tertullian (A.D. 145-220), prominent church theologian from North Africa, interpreted God's statements to Rebekah concerning the twins (Esau and Jacob) in her womb (Genesis 25:23) in the following manner: Esau, the older brother, represents the Jews; and Jacob, the younger brother, represents the Christian[s]. He indicated that God thereby revealed that the Christians would overcome the Jews and that the Jews would serve the Christians. Origen (A.D. 185-253), the president of the school of theology in Alexandria, Egypt, greatly influenced the Church's acceptance of the allegorical, or spiritualizing, method of interpreting the Bible in contrast to the literal, historical-grammatical method. This method allowed him to claim that the word "Israel" in the Bible can mean the Church, not national Israel. Cyprian (A.D. 195-258), Bishop of Carthage, stated that he "endeavored to show that the Jew, according to what had before been foretold, had departed from God, and had

---

[37] Found at http://baptistbulletin.org/the-baptist-bulletin-magazine/replacement-theology, last accessed 11/14/2016.

lost God's favor, which had been given them in past time, and had been promised them for the future, while the Christians had succeeded to their place, deserving well of the Lord by faith."[38]

Today, these errors continue on in the Catholic Church, which has instituted its own priesthood to copy that of Israel's priesthood as well as installing a continual sacrifice for sin in the Mass to replace the blood sacrificial system of the Law.

As mentioned, even the once stalwart Evangelical theologians have assimilated Replacement Theology by embracing Covenant Theology, the belief that God is done with the Jewish people or has not included them in as a national identity in the future.

Most recently, Palestinian Christians have updated the replacement theme by asserting that they, and not the Jewish people, are the true recipients of God's promises. Many mainline Protestant churches have embraced this theological aberration.

The Church Fathers who saw themselves as Israel had to discredit the real Israel, the Jewish people. They did so by making anti-Jewish theology an integral part of Christian apologetics. I cannot express that concept to you strongly enough. The Fathers turned out volumes of literature to prove that they were the true people of God, and that Judaism (Israel and the Jewish people) had only been a prelude to, or in preparation for, Christianity.

The Fourth Century

As we lay out the fourth century, and especially the centuries that followed, we cannot help but wonder and suspect a strong possibility that the Church was more unregenerate than regenerated by the **Blood** of Messiah. As the Church came into power in the fourth century, it turned on the synagogues with even greater intensity. Jewish civil and religious status was deteriorating, thanks to the influence the bishops had in the political arena. Laws were passed making it a capital offense for any Jew to make a convert; Jewish people were excluded from various professions, trades, and land ownership, denied all civil honors, and their autonomy of worship was being threatened. In every way, they were being discriminated against. In a vicious cycle, Christians felt that their belief in divine punishment was now

---

[38] Ibid.

supported by the growing evidence of Jewish isolation and harm put in place by human bias.

Let us continue to look at a few more Church Fathers as we move into the fourth century, starting with the Roman Emperor Constantine.

Constantine, Emperor of Rome (272-337 A.D.)

Constantine was the first Emperor to call himself a Christian (325 A.D.). When he did that, he made Christianity the official State religion in the Empire. As a professing Christian, Constantine adopted a policy of anti-Jewish laws. This meant that Judaism was no longer an approved religion by the State as it had been for centuries; Judaism had fallen from being an approved religion to being unapproved, and various forms of persecution followed.

Jerome (345-420 A.D.)

Jerome studied in Israel under Jewish rabbis, learned Hebrew, and then went on to produce the Latin Vulgate translation of the Scriptures. He stated that he had been delivered from Jewish opinions such as Premillennialism.[39] As a prominent Church leader, He even cursed and reviled Jews and took pleasure in their misfortunes.

Emperor Theodosius (reigned from 379-395 A.D.)

Theodosius professed to be a Christian and decreed that Christianity was to be the only religion allowed in the Empire. He expelled Jews from prominent positions and allowed Jewish property to be desecrated. He even decreed that a marriage between a Jew and a Christian would be regarded legally as adultery. He is noted for the Theodosius Code against the Jewish people.

Hilary of Potieres (Pictavium, Gaul) (310-367 A.D.)

Hilary of Potieres lived in France in the fourth century and spoke of the Jews as "a people who had always persisted in iniquity and out of its abundance of evil glorified in wickedness."[40]

---

[39] Ken Stewart, *Our Hope The Kingdom: The Return of the Messiah* (Bloomington, IN: WestBow Press, 2014), 42.
[40] Donald J. Dietrich, *God and Humanity in Auschwitz* (Piscataway, NJ: Transaction Publishers, 1995), 20.

Ambrose Bishop of Milan (340-397 A.D.)

In a letter he wrote to Emperor Theodosius, Bishop Ambrose defended a fellow bishop from Mesopotamia who had burned a synagogue at Callinicum and asked, "Who cares if a synagogue – home of insanity and unbelief – is destroyed?" In his letter, he misused the Prophet Jeremiah's words against Israel to vindicate the burning of the synagogue.

Gregory of Nyssa (331-396 A.D.)

This Church leader, who served as a bishop, gave the following indictment of the Jewish people, forgetting the origin of the Church as being almost uniformly composed of believing Jews:

> Slayers of the Lord, murderers of the prophets, adversaries of God, men who show contempt for the Law, foes of grace, enemies of their fathers' faith, advocates of the Devil, brood of vipers, slanderers, scoffers, men whose minds are in darkness, leaven of the Pharisees, assembly of demons, sinners, wicked men, stoners, and haters of righteousness.[41]

Do you begin to see and understand the rhetoric and the tone of the Church Fathers as they verbally afflicted the Jewish people and set in motion the outrageous attacks that have come down through the centuries? Look at the next example.

John Chrysostom (347-407 A.D.)

Known as the Patriarch of Constantinople, Chrysostom's legacy of anti-Semitism reflected the strongest attacks on Jews and Judaism by the Church Fathers. His teachings are found in his writings, the *Homilies of Chrysostom*, a collection of his Antioch sermons. Ironically, he is considered to be among the most beloved and admired in Church history. His name translates in Greek as "St. John, the Golden Mouthed." His discourses were prompted by the fact that many Christians were meeting on friendly terms with Jews, visiting Jewish homes, and attending their synagogues, which he viciously attacked. Understand the tremendous impact that Chrysostom had on the future generations of priests for centuries to come. The following are statements made by Chrysostom:

---

[41] Muriel Seltman, *The Changing Faces of Anti-Semitism* – Chapter 8 (England: Troubador Publishing Ltd, 2015).

The Synagogue was ... a criminal assembly of Jews... a place of meeting for the assassins of Christ...a house worse than a drinking shop... a den of thieves, a house of ill fame, a dwelling of iniquity, the refuge of devils, a gulf and abyss of perdition.

The Jews are the most worthless of all men. They are perfidious murderers of Christ. They worship the devil, their religion is a sickness. The Jews are the odious assassin of Christ and for killing God there is no expiation possible, no indulgence or pardon. Christians may never cease vengeance, and the Jew must live in servitude forever. God always hated the Jews. It is incumbent upon all Christians to hate the Jews.

The Jews sacrifice their children to Satan.... they are worse than wild beasts. The synagogue is a brothel, a den of scoundrels, the temple of demons devoted to idolatrous cults.

The Jews have fallen into a condition lower than the vilest animal. Debauchery and drunkenness have brought them to the level of the lusty goat and the pig. They know only one thing: to satisfy their stomachs, to get drunk, to kill, and beat each other up like stage villains and coachmen.

The synagogue is a curse, obstinate in her error, she refuses to see or hear, she has deliberately perverted her judgment; she has extinguished with herself the light of the Holy Spirit.[42]

I hate the Jews because they violate the Law. I hate the synagogue because it has the Law and the Prophets. It is the duty of all Christians to hate the Jews.[43]

Chrysostom further said that the Jews had become a degenerate race (sounding like Hitler and the Nazis) because of their "odious assassination of Christ for which crime there is no expiation possible, no indulgence, no pardon, and for which they will always be a people without a nation, enduring a servitude without end."[44]

---

[42] Fred Gladston Bratton, pp. 83-84. From Chrysostom's eight "Homilies Against the Jews" in *Patrologia Graeca* (Paris: Garnier, 1857-1866), 843-942.
[43] Ibid.
[44] Bratton, "Homilies Against the Jews." Seltman, *Changing Faces of Anti-Semitism* – Chapter 8.

In conclusion, the sermons of Chrysostom would become the foundation of homiletics in the centuries to come as the model to emulate in seminaries and schools. The natural result was that his message of hate was passed down to succeeding generations of priests and theologians. R. S. Storr, a nineteenth-century Protestant cleric, called Chrysostom "one of the most eloquent preachers since apostolic times who had brought to men the divine tidings of truth and love."[45] This Protestant clergyman ignored the anti-Semitism and poisonous venom against the Jewish people that poured out of Chrysostom's "golden mouth." Remember Jesus clearly stated and applied His teaching to love our enemies. Yes, the Church is to love Israel and not harm and slander the Jewish people.

A contemporary of Storr, Catholic theologian Cardinal John Henry Newman, described Chrysostom as a bright, cheerful, gentle soul with a sensitive heart.[46] Not toward the Jewish people was he a bright, cheerful, gentle soul with a sensitive heart! The impact of Chrysostom's words echoes off the pages of history as the Church continued to commit inhumane crimes against the Jewish people. Chrysostom further said that if a man is passionate to live for Christ, he will never have enough of fighting those who hate Christ (the Jews)."[47]

Apparently, the seeds of hatred that had become so intertwined with Church teachings also caused general spiritual blindness to Jesus' command to *love*. This spiritual blindness still exists and can only be corrected by correctly studying the Word of God regarding Israel and the Jewish people. This spiritual blindness will continue to the end of the Tribulation, as Jesus stated in Matthew 25:31-46 as referenced earlier, for Jesus references His physical brothers and sisters being persecuted by pagan and religious peoples after the battle of Armageddon.

Now let me move on to my last example of the hatred propagated by the Church Fathers. Augustine helped lay down a foundation for the Christian public to hate and mistreat the Jewish people down through the ages, and it did not end with the Holocaust. Anti-Semitism is out of the bag again today.

---

[45] Saint John Chrysostom, (Myrtle Beach, SC: The Order of Preachers, Independent) November 16, 2016. Online article.
[46] Found at www.cardinaljohnhenrynewman.com/chrysostoms-spiritual-renewal-cardinal-newman - dated July 3, 2015; accessed last on November 16, 2016.
[47] Sander L. Gilman and Steven T. Katz, *Anti-Semitism in the Time of Crisis* (New York, NY: New York University Press, 1991), 49.

Augustine the Bishop of Hippo (354-430 A.D.) in North Africa

Augustine rejected Premillennialism as being obsolete, and he developed a whole new view of the Kingdom of God concept of the Bible, called Amillennialism.[48] He taught that the organized Church is the Messianic Kingdom foretold in the Scriptures and that the Millennium began with the First Coming of Christ. He did this by using Origen's method of allegorizing the Scriptures. Through time, this teaching became official Church doctrine for centuries to come, continuing down through the Middle Ages. Because the Roman Catholic Church taught and believed that the Messianic Kingdom foretold in Scriptures had already arrived, the Church Fathers believed the Church had the right to enforce its beliefs and policies upon all people, because they believed they were the keepers of the Kingdom of God. This assumption carried over to its treatment of political rulers, pagans, and Jews. This played a key role in how the organized Church (the Catholic Church) acted throughout the Middle Ages.

Augustine also developed the theory of the Jews as a "witness people" to explain their continued existence. Allegorizing the Cain and Abel story, he stated that the Jews were marked by God when they murdered Christ, so they could not be destroyed. Yet their dispersion and misery served as testimony of their evil and a justification for viewing the Jewish people negatively.

In one of Augustine's sermons, he characterized the Jews as "willfully blind to Holy Scripture," "lacking in understanding" and "haters of truth."[49] Here are a few of his assertions:

- The true image of the Hebrew is Judas Iscariot, who sold the Lord for silver. The Jews can never understand the Scriptures and forever bear the guilt of the death of Christ.[50]

- The Jews are our attendant slaves, who carry, as it were, our satchels and bear the manuscripts while we study them.[51]

- These people have also become vagabonds, since they crucified God and our Lord.[52]

---

[48] Stewart, *Our Hope the Kingdom: The Return of the Messiah*, 42.
[49] Augustine of Hippo, *The City of God*, Book XVIII, Chapter 46.
[50] Augustine, Tractatus adversus Iudaeos; Patrologiae cursus completes, series Latina quoted from Augustine's *The City of God.*
[51] James Everett Seaver, *The Persecution of Jews in the Roman Empire – 300-438* (Lawrence, KS: University of Kansas Press, 1952) 52.

These questions need to be asked, such as "Was it then okay for Christian leaders to be haters of the truth of Scriptures? Could these readers dismiss the impact of maligning the Jewish people using speech? How could they excuse themselves from the evil of causing people to do the inhuman crimes that have been perpetrated again the Jewish people when the Bible clearly teaches that we are to be beyond reproach in our walk with the LORD and with the people that we interact with daily?" The Church Fathers had sown the seeds of hatred and intolerance, and Jews were to become the object of hatred and persecution all over Europe for centuries to come. That shameful heritage now operating in America and beyond is the result of applying the same kind of RT that so many Christian churches and organizations embrace today.

The anti-Semitism that the Church Fathers created century upon century led directly to their abuses of the Jewish people. History records the atrocities of the so-called Church: the expulsions from countries, accusations of Blood Libel, of poisoning springs and wells, of host desecration, and many other punishments based on false claims. Their falsehoods unleashed unspeakable crimes against the Jewish people that often are too gross and satanic to describe.

Lastly, I want to give you a classic example of allegorizing of Scripture, demonstrating how this technique is used to try to **replace** *Israel* with the *Church* by grossly misinterpreting God's plan. Here is an example of allegorizing Scripture used by Augustine as he reinterpreted the meaning of the parable of the Good Samaritan from Luke 10:25-37:

> A certain man went down from Jerusalem to Jericho = Adam
>
> Jerusalem = the heavenly city of peace, from which Adam fell
>
> Jericho = the moon, and thereby signifies Adam's mortality
>
> Thieves = the devil and his angels
>
> Stripped him = namely, of his immortality
>
> Beat him = by persuading him to sin
>
> And left him half-dead = as a man he lives, but he died spiritually, therefore he is half-dead

---

[52] Ibid., 53.

> The priest and Levites = the priesthood and ministry of the Old Testament
>
> The Samaritan = is said to mean Guardian; therefore Christ, Himself, is meant
>
> Bound his wounds = means binding the restraint of sin
>
> Oil = comfort of good hope
>
> Wine = exhortation to work with a fervent spirit
>
> Beast = the flesh of Christ's incarnation
>
> Inn = the Church
>
> The morrow = after the Resurrection
>
> Two-pence = promise of this life and the life to come
>
> Innkeeper – Paul"[53]

This is a completely radical departure of what God had intended for that passage to mean. None of the symbols in the allegorical interpretation relate to the context of the story. They are arbitrary, and assigned not because of the immediate or larger context of the passage, but based on the agenda of the one interpreting the data, to prove their own point of view, which therefore clashes with the truth of the Scripture passage.

Whenever an arbitrary assignment of value occurs, the meaning of the Scripture changes with the reasoning and wishes of the interpreter, covering the intent of God's inspiration by marrying it to the view of the interpreter. This, again, is how RT works. Its interpretations are rooted in an allegorical method of interpretation. If I may allegorize this allegory, look at the methodology as represented by two lovers walking hand in hand with the purpose of twisting Scriptures. Those two lovers are Allegory (purposeful misapplication of Scripture) and RT (purposeful distortion of Scripture).

In the big picture, the first four or five centuries in the Church saw the blatant de-judaizing of Jesus. The goal was to remove Jesus from His Jewish context and background to disassociate Him from Jews and Judaism. Over the centuries, the Church made Jesus into a blond, blue-eyed Gentile Messiah

---

[53] Gordon D. Fee and Douglas Stuart, *How to Read the Bible for All Its Worth: A Guide to Understanding the Bible* (Grand Rapids: Zondervan, 1993), 136.

with no trace of His Jewish ethnicity and heritage. The Christian Church broke its ties wherever it wished to do so and certainly deconstructed Jesus so that the Jesus Christ of Christianity was no longer a Jewish religious teacher.

Replacement theologians rearrange the Bible to fit their biases.[54] As a result, we have the death of the Jewish Church and later the slaughter of Jewish people. These are only a few brief statements, a preview of the organized Church's development of anti-Semitism after the first Apostolic century. From this point on, as the centuries piled themselves one upon another in continuous succession, this anti-Semitism only increased in intensity. Its capstone was the Holocaust of World War II, and it is heading to new levels of disregard and danger for Jewish people and the nation of Israel.

The Death of the Jewish Church

At the hands of the Gentile Church, which was becoming increasingly anti-Semitic, the organized Church was moving away from its Jewish roots and heritage toward a total and complete Gentile viewpoint. Jewish believers in Messiah were not accepted by the Church because the Jewish believers understandably wanted to keep their Jewish cultural and ethnic heritage. Jewish believers in Messiah were not accepted by the unbelieving Jewish population because they believed in the "Christian" Messiah, Jesus Christ. Hence, the Jewish Church was not embraced by the Church nor was it embraced by the Jewish community. The net result was the death of the Jewish Church because of their perspective of the Jewish background of Scripture. To the Church, anything – and I mean anything – that had a Jewish connection was viewed by the Gentile Church as Jewish, thus heretical! Next are just a few examples of the rejection of the Jewish background of Passover, by three Church councils.

Council of Caesarea: 196 A.D.

The resurrection of Yeshua (Jesus) would be celebrated on a Sunday each year during the Feast of Eshtar, a celebration of the pagan goddess of Egypt. So the Resurrection of Jesus was to be celebrated on a pagan, heathen holiday, not to be connected in any way with the Jewish Passover and the biblical Feast of First Fruits.

---

[54] Seltman, *The Changing faces of Anti-Semitism* – Chapter 8.

Council of Nicaea: 325 A.D.

This council declared that Yeshua's resurrection was to be observed on Easter Sunday with no attachment to the Jewish Passover.

Council of Antioch: 341 A.D.

The Council of Antioch decreed that anyone attempting to celebrate the Passover on the 14th of Nissan was to be excommunicated. Here is the unbiblical extreme that the Church Fathers forced upon the Church.

The Third and Fourth Centuries

The Jewish Church disappeared after the Church Fathers laid the groundwork for centuries of anti-Semitism in the organized Church. Because of all the anti-Jewish bias against Jewish believers in Jesus, the Jewish Church of believers was pushed out of existence because they did not want to lose their Jewishness, their ethnicity. It does not mean that there were no Jewish people coming to Faith, but it does mean that all Jewish believers had to give up their Jewishness. Despite persecution, there has always been a believing Jewish remnant down through history.

The On-Going Effects of Replacement Theology

Hopefully, after reading this partial expression of the anti-Jewish words, actions, and attitudes of the Church you will begin to realize that the early Church Fathers were not so holy or saintly as the Church makes them out to be. Yet today, everyone in the contemporary Church seems to want to go back to the early Church Fathers to get spiritual insights. Why don't we go all the way back to the Apostles Paul, John, and Peter for spiritual guidance and direction? They were all Jewish and had the Jewish perspective of God's salvation plan.

Here is what RT does and has done in relation to Israel by the hands of the Church Fathers:

- RT was introduced to the Church shortly after Gentile leadership took over from Jewish leadership in the second and third centuries.
- RT developed because the Church Fathers moved from the literal interpretation of Scripture to Origen's method of allegorizing the Scriptures. This shift was based on their desire to find a hidden meaning that did not exist.

- RT teaches that Israel, the Jewish people, and the Land of Israel have been **replaced** by the Gentile Christian Church, Gentile Christians, and Gentile nations in the purposes of God. More precisely, the Church is seen as the historic continuation of Israel to the exclusion of the Jewish people or Israel. The reason for this is because of the historical Christian charge that because Jewish people rejected Christ, turning Him over to the Romans for crucifixion, all Jewish people are thus guilty of killing God, the Jewish Messiah. Thus, RT states that Israel has now been **replaced** in God's plan. Without any biblical evidence for making such an assumption, they proceed to declare that by default, the Church takes the place of Israel, and the promises to Israel now apply to the Church.

- RT teaches that the Jewish people are no longer the chosen people of God. They are no different from any other ethnic group of people such as the English, German, Spanish, Russian, Asian, or African peoples.

- RT teaches that apart from repentance, the new birth, and incorporation into the earthly Gentile-led Church, the Jewish people have no future, no hope, and no calling in the plan of God. They are the same as any other ethnic group of people in the world – with no difference at all. Supposedly, God has forgotten about His promises to them or changed His mind in fulfilling them.

- RT teaches that since Pentecost as recorded in Acts 2, the term *Israel* as found in the New Testament now refers to the Church. They disregard that Acts 2 is referring to Jewish people coming to Faith in their Messiah.

- RT teaches that the promises, covenants, and blessings ascribed to Israel in the Bible have been taken away from the Jews (who have been **displaced** from God's promises) and these promises, covenants, and blessings have now been given to the Church, which has superseded Israel. However, they insist that the Jews are still subject to the *curses* found in the Bible as part of the same covenant agreements, as a result of their rejection of Christ. None of these curses are taken to apply to the Church.

- RT's form of theology became fertile soil from which Christian anti-Semitism grew; and its theology has now infected the Church for nearly 1,900 years. The Church – even taking into consideration conservative and fundamental believers – has largely not been able to shake it off to this present day.

Dispensationalists do not follow RT or use allegorical methods of interpretation. They believe, as I do, that the Scriptures are to be interpreted literally; we understand and accept that God needs no help from finite man to change or re-write what He is saying in His Word. He can speak quite well for Himself. The net result of reading in allegorical interpretation has been that RT has perpetrated teachings that are anti-Israel, anti-God of Israel, anti-Jewish, and anti-Bible.

RT has stripped the Jewish people of the covenants and promises that were made to them by God. They gladly relegate to the Jewish people the curses and assign the blessings of God to themselves. They gladly promote themselves as Israel in God's plan. According to them, the Church and its members, and not the Jewish people, are the elect, chosen people of God. This goes on and on.

I have been studying and teaching the Minor Prophets in Bible college, and I find the teachings of RT to depend on an unbelievable twisting of Scripture to fit a system of theology that has been satanically inspired to depreciate the Jewish people and to destroy them over the centuries. RT has become one of Satan's prime weapons against the Jewish people. When one reads the Prophets, one finds that God was angry with Israel; however, in the future, He will love them without hesitation. Any remembrance of their sin will be removed (Jeremiah 32:37-41; Hosea 2:18-20). Sadly, Replacement Theology has continued to be part of the foundational theology for the Roman Catholic, Greek Orthodox, Eastern Orthodox (Palestinian Christians), and Russian Orthodox churches and many denominations in Protestantism as well.

There are two basic methods of interpretation that are vying for the hearts of Christians today: The literal interpretation versus the allegorical interpretation of Scriptures. There are three systems of theological understanding: (1) Dispensational, (2) Covenant Reform/Replacement, and (3) Amillennial Theology. Based on one's method of interpreting the Scriptures, a person will either support Israel or attack Israel (the Jewish people). If a person interprets the Scriptures literally, from a dispensational perspective, that person will support Israel. If another person interprets the Scriptures allegorically from a Covenant/Replacement or Amillennial perspective, even though it is the same Scriptures being studied, that person will probably be opposed to Israel. If anyone teaches that we are in the Kingdom of God now and that Israel is totally rejected from having any place in the Kingdom and future prophecy, that teacher is aligned with Covenant and Amillennial interpretations as well as being theologically tied to Roman Catholicism, which accepted the foundation of RT.

People who accept RT do not necessarily use the words *Replacement Theology*, but fervently believe in the replacement of Israel by Christians and calling the organized Church the "new Israel." I have spent about a dozen hours going over a movie promoting this kind of teaching. I will not give the name of this pastor or church nor will I give the name of the movie and his church that produced it. This pastor is slick, smooth, and abuses Scripture, taking truth and twisting it. We must be biblically discerning against false teaching that seems to the undiscerning Christian to be good. I found out about this movie when a pastor called me and asked if I was familiar with it because one of the people in his congregation viewed it and thought it was pretty good.

In his presentation in the movie, the pastor gives a brief history of the Jewish people while interviewing rabbis and pastors of his persuasion. Then he moves into discrediting Jewish people because of the crucifixion of Jesus and wickedness over the years. He ends up saying that the Church Fathers labeled the Jewish as wicked people who are responsible for killing God. He states that the modern State of Israel is not a fulfillment of prophecy by God but was formed by the United States and the United Nations. He attempts to impress upon the listener that because Israel has not repented and accepted Jesus as their Messiah, the Jews today – while physically Jewish – are not real Jews. He teaches that the Church supersedes the Jewish covenants and that now it all belongs to the Church. Through the movie he is teaching RT but never once does he mention his theological bias or being anti-Jewish.

It is disheartening to see a conservative believer and pastor pick and choose Scripture to support his erroneous views. He makes no mention of passages such as Leviticus 26:36-44; Deuteronomy 29:24; Isaiah 59:20-21; Jeremiah 31:31-37; 32:37-41; Ezekiel 36:16-38; 37:1-28; Hosea 2:14-23; or Zephaniah 3:14-20 which without question show Israel's future restoration and regeneration as a nation.

Suggested Readings on History of Church Anti-Semitism

Finally I would like to give you a list of books if you have the interest to read about the atrocities of the Church. It is interesting reading, but it is not fun reading. I challenge you to become aware of the dark side of the Church. It is my prayer that you will understand the need to love the Jewish people because they are the physical brothers and sisters of your LORD Jesus Christ, as He Himself referenced them in Matthew 25:31-46.

Books

Brown, Michael L., *Our Hands Are Stained with Blood: The Tragic Story of the "Church" and the Jewish People* (Destiny Image: Shippensburg, PA, 1990).

Dimont, Max I., *Jews, God and History* (New York, NY: Mentor Book, 1994).

Heinrich, William H., *In the Shame of Jesus: The Hidden Story of Church-Sponsored Anti-Semitism* (JHousePublishing: Keller, TX, 2016), memorial edition. The author passed away in 2016 and I received permission to publish this book, which you can purchase through my website: www.PromisesToIsrael.org.

Melnick, Oliver, *They Have Conspired Against You: Responding to the New Anti-Semitism* (Keller, TX: JHousePublishing, 2007).

Nicholls, William. *Christian Anti-Semitism: A History of Hate* (Jason Aronson, Inc.: Northvale, NJ, 1995).

Telchin, Stan. *Abandoned: What Is God's Will for the Jewish People and the Church?* (Grand Rapids, MI: Chosen Books, 1997).

Thieme, R. B. Jr., *Anti-Semitism* (R. B. Thieme Bible Ministries: Houston, TX, 2003).

Magazine Articles

Israel My Glory, Friends of Israel Gospel Ministry, April/May 1993 (Bellmawr, NJ).

Israel My Glory, Friends of Israel Gospel Ministry, Sept/Oct 2014 (Bellmawr, NJ).

Chapter 3
Errors of Covenant Theology

Is the Background of God's Word Greek or Jewish?

Replacement, Covenant, and Amillennial theologians completely miss the central importance of teaching Scripture from a Jewish perspective and interpreting it literally. Even dispensationalists do not always fully recognize the importance of the Jewish perspective in understanding God's message to us! Instead, Covenant/Replacement theologians view the Scriptures from their own personal, theological position and bias, which was generated by viewing the Scriptures from a western, Greek perspective through the filter of bias against Jewish people, while using an allegorical approach to interpreting the Scriptures. These complex, anachronistic, and culturally-clouded approaches leave much to be desired.

In comparison, let me give simple points leading to interpreting God's Word when it is taken from its original perspective:

- The Scriptures are Jewish, authored by 40-plus Jewish men.
- The Scriptures are immersed in Jewish thought from the Middle East.
- The customs of Scripture are Jewish customs.
- The culture of Scripture is Jewish culture.
- The central focus of Scripture is Israel.
- The central focus of Scripture is not only Israel, but also specifically the Jewish Messiah.
- Israel is the world's timepiece.

- The Scriptures do not originate from a Greek background, a European background, or an American background, but they do originate from a Jewish background.

- The focus of Scripture is only temporarily on the Church, but start to finish, it is the story of Israel, its past, present, and glorious future!

- We as Gentile believers receive all the spiritual blessings of a Jewish New Covenant of which I give a detailed description in my book, *Israel's Only Hope: The New Covenant;*[55] we are grafted into the Body of Messiah – Jew and Gentile, one in Messiah.

- God is not done with Israel or the Jewish people; instead, one-third of Scripture is yet to be fulfilled as God completes the future plan He has described for them in Jeremiah 31:31-34.

This point, the Jewish frame of reference, needs to be understood by all believers. The Jewish background or frame of reference of the Scriptures is not taught by Evangelical, Conservative, or Fundamental Christianity, yet the Jewish perspective lays out the foundational understanding of the Covenants that God made with Israel. The Jewish perspective is the step in Dispensationalism that gives it even more power and authority to dislodge personal theological biases. Without this grounding, the understanding of the promises that God has made with national Israel and the Jewish people in general is pushed into the background subconsciously, resulting in a skewed understanding of the Jewish people and the State of Israel in the world today and lack of understanding of the very heart of God and His revealed plan.

What Are the Disconnects of Covenant and Replacement Theology?

We as Christians are suffering under 1,900 years of Replacement Theology (RT); we are suffering under the residual effects of bad doctrine and don't recognize it! The theology of most Bible-believing Christians has no practical, genuine interest in Jewish people. Few are interested in studying the Scriptures as God wrote them, because even we who take a dispensational view of the Bible have suppressed its obvious Jewish orientation that God used to convey the Scriptures.

---

[55] John B. Metzger, *Israel's Only Hope: The New Covenant* (Keller, TX: JHousePublishing, Purple Raiment Imprint, 2015).

I have been personally amazed at the apathy of fundamental as well as conservative believers. Sadly, pastors largely only give lip service to Israel. Too often, pastors, and even Bible School teachers, do not take the Jewish understanding of the Scriptures seriously because they miss the significance of it or have a bias against Israel and the Jewish people. You may say that is a rash statement, but when you look and listen, you only see a surface interest in Israel and not a deeply held practical and working conviction. Israel is for leading tours and enjoying vacations, or maybe for trying to convert a tour guide. Where in their ministries or teachings is love for the Jewish people systematically exhibited in their own locality?

When it comes to studying the Scriptures from a Jewish background and frame of reference, a pastor's response is to shift mentally into neutral. The sentiment is clear: The Jewish perspective is insignificant and unimportant to most pastors because it is Jewish! You may say this is an extremely critical statement, perhaps; but when you interact with conservative and fundamental believers as I have been doing for 20 years, you begin to see the pattern.

The alternative to Dispensational Theology is Covenant Theology. First let me say that although our theologies differ, I am speaking about my beloved brothers in Christ. While I love and respect them, Replacement theologians and Covenant theologians view Scripture from a very different perspective.

Covenant Theology, a Newcomer

Covenant Theology, also called Federal Theology, did not exist in the first-century Church among the Church Fathers, nor was it part of the Roman Catholic system of the Middle Ages. It did not exist at the beginning of the Reformation. However, dating from the fourth century, Augustine's Replacement/Amillennial Theology provided an inroad for the later development of Covenant Theology. The Reformers invented it because they did not "reform" or throw aside all of the erroneous doctrines of the Catholic Church. They held on to the Amillennial Theology of Augustine and RT of the early Church Fathers, making the Reformation incomplete!

Along with embracing the errors of the Church Fathers, the Reformers also kept the foundational teaching of allegorizing the Scriptures as presented by Origen. Thus, the Reformers fell short of removing the error of the very Church doctrine they were fighting against but instead incorporated many of the same errors into their reformed system of theology. Instead of reforming the error of an apostate church, they built Covenant Theology on the back of centuries of inaccurate teachings on the present and future state of the Jewish people and the nation of Israel. These errant teachings have persisted for over 1,300 years from the 2nd century to the Reformation. For an in depth look at this partial process of reformation, please see Appendix Four, an excellent article written by Dr. Andy Woods entitled "A Failure of the Reformation."

Covenant Theology came into being with the ministry of Kaspar Olevianus (August 10, 1536 – March 15, 1587) who was born in Trier, Germany. He was a friend of Calvin as a young man. Olevianus was a follower of Calvin and of the Reform persuasion. Covenant Theology started in the Reformed Churches of Switzerland and Germany, and then it was passed on to the Netherlands, Scotland, and England. In 1647 the Westminster Confession of faith, which embraced the new Covenant Theology, became the confession of faith for these European Church Reform denominations. It was then brought to America by the Puritans.

The basic definition of Covenant Theology, given by Louis Berkhof, himself a Covenant theologian, is stated as follows:

> The concept of the ***covenant*** became for the first time the constitutive and determinative principle of the whole system.[56] [Emphasis mine]

As the Reformers moved out of the corrupted theology of Rome, they proceeded to drag with them and implement the root of the problem by incorporating that root into the next system of theology called Covenant Theology. They failed to grasp and understand the importance of the perspective God used to send His message. God, Himself, gave eight biblical covenants in Scripture to help us understand His overall plan from Genesis to Revelation, and we will focus on that framework. Unfortunately, the Reformed Church did not move off its Gentile-Church, Greek focus to a Jewish focus on Israel and a Jewish Messiah as central.

Now what does the statement by Berkhof mean? Simply put, Covenant Theology uses the theological concept of *covenant* as an organizing principle for Christian theology. This means that all of God's dealings with mankind are bound up in three covenants that they have defined: the covenants of (1) Redemption, (2) Works, and (3) Grace. However, Covenant Theology has

---

[56] Louis Berkhof, *Systematic Theology* (2nd revised and enlarged edition; Grand Rapids, MI: Wm. B. Erdmann Publishing Co, 1941), 211.

a problem, for nowhere in the Scriptures are these covenants given by God as covenants. Instead, they have been inserted by a system of theology. What should take precedence: man's ideas or God's direct promises?

Wikipedia states the following regarding the three-covenant theory:

> These three covenants are called theological because, though **they are not explicitly presented as such in the Bible**, they are thought to be theologically implicit, describing and summarizing the wealth of Scriptural data. Within historical Reformed systems of thought, Covenant Theology is not merely treated as a point of doctrine or a central dogma, **but the structure by which the biblical text organizes itself**.[57] [Emphasis mine]

Please read that over again! This observation can be clearly seen; this system of theology was nonexistent in the Scriptures and has been inserted. It took root in the Reformed Theology of Calvin. It has absorbed the RT and Amillennial Theology[58] of Roman Catholicism so that today it is commonly referred to as Covenant/Replacement Theology.

It is always dangerous for theologians to imply or insert concepts into Scripture when the Scriptures do not clearly or directly teach those concepts. Though Covenant Theology uses the term *covenant* in its identification, it is not referring to the eight biblical covenants that God did make with mankind, three to Gentiles and five to Israel or the Jewish people. We will look closely at those eight covenants, but for now, let us review the three theological covenants of Covenant Theology: Redemption, Works, and Grace.

- (1) Covenant of Redemption:

Renald Showers, who references Louis Berkhof, states the following:

> The Covenant of Redemption was established between God the Father and God the Son. In this covenant the Father granted the

---

[57] Found at www.wikipedia.org/wiki/Covenant_Theology, second paragraph – last accessed October 24, 2016.

[58] Amillennial Theology teaches that the Second Coming of Jesus is not literal and that there is no literal 1000-year reign (or Millennium) of Christ on the throne of David. Therefore, they reject the Bible prophecies regarding God's future plan for Israel and the Jewish people, meaning that the prophecies in the Old Testament are fulfilled by the Church, who is the New Israel. They teach that Christ is currently reigning on the throne of David in Heaven and will not literally sit on the throne of David in Jerusalem.

Son to be Head and Redeemer of the elect. In return, the Son voluntarily agreed to take the place of those whom the Father had given Him.

The covenant of Redemption was established in eternity past. God knew that man would fall away from Him; thus, in eternity past God determined to provide redemption during the course of history for the elect.[59]

Notice the terms used, because there are truths that they speak of, but then they assume their theological system as an overlay on Scripture and imply what the Scriptures themselves do not say. For instance, the Scripture does say that Christ was the Lamb slain from the foundations of the world (Revelation 13:8), and it does say that Christ was foreordained (1 Peter 1:19-20), but it does not say that the Father and the Son made a covenant of Redemption; that is implied, going beyond what Scriptures said.

- (2) Covenant of Works:

Renald Showers once again states that the Covenant of Works was **made between God and Adam** in the beginning. Adam was the representative head of the human race, and God in the Covenant of Works required of Adam his "implicit and perfect obedience." However, nowhere is a Covenant of Works given by God in the Scriptures. Berkhof states that "the threatened penalty clearly **implies** such a promise."[60] [Emphasis mine]

What God did say in Genesis 3 was that Adam and Eve could eat of all the fruit of the trees of the garden except one. Imagine only one command to obey! If Adam disobeyed, he was promised death by God, which included spiritual death (separation from God) and physical death (separation from human life). Now notice again the words of Berkhof: "The threatened penalty clearly implies such a promise"[61] that if Adam violated the Covenant of Works, he would suffer death. However, nowhere in Genesis 2 – 3 is such a covenant given. For that matter, nowhere else in Scripture is such a covenant given. It does not exist; it is implied, and that is going beyond what

---

[59] Renald E. Showers, *There Really Is a Difference: A Comparison of Covenant and Dispensational Theology* (Bellmawr, NJ: Friends of Israel Gospel Ministry, 2013), 9. This book is a must read for you to understand the differences between their two systems of theology.

[60] Showers, *There Really Is a Difference*, 10.

[61] Berkhof, *Systematic Theology*, 215.

God said! Mind you, this is not just a point on an insignificant piece of Scripture but the foundation on which Covenant theologians build their entire theological system.

- (3) Covenant of Grace:

    According to this covenant, **God established the Covenant of Grace** (between Adam and God) because Adam broke the Covenant of Works. Berkhof defines the Covenant of Grace as "that gracious agreement between the offended God and the offending but elect sinner, in which God promises salvation **through faith in Christ**, and the sinner accepts this believingly, promising a life of faith and obedience."[62] [Emphasis mine]

    First of all, where in the Hebrew Scriptures is the Covenant of Grace specifically given? Nowhere! The absence of the specific promise in God's Word does not mean that God does not give grace to sinful human beings. God's promises that He reveals in His Word and the overall story of the Bible make clear that He will exercise grace throughout all of time. However, that the giving of His grace was part of a promise that He made directly with Adam is not recorded in Scripture.

How Does Dispensational Theology Differ from Covenant Theology?

God did make eight covenants that are part of His Word. These do relate to God's grace promised in Scripture. Do not confuse the three covenants that Covenant Theology implies with the Covenants that God made with Adam (promise of Messiah), Noah (rainbow), Abraham (Seed and Land covenants), Israel (restoration), David (the Messianic line), and the covenant given to Israel by Jeremiah (the New Covenant of forgiveness, regeneration, and the indwelling presence of the Holy Spirit) in Scripture. These Bible covenants are not one covenant in the same or continuous procession; they each have distinctions. The following chart,[63] used with permission from Mottel Baleston of Messengers Messianic Jewish Outreach ministry, I have found to be very helpful. You can also view the same chart in color, online at: www.arielm.org/outlines/o-mec-chart.pdf.

---

[62] Berkhof, *Systematic Theology*, 288.
[63] Mottel Baleston, *The Dispensations & Covenants* (San Antonio, TX: Ariel Ministries, 2006).

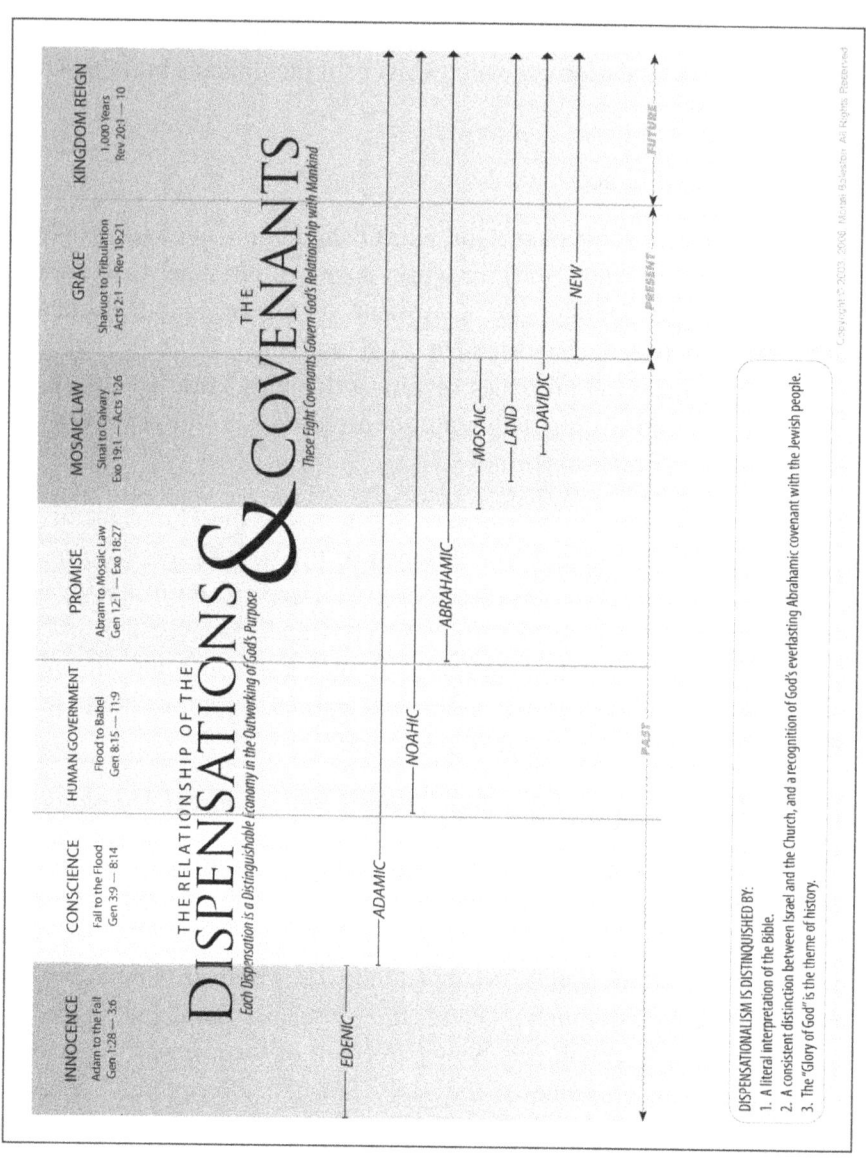

Figure 2.
The Relationship of the Dispensations & Covenants of the Bible

Covenant Theology's implied teaching on God's grace ignores any variations over history that God provided. For instance, under Mosaic Law, grace was dispensed through a sacrifice system. That system is distinct from how God dispensed His grace to Noah, and for that matter, to us.

As another example, the Mosaic Law and New Covenant are distinct; and the promises for each of them are distinct, one producing death and the other producing life. The Mosaic Law and New Covenant of Jeremiah are not recognized as distinct in the Covenant/Reformed covenant of Grace. The approaches of Dispensationalists and Covenant theologians are complete opposites. According to Dispensationalism, while God's grace is ongoing, God has dispensed it in distinct ways over time, according to His eight covenant promises. To Covenant theologians, God's various specific promises in Scripture are of little importance compared to the central importance of their implied interpretation of grace, as offered to Adam as an alternative to works.

These covenants that Covenant Theology takes as its central theological framework are implied covenants from theologians but are not covenants given by God in His Word. This must be noted carefully, and you must be biblically discerning. They use language that sounds good until you compare Scripture with Scripture, and then the system becomes man's arguments and theological systems and not God's Word. There is much more that can be said, but I am trying to kept it as elementary as possible.

Now we want to move on to some other points that separate Dispensationalism from Covenant Theology. There are three other areas where we are disconnected from our Covenant/Reform brothers.

- **The People of God:**

    Covenant Theology teaches that the Church existed in the Old Testament times and that Israel was a major part of the Church in the Old Testament. It often defines the Church as the continuing covenanted community. In other words, the Church consists of all the peoples throughout history who have had a covenant relationship with God. Thus, these people are essentially the same...[T]his issue of Israel and the Church being distinct is a major point of difference between Covenant and Dispensational Theology, ...[64]

What do Covenant theologians mean? First, they assert that the people of God, or "covenanted community," throughout history are all believers. They want you to believe that Enoch, Noah, Abraham, Moses, and David in the Hebrew Scriptures had to believe in Jesus Christ as their personal savior from sin. What Dispensational Theology recognizes is that there is only one common ingredient in the people of God through the ages: All are saved **by Faith** in the progressive revelation of God's Word throughout time.

The content of a saving Faith was different for Noah and Moses, both saved **by Faith**, and not in the finished work of Christ on the cross of Calvary before it happened. Because Scripture was progressively revealed, the full revelation of Jesus as the Savior of the World was not known in the Hebrew Scriptures. That would later be known when God took on flesh in the person of Jesus Christ (John 1:14).

What Differences Does It Make – God's Covenants or Man's Ideas about Grace?

Because Covenant theologians and Dispensational theologians disagree on what the Kingdom of God consists of and when it begins, taking a look at the subject is important. Lots of confusion exists regarding the subject of the Kingdom of God. God has a Kingdom program, and it is important to understand how this Kingdom program of God fits together. Understanding the usage and context when the term *kingdom* is used greatly helps us understand its meaning. In each instance in Scripture, God is referring to one of the following: (1) Mystery Kingdom, (2) the Messianic Kingdom, (3) the Theocratic Kingdom, (4) the Universal Kingdom or (5) the Spiritual Kingdom, which deals with the "people of God" issue. In the Scriptures, the context is always the priority; paying attention to the clues to the context of each use of the term will help us understand the meaning.

Again we must be discerning in our understanding, for there are **five Kingdom programs** of God referenced in Scripture. I have cited them below with permission from Arnold Fruchtenbaum.[65]

---

[64] Showers, *There Really Is a Difference*, 21-22.

(1) God's Universal, Eternal Kingdom: He Is in Charge, Not Any of Us

The **first** facet of **God's Kingdom program** goes by two names; it is sometimes called the **universal kingdom** or the **eternal kingdom**. These two programs demonstrate God's sovereign rule over His creation. The first name, **universal kingdom**, emphasizes God's extent of control over the entire universe. It is universal. It is also called the **eternal kingdom** because He is always in control. This all means that nothing inside the universe for all eternity has happened or will happen outside of His will.

Things will happen because of [God's] directive will as He decreed it, or by His permissive will (providence), because He so allowed it. But whatever happens, it all happens in the sovereign will of God, either by directive will or by permissive will. (See 1 Chronicles 29:11-12; Psalms 10:16; 29:10; 74:12; 90:1-6; 83:11-15; 103:19-22; 145; Proverbs 21:11; Jeremiah 10:18; Lamentations 5:19; Daniel 4:17, 25, 32; 6:27; Acts 17:24.)

(2) God's Spiritual Program

The second facet of the Kingdom program is the Spiritual program. The Spiritual Kingdom deals with the **rule of God in the hearts of the believers**. His Spiritual Kingdom is comprised of all believers who have experienced the new birth by the regeneration work of the Holy Spirit.[66] So from Adam onward the Spiritual Kingdom has existed, because there have always been believers who put their Faith in God and have the rule of God in their hearts. [These would be the people of God.] Now between Pentecost in Acts 2 and the Rapture, the Spiritual Kingdom and the Church are the same. The Church is part of the Spiritual Kingdom, in the eternal program of the Kingdom. But today the Church and the Spiritual Kingdom are the

---

[65] This section is taken from my personal transcription of Arnold G. Fruchtenbaum's tapes on *The Life of Messiah*, Volume 2 of Arnold's series called *Yeshua, The Life of the Messiah from a Messianic Jewish Perspective* (San Antonio, TX: Ariel Ministries, 2016).

[66] In contrast to this statement, I personally do not believe the regenerative work of the Holy Spirit is to be found in the Old Testament; however, that does not mean there were no saved people before the New Testament. The regenerative power of the Holy Spirit was released by Yeshua's sacrificial death, by the blood of the New Covenant. For more details on this subject, refer to my book, *Israel's Only Hope: The New Covenant, 2015.*

same thing, because today all believers are both part of the Church and the Spiritual Kingdom. The mistake that some theologians make is to equate the Kingdom of God with the Church throughout [Scripture]. They are only the same from Acts 2 to the Rapture. **The Spiritual Kingdom is much larger than the Church!** The Spiritual Kingdom was in existence before the Church was born and it will continue to exist in the hearts of believers when the Church is raptured. Matthew 6:33; 19:16, 23-24; John 3:3-5; Acts 8:12; 14:22; 19:8; 20:25; 28:23; Galatians 5:21; Ephesians 5:5; Colossians 1:13; 4:11; 1 Thessalonians 2:12; 2 Thessalonians 1:5; 1 Corinthians 6:9-10; 4:20. [Bolding is my addition.]

(3) God's Theocratic Kingdom

The third facet of God's Kingdom program is called the Theocratic Kingdom. The Theocratic Kingdom is God's rule over Israel, for Israel was a theocracy. This is God's special rule of His people Israel, the Theocratic Kingdom. This kingdom was established by Moses, and the Mosaic Law served as the constitution of the Theocratic Kingdom. This kingdom underwent two forms: the Meditatorial and the Monarchal.

> The **Meditatorial** form meaning [is] that He ruled His [T]heocracy through mediators, from Moses to Samuel. Samuel is the transition between the Meditatorial phase of the kingdom to the Monarchal phase.

> The **Monarchal** form was His rule over His Theocracy through the House of David. So from David to Zedekiah you had the monarchal form. In 586 B.C. the Theocratic Kingdom came to an end.

[The Theocratic Kingdom] began with Moses and ended with Zedekiah or the Babylonian destruction of Jerusalem. So at this point the *Times of the Gentiles* [began], and the Monarchal period [ended]. These *[T]imes of the Gentiles* will continue until the next phase of God's Kingdom program is established. Exodus 20 through 2 Chronicles 36 is the biblical record of the Theocratic Kingdom.

(4) The Messianic or Millennial Kingdom

The **fourth** facet of God's kingdom program also goes by two names, the **Messianic Kingdom** (Jewish term), or the **Millennial Kingdom**

(Gentile Church term). The term *Messianic Kingdom* emphasizes the Person who will rule over this kingdom, the Messiah, Yeshua. The term *Millennial* emphasizes the length of the kingdom, for 1000 years.

In the declining days of the Theocratic Kingdom, the quality of that kingdom began to decline because the kings of the House of David became more wicked[,] and the righteous less and less, so the Prophets mentioned the coming of a new kingdom, the Messianic Kingdom. The basis of the Messianic Kingdom is the Davidic Covenant in 2 Samuel 7:8-17; 1 Chronicles 17:10-16; Matthew 1:1; and Luke 1:32.

The Messianic Kingdom was a major topic of Old Testament prophecy. To this day most of what we know about the Messianic Kingdom comes from the Jewish Scriptures and not the New Covenant. Some passages are as follows: Psalm 2 and 72; Isaiah 9:6-7; 11:1-16; Jeremiah 23:5-6; 32:14-17; Ezekiel 34:23; 37:24; Hosea 3:4-5; Micah 4:6-8, 5:2; Malachi 3:1-4[.] (These passages are connected to the Davidic Covenant).

There was the Kingdom proclaimed by *Yochanan* the Baptist when Yeshua was present. In Matthew 3:2; 4:17; 10:5-7, the Kingdom was being offered by Him from the beginning of His ministry until the rejection of the Messiah in Matthew 12. Had they [Israel] accepted Him as the Messiah, this is the Kingdom that [could have been] established in their day. But this was the Kingdom rejected by Israel's leaders in Matthew 12, so that the Kingdom was then withdrawn.

One point of clarification, people have assumed that had Israel accepted Yeshua as Messiah that He would not have had to die. This is incorrect; the death of the Messiah was unavoidable because the issue of dealing with sin had to be by the shedding of blood. Whether Israel did or did not accept Him, He would have died anyway. The Atonement only comes by blood, not by kingly rule. [However,] the scenario would have been different:

> Israel would have proclaimed Him as their King, and the Romans would have seen that as an act of rebellion against the Roman Empire. So He would have been arrested by Roman authorities as He was tried by a Roman Judge, as He was, die a

Roman death, as He did and then be buried as He was. The difference is that after His resurrection three days later He would have dispensed with the Roman Empire and established the Messianic Kingdom. The issue would not be [whether] He died or not, He had to die for sin, His death was unavoidable. The issue [would be whether] the Kingdom [would] be established at this time[;] that was the issue. Israel's rejection was the means that God ordained for Him to die.

This is the kingdom that was rescinded from the generation of His day, and is destined to be offered to a future Jewish generation during the Tribulation as we read in Matthew 24:14; and this time around, Israel will accept Him as the Messiah (Isaiah 53; Zechariah 12:10-13:1). As a result of Israel's acceptance, He will then return (Zechariah 14:1-15); and He will then establish His Kingdom (Zechariah 14:16-21; Revelation 19:11-26). But since that Kingdom was rejected or rescinded, what happens in paragraph 64[67] is the introduction to a new facet of God's Kingdom program unrevealed before, called the Mystery Kingdom.

(5) The Mystery Kingdom

Now let us define **Mystery Kingdom** in its New Testament usage. Turn in your Bibles to Ephesians 3:2:

> *...if indeed you have heard of the stewardship of God's grace which was given to me for you; that by revelation there was made known to me the mystery, as I wrote before in brief. And by referring to this, when you read you can understand my insight into the mystery of Christ, which in other generations was not made known to the sons of men, as it has now been revealed to His holy apostles and prophets in the Spirit.*

---

[67] Paragraph 64 is in *The Harmony of the Gospels* by A.T. Robinson that Dr. Fruchtenbaum uses as he presents his teaching on *The Life of Messiah from a Jewish Perspective*. Arnold G. Fruchtenbaum, *Ariel's Harmony of the Gospels*, (San Antonio, TX: Ariel Ministries, 2016), 78-82. It is now an Ariel publication, stating on the front cover that it is "based on A.T. Robinson's *Harmony of the Gospels*."

So mystery in its New Testament usage means *a truth unrevealed in the Old Testament and then revealed for the first time in the new.* It does not have the common English meaning of mystery, but is something that was hidden in the Jewish Scriptures and now in the New Testament is revealed to us. Look at verses 9-10:

> *...and to bring to light what is the administration of the mystery which for ages has been hidden in God, who created all things; in order that the manifold wisdom of God might now be made known through the church to the rulers and the authorities in the heavenly places.*

Notice something hidden in God from the ages past only now revealed in New Testament times through the Apostles and Prophets:

> *Of this church I was made a minister according to the stewardship from God bestowed on me for your benefit, that I might fully carry out the preaching of the Word of God, that is, the mystery which has been hidden from the past ages and generations; but has now been manifested to His saints* (Colossians 1:25).

Again, [it was] a mystery that was hidden in the mind of God from the ages and generations, but now being revealed. Again[,] it is not something that cannot be explained, for Paul in these two passages states that it is now known. Of the various different mysteries in the New Testament, the one in #[5, above] has to do with the facet of God's Mystery Kingdom; and we get the name from Mark 4:11,

> *Unto you it is given to know the mysteries of the kingdom of heaven, but to them it is not given.*

They called it the Mystery Kingdom because that is [Yeshua's] name for it, so whatever we learn about this facet of God's kingdom program is something that was unrevealed in the Jewish Scriptures, revealed for the first time in the new. The Mystery Kingdom begins with the rejection of the Messiah in Matthew 12 and continues to the Second Coming. It tries to describe His rule on earth, while the King is physically absent and at the right hand of God the Father. Christendom probably best describes this kingdom because within

Christendom, under that umbrella you have everything called "Christian," both believers and non-believers.

This Mystery Kingdom is not the same as the Universal Kingdom because it is limited by time, from Israel's rejection to Israel's acceptance of Messiah. This Mystery Kingdom is distinct from the Spiritual Kingdom because this one includes believers and non-believers. It includes within its scope both the wheat and the tares.

This Mystery Kingdom is distinct from the Theocratic Kingdom for it is not dealing with God's theocratic rule over Israel. Within the Mystery Kingdom you have both Jews and Gentiles. By the same token, it is not the same as the Church, for the Church is only a part of the Mystery Kingdom but not the totality of it.

Finally, it is not the same as the Messianic Kingdom, because it is not ruled by the Messiah personally from David's throne in Jerusalem; and, furthermore, the Messianic Kingdom was anything but a mystery in the Jewish Scriptures. Most of what we know about that kingdom comes from the Jewish Scriptures, for it was a major area of revelation from the Jewish Scriptures.[68]

[End of quotation of Arnold G. Fruchtenbaum's teaching on the five Kingdoms of the Bible.]

Now let us move on to more specific points of distinction between Covenant/Reformed, RT, and the Dispensational approach. The first is replacement of Israel by the Church and the second is the usage of the allegorical method of interpretation.

- **Replacement of Israel by the Church:**

    The first-century Church did not teach the replacement of Israel by the Church when Paul, Peter, James, and John wrote their instructional teaching to the first-century Church. However, the early Church Fathers from the second century on, as illustrated in the chapter on RT, clearly showed that the Church taught that God had cast off Israel and that, by default, the Church had then replaced Israel as the people of God. Covenant Theology comes along and absorbs this and develops a system of theology around

---

[68] Arnold Fruchtenbaum, *Israelology: The Missing Link in Systematic Theology* (San Antonio, TX: Ariel Ministries, 1994), 604-614.

the replacement beliefs of the Early Church and attaches it to their Covenant of Grace. Notice this in the following quotation:

> The affirmation of the Jews as the people of God is tempered and colored by the Covenant Theology of Postmillennialism. This theology insists that it is the Church that is the people of God, and [in] the Old Testament the Church and Israel were the same [Covenant of Grace]. This is crucial to Covenant Theology. Their concept of the covenant of grace, the key foundation to Covenant Theology, with only one way of salvation with only one content of faith, requires them to hold to only one people of God. Since the Bible calls Israel the people of God and the Church the people of God, and if there can be only one people of God, it follows that Israel and the Church must be one and the same.[69]

As previously mentioned, there are several Kingdoms of God; and one of them deals with the Spiritual Kingdom of God, and that does include all believers from all time. However, the Spiritual Kingdom is not the Covenant of Grace that Covenant Theology holds to. If you look back into Genesis 1-12, you have clear covenant language being used in the following four covenants: Edenic (Genesis 1:28-30; 2:15-17), Adamic (Genesis 3:14-19), Noahic (Genesis 9:1-17) and Abrahamic (Genesis 12:1-3, 7). At the same time, there is no clear language used in Scriptures that Covenant theologians can claim concerning the Covenant of Grace. It also clearly ignores the clear language of the covenants and the distinctions that God makes between Israel and the Church. As was said before, they have implied an unbiblical covenant into Scripture that is not there to try and prop up their foundation concerning their unbiblical theological system. If you want a deeper theological discussion, please study the following books:

1. *Israelology,* authored by Arnold Fruchtenbaum and published by Ariel Ministries, San Antonio, TX, 1994.

2. *Dispensationalism,* authored by Charles Ryrie and published by Moody Press, Chicago, IL, 2007.

---

[69] Fruchtenbaum, *Israelology: The Missing Link in Systematic Theology*), 29-30.

3. *There Really Is a Difference,* authored by Renald Showers and published by Friends of Israel Gospel Ministry, Bellmawr, NJ, 1990.

Next we want to observe one of the most glaring abuses used freely by Covenant Theology to give so-called credence to their theological system.

- **Allegorical Interpretation of Scriptures:**

Webster Dictionary: "The expression by means of symbolic fictional figures and actions of truths or generalizations about human existence."[70]

In this section, we will look at a specific issue as it relates to the inherent danger of allegorizing Scripture, a method used by all systems of theology except Dispensational Theology. We have an all-sovereign God who is the author of speech, language, and grammar, who is completely capable of communicating His intended meaning. Covenant theologians limit the sovereignty of God and His being glorified in His redemptive program, which is incorrect. God receives glory not just in His redemptive program; He is sovereign in all things and He will receive glory in all things, not just in His redemptive program. Either way, we have man, who is *not* sovereign, who does *not* understand God; for even God says in Isaiah 55:8-9:

> *⁸ For My thoughts are not your thoughts, neither are your ways My ways, says the LORD. ⁹ For as the heavens are higher than the earth, so are My ways higher than your ways, and My thoughts than your thoughts.*

Let me give two illustrations and one application of falsely allegorizing Scriptures so that we can grasp the dangers of allegorizing the Scriptures unnecessarily.

(1) Covenant/Replacement and Amillennial theologies replace Israel as the people of God with the Church. They assert that the Church represents the people of God based on a false premise or assumption, since Scripture at no time directly states this.

(2) There are thirty First-Coming references regarding Messiah which were fulfilled literally in Scripture.[71]

---

[70] *Merriam-Webster's Collegiate Dictionary,* 32.

The pattern laid down in Scripture is a literal fulfillment; yet when it comes to the Second Coming of Messiah, Covenant/Replacement and Amillennial theologians want to allegorize or spiritualize the text, presenting it as symbolic instead of literal. Please let me illustrate this simply:

- Q. Was Jesus preceded by the voice crying out in the wilderness?
- A. *Yes, literally fulfilled.*
- Q. Was Jesus born of a virgin?
- A. *Yes, literally fulfilled.*
- Q. Was Jesus born in Bethlehem of Judea?
- A. *Yes, literally fulfilled.*
- Q. Was Jesus the Prophet like Moses?
- A. *Yes, literally fulfilled.*
- Q. Was Jesus riding on a colt of a donkey into Jerusalem?
- A. *Yes, literally fulfilled.*
- Q. Were Jesus' hands and feet pierced?
- A. *Yes, literally fulfilled.*
- Q. Was Jesus from the tribe of Judah?
- A. *Yes, literally fulfilled.*
- Q. Was Jesus the son of David, meaning in the ancestry line of David as prophesied?
- A. *Yes, literally fulfilled.*
- Q. Was Jesus the vicarious, voluntary sacrifice for sin?
- A. *Yes, literally fulfilled.*
- Q. Did Jesus arrive at the promised time as Daniel said?
- A. *Yes, literally fulfilled.*

These and many other prophecies were literally fulfilled; they were not allegorized or spiritualized by the authors of Scripture. I could fill a book with the promises of God that were literally fulfilled in the life of Israel as well as in the life of Jesus Christ—literal fulfillment, literal fulfillment, literal

---

[71] Arnold G. Fruchtenbaum, *Ha Mashiach* (San Antonio, TX: Ariel Ministries Press, 2015).

fulfillment!! Yet for the Second Coming of Scripture, it is all symbolic, spiritualized, or allegorized by "scholars" within the Covenant/Replacement and Amillennial theologies. Now the same authors of Scripture also reference the Second Coming of Christ. They prophesy that the Messiah will set up a future, earthly, physical kingdom that will endure for 1,000 years. They all speak of the seven years of the Tribulation before the Kingdom, and prophesy that God will fulfill all the covenants He made with Abraham, David, and Israel. The Second Coming passages are just as literal as the First Coming passages, yet Covenant/Replacement and Amillennial theologians want to spiritualize them and remove the literal meaning that God placed upon them.

The abuse of Scriptures by religious scholars of a Covenant/Replacement persuasion can be seen in the chapter and verse headings as given in the Thompson Chain Reference Bible.[72] I picked out some very obvious examples in the Prophets. None of these passages in any way relates to the Church, yet look at the implied headings inserted in this Bible version over these passages in the Hebrew Scriptures:

Table 1. Replacement Theology's Bias in Bible Headings

Scripture Ref.	Imposed Headings
Isaiah 19:18	Calling of Egypt into the Church.
Isaiah 30:18	His mercy to the Church.
Isaiah 33	God's judgments against the enemies of the Church.
Isaiah 34:1-15	Judgments wherewith God avenges His Church.
Isaiah 41:1-20	God speaks of His merciful providence in regard to His Church.
Isaiah 44:1-8	God's Church comforted.
Isaiah 45:1-4	God calls Cyrus for His Church's sake.
Isaiah 49:13	God's love to the Church perpetual.
Isaiah 52:1-6	The Church roused with God's promise of free redemption.
Isaiah 54	The Church comforted with gracious promises.
Isaiah 56:9-12	The Church distressed by blind watchmen.
Isaiah 60:1-14	Glory of the Church in the abundant access of the Gentiles.
Isaiah 61:6-11	Restoration and blessedness of the Church.
Zechariah 9:1-8	God defends His Church.

---

[72] Frank Charles Thompson, *Thompson Chain Reference Bible*, (Indianapolis, IN: B.B. Kirkbride Bible Co., Inc. 1964).

With such odd insertions, misguided men are saying that their interpretations of various biblical passages are better understood from their own perspective rather than God's. Man's word becomes superior to God's Word; man is taking authority that is not his and placing or making God's interpretation secondary to or beneath man's interpretation. Just sit there and ponder that thought before reading on! The words below express a blunt point:

God's authority and interpretation become Subservient to Man's Authority and Interpretation when allegorized!

Chapter 4
What Is Dispensationalism?

John Nelson Darby (November 18, 1800 – April 29, 1882) was born in Westminster, London, and was a member of the Plymouth Brethren Assembles. He has been given the title of the Founder of Dispensational Theology. However, he only popularized what was believed and held by numerous believers going back to the 1500s. Dispensational Theology grew up at the same time as Covenant Theology, even though the Covenant school of theologians likes to say that Darby was the "new kid on the block" theologically.

A History of Dispensationalism

Although Dispensational Theology was not developed by the early Church, some, like Clement of Alexandria and Augustine, did recognize three or four distinct ways of the workings of God in the world. However, while saying that, the Apostle Paul taught and handled the Scriptures dispensationally as he wrote to the churches.

The first person to develop a genuine dispensational scheme in a systematic fashion was the French philosopher Pierre Poiret (1646-1719), born in Metz, France. In *The Divine Economy*, he developed seven dispensations covering the scope of Scriptures and history. His work was published in Holland in 1687. This was about a century after Kasper Olevianus began to develop Covenant Theology.

In 1699, John Edwards (1639-1716) published a well-developed, dispensational scheme in his book entitled *A Complete History and Survey of All the Dispensations*. Also, Isaac Watts (1674-1748), the hymn writer, presented Dispensationalism in an essay that he wrote called "Harmony of all Religions which God Ever Prescribed to Men and all His Dispensations towards Them." However, it was not popularized until the nineteenth century under the ministry of John Nelson Darby. Dispensational teaching became popularized by the *Scofield Reference Bible,* published in 1909.

Another name that helped to popularize dispensational teaching was a Presbyterian minister in St. Louis, Missouri, by the name of James H. Brookes. In 1909, in St. Louis, the Brookes Bible Institute was established; and according to their web-pages, Brookes was the father of Dispensationalism.

A new book by William C. Watson [73] pushes the date for the beginning of Dispensational Theology back to the seventeenth and eighteenth centuries as men began to discern from Scripture that the Church and Israel were distinct from each other. Many different men who preceded Darby became cognizant that God in the future would gather Israel in unbelief and bring them back to the Land in preparation for Israel embracing Jesus Christ as their Messiah. We will look into this plan as it is revealed in God's Word.

So in reviewing the history of the two theological systems today, Dispensationalism is the newest, coming about a century after the development of Covenant Theology. Both were developed many centuries after Amillennial Theology was established by Augustine and RT was established by the early Church Fathers.[74]

Turning our attention to Dispensational Theology and why it is helpful in discerning the relationship between Israel and the Church, we will start with a definition. The word translated "dispensation" is the New Testament word *oikonimia*, from which the English word economy is derived. The *oikonimia* is the combination of two words in the Greek meaning house "*oikos*" and "*nemo*" meaning to "dispense, manage, or hold sway" which then literally means "house dispensing" or" house managing." So a very simple definition would be to administer a household by God. It is the divine administration of God upon the earth in the form of dispensations, each one being set by God in His time as it relates to His progressive revelation of Scripture. Walking "by Faith" is a principle that is always at work throughout history, as man is to walk obediently to the known will of God in Faith.

In practice, what is Dispensationalism and how does it work? We will be looking at several points that will help us describe this system of theology.

---

[73] William C. Watson, *Dispensationalism before Darby: Seventeenth-Century and Eighteenth-Century English Apocalypticism* (Silverton, OR: Lampion Press, 2015).
[74] Showers, *There Really Is a Difference*, 29-30.

Again a dispensation is defined as a "specific way by which God administers His program and His will in the world, and on the other hand, it covers a designated period of time."[75] Fruchtenbaum further states:

> As to its content and meaning, a Dispensation is a stewardship, a responsibility, or an administration. As to time, it is an age, because every Dispensation covers a period of time. Within each Dispensation, God administers His economy, His rule, His authority, and His program in some different way than the previous Dispensation.[76]

Why did Dispensationalists hold to this system of theology? How is it different from Replacement, Covenant and Amillennial Theologies? When you view Scripture from the literal understanding, without adding allegory or spiritualization to the Scriptures, you will remove your own personal biases. As a result, you will easily align yourself with a dispensational understanding of Scripture.

The major key to understanding the Bible is the literal interpretation of Scripture, which is also called historical-grammatical interpretation. By looking at Scripture from God's point of view, we are able to grasp the very heart of God and His program for the earth. Remember that by the time Luther nailed his ninety-five theses on the church door, the Roman Catholic Church had corrupted every aspect of theology by the use of allegory, spiritualization, and Church tradition. The doctrines of God, Christ, Holy Spirit, Sin, Salvation, the Church, and Man were in dire need of being reformed based on biblical interpretation instead of man's interpretation. One of the last doctrines to be corrected was the doctrine of Eschatology, or future things. This is the doctrine that God has raised up to guide us in the last days, to remove the spiritual blinders from the eyes of His people regarding His plan for Israel. Clear dispensational teaching clarifies God's direct message to us that has been so clouded by all the allegorical and spiritualization of Scripture, so devastating to our understanding of how the Last Days will begin, whom they deal with (Israel), and the outcome of God's plan.

As background for this study, remember that the issues we will be considering have been controversial. Wars have been fought over differences

---

[75] Arnold G. Fruchtenbaum, *The Dispensations of God, Manuscript #41* (San Antonio, TX: Ariel Ministries), 4.
[76] Ibid.

in religion, and the lives of theologians have been lost in the quest for truth. For example, the Roman Catholic Church burned John Huss (1371-1415) at the stake because he did not sing their tune. It was the Reformers, men who wanted to reform the doctrinal errors of the Roman Catholic Church, who also hunted down and murdered Anabaptists because they rejected infant baptism, just as the Roman Catholic Church had done to those who rejected their doctrines. It was the Reformers who corrected some theology, but when it came to Israel's future, they murdered the first Gentile Zionist, Frances Kett (in 1587 or 1589) by burning him at the stake because he believed that God had a plan for Israel's future! One author expresses the following statement:

> Today it is difficult to imagine that a Christian was once martyred for teaching that God still had a plan for the Jewish people. Yet a devout man named Francis Kett was burned at the stake for expressing that belief and insisting that the Bible prophesied a return of the Jews to their ancient promised land. He is considered to be the first Gentile martyr to die for the return of the Jews to their divinely Promised Land. He would not recant, but boldly announced what has been fulfilled in the past two centuries.[77]

The Reformation did not immediately clean up the corruptions of the Roman Catholic Church, but it developed over the next couple of centuries, into the eighteenth and nineteenth centuries, where this last aspect of theology, God's future for Israel, was finally beginning to be corrected. So while Dispensational Theology may be slightly younger than the other systems of theology such as Covenant Theology, it was developed over a period of time as people began to see that Israel did have a future after being suppressed for over eighteen centuries.

As the Protestant movement slowly cleaned up the corrupted theology of Roman Catholicism, there were very positive corrections made. However, the theology of Israel was slow to emerge because of a fatal flaw in the Reformers and those who followed. That flaw was the continued use of allegorical interpretation of Scripture as it related to Israel and future events which also relate to Israel. I would encourage you to pause and read Appendix Four of this book, an article by Dr. Andy Woods on what the

---

[77] Heinrich, *In the Shame of Jesus*, 113. Original published by Evidence of Truth Ministries, 2008 in Witmer, PA. Frances Kett is also referenced by ICEJ – International Christian Embassy Jerusalem – www.int.icej.org?media/history-christian-zionism.

Reformation accomplished and failed to accomplish as it relates to correcting Church biases against Israel and the Jewish people.

Let me introduce something that is new, but is not new, because it has been suppressed first by Replacement Theology, then by the Amillennial Theology of Roman Catholicism, and then finally by Reform Theology of the strain of Calvin's Reformers. What is it?

The Jewish Background of the Scriptures

The Bible is clearly a Jewish book. This point, the Jewish frame of reference of the Old and New Testaments, needs to be understood by all believers. The Jewish background or frame of reference of the Scriptures is not taught by Evangelical, Conservative, or Fundamental Christianity. It seems a paradox that they attempt to lay out a foundational understanding of the covenants and dispensations that God made with Israel. The understanding of the promises that God has made with national, ethnic, physical Israel and the Jewish people in general have been pushed into the background for nearly nineteen centuries, resulting in a skewed understanding of the Jewish people and the State of Israel in God's eyes. Losing this focus affects how the Church views Israel in the world today. The Church has missed understanding the very heart of God as He revealed His plan for Israel's future.

We as Christians are still suffering under the 1,900 years of RT and its theological brothers. We are suffering under the residual effects of bad doctrine and don't recognize it! Our theology, though dispensational, has RT embedded in it. The fruit of this error today is that the Church has no practical, genuine interest in Jewish people, or the study of the Scriptures as God wrote them. Although we see the Scriptures dispensationally, the heart of our own understanding has been tarnished.

I have been personally amazed at the apathy of fundamental and conservative believers; pastors largely only give lip service to Israel. Many believers are more interested in tours to Israel to walk on holy places than to discern God's will toward the Jewish people, despite it being a main theme of the Bible from start to finish. Even though Dispensational Theology requires understanding of Israel's place in Scripture and in relation to God, they themselves have no significant personal interest in Israel because it's Jewish. You may say that is a rash statement, but when you look and listen as I have for 20 years, you only see a surface interest in Israel and not a deeply held conviction. This apathy for what God has stated in His Word about Israel has another important impact; it has contaminated our view of Missiology (Missions), but that I will cover later in this book.

The following facets of Dispensationalism will help us understand the radical difference between the other three theologies and Dispensational Theology. When we recognize God's pattern in His Word, we can grasp and understand His plan of the ages as it relates to Israel and the Jewish people.

The Facets of Dispensations

There are seven dispensations that deal with life on the earth, and seven specific elements or facets involved in each Dispensation:[78] (An eighth Dispensation, called the Eternal Order, deals with life in the new heavens and earth, but we will not focus on that.)

- First, each dispensation has one or more names, which somehow show what the basic rule of life was for that particular Dispensation.
- Second, each Dispensation has a chief person to whom special revelation is given.
- Third, each Dispensation provides a responsibility to man because each Dispensation begins with new revelation requiring a human response.
- Fourth, there is a specific test for mankind in each Dispensation.
- Fifth, following the test comes a specific failure.
- Sixth, there is a judgment that brings the Dispensation to an end.
- Seventh, each Dispensation has something in it that characterizes divine grace.

Before I move on to brief descriptions of these seven facets of Dispensationalism, there is another principle that I believe we need to understand as we study the Scriptures. That is, what did the followers of God know at a given time? Take Noah as our first example. Noah was obedient to God with the information that he received from God (Genesis 7 - 9), which

---

[78] The seven dispensations we are focusing on are the Economies of Innocence, Conscience, Human Government, Promise, Law, Grace, and the Kingdom. There is one additional dispensation known as the Eternal Order.

was more than those who preceded him like Adam or Enoch (Genesis 2 - 5). Noah responded **in Faith** to the known will of God in his time just as Adam and Enoch responded to God **in Faith** on the content of what had been revealed to them by God. The same can be said of Abraham (Genesis 12 - 22), who had more revelation than Noah; Abraham acted **in Faith** and was obedient to God based on His knowledge of God's will. The content of their Faith was different, and they had to exercise Faith within the revealed will of God at the time. This process goes on and on as the progressive revelation of God's Word was given to others, such as Moses, David, Isaiah, and so on.

For each of the seven Dispensations, I will give Scripture references and details on the seven facets just described above.

- Economy of Innocence - conditional
    1. Name: Freedom
    2. Adam – Genesis 1:26 through 3:6 (See specifically 1:28-29; 2:15-17, 24.)
    3. The basic content of the Edenic Covenant contained two aspects: responsibility to the earth and to the Garden of Eden. Concerning the earth, Adam and Eve were responsible to subdue it, to replenish it, to multiply on the earth, and to take control of it in general. Concerning the garden, they were responsible to till the Garden.
    4. One specific test was that they were not to eat or partake of the tree of knowledge of good and evil.
    5. They violated the one and only law, by eating of the fruit of the tree of knowledge of good and evil.
    6. They were expelled from the Garden and the curse of sin was placed upon men and women.
    7. Grace is shown by the promise of the Seed of the woman, the coming redeemer – Genesis 3:15.

- Economy of Conscience - unconditional
    1. Name: Self-Determination
    2. Adam and Eve – Genesis 3:7-8:14
    3. Adam was to be obedient to the Adamic Covenant.
    4. The test involved two things: man's obedience to the dictates of conscience in the knowledge of good and evil, and man's response to failure by a proper and acceptable sacrifice.

5. Man's failure is seen in Cain and the evil of man's heart in Genesis 6.
6. All life was to be destroyed by a worldwide flood.
7. God's Grace is demonstrated by God saving Noah and his family in the ark.

- Economy of Human Government - unconditional
    1. Name: Civil Government
    2. Noah – Genesis 8:15-11:9
    3. Mankind was to be obedient to the Noahic Covenant.
    4. The specific test was for mankind to spread out over the earth.
    5. Man's failure was that of rebellion: They stayed in one place and built the tower of Babel contrary to the known will of God.
    6. Judgment came in the form of God changing their languages so they could not communicate and had to disperse.
    7. God's Grace provided a believing remnant.

- Economy of Promise - unconditional
    1. Name: Patriarchal Rule
    2. Abraham – Genesis 11:10 through Exodus 18:27
    3. Man's responsibility was to obey the promises of the Abrahamic Covenant.
    4. The specific test was for Abraham, Isaac, and Jacob to stay in the Land that was promised.
    5. Israel's failure was the tendency not to stay in the Land promised.
    6. Man's failure led to the Egyptian bondage of the descendants of Jacob.
    7. God's Grace preserved His people, whether they were inside of outside of the Promised Land.

- Economy of Law - conditional
    1. Name: Mosaic Law
    2. Moses (Israel) – Exodus 18:28 through Acts 1:26
    3. Israel was to be obedient to the 613 laws of Moses, and they were to be obedient to the Prophets.
    4. The test was to be obedient to the 613 laws and to accept the Prophet that would come.
    5. Israel's failure was the violation of the 613 laws of Moses and the rejection of the Prophet, the Messiah, when He came.

6. Israel's failure resulted in the 70 A.D. destruction of Jerusalem and the Temple with the worldwide dispersion of Israel.
7. By God's Grace, the rejected Messiah, the Prophet like Moses, became the substitutionary sacrifice for the sins of mankind, who would place their Faith and trust in Him.

- Economy of Grace - unconditional
    1. Name: Age of Grace
    2. Paul the Apostle – Acts 2:1 through Revelation 19:21
    3. Both Jew and Gentile were to be obedient to the New Covenant.
    4. The specific test is, "Will man accept the free gift of salvation by the simple act of Faith in the person of Yeshua the Messiah?"
    5. Man's failure to embrace God's free gift will result in the Great Tribulation.
    6. Man's failure to embrace God's free gift will result in the greatest judgment of man outside the flood of Noah's day.
    7. God's Grace will be seen in God removing the Body of Messiah from the earth before the Great Tribulation.

- Economy of the Kingdom - unconditional
    1. Name: Millennial or Messianic Kingdom
    2. Messiah – Revelation 20:1-10
    3. Obedience to the New Covenant and obedience to the Messianic King, physically reigning on earth in Jerusalem.
    4. Everyone born into the Kingdom will have to personally accept the Messianic King as personal Lord and believe the same Gospel of the age of Grace.
    5. Man's failure is that he will revolt against the Lord and reject the salvation that was offered and try to attack and overthrow the Messiah in the Holy City.
    6. All these invading armies will be destroyed by fire out of Heaven.
    7. God's Grace will be shown by fulfilling during the Kingdom all the promises and covenants that He made; every man will sit in safety and security, immortality for all the saved.

- The Eternal State – the New Heavens and the New Earth – Revelation 21-22

All of the points on the seven Dispensations are brief; if you desire to study further and more completely, please refer to Arnold Fruchtenbaum's

The Dispensations of God, Manuscript #41, available as a free pdf download at *www.arielm.org/dcs/pdf/mbs041m.pdf.*[79]

What becomes ever so clear as you move through Scripture is that it is a progressive revelation of God to man. God did not bestow all of His truth on Adam or Noah, nor did He give it all to Abraham or Moses. He revealed Himself progressively, piece by piece. Over time, He revealed His plan for all mankind, and the necessity for man by Faith to believe in God, based on what He had revealed to mankind up to and including that time.

We, the Church, do have the completed revelation of God! The last writer of the Scriptures, the Apostle John, put the period at the end of God's revelation of Himself and His plan to redeem us, as we by Faith trust Him as our Savior from sin. Noah, Abraham, Moses, David, or Isaiah could not fathom the things that would be revealed; they were responsible for what they knew and lived obediently "by Faith."

The system of theology called Dispensationalism is not built on imposing the theology of man to a text; it is rather the theology that God placed clearly in the text, literally, clearly understood without the interference of man's allegorical interpretation and spiritualization. Dispensational Theology is intended to stay true to what God reveals literally in the Bible, without man's theological biases of the biblical text being used to make it say things that it simply does not say.

One of the biggest points of disagreement between Dispensational, Replacement, Covenant Reform, and Amillennial theologies is that the Dispensationalist sees a clear distinction between Israel and the Church. Why? Because God has made a clear distinction between the two as He wrote His Word and gave it to us.

Progressive Dispensationalism

One other point that I will be brief with is the relatively new teaching called Progressive Dispensationalism (PD). This is a confusing and complex point of view for the layperson to understand. So let me give you a few pointers to help you get a grasp on the new, compromising issues surrounding Progressive Dispensationalism. Let me begin by being as simplistic as possible to a non-simplistic theological position.

---

[79] Fruchtenbaum, *The Dispensations of God, Manuscript #41.*

The movement arose out of the Dispensational Study Group which first met on November 20, 1986, in connection with the annual meeting of the Evangelical Theological Society in Atlanta, Georgia. Five years later, at the 1991 meeting, it was first labeled or introduced as "Progressive Dispensationalism." The purpose of the Study Group appears to have been to clarify Dispensational issues in order to **bridge the gap** between Dispensationalism and Covenant Theology, thus following a conscious movement toward Covenant Theology. The heads of the movement are Darrell Bock of Dallas Theological Seminary; Craig A. Blaising, now at Southern Baptist Theological Seminary; and Robert L. Saucy of Talbot Theological Seminary. In the period 1992-93, each of these three men authored books presenting this movement.

History and religious beliefs provide insight regarding the harm that can be done by espousing false doctrine. In the second century, when Origen along with Justin Martyr and others paved the way for RT to thrive, they did not foresee the atrocities that would be perpetuated upon the Jewish people as a result. They did not live to see all the criminal acts done in history as their words and acts rolled up into a crescendo with the Holocaust against God's chosen people. I am not saying that PD will have the same result as Replacement did, but one must wonder what the effect over time will be to the Jewish people 100 or 200-years-plus from now. What will the outcome be, theologically and practically, to continue to avoid proper acknowledgment of God's plan for Israel and the Jewish people?

The basic problems of this movement are summarized by the words *compromise* and *confusion* and relate to the relationship of two systems of theology: Replacement Covenant Theology on one side and Dispensational Theology on the other. In some areas, the two systems are being merged together. PD *blurs the distinctions* between two theological viewpoints on Israel and the Church as well as the future Millennial reign of Messiah. It appears that those who promote PD are trying to find common ground for agreement between two diverse systems of theology. This blurring serves only to confuse and compromise Bible believers. Here is only one of numerous problems:

- Dispensationalism stands firmly on literal interpretation of Scripture; whereas, Progressives have come up with a new hermeneutic (method of interpretation) called "complimentary hermeneutic" where they *modify* the literal hermeneutic approach. While using literal interpretation much of the time, they on critical passages ***blur the distinction*** between Israel and the Church while ***minimizing*** and ***de-emphasizing*** the prophetic importance and position of modern-day Israel. They also de-emphasize and minimize the distinctiveness of the Church and the uniqueness of the Millennium.

- Progressives use (or allow) the New Testament to ***introduce changes and additions*** to the Old Testament revelation. By using "complimentary hermeneutics," they further introduce into God's Old Testament promises much more than they contain.

- To illustrate, PD has changed the understanding of the issue of the Throne of David that Messiah will reign upon. Compare and contrast:

    Dispensationalism states that David's throne is an earthly throne that Messiah will reign from physically and literally in Jerusalem during the Millennial Kingdom of Messiah, at which time He will fulfill the Abrahamic, Land, Davidic, and New Covenants.

    Progressives say that when Christ ascended to heaven, He inaugurated the Messianic Kingdom, which means the Church age and the Kingdom are now merged together, no longer distinct. To Progressives, Christ is now sitting on the throne by the Father; and that throne is the throne of David that has been transferred from an earthly sphere to a heavenly sphere. That is Covenant Replacement theology and NOT Dispensationalism.

How do Progressives go about making such changes? By using their new "complimentary hermeneutic," they tweak the literal sense of the Bible to create new concepts that are not biblical. To illustrate further, in Acts 2:30c, Peter said, *He* (God the Father] *would raise up Messiah to sit on his* [David's] *throne*. They implant by complimentary hermeneutics something that the text of Acts 2 does not say or imply! What Acts 2:30-36 states is that Messiah's resurrection and exaltation at the right hand of God on the heavenly throne guarantees His future reign on the earthly Davidic throne as David's Lord and greater descendant (Psalm 110:1). PD theologians insert a shortcut, that the throne in heaven becomes David's throne. That goes completely against the context of Acts 1-2 and against what the Apostle James said at the Jerusalem Council. In Acts 15:16, James used the phrase the *tabernacle of David* and states that David's throne has been in ruin (which we know has been true since 586 B.C.). James further states that David's throne was still in ruin after Messiah's ascension to heaven. Progressives conveniently ignore this clear statement by the Apostle James to insert their new, theological teaching. As a result, they claim falsely that Messiah is currently reigning from David's throne in heaven and that the Messianic Kingdom is now inaugurated and beginning to be fulfilled. This sounds like Amillennial Theology, which claims that there is no Millennial Kingdom; but there is a difference. Progressive Dispensationalism's take on the Millennial Kingdom has been described as being "already, but not yet," meaning it was inaugurated but it is not yet in effect.

- To again illustrate further from Acts 1:3, 6-7, 9 and 11. Look at the following passages:

  - Acts 1:3b – *and speaking of the things pertaining to the kingdom of God.*

  - Acts 1:6 – *When they therefore were come together, they asked of Him, saying, Lord, will Thou at this time restore again the kingdom to Israel?*

  - Acts 1:7 – *And He said unto them, It is not for you to know the times or the seasons, which the Father hath put in His own power.*

  - Acts 1:9 – *And when he had spoken these things, while they beheld, He was taken up: and a cloud received Him out of their sight.*

  - Acts 1:11 – *You men of Galilee, why stand you gazing up into heaven? This same Jesus, which is taken up from you into heaven, shall so come in like manner as you have seen Him go into heaven.*

In verse 3, Jesus was giving the disciples some additional teaching on the Kingdom of God. Now in verse 6, you can clearly see what is on the minds of the disciples. They ask Him if He is now going to restore the Kingdom, the promised Davidic Kingdom. Then look again at Jesus' response to the disciples in verse 7. Simply, *It is not yours to know; it is in the Father's own power.* Then in verse 9, Jesus ascends to heaven; and in verse 11, there are two angels who tell those witnessing His ascension that as He went up to heaven, He will return to earth.

Yeshua did not answer His disciples' question about the setting up of the promised Kingdom. Now understand, they were moments away from His ascension; and if the Progressives are right, Yeshua could have just as easily said, "You are mistaken about this Jewish concept of the earthly throne and the Kingdom in Israel. The throne of David has been transferred to the throne of God in heaven where I will ascend, and I will shortly begin to reign from there." Jesus did not say that nor did He imply that in any way.

What was briefly looked at is only one point of numerous points that could be given. The many subtleties in the teaching of PD are difficult for the average believer to grasp. Thomas Ice, a well-respected Dispensational theologian, said with respect to PD that it is "difficult [to] read because of its erudite technical style …. It is sometimes hard to get a grip on what is precisely being said, even after reading a passage several times."[80]

This new Progressive theology is difficult to grasp, and even more difficult to understand are the nuances as it encroaches into other areas of theology. Most people who follow Progressive teaching will not even be aware of the overall impact. While I am in no way applying a political viewpoint to founders of PD theology, I would like to propose an example:

> What is the difference between capitalism and communism? Politically and philosophically they are not compatible in any way, just as Covenant/Replacement and Dispensationalism are not theologically compatible in any way. If we add another political viewpoint, such as socialism within the American context, what is the impact of that? In the example, let's say that Socialism operates in a capitalist society while teaching the tenets of Socialism/Communism. Now politically and philosophically, Socialism is more closely related to Communism than it is to Capitalism, yet it operates within a capitalistic society. So Progressive Dispensational, while operating within Dispensationalism, is far more related to Replacement/Covenant Theology than to Dispensational Theology. The movement, the direction, of PD is toward Replacement/ Covenant Theology and is not a clarification of Dispensationalism. It is completely possible that PD will ultimately lead its followers into Covenant Theology, which

---

[80] Thomas Ice, "A Critical Examination of Progressive Dispensationalism," *Biblical Perspectives*, Vol. 5, No. 6, November-December, 1992.

is the enemy of Dispensationalism, Israel, and God's future plan for Israel.

(Remember, I am not trying to make an equivalency between PD and any political view; this is just an illustration of how belief systems can influence one another.)

The problem today as well as yesterday is that people do not learn from the past! We need to help each other to understand history for our benefit. For example, Socialism in history was not an important tenet of American ideology. It has gained prominence through many subtle encroachments. We can use its example of how challenging views such as Progressive Dispensationalism can become integrated in place of more traditional viewpoints when a subtle approach is used.

I will start with the 1930s even though the infiltration of Socialism into American politics began before that. In the 1930s, the Humanist society put their philosophy in writing and called it the Humanist Manifesto.[81] They have implemented that philosophy to the letter. Then in the 1940s, John Dewey articulated it to the general society. President Roosevelt implemented some of it into American society with his New Deal programs. Its advancement continued into President Johnson's era with the Great Society and the eradication of poverty. Our colleges and universities then began to teach socialism to a new generation. That generation then began to teach it in other colleges as well as teaching it to our children in our secondary educational system, which is made up of Federal/State schools). The advancement of a socialistic outlook now encompasses our educational system and media outlets, where it is promoted to the general, naïve citizen.

From a religious perspective, we have had Liberalism denying the foundations of our faith and Humanism teaching evolution to the point that today our society has been completely compromised and contaminated. Today we have one of the two parties principally that have swallowed the Socialism "Kool-Aid" with the help of the other political party and have passed legislation so that now, today, we have approximately 50 percent of our society with their hands wide open to receive all the social benefits. Now, today, we are only a generation away from being a complete Socialistic nation, the same kind of government that Communism has, which takes from the rich and the middle-class through taxation and gives to the poor and

---

[81] Roy Wood Sellars and Raymond B. Bragg, *Humanist Manifesto* (Washington, DC: American Humanist Association, 1933).

aliens in society. The only difference at this point for us nationally, is that we do not have a dictator/despot as a national leader yet. Bending the truth usually has this progression, because the propagation of a false teaching requires enforcement to succeed.

This is the danger of Progressive Dispensationalism. It is actively blurring the distinctions between Dispensationalism and Covenant Theologies. As history shows over and over again, it will inflict as a cancer into the whole body of Messiah and eventually destroy the body. In our case, it will destroy a large part of Dispensationalism and the Church's understanding of God's place for Israel in His plan.

If I am right, there will always be believers who will have strong ties to Israel with clear teaching that is unbiased and literal in its interpretation. Yet, Christendom will become less and less friendly to Israel and the religionist world will move increasingly towards a theology that is unfriendly to Israel. It will increasingly become a theology that shows a bias against Israel as a larger portion of the world, the religious world, will be collectively *Poking God's Eye.*

We have already seen through history that Christian theology has not been friendly to Israel or the Jewish people. If Dispensational Theology is compromised, could that possibly open the door theologically for the future events of the Last Days? Bear in mind that when the rapture of the Church occurs, Dispensational believers will be caught up to be with their LORD in the sky, then to heaven, and that will include many Covenant believers. However, that vacuum in the world will leave only the apostate church, which is religiously anti-Israel.

Sadly, Dispensationalists are not teaching Dispensational Theology in schools and seminaries that once were strongholds for Dispensationalism, but instead they are setting up future students to be hit broadside with a form of theology that they will not be able to defend themselves against, thus becoming Covenant/Replacement theologians themselves!

Summary of Dispensationalism

Dispensationalism is the last great clarification of the corruption of Church doctrine of the past in the understanding of God's Plan of the Ages (the Economies of God). Dispensationalism is a strong defense against biblical error, whether it relates to salvation, redemption, the place and position of Israel, the place and position of believers in all ages, the literal fulfillment of the covenants, or the promises that God made to Israel, the Chosen vehicle of God, to bring it all about. If we want to see it God's way, we have to work to focus on God's perspective and not human bias.

Chapter 5
Israel: Violent Perpetrator or Defender of Their Country?

Three theological systems (Replacement, Amillennial, and Covenant) have long influenced the foundations and religious opinions surrounding the Church. Traditionally, these viewpoints have provided a basis, in varying degrees, for anti-Jewish speech and anti-Israel rhetoric. Anti-Semitism now infuses the secular propaganda machine that influences all our spheres of life: workplace, politics, foreign policy, college campuses, and more. As a result, we are being led by people who have no spiritual insight into the Last Days as God moves the world into its final chapter of Gentile rule. The Antichrist will make his final, futile attempt to annihilate Israel and all the Jewish people from the face of the earth, with many following along, unaware of their ignorance or complicity.

The news media in American as well as European networks are purposely distorting the events that have taken place in Israel, the West Bank, Gaza, and Lebanon to put Israel in a bad light. These are humanistic secular networks that have no spiritual insight, no knowledge or background of the Bible, and they are in general devoid of moral, right-and-wrong, biblical discernment. The media have simply become the propaganda machine of the radical left in America, echoing Christian bias against the Jewish people.

We see Protestant, Orthodox, and Catholic churches calling for boycotts against Israel and walking hand in hand with nations accusing Israel of being occupiers. Please understand; Israel has not always responded in the right way, but even with that being understood, shortcomings on the part of Israel do not remove the Abrahamic Covenant and God's promises to Israel.

We see Christians nodding in agreement as Israel is called an apartheid nation and racist. Some extremists have even called Israel a Nazi regime because when they defend their people from attacks, they wind up killing innocent children, young people, and adults who are purposely placed in danger by inflammatory, radical Islamists. Nations and religions are siding with Palestinian Christians and Muslims in telling the world that Israel is a monster, inflicting injustice on these innocent peoples. The problem is that few people have the intellectual integrity to research the facts for themselves without bias.

I again must state, Israel is an unregenerate nation, just like the United States of America and Europe. We also have done many things wrong as a nation such as the following:

- The United States has not kept one treaty with the Native Americans, but slaughtered them and then used forced marches to resettle them in undesirable places. We on the East Coast, the Midwest, and the West live on occupied land that belongs to the Native Americans.

- We have a history of oppression of the Black people in America; and, shamefully, the KKK is still alive. The United States' attitude and actions against Black people over the years can easily be called into question, and many injustices have plagued our nation, which is supposed to be the Land of the Free.

- Our country took lands from Mexico and then developed them into States like New Mexico, Arizona, and California.

- Japanese-American citizens were interned by our government in World War II because they looked different and were feared as enemies, whether or not there was any evidence against them.

Israel has done wrong things, too. Even though they are in unbelief as a nation, they are still the chosen people of God.

You say that I am being very hard on Christians and secular news outlets? Well, I am! They are shaping history, yet they do not recognize the seriousness and error of their anti-Jewish position, and, may I add, their anti-God position. If you think I am wrong, then I challenge you to follow this study through and see what God has plainly said in His Word.

There is a principle that all people should use before making a judgment for or against Israel: To every instance there are two sides, and each side needs to be vetted completely before arriving at a decision. What is the story on Israel? Who is in the right? Who is honest with the facts both biblically and historically? This book is not a study of the Muslim/Christian/Israeli conflict, but we do need to understand a few historical facts before we engage in the study of the blessings and cursings of the Abrahamic Covenant, which is the theme of this book.

Before we view the eighteen facts concerning Israel and the Land, let us remember that we are looking at a modern-day miracle. Let me quote from another author:

> Israel should have ended as a nation and probably as a people in 586 B.C., but it survived. Israel definitely should have ended as a nation in 70 [and 135] A.D., but as the ancient Bible prophets wrote, the nation was literally reborn. After ceasing to be a nation for almost 1,900 years, on May 14, 1948, Israel was once again a nation. This was followed in June 1967 with a united Jerusalem once again the capital. The Hebrew language had become almost extinct, but yet today the Israelis speak Hebrew. They speak the same language as their ancestors. They kept the same religion while in exile. There is simply no nation like Israel.[82]

Satan did everything possible to destroy Israel as a people, religion, culture, and ethnicity; yet here they are! The Romans changed the name of the city of Jerusalem to Aelia Capitolina and changed the name of the Land of Israel to Palestine, yet today we have Jerusalem and Israel once again. You have today a fossil nation and a fossil language and people alive and well (Ezekiel 37). Israel has been indestructible and will continue to be indestructible regardless of what America, Europe, the United Nations, or the Islamic nations attempt to do (Jeremiah 31:35-37). Was it a fluke? No, it was foretold by the Prophets over 2,600 to 3,400 years ago (Deuteronomy 30), and here we stand today looking at an absolute miracle of God.

Eighteen Facts about Israel

Now consider these eighteen facts listed below as they relate to the background of Israel returning to the Land amid radical, unprovoked attacks on Israel:

- **FACT ONE**: There has never been a Palestinian government over the people of that land area. Not since the fall of the Jewish

---

[82] John McTernan and Bill Koenig, *Israel: The Blessing or the Curse* (Hearthstone Publications: Oklahoma City, OK, 2002), 16-17.

state in 70 A.D. have the people of that area ever sovereignly ruled themselves; the area was always ruled by outside powers such as Babylon, Egypt, Syria, Turkey, and, lastly, Britain. From 70 A.D. until 1948, this land area we call Israel did not have self-government; but in 1948, Israel was established as a modern nation. Self-government was absent for almost 1,900 years. Dr. William Heinrich stated:

> During the Islamic occupation, Jerusalem was never a capital city. To [Muslims], Baghdad, Damascus, and Cairo were the centers of imperial power while Jerusalem was a small city that had no major highways or rivers, and was located on an inconvenient mountaintop. Jerusalem was never a site of great Islamic schools, Islamic ideas, or theologians. In fact, throughout much of history, the Muslims looked down upon Jerusalem Arabs in the same way that, in the time of Jesus, Temple leaders looked down upon the Jews of Galilee. [Jerusalem] only had significance to Muslims when it was the traditional "city of the prophets," howbeit, all those prophets were Jewish. Jerusalem was never a capital to non-Jewish people. Therefore, to say that Jerusalem is the holy city of three faiths is at best a myth. Historically, it was the holy city only for Judaism and Christianity. In fact, throughout Islamic history, other [cities] such as Damascus were often more holy than the City of Zion.[83]

- Romans and Byzantines ruled until 638 A.D.

- Muslims captured Israel and Jerusalem in 638. Thus began the Muslim rule of the Land by the Caliphs from Damascus and Baghdad until 1072.

- Crusaders ruled from 1099 until 1291.

- Muslim Mamelukes of Egypt ruled from 1291 until 1516.

- Muslim Ottoman Turks of Turkey ruled from 1516 until 1917.

- The British were given the mandate by the League of Nations to rule from 1918 until 1948.

---

[83] Heinrich, *In the Shame of Jesus*, 85.

- **FACT TWO**: The Land was a wasteland and barren of people, according to Mark Twain, who visited it in 1867. He wrote for the Alta Californian, a San Francisco paper. A report from the British Consulate in 1857 also made a similar comment.
  - Palestine sits in sackcloth and ashes … desolate and unlovely.[84]
  - The country is in a considerable degree empty of inhabitant; and, therefore, its greatest need is of a body of population. (British Consulate in 1857)
- **FACT THREE**: The vast majority of the peoples in the Land today are Muslim immigrants from other countries to Palestine who came for jobs that the Jewish people were providing.[85] The vast majority of Jewish people in the Land are also immigrants from all over the world that have come home to the Land that was promised by God to Abraham and his descendants. (See Appendix 3 for over 200 Land references.)
- **FACT FOUR**: The Jewish people called Zionists began to return to Israel in the 1880s first from Russia. They purchased the Land they settled on at highly inflated prices from Muslim overlords. However, there has always been a small Jewish presence in the Land as well as a Christian and Muslim presence.
- **FACT FIVE**: In 1917 the British Balfour Declaration, passed by the League of Nations, promised the Jewish people a land in Palestine. The land area involved was geographically Israel and Jordan as we know them today.
- **FACT SIX**: In 1919 the Mufti of Jerusalem, Haj-Amin el Husseini (who would become the mentor to Yasser Arafat) and who had been appointed by the British government, spread inflammatory words that the Jewish people were going to take over the Temple Mount. Muslim riots broke out in 1919 and 1920 (referred to as "Bloody Passover" and taking place in Tel Hai settlement in Upper Galilee). Attacks occurred in 1921 in Jaffa, Rehovot, and Petah Tikva. In 1929 and 1936, attacks resulted in hundreds of Jewish people being murdered. Great Britain is solely responsible for laying the groundwork for the

---

[84] Mark Twain, *The Innocents Abroad;* last accessed online November 16, 2016.
[85] Joan Peters, *From Time Immemorial: The Origins of the Arab-Jewish Conflict Over Palestine* (JKAP Publications, 1984).

conflict in the Mid-East today. So from that day to the present, Jewish people are continually being attacked by radical Palestinian, Muslim attackers. History also notes that the Mufti of Jerusalem had extremely strong and close personal ties with Adolph Hitler and the Nazi murder machine in Europe.

- **FACT SEVEN**: During the 1920s through the mid 1940s, the British government caved into the demands of Muslim countries that surrounded Palestine and restricted many Jewish immigrants from going to Israel. When Jewish people were trying to escape the impending Holocaust of Nazi Germany, Britain restricted Jewish immigration because of oil dependence on Muslim and Arab nations. They did not want to offend the newly created Muslim/Arab nations like Iraq, Saudi Arabia, Jordan, Syria, and others carved out under British and French leadership through the League of Nations, predecessor of the United Nations.

- **FACT EIGHT**: During and after the War of Independence of Israel in 1948, some 900,000 Jews were expelled from Islamic nations; and their property was confiscated. They were promised a fair price for their homes and businesses, but the Islamic countries reneged and kept it all.

- **FACT NINE**: Because of her war of Independence in 1948, Israel did expel some Muslims from the Land, but the Muslim nations were responsible for the vast majority of expulsions. Unlike the Jewish people, Muslim countries kept Palestinian Muslim people in refugee camps to instill hatred and use them as pawns in their political/religious chess game against the Jewish State. Here is a series of documented statements by the Muslim governments and newspapers themselves:

    - Since 1948, we have been demanding the return of the refugees to their homes. While it is we who made them leave .... We brought disaster upon ... Arab refugees, by inviting them and bringing pressure to bear upon them to leave ... We have rendered them dispossessed ... We have accustomed them to begging.... We have participated in lowering their moral and social level.... Then we exploited them in executing crimes of

murder, arson, and throwing bombs upon men, women and children – all this in service of political purposes.
—*Haledal Azm – Syrian Prime Minister – 1948-49*

- The Arab exodus from other villages was not caused by the actual battle, but by the exaggerated description spread by Arab leaders to incite them to fight the Jews.
—*Yenes Ahmed Assad, refugee from the town of Deir Yassin – April 9, 1953*

- The Arab exodus, initially at least, was encouraged by many Arab leaders, such as Haj Amin el Husseini, the exiled pro-Nazi Mufti of Jerusalem, and by the Arab Higher Committee for Palestine. They viewed the first wave of Arab setbacks as merely transitory. Let the Palestine Arabs flee into neighboring countries. It would serve to arouse the other Arab peoples to greater effort, and when the Arab invasion struck, the Palestinians would return to their homes and be compensated with the property of Jews driven into the sea.
—*Kenneth Bilby in New Star in Near East (NY), 1950*

- The Arab States encouraged the Palestine Arabs to leave their homes temporarily in order to be out of the way of the Arab invasion armies.
—*Falastin (Jordanian newspaper, February 19, 1949)*

- We will smash the country with our guns and obliterate every place the Jews seek shelter in. The Arabs should conduct their wives and children to safe areas until the fighting has died down.
—*Nuri Said, Iraqi Prime Minister, quoted in Sir Am Nakbah, 1952*

- **FACT TEN**: Israel attacked Egypt within hours of being attacked by a Muslim coalition in the 1967 conflict, called The Six-Day War.

- **FACT ELEVEN**: Israel was again attacked in 1973 – the Yom Kippur War.

- **FACT TWELVE**: In 1980, Israel was being attacked by radical Hezbollah in Lebanon, with rockets and armed radicals attacking northern Israel from Lebanon.

- **FACT THIRTEEN**: In the 1980 to 1990s, Israel had to deal with a major outbreak of suicide bombers and other murderers of Jewish people, as well as the initiation of the First Intifada. This uprising was enacted by Muslim Palestinians radicalized by their leaders to shoot Israelis and set off bombs in busy shopping areas and on busses. The radicals indiscriminately murdered Jewish people at bus stops, restaurants, and on the streets of Israel. Additionally, by staging riots and throwing rocks at the military (IDF), they instigated unrest in Israel.

- **FACT FOURTEEN**: Israel greatly desires peace and not war and violence. Israel has demonstrated that time and time again. However, they have been pushed to defend themselves because of radical Islam's admitted agenda to oust Israel from the Land.

- **FACT FIFTEEN**: In 2000, Arafat, the leader of the Palestinian Liberation Organization (PLO), initiated the Second Intifada after Arafat, representing the Palestinians, rejected a national homeland presented by Israel being brokered by the Clinton administration.

- **FACT SIXTEEN**: In 2014, Israel invaded Gaza to destroy the sources of the over 4,000 rockets that were fired into Israel. Israel also targeted underground tunnels used to smuggle Hamas radicals into Israel undetected to commit mass murder. Israel destroyed the tunnels that Hamas had constructed ***with millions of U.S. aid dollars*** that we sent to them for "humanitarian purposes." Hamas dug the tunnels in order to send radicals dressed as Israeli soldiers into Israel to murder hundreds if not thousands of Israelis in Israel.

- **FACT SEVENTEEN**: Today we still have the descendants of the first refugees in the same refugee camps of Palestinians that still exist from over 65 years ago. Question? Where are the refugee camps of displaced persons from World War II with millions of displaced persons? There are none; at least Europe had the moral integrity to care for their own people. The fact that there are Palestinian refugee camps still active in the Arab world shows a combined conspiracy to maintain a cesspool of hatred against Israel by the UN, Arab States, and, later, the PLO, led by Yasser Arafat. Together, they have been successful in dehumanizing Palestinians as well. Interestingly, that population has grown dramatically since 1948 with little to no help to relocate and settle them from the Arab host nations they fled. The United Nations estimated that over 725,000 Arabs fled from Palestine between April and December 1948. The Israelis estimated that figure between 550,000 and 600,000 during that same time frame.[86]

Yet there were more Jewish people evicted from Muslim countries during the same time frame, with no Jewish refugee camps existing. Question: Why are there Palestinian refugee camps and no Jewish refugee camps? Have you ever tried to find out why? You may be surprised to discover how cold and heartless the Muslim States have been, refusing to meet the needs of these people that they, in reality, disposed of themselves!

Here are the figures of Jewish people who had to flee for their lives after the establishment of the State of Israel in 1948 through 1972 from the following countries: Morocco (260,000), Algeria (14,000), Tunisia (56,000), Libya (35,666), Egypt (29,525), Lebanon (6,000), Syria (4,500), Iraq (129,290), and Yemen and Aden (50,552) That is a total of 643,533 Jewish people who fled to Israel. Moreover, an additional 260,000 Jewish immigrants from those same Arab countries chose to go to Europe and the Americas.[87] That is a grand total of 903,533 Jewish people forced to flee. Question: Where are the Jewish refugee camps? There are none! Question: Why are there still refugee camps of Arabs today?

- **FACT EIGHTEEN**: Islam wants to claim Jerusalem and the Temple Mount as their third most holy site, yet consider the following quote:

  > Islam does not recognize the covenant with Isaac and Jacob, but instead believes God made a covenant with Abraham and Ishmael. Islam believes that the Koran and not the Bible is the Word of God. The Koran fails to mention Jerusalem even once, and it does not mention

---

[86] Martin Gilbert, *The Routledge Atlas of the Arab-Israeli Conflict, 7th Edition* (New York, NY: Routledge Taylor & Francis Group, 2002), 47.
[87] Ibid.

> the rebirth of the nation of Israel. Jerusalem is mentioned 811 times in the Bible. The rebirth of Israel is on page after page in the Bible, while the Koran is silent.
>
> The [1948] rebirth of Israel shows [the] authority of the Bible as the Word of God. God's everlasting covenant together with the rebirth of Israel is like an anvil against the Koran. Israel is proof the Koran and Mohammed are false.
>
> This tension between Israel and the Koran can never be peacefully resolved. For Islam to recognize the nation of Israel would be an admission that the Koran and Islam are wrong.[88]

Islam and other haters of Israel use rhetoric to try to present the lie that the Jews in the Land are not real Jews. As far as the Church was concerned, Jewish people were considered to be Jews during the pogroms (riotous, violent, anti-Semitic attacks) in Russia, Poland, and the Ukraine, when they were being slaughtered and persecuted. In Nazi Germany, they were Jews to be destroyed; but now, all of a sudden, when they wish to migrate to their homeland, Jewish people are seen as some other ethnicity that did not originate in the Land. What a double standard! What ignorance that intelligent people would not see the hypocrisy of such propaganda.

Radical Islamic Palestinians are actively attempting to deny the previous presence of Jewish people in the Land. They are destroying as many of the Jewish ties to the Land as they can, and they use propaganda to try to turn the world against Israel, saying despite the evidence to the contrary that Israel never existed in the Land.

Is Israel the Problem?

Israel is called an occupier by Americans, Europeans, and Palestinians, an interesting charge made by intellectually dishonest Americans and Europeans. Lands that Israel captured in the Six-Day War are similar to other conflicts in the world where territory is taken strategically. The United States is also an occupier of the lands that we took from the Native Americans, as well as Mexico. These Americans that charge Israel have a double standard.

---

[88] McTernan and Koenig, *Israel: The Blessing or the Curse*, 53.

We live in our "occupied" land in America and then condemn Israel for holding Land that is theirs by the legal right of God.

Israel has a document that goes back 4,000 years: the Holy Scriptures. Israel is charged as being racist, and Christian Zionists are also viewed as racist. They have been called Nazi, which is purely intellectual dishonesty. Most of the younger (not to exclude the older generation) generation today in the U.S. and Europe do not have the intellectual honestly to go back and understand that Hitler and the Nazis were inhumane, brutal murderers of not just the Jewish people, but also of millions of others they detested. That conflict, World War II, caused the death of 45 million people in the European theater. There can be no more equivalency claimed when Israel is defending its own borders and people against enemies.

Theologically dishonest Palestinian Liberation Theology (PLT) abuses Scripture to justify a political agenda for justice, which in itself is unjust. The growth of PLT has been spear-headed by *Sabeel Center*, the Jerusalem-based ecumenical organization for Palestinian Christians (see Appendix One), with its primary speaker being Dr. Naim Stifan Ateek.[89] I would encourage everyone to read the September/October 2014 issue of *Israel My Glory* magazine from the Friends of Israel Gospel Ministry where they deal with a number of relevant issues relating to Israel and Christians who support Israel.[90] Articles entitled "The Art of Reframing: Palestinian Liberation Theology" (pp. 20-23), "Dr. Ateek's Rose-Colored Glasses" (pp. 24-26), and "Evangelicals against Israel" (pp. 30-33) reveal the unbiblical anti-Semitism that is misleading believers, trying to discourage them from supporting Israel.

The conference called "Christ at the Checkpoint" is a coalition of Protestant, Catholic, and Orthodox leaders and individuals who are opposed to so-called injustice of Israel towards the Palestinians while completely ignoring the historical events that caused the Israeli response.

What keeps the constant conflict going in Israel? What has caused the violence in the Land against the Jewish people is totally one-sided and orchestrated by Islamic countries around Israel that have sought to drive Israel into the sea to recapture the land for Allah. It is a religious war on the

---

[89] Ateek was born in a Palestinian village of Beisan (Beth Shean) in 1937 and became a Palestinian priest in the Anglican Church in 1967.
[90] *Israel My Glory,* published by Friends of Israel Gospel Ministry, September/October 2014. See www.FOI.org for contact information.

part of the Muslims on one side. From the Palestinian Christian side, the fuel is RT, once again the foundation for hurtful, unjust attacks on Israel and the Jewish people.

Christians have the unbiblical idea that they will work toward bringing in the Kingdom of God. Yet it is only God who will be able to do that, not unbiblical Replacement/Covenant or Amillennial Theology. The Kingdom of God is about Israel, not the Church, and by that I mean we as the Church will be reigning with Christ. However, it is not about us; it is about Messiah and Israel. The Church will have absolutely nothing to do with the bringing in of the Millennial Kingdom; only Christ, Himself, will do that. You may ask what part the Church will play in the End Times. Absolutely none. Our commission is to preach the Gospel of Jesus Christ to the world until God takes us home and unleashes His wrath upon a wicked and corrupted world.

By the way, Amillennialism teaches that the Kingdom of God is now, today. Since the world is still broken and full of violence, they must believe God is doing a crummy job with His Kingdom. Nevertheless, that is the teaching from the Catholic Church and Orthodox religions today.

Movies have been made that are completely lopsided in only showing Israel's response but excluding the mountains of documented history that always point to the instigator, the aggressor: Islam and its radical agenda against Israel. Those who support their agenda have shrewdly put together films that are very unbalanced, movies like *With God on Our Side* or *Little Town of Bethlehem* or *The Stones Cry Out* to show what they describe as harsh and ruthless military responses on the poor, defenseless Palestinians. It is all a lopsided, one-sided propaganda machine against Israelis protecting themselves. If Islam would stop being the aggressor and stop teaching hatred and the murder of Jews and acknowledge Israel's right to exist, there would be peace! However, if Israel gives in, they will be overrun and massacred and cease to be a nation.

Most people are blinded by their own unbiblical human bias against Israel. We are all biased, either to human ideas on the negative side, or on the positive side by the written Word of God; but many are in the fluid position of denying their allegiance to God in favor of anti-Semitism. Believers in Christ need to wake up and view the evidence, both biblical and historical. Believers, and American citizens in general, are in the process of swallowing the biggest lie, that Islam is a peaceful religion. Do your research; Islam holds sway over 1 billion people by intimidation, leading to spiritual and physical slavery for their masses today. A retired Admiral in the U.S. Navy, James Lyon, made the following statement in Washington, D.C., in February 11, 2015:

> The country of Turkey has said, "Islam is Islam, There are no modifiers. Democracy is the train that we take to our ultimate objective." He could not have said it better. Until you recognize that Islam is a political movement masquerading as a religion, you are never going to come to grips with it.... The Obama Administration has a strategy; it is very simple and any thinking American should be able to grasp it. It [Obama's Administration] is anti-American, anti-Western; it is pro-Islamic, pro-Iranian and pro-Muslim Brotherhood.[91]

Most Americans and Europeans, both individuals and their leaders, are in denial of the present threat of Islam to their nations, culture, and freedoms. They talk about it and do nothing to counter it. This statement was made in the context of all the Islamic threats that America and Europe face today. Lyon's assessment of Islam hits the bullseye dead center.

Israel has had to deal with the radical Islamic threat for almost 100 years, going all the way back to 1919 and the Mufti of Jerusalem (Haj-Amin el Husseini) who instigated the first riots against the Jewish people. This carries over to the Palestinian problem that Israel is dealing with today. You can judge Israel for perhaps not always responding correctly, but how would America respond if we were in their shoes?

It is easy to project blame on Israel for the tensions with the Palestinians, but it is quite another thing when one has to deal with terrorism rather than just sitting on the sidelines while criticizing those facing it. The Islamic radicalism that Israel has been dealing with is coming to America! You may remember these fairly recent events:

- 250 U.S. Marines murdered in Lebanon (October 23, 1983).
- U.S.S. Cole attacked in Yemen (October 12, 2000).
- Twin Trade Towers bombed in New York City (2001).

---

[91] Retired Admiral James "Ace" Lyon, February 11, 2015 in Washington D.C. Recorded from You Tube.

- Unarmed military personnel murdered at Fort Hood (November 5, 2009).
- Innocent civilians murdered at the Boston Marathon bombing (April 15, 2013).
- Murder of unarmed American civilians by terrorists in San Bernardino, CA (December 2, 2015).
- Mass slaughter of civilians in an Orlando, FL, nightclub (June 13, 2016).

These kinds of events will become more frequent in the coming years. Just as this book is being completed, three attacks have all fallen together in a two-day period: home-made bombs being set up in Chelsea, NY, and Seaside Park, NJ, and a knife attack on civilians enjoying time at a shopping mall in St. Cloud, MN, all in September 2016.

Returning to Israel, Americans frequently fail to research past events so that they can understand present events. Americans have at their fingertips the capability to research past and present events but tend to only view one side because of bias, which then gives a distorted position or viewpoint. Many Christians do not have biblical clarity to understand the situation from God's perspective. Instead, they fall prey to godless, secular news media, to human propaganda, whether from carnal Christian sources or unbiblical sources.

Jewish people have suffered immensely at the hands of Christians for over 1,800 years, as I pointed out in chapter two with the beginning of Replacement Theology. The crimes committed against them are often unimaginable. To speak of those atrocities brings great sorrow of heart. Jewish people have been persecuted in every imaginable way. Jewish people have been hated by the organized Church, which has been the most anti-Semitic organization on the planet, for no other organization outside of the Church has done more anti-Semitic acts.

In the footnote below, I will recommend some good books to read about Church history, which is rarely presented in secular or religious schools of higher education.[92] Because of the atrocities committed by Christians over

---

[92] Heinrich, *In the Shame of Jesus*. Michael Brown, *Our Hands are Stained With Blood* (Destiny Image: Shippensburg, PA, 1992).

the centuries, Jewish people naturally look at Christians potentially as their enemies.

Palestinian Christians are one special case where Israelis hold a suspicious, negative view of Christians. Palestinian Christians were not the aggressor militarily in the current conflicts in Israel, but they have instead been caught in the middle between Israel and the radical Palestinian Muslim elements. Both historically are not trusted by Israel because of past negative involvement with both groups over a period of centuries.

You may say I am biased towards Israel and against the Palestinian people, both Muslim and Christian, but I am not. The pain that has been inflicted on Palestinian Muslims and Palestinian Christians by the radical Islamists is deplorable, and the harm they have inflicted on Israel, who is not the aggressor, is equally deplorable. The radical Islamists have been stirring the pot of hatred and violence for 100 years. *Who* is inflicting the pain and misery? *Who* is triggering the violence and injustice? The answer will shock most people, especially those who support the Palestinian cause.

War is messy. War is not fair. War causes pain on both sides, but who is the perpetrator of the injustices? The perpetrator is not Israel, but radical Islam, who hates Israel and who has placed the Palestinian Christians in the middle. The situation is disguised by intentionally slanted news coverage, media portrayals, and rhetoric that support a political agenda, and not a balanced view regarding the causes and perpetuation of the Palestinian crisis. For their part, Palestinian Christians are now heavily using RT today, known as Palestinian Liberation Theology, to poison the hearts and minds of novice Christians in America who do not have the biblical knowledge and intellectual integrity to honestly research it for themselves and recognize truth from error. Others already have their minds made up because of their anti-Semitic biases and do not care to take an honest, balanced, biblical approach.

The main aim of Islam in the Middle East and the rest of the world is to forcibly convert the world to Islam. Those who believe otherwise are naïve and gullible. If Islam does prevail, the world will be thrown into the darkest period it has ever experienced, by contrast making the Dark Ages of the Middle Ages look bright.

Islam as a political force removes all religious liberties, all civil liberties, all personal liberties, all political liberties, and all intellectual liberties. Women, you would lose ALL your hard-fought-for rights, only to be considered as a sexual toy and personal servant to be used by men. Why do Americans fail to counter Islamic extremism? They are afraid of being called Islamophobic. America, do your research on the history of Islam and its tactics and understand that there is nothing good or righteous that comes out of Islam. Understand that Islamic culture is a culture of hatred, oppression, and death to all who disagree with it. Take a good look at ISIS and understand this is the Islam that conquered the Middle-East and North Africa in the seventh and eighth centuries. Look at the hotspots in the world. Most of them are where Islam is fighting other Islamic people or killing Christians and Jewish people, such as in the conflicts surrounding Iran and the civil war in Syria.

I attended a conference called the Lausanne Consultation for Jewish Evangelism in March, 2014, at Wheaton College. An invitation was given to Gary Burge, who is a huge supporter of the Palestinian Christian and Muslim cause. As I listened to him and the moderator discuss the opposite sides of the issues, I had to give Burge credit for not calling for the defeat and dismantling of the State of Israel. However, as I listened to him tell his perspective, I began to realize he has done the same thing that most Americans, including the news media, have done. He has focused on Israel's hard-line response to many Palestinian attacks, and he is absolutely ignoring the Abrahamic Covenant. He looks at the Israeli response to Palestinian and Muslim violence at checkpoints and Israel's defensive bombing of cities from which attacks are launched while purposely passing over the crimes of the instigators.

I spoke with Gary Burge privately after the meeting and thanked him for coming and sharing his position so that we could understand this movement against national Israel better. But then I referenced all of the illustrations that he had used to point to Israel's aggressive behavior over the last 30 years. I then asked, "Are not these past 30 years the effects and not the cause of the actual Muslim/Israeli tensions?" I then asked him if the root cause of the conflict springs from the radical Islamic element that instructs children, teenagers, and the general population to hate Jewish people and to annihilate the State of Israel. After all, the Mufti of Jerusalem from 1919 through World War II incited hatred and violent conflict with Israel. Overall, is it the radical Islamic element that has been foremost in murdering other Muslim people who wanted to live in peace with Israel?

I found Mr. Burge's answer surprising in light of what he is personally promoting. He said that yes, the cause of the problem has been the radical

Muslim element. I would add to his yes that the radical Islamic element still does instigate the violence in the area. So the problem does not weigh upon the shoulders of the Israelis but with the radical, unregenerate Islamic heart that is completely corrupted by centuries of hatred and in need of salvation through Jesus Christ.

This book was written to express what God says about the matter as He weighs into the discussion and His attitude towards Israel from His very Word, the Bible. America is in the process of becoming anti-Israel, which is just another form of anti-Semitism. The ramification of movements such as Palestinian Liberation Theology, Christ at the Checkpoint, and the Bethlehem Bible College, who embrace RT, is a self-perpetuating hatred of Israel and the Jewish people. They are actively ***Poking God's Eye***, blinded by their own hatred. These organizations rely on the false belief that God is done with Israel. The retribution that they and the people influenced by them will receive at the hands of God is frightening as it relates to the blessings and cursings of the Abrahamic Covenant. One can pray that their perspectives will change, so that that they will experience the blessings God has reserved for those who honor the Jewish people. May they come to live in peace!

What we are about to see in the blessings and cursings of the Abrahamic Covenant is that it is just as active today in the mind and heart of God as it was when He gave it to Abraham 4,000 years ago. This is a subject that I have found almost no information on, and Christians need to understand that their position against Israel is also a position of being against God, Himself. Much more could be written on the history of the Arab/Israeli or Christian conflict, but that is not the purpose of this book. We want to look at Scripture and see what God has to say about our responses to Israel.

Chapter 6
The Character of God – His Integrity

For Christians, true believers, who take a negative position against Israel: God will not turn a blind eye to your action! He will not judge a believer on the basis of His salvation, for that has already been dealt with at the cross of Calvary. However, He will definitely judge His sons and daughters at the Judgment Seat of Christ, better known as the Bema Seat, in relationship to rewards. That is a different subject, but it will suffice to say, many believers will forfeit their rewards at the Bema Seat because of their present sins, including acts of anti-Semitism.

In going through the upcoming chapters, the Scriptures are clear. If you touch Israel, the pupil of His eye, He will touch you (Zechariah 2:8), and it will not be a loving touch. That will be born out as we go through the Scriptures.

God stands by His promises that He makes to the Jewish people; His character is at stake; His Word is at stake! When people do not keep their word, you lose trust and confidence in them. If God does not keep His covenants with Israel, how can you have any confidence that He will keep His promise of salvation with you?

You may say that when Jewish people turned Jesus over to the Romans in the first century to be crucified, God was finished with them. If you read through the Prophets, they repeat time and time again throughout their writings that God is not finished with Israel; for the blood sacrifice of Christ on the cross was already placed into God's plan of redemption with their future in mind. If God has abandoned them based on their shortcomings, take a look at the Church. We Christians, who have the complete revelation of the Scripture, including the Roman Catholic, Eastern Orthodox, Russian Orthodox, and Protestant churches, are largely apostate bodies. Why should God keep His promises of salvation for us? Why should He not cast off the Church as an apostate body as some say He cast off Israel?

We clearly recognize that there was always a faithful remnant in Israel, and there is a faithful remnant among the Church; but the Church is largely apostate. The Church today is in a deplorable condition:

- More and more, the Church has replaced the Bible, His Word, with the addition of Church authority, tradition, and works, just as the Jewish people did with rabbinic law.

- The apostate church has removed the literal interpretation and replaced it with allegorical interpretation, making the depraved creature the authority over God and His Word.

- In some camps, salvation is seen as a matter of works rather than by Faith through grace alone.

- Other "christian" groups have added other books to the Bible that were not accepted by Judaism and early Christianity: the Apocrypha and Pseudepigrapha. Today we have the *Book of Mormon* and Mary Baker Eddy's *Science and Health with Keys to the Scriptures* (Christian Science), and of course the Jehovah Witnesses' New World Translation of the Bible.

- The Church has in the past forcibly converted people to Christianity by the sword, just as Islam has done.

- The Church has murdered untold numbers of people who believed differently from Christians, just as Islam has done in the past and is doing today.

- The Church has sanctioned mobs to murder, rape, and pillage Jewish communities for centuries, and even was doing it in the name of Jesus with their crosses raised high.

- Today the Church at large has a social/political gospel with very little responsibility to the teachings of Scripture, as in the example of Palestinian Liberation Theology.

- Today, many Protestant Christians deny the resurrection, the virgin birth, the inspiration of the Scriptures, as well Genesis 1-11 as fictitious stories and myths. The Church largely supports the teaching of evolution as fact over and against the creation story presented in the Written Word of God.

- Today, many Evangelical Churches are in the entertainment business and preach a warm, fuzzy gospel in the manner of Joel

Osteen or the prosperity gospel in the manner of Benny Hinn. There are so many false teachings today.

- Today, new heresies and heretics spring up at every turn, and the Church is embracing them and not regarding the many, many warnings of the Apostles against false teaching.
- Today, the Church has cast off absolute Truth and replaced it with relativism and evolution and political correctness.
- Today, even most fundamental and conservative churches are apathetic in their faith.
- Today the Church has lost sight of its mission to preach the Gospel. It is not a state like the Vatican, with diplomatic status, or a state church controlled by the government, as in European countries. God's purpose for the body of believers rests within the hearts of true believers, and not in any secularized system, but only to the degree that they grasp His plan. Will the Great Commission continue to recede as the central mission of Christ's bride, the Church, as believers are opposed by secular powers? Can our faith and convictions survive the growing opposition to the Christian Church, the salvation message, and Bible truth during the current age of humanist opposition, government intervention, and public ridicule? We can, of course, but education in God's Word is essential. He who has an ear, let him hear. He who has an eye, let him see.

The sins of the Church today are legend. So why has God not cast off the Church for denying Him? God keeps His word; He is not fickle like man who does not keep His word or live by it.

I have listened to Covenant/Replacement pastors and scholars take Scripture and twist it like a pretzel so that they can lift themselves up and shove the Jewish people down. From conservative Christian circles, many of these men are born again, saved people who have a fascination with the artificial standing that they make for themselves. I have learned over these past 70 years that whenever anyone tears people down, it is to raise oneself up.

The Church is having a love affair with the world system, and as Christians we are empty, cracked vessels that no longer hold water. As a sad result, we lack vision, passion, and sacrificial living to take the Gospel of

Christ to a world that is either lost because they have never heard the Good News, or are living in dead churches just going through the motions. By God's grace, there is still a remnant that knows the truth and lives by it!

God has put in place blessings and cursings to grab our attention, and He has also made His position regarding Israel and the Jewish people manifest in His Word. Let us examine God's message to us regarding His heart for the Jewish people and how He wants us to respond to them. It is not just an exercise in theology, but it makes a real difference in how we apply our faith, and what we will and will not choose to do as believers in Jesus Christ.

Blessings and Cursings

The Abrahamic and Mosaic Covenants both speak of blessings and cursings, but they are directed to two different people groups. Read carefully and understand what is about to be said:

- **The Blessings and Cursings of the Abrahamic Covenant in Genesis 12:3 relate solely to the Gentile population on the earth.** They have absolutely nothing to do with blessings and cursings to Jewish people based on their adherence to the Mosaic Law. To the contrary, the blessings and cursings listed in Genesis 12:3 have everything to do with how Gentiles treat Jewish people. If we bless Jewish people, we will be blessed. If we curse Jewish people, we will be cursed.

- **The Blessings and Cursings of the Mosaic Covenant in Deuteronomy 28 have to do solely with the Jewish people and not the Gentiles.** God promised to bless Israel if His people obeyed the Mosaic Law, with so many blessings that it would be all they could do to absorb them all. However, if they chose to disobey the Mosaic Law, God promised to send cursings upon them, more than they could handle.

- So we have two sets of blessings and cursings: **one set is *directly related to the Gentile population*** of the earth in the Abrahamic Covenant, and **the second set is *directly related to the Jewish population*** in a covenant they made with God to keep the Mosaic Law.

This principle of blessing and cursing generally is not thought through by the average person, whether they are true believers or not. Now much of Christendom is ready to say that the Jews are cursed because of what they have done to Messiah; and because of that, they have poured out upon the Jewish people unspeakable atrocities. Such actions are a gross violation of the Abrahamic Covenant, and God will hold the Gentiles accountable for their behavior.

Unbelievers will be held accountable at the Great White Throne Judgment, and true believers in the Messiah will be held accountable at the Bema Seat Judgment. People are not condemned to hell because of anti-Semitism. Their works could be judged perhaps in their lifetimes, receiving God's cursings as they live on the earth. However, only because of unbelief is anyone judged at the Great White Throne Judgment, where those who have not put their trust in God will enter into hell, the Lake of Fire.

True believers can also be judged in their lifetimes, receiving God's curses or His blessings, depending on how they treat the Jewish people. However, when they are justified by God, their salvation is secure; and all their past deeds are forgiven. All true believers will stand before a Jewish Judge who will reward them for deeds done in the flesh or deeds done in the light, generated by the ministry of the Holy Spirit. Those works done in the flesh will be burned up, and those deeds done in the Spirit will endure like gold, silver, and precious stones (1 Corinthians 3:13-15). So be forewarned. If you are among that group that attacks Israel, your anti-Semitic acts done in the flesh will limit your rewards when you stand before that Jewish Judge at the Bema Seat of Jesus Christ.

Most people have not considered the fact that many Gentiles are under the curse of God because of how negatively they have treated and are still treating the Jewish people. If you want to say that Israel is cursed of God, then in so doing you should understand you are also cursed of God as to how you have treated the Jewish people. An example is given in Matthew 25:31-46. This is the thread that we want to trace through Scripture so that we as Gentiles understand what God has placed before us, namely the Jewish people and how we are to treat them.

The Covenants

God has given to mankind eight covenants. The first three apply to the Gentile world, and the next five to the Jewish world. There are two types of covenants: conditional and unconditional. Arnold Fruchtenbaum gives a definition for both types:

A **conditional covenant** is a bilateral covenant in which a proposal of God to man is characterized by the formula: If you will, then I will, whereby God promises to grant special blessings to man providing man fulfills certain conditions contained in the covenant. Man's failure to do so often results in punishment. Thus one's response to the covenant agreement brings either blessings or cursings. The blessings are secured by obedience, and man must meet His conditions before God will meet [H]is. Two of the eight covenants of the Bible are conditional: the Edenic Covenant and the Mosaic Covenant.

An **unconditional covenant** is a unilateral covenant and is a sovereign act of God whereby He unconditionally obligates Himself to bring to pass definite blessings and conditions for the covenanted people. This covenant is characterized by the formula: I will, which declares God's determination to do as He promises. Blessings are secured by the grace of God. There may be conditions in the covenant which God requests the covenanted one to fulfill out of gratitude, but they are not themselves the basis of God's fulfilling His promises. Six of the eight covenants are unconditional: the Adamic Covenant, the Noahic Covenant, the Abrahamic Covenant, the Palestinian or Land Covenant, the Davidic Covenant, and the New Covenant.[93]

Here is a list of the eight Covenants that God really did give in His Word to help us grasp His heart and understand Scripture.

- The **Edenic Covenant** was cancelled by man's fall.

- The **Adamic Covenant** is still in effect today.

- The **Noahic Covenant** is also still in effect today. Non-believing Gentiles will be judged by God in relationship to their not keeping the Noahic Covenant. They will receive the wrath of God in the Tribulation. (There are no Christians in the Tribulation. Notice that in the second sentence I said *Gentiles*, not *Christians*.) Most Gentiles do not give any consideration to the external moral constraints of government provided for the Noahic Covenant; but God does, and He will judge.

---

[93] Arnold G. Fruchtenbaum, *The Eight Covenants of the Bible – Manuscript # 21* (San Antonio, TX: Ariel Ministries, 2005), 5.

- The **Abrahamic Covenant** promises the national existence of Israel as a people and nation; they are indestructible.
- The **Mosaic Covenant** was to keep the Jewish people separate from the Gentiles because of the promises and the covenants until Messiah came and fulfilled the standards of the Law perfectly, at which time the Law ceased.
- The **Land Covenant** is the promise of the Land to national, ethnic, physical Israel.
- The **Davidic Covenant** is the promise that a son of David will reign physically over Israel and the world on his throne from Jerusalem throughout the 1,000 year Millennial period.
- Lastly, the **New Covenant** promises regeneration for Jewish people and the Gentiles. It greatly helps us in understanding more fully God's salvation plan through the ages.

Below is a listing of the eight covenants between God and Israel, with their Scripture references.

Table 2. God's Eight Covenants

COVENANTS	
Edenic Covenant	Genesis 1:28-30; 2:15-17; Hosea 6:7
Adamic Covenant	Genesis 3:14-19
Noahic Covenant	Genesis 9:1-17
Abrahamic Covenant	Genesis 12:1-3, 7; 13:14-17; 15:1-21; 17:1-21; 22:15-18
Mosaic Covenant	Exodus – Deuteronomy
Land Covenant	Deuteronomy 28-29
Davidic Covenant	2 Samuel 7:11-16; 1 Chronicles 17:10-14
New Covenant	Jeremiah 31:31-34; Ezekiel 36:26 and 27

In this book we are focusing on one aspect of the Abrahamic Covenant, the outworking of the blessing and cursing of that covenant. Genesis 12:1-3, 7 is foundational in understanding this covenant, for there are three aspects to this covenant that God will develop into three additional eternal unconditional covenants. First, look with me at Genesis 12:

> *¹ Now the LORD had said unto Abram, Get you out of your country, and from your kindred, and from your father's house, unto* **a land that I will show you***: ² And I will* **make of you a great nation***, and I will bless you, and make thy name great; and you shall be a blessing: ³ And I will bless them that bless you and curse him that curses you:* **and in you shall all the families of the earth be blessed.**
>
> *⁷ And the LORD appeared unto Abram, and said,* **Unto your seed will I give this land***: and there he built an altar unto the LORD, who appeared unto him.*

In this passage, there are several *I will's* of God as He makes this unconditional covenant with Abram. These three aspects of this covenant stand out and need to be understood. In the Abrahamic Covenant, these three aspects are as follows:

1. **Land** aspect in verses 1 and 7.
2. **Seed** aspect in verses 2 and 7.
3. **Blessing** aspect in verse 3, that God will develop in His progressive revelation of Himself to Abraham and the Jewish nation, that all the families of the earth will be blessed.

In Genesis 12:3, God states to Abram, *and I will bless them that bless you and curse him that curses you*. This passage must be understood in the light of the growing anti-Semitism from the Church, Europe, and the Muslim world. God will not tolerate anti-Semitism, and those individuals and nations who perpetrate it will be judged accordingly.

The following point must be understood by all peoples. Nowhere in Scripture does the Abrahamic Covenant promise salvation; it promises the national existence of Israel. Israel as a people is indestructible! Out of the Abrahamic Covenant, God will develop three other covenants directly connected to each of the three aspects laid down in the Abrahamic Covenant: Land, Seed, and Blessing:

- The Land aspect of the Abrahamic Covenant will be expanded by God into the Land Covenant of Deuteronomy 29-30.

- The Seed aspect of the Abrahamic Covenant will be expanded by God into the Davidic Covenant of 2 Samuel 7:11-16 (with Solomon in view) and 1 Chronicles 17:10-14 (with Messiah, son of David in view).

- The Blessing aspect of the Abrahamic Covenant will be developed by God into the New Covenant of Jeremiah 31:31-34. This is a marvelous subject for studying and understanding the heart of God to save both Jew and Gentile from their sin when they put their Faith and Trust in Him. I would encourage you to read my book *Israel's Only Hope: The New Covenant*.[94]

- These four covenants will be interconnected and interlocked together throughout the Scriptures. They are individual covenants that God interrelates to reveal His plan for Israel, His covenant people.

Table 3. Interrelationship of Abrahamic Covenant with Land, Davidic, and New Covenants

ABRAHAMIC COVENANT		
LAND ASPECT:	SEED ASPECT:	BLESSING ASPECT:
LAND COVENANT	DAVIDIC COVENANT	NEW COVENANT

Land Covenant

The Land Covenant is the promise that the Land of Israel belongs to God, who gave it to Abraham and his descendants and to no one else. In fact, in Joel 2:18, the LORD says that He is *jealous for His land*. It was *His land* that He promised to Israel in the Abrahamic and Land Covenants. He promised it to Israel and not to the Church, the Palestinian Christians, or the Muslims. Although the Land Covenant does not promise salvation, it is the title deed to the Land which Israel possesses by God's decree.

Today the issue is the ownership of the Land between Israel and Palestinians, who both claim it. Who has the right to the Land: Palestinians or Israel? Let us look at what God, Himself, says about the Land. I will elaborate more on the Land Covenant in the next chapter. Appendix Three lists over 200 verses on the ownership of the Land.

---

[94] Metzger, *Israel's Only Hope: The New Covenant*.

Davidic Covenant

The Davidic Covenant is the promise to David that one of his sons will re-establish his throne (Isaiah 11:1), dynasty, and house eternally in the future. The Son of David will come and reign on David's throne physically in Jerusalem. Once again, this covenant does not promise salvation; it promises that the Son of David will reign physically over the whole world from David's throne in Jerusalem.

New Covenant

The New Covenant is named in Jeremiah 31:31-34 and referenced by other prophets, such as in Ezekiel 36:26-27. This New Covenant has three key ingredients:

- A new heart – regeneration
- A new spirit – indwelling of the Holy Spirit
- Removal of all sin

This promise to regenerate the hearts of the Jewish people is unique to this covenant. This is a future event yet to happen. All Israel will embrace Jesus as their Messiah and LORD at the end of the Tribulation period, the time of Jacob's Trouble. This is the only covenant that promises salvation.[95] It is also through this covenant that God opened the doors of salvation to Gentiles without their becoming Jewish.

With all this in mind, we are ready to see what God teaches us about the ownership of the Land, as we look at the actual outworking of the Abrahamic Covenant in the Bible as well as in history.

So to recap this chapter, God has set the eternal covenants in motion. He has given them. He will implement them, and He will fulfill them in the lives and hearts of the Jewish nation called Israel. The integrity of God's character and Name is at stake as Ezekiel 36:17-38 clearly states, even though Israel has profaned His Holy Name, He will bring these covenants to fulfillment to glorify His Name that was profaned.

---

[95] Ibid.

Chapter 7
Who Has Ownership of the Land?

Today there is increasing anti-Israel sentiment in the world, including the growth of anti-Israel rhetoric and actions among Evangelical Christians. Some blame Israel for all the turmoil in the Middle East. There is a propaganda war being orchestrated by Palestinian Christians on one side and radical Islam on the other. They both claim that Israel has no right to live within her borders. Both of these have a blemished theological base, with Palestinian Christians grounded in Covenant/Replacement Theology and radical Islam based on human invention rather than biblical theology and its evidence.

The Land Covenant

Genesis 12:1-3, 7

So one more time, before going into the outworking of the cursings and blessings of the Abrahamic Covenant, we need to understand the Land Covenant and its connection with the Abrahamic Covenant.

The unconditional Land Covenant is intrinsically interwoven into the unconditional Abrahamic Covenant as well as the conditional Mosaic Covenant, yet the Land Covenant is a distinctive covenant from the Abrahamic and Mosaic Covenants. Let us begin again with the foundational document, the Abrahamic Covenant in Genesis 12:1-3, 7:

> *¹ Now the LORD had said unto Abram, Get you out of your country, and from your kindred, and from your father's house, unto* **a land** *that I will show you: ² And I will make of you a great nation, and I will bless you, and make your name great; and you shall be a blessing: ³ And I will bless them that bless you, and curse him that curses you: and in you shall all families of the earth be blessed.*
>
> *⁷ And the LORD appeared unto Abram, and said, Unto your seed will I give* **this land:** *and there he built an altar unto the LORD, who appeared unto him.*

Genesis 13:14-17

In this passage, we see that the LORD has chosen Abram in His first announcement in Genesis 12, but it is not the last of the covenant announcements of God. Notice very clearly in verses 1 and 7, the Land is a predominant part of the Abrahamic Covenant. Now look at Genesis 13:14-17, which is the second announcement of the Land in the Abrahamic Covenant, as the LORD spells it out even more clearly:

> *14 And the LORD said unto Abram, after Lot was separated from him, Lift up now your eyes, and* **look** *for the place where you are* **northward**, *and* **southward**, *and* **eastward**, *and* **westward**: *15* **For all the land which you see**, *to you will* **I give it**, *and* **to your seed forever.** *16 And I will make your seed as the dust of the earth: so that if a man can number the dust of the earth, then shall your seed also be numbered. 17* **Arise, walk through the land in the length of it and in the breadth of it; for I will give it unto you.**

In this passage, the LORD simply lays out His promise in a very clear, precise way. There is no mistaking what He said. Here the promise is clarified to Abram; and it is so clear, it really needs no further comment.

More Confirmations: Genesis 17, Genesis 22:15-18, and Genesis 26:3-4

The third announcement of the Abrahamic Covenant is the confirmation of that covenant by the Word of the LORD and the Shekinah of the LORD that was given in Genesis 15. Genesis 17 and 22:15-18 are the final two announcements by God of the Abrahamic Covenant. Next, the Abrahamic Covenant, that includes the Land, is confirmed with Isaac. Notice what the promise to Isaac contains in Genesis 26:3-4:

> *3 Sojourn* **in this land**, *and I will be with you, and will bless you,* **for unto you and unto your seed, I will give all these countries,** *and I will perform the oath which I swore unto Abraham your father; 4 And I will make your seed to multiply as the stars of heaven,* **and will give unto your seed all these countries;** *and in your seed shall all the nations of the earth be blessed.*

Reconfirmation of the Land Covenant to Abraham and His Descendants

Notice one of the key ingredients of the reconfirmation of the Abrahamic Covenant to Isaac. The Land that was personally promised to Abraham is also personally promised to Isaac as well. Then the promise was reconfirmed to Jacob, the son of Isaac. So it was passed on to the second and then the third generation from Abraham. Notice how God with clarity states the promise in Genesis 28:4, 13 and 35:12 to Jacob:

> $^{28:4}$ *And give you the blessing of Abraham, to you, and to your seed with you; that you may* **inherit the Land** *wherein you are a stranger, which God gave unto Abraham.*

> $^{28:13}$ *And, behold, that LORD stood above it, and said, I am the LORD God of Abraham your father, and the God of Isaac:* **the Land** *whereon you lay, to you will I give it, and to your seed;* ^{14} *and your seed shall be as the dust of the earth, and you shall spread abroad to the west, and to the east, and to the north, and to the south: and in you and in your seed shall all the families of the earth be blessed.*

> $^{35:12}$ **And the Land** *which I gave Abraham and Isaac, to you I will give it,* **and to your seed after you will I give the Land**.

Carefully go back over all these verses and observe the personal promise to Abraham, Isaac, and Jacob that the Land was given to them personally by God. Also notice that each passage clearly states that the inheritance of the Land will be passed on to their descendants. There is no misunderstanding the words of Moses; God spoke clearly through him.

David L. Cooper's Principle of Applying Literal Interpretation to the Bible

Now before moving on to the next passage, let me repeat the principle of interpretation that we use in Ariel Ministries; it is called the Golden Rule of Interpretation. Many others use the same principle without quoting it. It is as follows:

> When the plain sense of Scripture makes common sense, seek no other sense; therefore take every word at its primary, ordinary, usual, literal meaning unless the facts of the immediate context, studied in the light of related passages and axiomatic and fundamental truths, indicate clearly otherwise. (David L. Cooper)

The basic idea is that God is completely capable of speaking for Himself without the supplemental or editorial help of theological scholars who are well over 2000 years removed from when God spoke. Telling the omniscient and omnipotent God that they, the dust of the earth, can better tell us what God said, goes against the literal interpretation of God's Word.

Those of us with a dispensational approach do not reinterpret the Bible from our own perspective, but we instead view the Bible from a Jewish perspective as we take His Word literally. This is extremely important to understand as we get into the Land Covenant and how Covenant Theology puts an unbiblical spin on what God, Himself, said.

Covenant theologians are in so many words saying that the covenants to Israel have been cancelled because of disobedience of Israel and for their being directly responsible for the death of Christ. As a result of these basic misperceptions, Covenant theologians teach in error that the Church has become the new inheritor of the covenants. That is an unbiblical myth! Imagine Covenant Theology that teaches and stresses the sovereignty of God, but in their theological system they are telling the Sovereign God that He needs the help of imperfect, fallible man to reconstruct His Word. Instead of believing what the Sovereign God has clearly stated, they bend God's Word to fit their theological biases.

To be fair, Covenant theologians who teach the sovereignty of God only do so as it relates to the redemption process of the so-called elect. So they actually teach a limited sovereignty, while we in Dispensational Theology teach the sovereignty of God in every sphere of life. God's will is accomplished in all areas, for God is sovereign over all!!

The Land Covenant in Leviticus and Deuteronomy

As we move through the following verses, notice how clearly our Sovereign God articulates His Word as it relates to the Land Covenant and its interaction with the other unconditional covenants. Look with me at the words of Moses in Leviticus and Deuteronomy as he prophetically lays out God's revelation of the future of Israel and her restoration.

> *But I have said unto you,* **You shall inherit their land,** *and* **I will give it unto you to possess it**, *a land that flows with milk and honey: I am the LORD your God, which has separated you from other people. (Leviticus 20:24)*

Moses was here speaking of the Land as he addressed the Exodus generation. They were to receive it, as God promised to Abraham, Isaac, and Jacob. Then, in Leviticus 26:40-46, Moses reflects that Israel's rebellion did not catch God off guard. God, through His servant Moses, tells His people of their future iniquity and trespasses. They will consistently walk contrary to all the judgments and statutes that God gave them; yet with all that our

Sovereign God says in verse 44, He maintains: *I will not cast them away, neither will I abhor them, utterly, and to break My covenant with them: for I am the LORD their God.* These verses are only part of the section as to what God is going to do; for that, read all of Leviticus 26.

Now let us look at all seven verses in Leviticus 26:40-46:

> *⁴⁰ If they shall **confess their iniquity**, and the **iniquity of their fathers**, with their **trespass which they trespassed against Me**, and that also they have **walked contrary unto Me**; ⁴¹ And that I also have walked contrary unto them, and have brought them into the land of their enemies; if then their **uncircumcised hearts** be humbled, and they then accept of the punishment of their iniquity: ⁴² **Then will I remember My covenant with Jacob**, and also **My covenant with Isaac**, and also **My covenant with Abraham** will I remember; and **I will remember the Land**. ⁴³ The Land also shall be left of them, and shall enjoy her Sabbaths, while she lies desolate without them: and they shall accept of the punishment of their iniquity: because, even because they despised My judgments, and because their soul abhorred My statutes. ⁴⁴ And yet for all that, when they be in the land of their enemies, **I will not cast them away, neither will I abhor them, to destroy them utterly, and to break My covenant with them:** for I am the LORD their God. ⁴⁵ But I will for their sakes remember the covenant of their ancestors, whom I brought forth out of the land of Egypt in the sight of the heathen, that I might be their God: I am the LORD. ⁴⁶ These are the statutes and judgments and law, which the LORD made between Him and the children of Israel in Mount Sinai by the hand of Moses.*

Notice Israel is not even in the Land yet; but God, through the mouth of Moses, is prophesying the sin of Israel, her iniquity and trespasses in which His people will walk contrary to the law because of their uncircumcised hearts. The word *remember* does not mean that God forgot; it means that when Israel confesses their sins and embraces Him, then He, the Sovereign God, will act upon the promises He personally made to Abraham, Isaac, and Jacob.

Now as this future chapter is given, just as the Prophets will confirm it in their own day, the Sovereign God, who will bring all things to His glory, will not cast Israel away. But Covenant and Replacement Theology says, "Okay, but they rejected the incarnate Christ." That is right, but it is nothing new. He was already rejected by them all the way back in Exodus 32 with the Golden

Calf, and that was only a foretaste of what they would do.[96] The one who communicated with Moses was the second Person of the God-head, the one we call Jesus Christ; He was the God of Israel as He even references in Matthew 23:37:

> *O Jerusalem, Jerusalem, you that killed the prophets, and stoned them which are sent unto you, how often would* **I** *have gathered your children together, even as a hen gathers her chickens under her wings, and you would not!*

Now the word **I** is buried in the middle of that verse; people just read over it, for we never connect the meaning that Jesus was referencing to His activity as the God of Israel in the Hebrew Scriptures. Jesus did not say that the Father wanted to gather His chosen people; **He** says that He, Himself, wanted to gather them together and protect and nurture them as their Sovereign God. He is speaking not only of His desire to protect them, but that it was He, Himself, who sent the Prophets that they killed and stoned. He may have been rejected physically before the Sanhedrin and Pilate, but He was rejected by Israel throughout biblical history.

Now, going back to Deuteronomy 5:16, we find that He, the LORD through Moses, emphasizes again the Land which He would give them.

> *Honor your father and your mother, as the LORD your God hath commanded you; that your days may be prolonged, and that it may go well with you,* **in the Land which the LORD your God gives you.**

Then in Deuteronomy 11:21, it is clearly stated that this is the Land that He swore to the fathers, meaning to Abraham, Isaac, and Jacob.

> *That our days may be multiplied, and the days of your children,* **in the Land which the LORD swore unto your fathers to give them,** *as the days of heaven upon the earth.*

Then Moses moves to the teaching on the Land Covenant to the new generation that was about to enter the Land under the leadership of Joshua. In Deuteronomy 29-30, you have a thorough stating of the Land Covenant that was given to them. Let me share a couple of verses with you from Deuteronomy 29. Please take your Bible and read this entire passage before

---

[96] For a further in-depth study, see my book *Discovering the Mystery of the Unity of God*, published by Ariel Ministries in 2010, San Antonio, TX.

going further. In verse one, God states the covenant and then contrasts it with the Mosaic Covenant:

These are the words of the covenant, which the LORD commanded Moses to make with the children of Israel in the land of Moab, beside the covenant which He made with them in Horeb [Mt. Sinai].

Notice that God made two covenants with the Exodus generation of Israel in the wilderness: first the Mosaic Covenant from Exodus 20 through 24 a year into their journey, and then the Land Covenant at the end of the wilderness journey forty years later. These two covenants were made with Israel, and notice that the Sovereign God makes a clear distinction between them. The second covenant is not an extension of the Mosaic Covenant, but a different distinct covenant about the ownership and possession of the Land.

In the section of verses from Deuteronomy 29:1 through 30:1-10, Moses gives the whole "history" of Israel ahead of time, before it happens: their sin, rebellion, idolatry, and the violation of the laws of Moses as well as their future restoration. Notice in Deuteronomy 29:13 that this covenant is an extension of the Land promise given to Abraham that we covered in Genesis 12 and 13:

[13] That He may establish you today for a people unto Himself, and that He may be unto you a God, as He hath said unto you, and as He hath sworn unto your fathers, to Abraham, to Isaac, and to Jacob.

Then in Deuteronomy 29:20-21, 27 Moses references the curses that are clearly given in Deuteronomy 28:15-68. Israel was unfaithful, and the Jewish people were judged severely by God; but we see by the same prophecy that in the end, the same Sovereign God will restore them when they confess their sin and place their Faith in Him and Him alone.

Next, as we read Deuteronomy 30:1-10, we can discern these three observations made by Dwight Pentecost in his book, *Things to Come: A Study in Biblical Eschatology*:

1. The Land Covenant reaffirms to Israel their title deed to the Land of Promise.

2. The conditional Mosaic Covenant did not render the unconditional Abrahamic Covenant null and void.

3. [The passage] is an elaboration of the Land aspect of the Abrahamic Covenant and reaffirms Israel's right to the

Land even after a long history of disobedience arising out of unbelief. While the enjoyment of the Land may be conditioned by obedience, the ownership of the Land is not.[97]

Now let us look at Deuteronomy 30:1-10 and then we will view a short outline of the prophetic events that will happen in Israel's future.

[1] And it shall come to pass, when all these things are come upon you, the blessing and the curse, which I have set before you, and you shall call them to mind among all the nations, whither the LORD your God has driven you,

[2] And shall return unto the LORD your God, and shall obey His voice according to all that I command you this day, you and your children, with all your heart, and with all your soul.

[3] That then the LORD your God will turn your captivity, and have compassion upon you, and will return and gather you from all the nations, whither the LORD your God has scattered you.

[4] If any of you be driven out unto the outermost parts of heaven, from thence will the LORD your God gather you, and from thence will He fetch you.

[5] And **the LORD your God will bring you into the land which your fathers possessed, and you shall possess it**; *and He will do you good, and multiply you above your fathers.*

[6] And the **LORD your God will circumcise your heart**, *and the heart of your seed, to love the LORD your God with all your heart, and with all your soul, that you may live.*

[7] And the LORD your God will put all these curses upon your enemies, and on them that hate you, which persecuted you.

[8] And you shall return and obey the voice of the LORD, and do all His commandments which I command you this day.

[9] And the LORD your God will make you plenteous in every work of your hand, in the fruit of your body, and in the fruit of your cattle, and in the fruit of your land for good: for the LORD will again rejoice over you for good, as He rejoiced over your fathers:

---

[97] Dwight Pentecost, *Things to Come: A Study in Biblical Eschatology* (Grand Rapids, MI: Zondervan, 1964), 95-96.

¹⁰ If you shall hearken unto the voice of the LORD your God, to keep His commandments and His statutes which are written in this book of the law, and if you turn unto the LORD your God with all your heart and with all your soul.

Eight Points Moses Makes About Israel (Deuteronomy 30:1-10)

In these ten verses, the Sovereign LORD through Moses makes eight points concerning Israel. As you read, look for answers to the following two questions: "Where is the covenant cancelled because of sin and unbelief? Where is the Land given to another group of people, be it the Palestinians or the Church?" Here are the eight points:

1. Moses prophetically spoke of Israel's coming disobedience to the Mosaic Law and their subsequent scattering over all the world (29:2-30:1).
2. Israel will repent (30:2).
3. Messiah will return (30:3).
4. Israel will be regathered (30:4).
5. Israel will possess the Promised Land (30:5).
6. Israel will be regenerated (30:6).
7. The enemies of Israel will be judged (30:7).
8. Israel will receive full blessing, specifically, the blessings of the Messianic Kingdom (30:8-10).

This passage and the eight points give special importance to the Land Covenant as it reaffirms Israel's title deed to the Land. Although Israel would prove to be unfaithful and disobedient, the right to the Land would never be taken from her. Her enjoyment of the Land (30:9-10) is conditioned on obedience; ownership of the Land (30:1-8) is unconditional. Furthermore, it shows that the conditional Mosaic Covenant did not lay aside the unconditional Abrahamic Covenant.

It might be taken by some that the Mosaic Covenant displaced the Abrahamic Covenant, but the Land Covenant here shows that this is not true. The Land Covenant is an enlargement of the original Land aspect of the Abrahamic Covenant. It amplifies the Land aspect and emphasizes the promise of the Land to God's people **in spite of their unbelief.**

Covenant/Replacement Theology[98] tries to say that the Land Covenant was fulfilled in Joshua 11:23 where it states:

> *So Joshua took the whole land, according to all that the LORD said unto Moses; and Joshua gave it for an inheritance unto Israel according to their divisions by their tribes. And the land rested from war.*

This is a general statement and not a statement of totally conquering and settling in all the Land, for we find the following record in Judges 1:21-36:

1. Judah did well, but could not drive out the inhabitants of the valleys because of their iron chariots. Judah did not take Jerusalem until the time of David (2 Samuel 5:6-9), or the city of Gezer until the time of Solomon (1 Kings 9:16).

2. Benjamin did not take Jerusalem.

3. Manasseh did not take Beth-shean, Taanach, nor Dor and Megiddo.

4. The victories of Ephraim, Zebulun, Asher, and Naphtali were incomplete.

5. Dan was forced by the Amorites into the mountains, and many of this tribe would relocate to the northern part of Israel, which became known as Dan.

6. In Judges, all the tribes of Israel went through the repetitive cycle of sin to deliverance that eventually led to them falling into bondage to foreigners under God's judgment.

7. The Philistines were not conquered.

8. Phoenicia was never attacked.

9. The Jewish people lived in other areas of the Land of Israel, but only put the Canaanites under tribute (taxation) instead of removing them from the Land. Thus the Canaanites became a thorn in their side.

So when the whole context is studied, we find in the Hebrew Scriptures that Israel did not possess, dwell, and settle in all of the Promised Land, nor

---

[98] Fruchtenbaum, *Israelology: The Missing Link in Systemic Theology*, 212.

has it happened in Jewish history since. Simply stated, Israel has never controlled and dwelled in all the Land promised. However, according to the Land Covenant promises given by God, the Jewish people will someday in the future be given all the Land promised in the Land Covenant.

Promises for Israel's Restoration

Now let us turn our attention to a sampling of passages from the Prophets as they state time and time again that Israel will sin and be punished but eventually will be restored. It is true they were to receive severe judgment by the hand of God, but that also, by that same hand of God, and upon their confession to Him of their sin, He will restore Israel and fulfill the Land contract that He made with Abraham, Isaac, and Jacob and to all the believing seed of Israel, the Jewish nation. In **Isaiah** 14:1-2 notice that when Israel is restored, they will possess the Land.

> *¹ For the LORD will have mercy on Jacob, and* **will yet choose Israel,** *and* **set them in their own land:** *and the strangers shall be joined with them, and they shall cleave to the house of Jacob. ² And the people* [Gentiles] *shall take them, and bring them to their place: and* **the house of Israel shall possess them in the land of the LORD** *for servants and handmaids: and they shall take them captives, whose captives they were; and they shall rule over their oppressors.*

Can it be any clearer? This is not the Church as Replacement theologians dictate and Palestinian Christians perpetrate. I am not treating the Palestinian condition lightly. Remember, as I said in the previous chapter, the Palestinians have been used as pawns in the hands of radical Palestinian Muslims. Their stance is not biblical, but reflects a political agenda helped along by the greater ambitions of radical Islam.

Now, let us look to the words of the LORD through the pen of the Prophet **Jeremiah** in chapter 16:13-15:

> *¹³ Therefore* **will I cast you out of this land into a land** *that you know not, neither you nor your fathers; and there shall you serve others gods day and night; where I will not show you favor.*
>
> *¹⁴ Therefore,* **behold the days come says the LORD**, *that it shall* **no more** *be said, The LORD lives,* **that brought up the children of Israel out of the land of Egypt**;

15 **But,** *the LORD lives,* **that brought up the children of Israel from the land of the north, and from all the lands whither He had driven them: and I will bring them again into their land that I gave unto their fathers.**

Long before Abraham's descendants had even entered into the Land to begin with, Moses prophesied that the Jewish people would be dispersed from the Land due to their disobedience. God did cast Israel out of the Land by the hands of the Assyrians in 722 B.C. and Babylonians in 586 B.C. by way of captivities. Later, after many Jewish people had returned to the Land, the Romans expelled the Jewish people from the Land again in 70 and 135 A.D. This status of being dispersed continued until fairly recently, when Israel once again became a State in 1948, after years of Jewish people regathering there.

Moses, along with the Prophets, also spoke directly to the regathering of Abraham's descendents, through Isaac and Jacob, to the very Land that they were expelled from. In verse 14, the phrase: *behold the days come says the LORD* is a prophetic future statement. Israel will no longer be remembering the deliverance from Egypt which they have practiced since Exodus 12 with the celebration of the first Passover. The reason is because they will be remembering God's greater deliverance of them from the nations as the LORD fulfills the Abrahamic Covenant with the people of Israel by His returning them to the Land of their fathers.

In reading the following verses, I cannot understand the disservice that Replacement and Covenant Theology places upon God to completely dishonor His Word by lifting up their words above the Living Word of God. Let us continue in Jeremiah 32:37, 41 and see what else the Sovereign Creator, the one who called Israel to be His people, says about Israel:

37 Behold I will gather them out of all countries, where I have driven them in My anger, and in My fury, and in great wrath; and I will bring them again unto **this place***, and I will cause them to dwell safely.*

41 Yes, I will rejoice over them to do them good, and **I will plant them in this land** *assuredly with My whole heart and with My whole soul.*

In these verses you have an outburst of emotion from the LORD, both negatively in Jeremiah 32:37, and positively in verse Jeremiah 32:41. Verse 37 states, He will gather them from all the countries that He dispersed them to in His *anger, fury,* and *great wrath.* Then notice *I will bring them again unto this place.* This place, what place? This place is from where Jeremiah was writing: Jerusalem in the nation of Israel. Now look in verse 41 at the positive emotional outburst of God in that He *will rejoice over them* and *will plant them in this land,* Israel, with all His *whole heart* and with all His *whole soul.* That is a very intense emotional response by God concerning His restoration of Israel in the future in the Land that their fathers possessed.

Now let us move from Jeremiah to **Ezekiel**. I am not going to quote all of Ezekiel 16 with its 63 verses, but let me give you a basic outline of what happens in these verses as God speaks of Israel in its infancy, marriage, adultery against God – their violation of the Mosaic Law – and finally of Israel's dispersion. In spite of all this, God will act (remember) and restore Israel by way of the New Covenant to the Land of their fathers. Look at the outline:

Table 4. Ezekiel 16: Israel's Relationship to God Described

Ezekiel 16	Stage in Israel's Relationship with her God
Verses 1-7	Childhood: God's paternal love for Israel in her infancy.
Verses 8-14	Marriage: Israel as the wife of Yahweh at Mt. Sinai.
Verses 15-34	Israel as an adulteress.
Verses 35-52	Israel punished by her God with worldwide dispersion.
Verses 53-59	Israel guilty of violating the Mosaic Law.
Verse 60	God remembers the Land Covenant of her youth.
Verses 61-63	God says, *I will establish a New Covenant, resulting in her salvation.*

God's Judgment vs. His Unconditional Covenant with Israel

These verses very clearly show that one provision of the covenant has already been fulfilled: the worldwide scattering of the Jewish people. This partial fulfillment was literally fulfilled, and this indicates a future literal fulfillment of the yet unfulfilled portions will take place, an implication that the covenant is unconditional. God fulfilled in the short-term what He promised, assuring that He will also fulfill that which is yet future. Now look at the last four verses of Ezekiel 16:

> ⁶⁰ *Nevertheless* **I will** *remember* **My covenant** *with you in the days of your youth, and* **I will** *establish unto you an* **everlasting covenant**. ⁶¹ *Then you shall remember your ways, and be ashamed, when you shall receive your sisters, your elder and your younger: and* **I will** *give them unto you for daughters, but not by your covenant.* ⁶² *And* **I will** *establish My covenant with you and you shall know that I am the LORD:* ⁶³ *That you may remember, and be confounded, and* **never open your mouth anymore because of your shame**, *when I am pacified toward you for all that you have done, says the Lord GOD.*

Notice the *I will*'s of God. You have two covenants referenced here. In verse 60, *My Covenant* refers to the Mosaic Covenant; and *everlasting covenant* is a reference to the New Covenant of Jeremiah 31. When God establishes His everlasting covenant with them (Jeremiah 31:31-34) all Israel will remember their sin and sins, yet they will not open their mouths for shame, indicating their redemption. Here again, the LORD, through the pen of Ezekiel, references their sin and shame and their restoration. This is national Israel; and we saw in preceding verses that at that time, He will place them back in their Land, the Land of their fathers. This is a prophetic passage, and God is referencing a future time when the New Covenant will regenerate Israel, something which the Mosaic Covenant as a temporary covenant could not do, and it is guaranteed. This would be referencing the period of time called the Messianic Kingdom when Israel is a saved nation in the Land.

Continuing in Ezekiel, we see God pointing out Israel's sin that made Him angry and furious with great wrath at their sin. Yet with all that, He will glorify His Name through them; and He will bring them into the same Land that was given to their fathers. Look at Ezekiel 20:41-44:

> ⁴¹ *I will accept you with your sweet savor,* **when I bring you out from the people, and gather you out of the countries wherein you have been scattered;** *and I will be sanctified in you before the heathen.* ⁴² *And you shall know that I am the LORD,* **when I shall bring you into the land of Israel, into the country for which I lifted up My hand to give it to your fathers.** ⁴³ *And there shall you remember your ways, and all your doings, wherein you have been defiled; and* **you shall loathe yourselves** *in your own sight for all your evils that you have committed.* ⁴⁴ *And you shall know that I am the LORD, when I have dealt with you for My name's sake, not*

according to your wicked ways, nor according to your corrupt doings, O you house of Israel, says the LORD God.

In Ezekiel 16:60, God states that the people of Israel will be so ashamed of themselves that they will not open their mouths; in Ezekiel 20:43, they will loathe themselves. With all their sin in the Hebrew Scriptures and the rejection of Yeshua they will have great shame and loathe themselves because of their evil doings. Two of the most magnificent words in Scripture are **but God**. Israel will experience shame and self-loathing because of their sins and rejection of their Messiah, **but God** will provide as He promised. When the **Blood** of Yeshua became the propitiation of their sins,[99] Yeshua set in motion the removal of all sin as far as the east is from the west; that's the New Covenant. He did not cover their sin but removed their sin as far as the east is from the west and forgave them upon their placing their Faith and trust in the God of Israel alone, Yeshua the Messiah, the Promised One. A sinful nation will be restored to the Land because of the **Blood** of the New Covenant given at Calvary. Their rejection of Him paved the way for their own salvation and ours as Gentiles, too.

The Value of Language

Now let me step back for a minute before I continue as we review all these passages on Israel's sin, judgment, and future restoration. I hope you have gone by now to the third appendix of this book and read all the passages that relate to Israel, the Land, and her restoration. Let me ask a question. What is the value of language if we re-interpret God's intended meaning out of it? That does not place us on the "Solid Rock" but upon the shifting sands of fickle man. The quotes I want to give are unrelated to the subject but not to the underlying substance of the foundations of Scripture.

The quotes below have to do with the Creation/Evolution argument that is going on in our churches, Bible schools, and seminaries as well as Christian schools. Look at the statements of three atheist evolutionists as they chide theologians:

- Atheist and God hater **Bill Maher** states, "If [the Bible is] not 100 percent true, I would say the whole thing [the sum of all the writings that follow Genesis] falls apart."

---

[99] See Isaiah 53:11. The word *satisfied* has the same meaning as when Paul in Romans 3:25 uses the word *propitiation*. It means that the blood of Messiah satisfied all of God's holy, righteous demands, freeing Him to act on our behalf.

- **Richard Dawkins** said, "Sophisticated theologians are quite happy to live with evolution. I think they are deluded. I think the Evangelicals have got it right in that there really is a deep incompatibility between evolution and Christianity."
- **T.H. Huxley** – advocate of Darwinian evolution has more insight than many Christians today when he says,

> If divine authority is not here claimed for in Genesis 2:24, what is the value of language? And again, I ask, if one may play fast and loose with the story of the Fall as a "type" or "allegory," what becomes the foundation of Pauline theology?"
>
> [Huxley] points out that once allegory is introduced as the main way of interpreting Scripture, New Testament theology, which has the Old Testament as its foundation, becomes a shaky basis that not even Paul could have built upon. Huxley even says later that "the position they [meaning evolution-accepting Christians] have taken up is hopelessly untenable."[100]

These three atheists quoted above take Christians and scholars, including Replacement, Amillennial, and Covenant theologians, to task for being completely inconsistent. When they apply allegorical interpretation to the Bible, "the whole thing falls apart," "…they are deluded," the "position they have taken up is hopelessly untenable." Let us return to further investigation of the Land Covenant using the literal approach of interpretation.

Ezekiel and the Land Covenant

Now look again, for Ezekiel is not finished. He has more to say about Israel and Israel's Shepherd. Before we focus on the significance of what Ezekiel is saying, look forward with me to John 10:11, 14-16, where Jesus/Yeshua reveals His identity as a shepherd:

> [11] *I AM the Good Shepherd: the Good Shepherd gives His life for the sheep.*
>
> [14] *I AM the Good Shepherd, and [I] know My sheep, and am known of Mine.* [15] *As the Father knows Me, even so* **I know** *the Father: and*

---

[100] Ken Ham, *Six Days: The Age of the Earth and the Decline of the Church* (Green Forest, AR: Master Books, 2014), 96-97.

I lay down My life for the sheep. ⁱ⁶ *And other sheep I have, which are not of this fold: them also I must bring and they shall hear My voice; and there shall be one fold, and one Shepherd.*

As we read Ezekiel 34:11-14, reflect back on what Yeshua said about His sheep and the voluntary laying down of His life for His sheep. Also notice the phrases that speak of the Land:

¹¹ For thus says the Lord GOD; Behold, I, even I, will both search My sheep and seek them out. ¹² As a shepherd seeks out his flock in the day that he is among his sheep that are scattered; so will I seek out My sheep, and will deliver them out of all places where they have been scattered in the cloudy and dark day. ¹³ And I will bring them out from the people, and gather them from the countries, and **will bring them to their own land and feed them upon the mountains of Israel** *by the rivers, and in all the inhabited places of the country. ¹⁴ I will feed them in a good pasture, and* **upon the high mountains of Israel** *shall their fold be: there shall they lie in a good fold, and in a fat pasture shall they feed* **upon the mountains of Israel**.

Here God is taking on the position of a shepherd who seeks for his lost sheep that have been scattered, and He promises to bring them out from the people (Gentiles) and will bring them back to their own Land and provided for them. Yeshua in John 10 states that He is that shepherd of those sheep that are scattered from Him, but He will lay down His life voluntarily for His sheep. Yeshua said that He has another flock of sheep; these will turn out to be Gentile believers in Him. Notice that He will make the two flocks one, a prophecy of the union of Jewish and Gentile believers together (Ephesians 2:14-15). He was speaking of the future Church that was not then in existence.

Imagine what blessings our Replacement and Covenant brothers have missed because of the wholesale rejection and replacement of Israel. It is hard for finite man to grasp the love and commitment of the Sovereign God of Israel for His people Israel to even include us Gentiles in that plan. God is not finished with Israel. This same Sovereign God will glorify His Name through Israel when they embrace Him as their God and the reality of His Land Covenant with Israel is fulfilled.

Now we will continue to look at what else Ezekiel states in 34:22-27 about His flock:

> ^{22} *Therefore will I save My flock, and they shall no more be a prey; and I will judge between cattle and cattle.* ^{23} *And I will set up one shepherd over them, and he shall feed them, even My servant David; he shall feed them and he shall be their shepherd.* ^{24} *And I the LORD will be their God and My servant David a prince among them; I the LORD have spoken it.* ^{25} *And I will make with them a covenant of peace, and will cause the evil beasts to cease out* **of the land***: and they shall dwell safely in the wilderness, and sleep in the woods.* ^{26} *And I will make them and the places round about My hill a blessing; and I will cause the shower to come down in his season; there shall be showings of blessing.* ^{27} *And the tree of the field shall yield her fruit, and the earth shall yield her increase, and* **they shall be safe in their land***, and shall know that I am the LORD when I have broken the bands of their yoke, and delivered them out of the hand of those that served themselves of them.*

Now in the next passage in Ezekiel 36, I am only picking out three verses to share below, but the entire section needs to be read. Ezekiel 36:16-18 is a great section to show God's love for a people that are not worthy of it because His Name has been profaned by them before the Gentiles. Then, starting with verse 20, we read that the Sovereign God will glorify His Name by doing a work in the hearts of Israel and will bring them back to the Land, the Land that their fathers possessed. Look at Ezekiel 36:20, 24, and 28 that reaffirm the relationship of Israel with the Land three times in close succession:

> ^{20} *And when they entered unto the heathen wherever they went, they profaned My holy name, when they said to them, These are the people of the LORD, and are gone forth out of* **His land***.*
>
> ^{24} *For I will take you from among the heathen, and gather you out of all countries, and* **will bring you into your own land***.*
>
> ^{28} **And you shall dwell in the land that I gave to your fathers***; and you shall be My people, and I will be our God.*

Look at the emphasis on Israel being returned to the Land. This is not my emphasis; it is God's emphasis contrary to the teaching of Replacement/Covenant Theology. By the way, notice verse 20: Again, whose Land is it? It is God's Land which He promised to Abraham and to his seed.

You may say I am going overkill on this point of Israel inheriting the Land, and my answer is, yes. Why? Because for over 1,800 years, RT and later Covenant Theology have been teaching that God is finished with Israel and is now working solely with the Church, which they call the New Israel. Israel is given the curses, but the Church supposedly now receives all the blessings promised to Israel. Where do Moses and the Prophets state such a thing? They don't, but finite scholars do! They have polluted the Word of their own Sovereign God by their own unbelief in the Word of God.

Let us examine one final section of Ezekiel in 39, verses 28-29:

> *^{28} Then shall they know that I am the LORD* **their** *God, which caused them to be led into captivity among the heathen:* **but I have gathered them unto their own land**, *and have left none of them anymore there. ^{29} Neither will I hide* **My** *face any more from them: for I have poured out* **My** *Spirit upon the house of Israel, says the Lord GOD.*

Again and again, God says that He will restore Israel and He will place them in their Land. Notice the possessive terminology that He has used.

The Land Covenant in Joel

Now look at Joel 2:18 where God says, *Then will* **the LORD be jealous for His land**, *and pity His people.* Look at the words of the LORD. He is *jealous for His land*, not the churches' land, not Palestinian land, but His Land which just happens to be the Land that He promised to Abraham, Isaac, and Jacob and to their descendants. It is this Land that the Sovereign God promised and reaffirmed throughout the Prophets. Notice also that God will pity Israel because of all that they have suffered at the hands of anti-Semites throughout the centuries and even today.

The next verse has my curiosity up. Could the anti-Semites in Europe, America, and the United Nations actually pull off a Two-State plan? I cannot answer that question, for I am not a prophet nor the son of one; but look at the Word of the LORD in Joel 3:2 where that terminology comes up:

> *I will also gather all nations, and will bring them down into the valley of Jehoshaphat, and will plead with them there for My people and for My heritage Israel, whom they have scattered among the nations, and* **parted My land**.

Here God speaks through Joel of the parting of His Land, and notice the personal pronoun, it is God's – the Sovereign LORD's – Land and not anyone else's. He as the owner can give it to whomever He wishes; and according to the Abrahamic Covenant and the Land Covenant, He, the

Sovereign LORD, gave it to Abraham, Isaac, and Jacob and to all their descendants.

When will the Land be parted? Could it become a reality before the Tribulation begins as a result of the United States, Europe, and the United Nations pushing Israel to give up land, the so-called Two-State Plan? Or could it take place in the middle the Tribulation when the Antichrist breaks his false covenant of peace (death – Isaiah 28:14-18; Daniel 9:27) with Israel and it becomes a covenant of death (Isaiah 28:15) as he pursues his desire to annihilate Israel from off the planet? Again I do not know. What I do know is the charge that the LORD makes here in Joel that the Land will be parted, and the Sovereign LORD will judge those nations for parting His Land.

In one last reference in Joel, the LORD clearly shows the Land as the possession of Israel from generation to generation, for at that time He will dwell in Zion. So Joel 3:17-21 clearly sees the Land belonging to Israel as these verses state:

[17] So shall you know that I am the LORD your God dwelling in Zion, My holy mountain: then shall Jerusalem be holy, and there shall no strangers pass though her any more. [18] And it shall come to pass **in that day***, that the mountains shall drop down new wine, and the hills shall flow with milk, and all the rivers of Judah shall flow with water, and a fountain shall come forth of the house of the LORD, and shall water the valley of Shittim. [19] Egypt shall be a desolation, and Edom shall be a desolate wilderness, for the violence against the children of Judah, because they have shed innocent blood in their land. [20]* **But Judah shall dwell forever, and Jerusalem from generation to generation.** *[21] For I will cleanse their blood that I have not cleansed: for the LORD dwells in Zion.*

The Land Covenant in Other Prophetic Passages

We will now observe that the Prophets Amos, Obadiah, Micah, Zechariah, and Hosea are in complete agreement with Moses and the other Prophets as they all clearly recognize that the Land belongs to Israel. They confirm that once God settles them in the Land, they will never again be moved; they will become the faithful wife of Jehovah because of the New Covenant. Look at Amos 9:15 to see this Prophet's confirmation of the Land Covenant.

And I will plant them upon their land, *and* **they shall no more be pulled up out of their land which I have given them**, *says the LORD your God.*

Obadiah 17 simply confirms that there will be a deliverer in Zion and Israel shall possess their possessions.

But **upon mount Zion shall be deliverance**, *and there shall be holiness; and* **the house of Jacob shall possess their possessions**.

Micah 4:7 is an interesting verse because he mentions that Israel was cast off; but, as we have seen in the words of other Prophets, Israel will be regathered to the Land and the LORD shall reign over them, Israel forever.

And I will make her that halted a remnant, **and her that was cast far off** *a strong nation: and* **the LORD shall reign over them in Mount Zion from henceforth, even forever**.

Then we have the words of the Prophet Zechariah that I will reference in 3:8-9 as God speaks of Messiah as *My servant the BRANCH,* saying that He *will remove the iniquity of that Land in one day.* Again, here is the restoration of Israel; and as will be seen in Zechariah 9:16, all of this will happen in connection with the Land. Look at these two verses:

3:8 Hear now, O Joshua the high priest, you, and your fellows that sit before you: for they are men wondered at: for, behold, I will bring forth My servant the BRANCH. 3:9 For behold the stone that I have laid before Joshua; upon one stone shall be seven eyes: behold, I will engrave the graving thereof, says the LORD of hosts, and **I will remove the iniquity of that land in one day**. [Also see Romans 11:26-27.]

9:16 And the LORD their God shall save them **in that day** *as the flock of His people: for they shall be as the stones of a crown, lifted up as an ensign* **upon His land**.

Throughout the whole story of the Prophet Hosea and his wife Gomer, God uses this book as a picture of His relentless love for Israel. Israel will become the faithful wife of Jehovah; although Hosea and Gomer were divorced, just as Hosea brought Gomer back to his household to remarry her, God shows that He will likewise be faithful to bring His wife Israel back to Him and remarry her. Hosea 2:19-20 declares emphatically God's abounding love for Israel:

> *^{19} And* **I will betroth** *you unto me forever; yes* **I will betroth** *you unto me in righteousness, and in judgment, and in lovingkindness, and in mercies. ^{20}* **I will even betroth** *you unto me in faithfulness: and you shall know the LORD.*

What an awesome picture of God's love for Israel!

Turning to Zephaniah 2:17, the Prophet speaks of Israel in the Kingdom with God dwelling in their midst:

> *The LORD your God in the midst of you is mighty; He will save,* **He will rejoice over you with joy***;* **He will rest in His love***,* **He will joy over you with singing***.*

Look at the words of love and joy that God will have over Israel when she becomes the faithful wife; His love is amazing! This is the only verse in all of the Bible that references God singing, and He does so over Israel.

In all of these passages from Moses and the Prophets, it rings clear and absolute that even though Israel has sinned greatly, the Sovereign God will regather the Jewish people. He will restore them, and He will fulfill His covenant with the patriarchs and their descendants. Replacement and Covenant Theology can teach the opposite; the problem for them is that they are going against their God whom they say is sovereign, leading to a contradiction of positions.

Let me spotlight one other false theological connection that Amillennialism makes through the Roman Catholicism and Orthodox Churches. Again, the lack of literal interpretation of the Word of God has caused Amillennialists to hold onto their bias against Israel. They discount completely the fulfillment of all the covenants in the Millennium, for they say that the Kingdom of God is now. Can you imagine such a ludicrous thought? Suggesting that the Kingdom of God is now is a great reproach to the integrity and character of God and does great harm to His Holy Name. In doing so, the Church, like Israel, has polluted His Holy Name. God's Word shows that He, the Sovereign LORD, is LORD over everything and not just in the covenants' redemptive motif. The Sovereign of the universe is faithful and will provide for His wife Israel, just as He has provided a glorious future for His bride, the Church of true believers, Jew and Gentile, one in Messiah.

Now let us move into the blessings and cursing of the Abrahamic Covenant.

PART 2

The Abrahamic Covenant:
How We Bless or Curse God

Chapter 8
The Residual Effects of the Blessings and Curses of the Abrahamic Covenant

Introduction

I have chosen a subject that, to the best of my knowledge in all my 56 years as a believer in Messiah, has had very little attention given to it: the Abrahamic Covenant. I do not ever remember seeing anything written on it. This subject was introduced to me by the scattered references from Arnold Fruchtenbaum's teachings over the years. Comprehending it is so important in our understanding of the Scriptures in general. An author that I can no longer remember once said:

The most central portion of all Scripture is the Abrahamic Covenant; everything else is commentary on it.

Blessings and Curses of God (Genesis 12:1-3)

Can the Abrahamic Covenant be that important? The answer is a resounding yes! Once you see the interweaving of the other covenants that come out of it, you will all be amazed at the tremendous significance of understanding and grasping this covenant. In this study, we will be dealing with only two of the fourteen provisions in the Abrahamic Covenant, and these two have received very little attention.

Let us begin again with Genesis 12:1-3. We want to study the ramifications of the outworkings of the blessings and cursings of the Abrahamic Covenant and see their residual effects, the outworkings of the blessings and cursings that relate to how we as Gentiles treat the Jewish people.

> *¹ Now the LORD had said unto Abram, Get you out of your own country, and from your kindred, and from your father's house, unto a land that I will show you. ² And I will make of you a great nation, and I will bless you, and make your name great; and you shall be a blessing: ³* **And I will bless them that bless you, and curse him that curses you: and in you shall all families of the earth be blessed.**

Notice in particular verse 3 is covering what I believe to be completely uncharted waters to almost all believers in Christ in seeing the ramifications of the neglected teaching on the actual blessings and cursings motif of the Abrahamic Covenant. Yet as this book is written, I am not aware of any written resources to refer to, except for the Scriptures, material from Arnold Fruchtenbaum,[101] and a few pages by John F. Walvoord, who deals with it in a general sense.[102] I am sure there are scattered articles in theological journals, but only scholars read them; the laity of the church does not. Yet in my understanding, I see two things to expound upon, to comprehend the impact of the blessings and curses as they are reflected throughout the Written Word as well as history.

1. First, what impact have these blessings and cursings had on the Gentile nations and individuals through recorded biblical history as well as post-biblical history?

2. Second, does the Church's lack of blessing Israel, the seed of Abraham, have anything to do with our worldwide missions outreach? The Church is to evangelize the world for Christ, but can that be completely realized when we violate the LORD's words through Paul in Romans 1:16?

For I am not ashamed of the gospel of Christ: for it is the power of God unto salvation to everyone that believeth; **to the Jew first**, *and also to the Greek.*

---

[101] Arnold G. Fruchtenbaum, *The Remnant of Israel: The History, Theology, and Philosophy of the Messianic Jewish Community* (San Antonio, TX: Ariel Ministries, 2011), 71-95.

[102] John F. Walvoord, *Major Bible Prophecies* (Grand Rapids, MI: Zondervan Publishing House, 1991), 42-43.

Regarding Gentiles and the Abrahamic Covenant

Regarding the impact of the cursings and blessings, Arnold Fruchtenbaum has often taught that God will deal with individuals and nations who curse Abraham and his descendants with the following principle: curse for curse, a curse to them in kind. God will also bless those who bless the Jewish people with blessings in kind.

My focus on the impact on missions when the focus on Israel is neglected is subjective; but I believe with the pattern laid down in Scripture, it is a valid approach and a valid question to be asked of pastors, missionaries, and especially mission agencies and their executives. My question for the Church is, if we ignore God's procedure for evangelism by **withholding** the Gospel from Jewish people, who are to be reached first with the Gospel, are we blessing or cursing Israel?? We will look at this subject at the end of this book, but first let's review what the Scriptures have to say about the theme of Blessing and Cursing as it relates to Gentiles and the Abrahamic Covenant.

Our study will cover the following areas with the outline taken from Arnold Fruchtenbaum's book *The Remnant of Israel*:[103]

- Study of Genesis 12:1-3.
- The outworkings of the Blessings and Cursings on an individual level.
- The outworkings of the Blessings and Cursings on a national level.
- The outworkings of the Blessings and Cursings in the inter-testament period.
- The outworkings of the Blessings and Cursings in the New Testament.
- The outworkings of the Blessings and Cursings in post-biblical history.
- The outworkings of the Blessings and Cursings in prophecy.
- The outworkings of the Blessings and Cursings in Church missions today.

---

[103] Fruchtenbaum, *The Remnant of Israel*.

In Genesis 12:1-3, God appears to Abram and gives him some promises as well as specific *I will's* of God. Let us follow them through Scripture and learn the heart of God for His people Israel. Let us begin with the text before us, which was quoted for you at the beginning of this chapter. This passage and the other covenants related to it are the most important covenants made by God to Israel.

Before going into the passage, we will look at some of the background for this passage as a precursor to the Abrahamic Covenant. There are several interesting observations to be made:

1. In chapters 1 – 11 of Genesis, God begins with blessing via the creation of the heavens and the earth with man created and placed on the earth. However, God revealed to us the origin of sin and the curse connected to it; then sin is judged with God's cursing: the worldwide flood of Genesis 6-9. Next, because of the sin of those descendants at Babel, God cursed man again by changing their languages, thus forcing them to scatter and populate all the earth as His original command to them states in Genesis 9:1 and 11:1-9. So these passages in the earlier chapters of Genesis, after creation, primarily deal with cursings after God had initially blessed the creation. In the remainder of Genesis, chapters 12 – 50, God deals with blessing the people of the earth through Abraham in the Covenant that was given to him.

2. From Adam to Noah are 10 generations, beginning with blessing and ending with cursing and death in Genesis 5. From Noah to Abram are also 10 generations, beginning again with a blessing but ending again with the cursing of dispersion because of mankind's rebellion at the Tower of Babel.

3. Genesis begins with great blessings in the creation, but after the Fall, Scripture deals with God's curse because of sin: death, dispersion and separation through chapter 11 of Genesis. In chapter 12 we read of great blessing again, both physical and spiritual, with the announcement of the Abrahamic Covenant.

4. Under Nimrod, people wanted to make a name for themselves (Genesis 11:4); but in the Abrahamic Covenant, God states in contrast that He will make Abram's name great (Genesis 12:2).

5. Each of the heads of people – Adam, Noah, and Abram – had three sons. God chose Seth, the third-born son of Adam and Eve, to carry the Messianic line to replace Abel, the second-born who was murdered by their first-born, Cain. Noah had three sons, with the first-born being Shem, who is in the Seed line of the Messiah. Japheth is the second-born son of Noah (Genesis 10:21) but is always listed last after Ham. Of Terah's three sons, God chose the third-born – Abram – to carry the Messianic line. So God does not always use the firstborn.

6. The world again was becoming corrupted, so God chose a man, Abram, to make provision for deliverance. That does not mean there were not others walking faithfully with the LORD, such as Job and Melchizedek, who were contemporaries of Abram.

7. One observation on the phrase *I will curse*: It is a verb phrase related to the words of cursing used in Genesis 3:14 (where it applies to the serpent); 4:11 (applying to Cain); and 9:25 (to Canaan).[104]

With the background of God's cursing and His complete desire to bless, not just Abram, but all the families that are derived from the 70 nations of Genesis 10, let us re-read Genesis 12:1-3, 7 with our emphasis on verse 3:

> *¹ Now the LORD had said unto Abram, Get you out of your own country, and from your kindred, and from your father's house, unto a land that I will show you. ² And I will make of you a great nation, and I will bless you, and make your name great; and you shall be a blessing:* ³ **And I will bless them that bless you, and curse him that curses you: and in you shall all families of the earth be blessed.**

---

[104] John D. Currid, *An Evangel Press Study Commentary: Genesis 1:1 to 25:18* (Webster, NY: Evangel Press, 2003), 253.

⁷ And the LORD appeared unto Abram, and said, Unto your seed will I give this land: and there he built an altar unto the LORD, who appeared unto him.

The Fourth "I Will" of God Regarding Abraham

First we need to recognize the five *I will's* of God before zeroing in on verse 3. They are as follows:

1. *Get you out of your country, and from your kindred, and from your father's house, unto a land that* **I will** *show you.*

2. **I will** *make of you a great nation.*

3. **I will** *bless you, and make your name great; and you shall be a blessing.*

4. **I will** *bless them that bless you, and curse him that curses you: and in you shall all the families of the earth be blessed.*

5. *Unto your seed* **will I** *give this land.*

Much can be said about these five points, but we want to focus on the fourth *I will*. God gave a personal as well as a national promise that whoever blesses Abram and his descendants (Israel) God will in turn bless. But the opposite side of the coin is that whoever curses Israel, God will curse. Several authors lay out the parameters to the blessings and cursings as they relate to Israel in the following six quotations:

> Bless [*barak*] and curse [*'arar*] are integral motifs in Genesis. In chapters 1-11 "curse" is the consequence of unlawful behavior: Now "curse" is explained by how a people mistreats Abram, the appointed heir of the blessing. Later events in the lives of the patriarchs illustrate this promise. Pharaoh and Abimelech suffer because of Abram and Sarai (12:7; 20:17-18); Laban learns to temper his anger against son-in-law Jacob (31:29); and both Potiphar and Pharaoh benefit from the Lord's blessing on Joseph (39:2-6; 47:5-15). ... The two occurrences of the word translated "curse" are two different Hebrew words. "Whoever curses" renders the (*piel*) participle of *qll*, which in the basic stem (*qal*) means "to be small, insignificant." The *piel* stem carries a declarative sense, "to declare insignificant, to ridicule." The second occurrence of "curse" is the common word in

Genesis for curse ['arar]. Some derive from this difference that the severity of the two "curses" is different. Those who dare to treat Abram "lightly" (qll) will receive the greater weight of God's "curse" ['arar]. But the parallel effect of the language supersedes any lexical difference in nuance; this is seen later by the repetition of the promises made to Jacob where 'arar ("curse") occurs instead qll.[105]

Matthews lays out the two different usages of the word *curse*, and now the emphasis will move from a general curse from God, to a specific curse to anyone who speaks and does evil to Abram and his seed. This does not mean that God's general curse expired, for it still applies to anyone who is rebellious against God in one's attitudes and conduct toward Abraham, Isaac, Jacob and their descendants, Israel. The point is that now, whether Israel is right or wrong, their national identity is at stake; anyone who curses Abram or his descendants will equally receive the curse of God. So we have a general curse against mankind for rebellion against God and a specific curse against all Gentiles who would curse Abram. Now look with me at the second quotation:

> The blessing and cursing of men were to depend entirely upon their attitude towards him [Abraham], and all the families of the earth were to be blessed in him.
>
> קלל, lit., to treat as light or little, to despise; denotes "blasphemous cursing on the part of a man:"
>
> ארר judicial cursing on the part of God.
>
> It appears significant, however, "that the plural is used in relation to the blessing, and the singular only in relation to the cursing; grace expects that there will be many to bless, and that only an individual here and there will render not blessing for blessing, but curse for curse."[106]

Here Keil and Delitzsch emphasize that now the blessing and cursing of men will depend on man's attitude toward Abram and his descendants. It is also interesting to note that the blessing is plural (towards *them*) indicating that many will receive the blessing from Abraham and his descendants. But

---

[105] Kenneth A. Matthews, *The New American Commentary: Genesis 11:27-50:26* (Nashville, TN: B&H Publishers, 2005), 115-116.
[106] C. F. Keil and F. Delitzsch, *Commentary on the Old Testament: The First Book of Moses - Genesis* (Peabody, MA: Hendrickson Publishing, 2006), 123-124.

the curse is in the singular (towards *him*) which indicates that there will be those individuals or individual nations who choose to curse Abram or Israel who will receive the curse. A rabbinic commentary states the same thing:

> **Those** *that bless you* – This word is in the plural
> **And he** *that curses you* – This word is in the singular.[107]

This is the pattern that is being laid out as we see the implications from this verse being backed up by references throughout the Scriptures. John Sailhamer helps us to focus in on God's intention:

> What God declared is that His attitude toward Abram's fellow men would be determined by their attitude toward Abram. Those who acted favorably toward Abram would win the favor of God. Those whose inclination to Abram was hostile and evil could come under the curse of God. This clearly indicated that Abram stood in a distinctive relationship to God.[108]

If you love Abram, then God will love you. If you hate (curse) Abram, God takes it very personally. Abram and his descendants stand in a unique place in the mind and heart of God and should equally stand in ours. So the core issue is, if you treat Abram and his descendants poorly, expect God's *arm* to fall upon you. If you treat Abram and Israel well, expect God's hand of blessing upon you. This extends to Gentile individuals or nations.

How We Bless or Curse God

The next quotation by Allen Ross gets even closer to the core of the issue:

> To bless or curse Abraham was to bless or curse Abram's God.[109]

That is a profound statement. Do we really believe that? Hopefully, as we go through the Scriptures, God will reinforce His will and His heart to us. Because God has chosen Abram to be the instrument through whom He will bless *all the families of the earth,* God takes the treatment by Gentile individuals and nations very seriously. If Abram is blessed, it is the same as

---

[107] H. Norman Strickman and Arthur M. Silver (translators), *Ibn Ezra's Commentary on the Pentateuch: Genesis (Bereshit)* (New York, NY: Menorah Publishing Company, 1988), 150.

[108] G. Charles Aalders, *Bible Student's Commentary: Genesis vol. 1* (Grand Rapids, MI: Zondervan, 1981), 269.

[109] Allen Ross, *The Bible Knowledge Commentary: Old Testament* (Wheaton, IL: Victor Books, 1985), 47.

blessing God. However, to curse Abram and his seed is to curse God Himself. We do not want to be in that position, as recipients of God's wrath, anger, and indignation. This is serious, and too many people today do not take it seriously and will receive God's wrath.

Israel of God (the remnant out of Israel who are now believers in Messiah) is the covenant people of God through whom He has chosen to reveal Himself. Non-believing Jews are not part of the remnant, and Gentiles are not part of this remnant. God has given clear boundaries to the fact that he who blesses the Jewish people will himself be blessed and he who curses the Jewish people could receive His curse, kind for kind. To be honest, I would not want to receive God's backhand of discipline for any negative words or acts against Israel, whether experienced individually or nationally.

Even though the blessings are mentioned throughout the Torah as well as in the Prophets and the Writings, the Abrahamic Covenant echoes off of every page in the Tanakh. John Sailhamer follows the blessing of God promised through the book of Genesis in the following quote:

> Most notable is the frequent reiteration of God's "blessing" in [Genesis] 1:28 (and 9:1) throughout the narrative of Abraham and his descendants (12:1-3; 13:15-16; 15:5, 18; 17:6-8; 22:17-18; 25:11; 26:2-4; 27:27-29; 49:28).[110]

This Abrahamic Covenant will overshadow all other covenants made with Israel. It is the foundation for all the others. In the blessing, we will note that God had a blessing for Ishmael because of Abraham's love for Ishmael in Genesis 17:20. Isaac's blessing given to Esau was a restatement of what God said to Rebekah in Genesis 25:23. It was a statement of submission of Esau (Edom) to Jacob (Israel) and not a true, genuine blessing, as most people misread it. Also notice as well the descendants of Ishmael are with us today and the descendants of Esau (Edom) are non-existent today. We will see why Edom is not represented today a little later.

Bruce Waltke, regarding God's resolve and unbending attitude towards anyone that blesses or curses Abram and Israel, states that the *I will bless* and *I will curse* of God is eternal and irrevocable:

> The statement is in a form indicating resolve ("I will bless"), intentioned toward plural recipients ("those who bless"). Then it

---

[110] John H. Sailhamer, *The Expositor's Bible Commentary: Genesis* (Grand Rapids, MI: Zondervan, 1990), 112.

shifts to a simple statement of fact ("I shall curse") and a singular recipient ("whoever curses"; see also [Genesis] 27:29; Numbers 24:9).[111]

This is serious stuff, and the Church today is naive and ignorant at best of the impact and reality of God's words in Genesis 12:3. The unsaved world largely is oblivious to the Abrahamic Covenant. I spoke recently with a Navajo pastor, a Native American, who informed me that the leadership of the Navajo Nation does not support Israel today, but instead they support the Palestinian Muslims and Christians. What a shame for the Navajo Nation, who has suffered so much already at the hands of "white man's justice" to also receive the curse of the God of Israel upon themselves. Whether people know it or not, the Abrahamic Covenant is just as real today as when it was given to Abram. God's blessing will be immediate; and God's judgment is sure, although the timing is His. His judgment will either be immediate or postponed to a future time.

---

[111] Bruce K. Waltke, *Genesis* (Grand Rapids, MI: Zondervan, 2001), 206.

Chapter 9
The Outworking of the Abrahamic Covenant Individually

Throughout this section I will not be quoting the lengthy passages of Scripture for each of the example used to show the Outworking of the Abrahamic Covenant.

King of Egypt – Cursing
Genesis 12:10-15

In this section, we will look at the individuals who were blessed or cursed because of their attitude or treatment of Abram and his descendants. This incident was early in Abram's walk with the LORD; and even though he trusted the LORD by separating from his family in Haran, he was still learning to trust his LORD in all things. That included trusting Him for the safe keeping of himself and his wife Sarai.

Verse 10 tells us that there was a famine in Canaan, so Abram went to sojourn in Egypt for food. *To sojourn* means that you are only staying temporarily, so this was not a permanent move in his own thinking. Now the text in the preceding verses tells us of Abram's fear and lack of trust in his LORD. Remember, Sarai was his half-sister, so the story he tells is true, well, actually a half-truth cloaked to lead a person to come to another conclusion. Because Abram was afraid for his life, Sarai was to say that she was his sister. Abram was afraid that someone would kill him to take her. He did not count on Pharaoh taking her! He had no time to negotiate, which could have allowed him (and Sarai) time to escape the area. Pharaoh saw her and took her for his wife. Pharaoh's understanding was that Sarai was Abram's sister because of the half-truth Abram told. So Pharaoh thought, according to the customs of the day, that Sarai could be taken and placed in his harem.

Unbeknownst to Pharaoh, his action was a direct threat to the Seed line of Abraham as well as the people that God would choose for His Name. Pharaoh gave, as it were, the bride price to Abram, which consisted of *sheep, and oxen, and he asses, and menservants, and maidservants, and she asses, and camels* (vs. 16). But God sent plagues upon Pharaoh and his entire house because of Sarai. The Scripture does not tell us how, but Pharaoh figured out that Sarai was Abram's wife and confronted Abram; he gave Sarai back to Abram and ushered them out of Egypt.

So the whole house of Pharaoh was afflicted and cursed because of putting the whole plan of God at risk by taking Sarai. Abram was wrong; and at least this time, Egypt was innocent with its dealing with Israel. Abram did not have to return the bride price, so he left richer than when he came. So in verse 17, the outworking of the Abrahamic Covenant was working against Egypt.

Abimelech – Cursing, Part 1
Genesis 20:1-18

Here again we have the same story line, the same half-truth and lie. Notice Abram's thought process in verse 11:

> *...because I thought, surely the fear of God is not in this place; and they will slay me for my wife's sake.*

Now Abimelech did not know the truth of the matter when he took Sarai, just like Pharaoh had not known. In verses 3-7, God speaks to Abimelech in a dream. Notice in verse 3 that God is blunt and to the point, *you are but a dead man, for the woman which you have taken; for she is a man's wife.* Abimelech's response is that he did not know; he said he was innocent of this, to which the LORD responded, yes, He knew that. Notice the important words of verse 6, that God had withheld her from him, so that Abimelech would not be *sinning against Me* [God]. Abimelech would have sinned against God because he would be a genuine threat to the redemptive plan of God, for out of Abraham and Sarah would come Isaac and eventually the Messiah, Himself. If this situation had continued, Isaac would not have been born; so Abimelech's action, even though he was unaware of its significance, was sinning against God who made the covenant with Abraham. Fruchtenbaum states the following:

> The above two passages [Genesis 12 with Pharaoh and Genesis 20 with Abimelech] indicate the first real attempt to destroy the Jews.

God had already promised that He would bless the Gentiles through the Jews and that the Jews would continue through Abraham's son Isaac. Now both of these incidents occurred before Isaac was born, and I see here a definite attempt to keep Isaac from being born by taking his future mother away. If Satan could keep Isaac from being born, then the Jews would die out with the death of Abraham. Unknowingly, Abimelech cursed Abraham in such a way as to destroy the Jews, and now God curses Abimelech. When God operates on the cursing aspect of the Abrahamic Covenant, He works on the sub-principle of curse for curse in kind.[112]

Now Abimelech cursed Abram by potentially attacking the whole Seed of Abram by the fact that Isaac would not be born from a union of Abraham and Sarah. So in verse 18, God said that He closed all the wombs of the house of Abimelech as curse for curse. The outworking of the Abrahamic Covenant was clearly applied.

Abimelech – Cursing, Part 2
Genesis 26:7-16

In this passage, Isaac is caught playing the same game as his father Abraham, except this time Isaac has told an outright lie. Now Abimelech (the Philistines) did not take Rebekah, but they saw that she, too, was a good-looking woman. Then you have Isaac and Rebekah showing affection to each other, and Abimelech confronts Isaac. Abimelech states that if one of the people had lain with her, the guilt would have been upon them because of Isaac's lie. Now nothing happened here as a curse, but the potential was there. Did Abimelech (a dynastic name for the king) know and look up in their records and find the story of Abram and Sarai? Was that why he did not take her? That is an assumption which cannot be answered, but the real possibility remains. Abimelech avoided being cursed by doing a little research and avoiding sin.

Laban – Blessing/Cursing
Genesis 30:27-30, 34-36, 43; 31:1-10, 24

In this text, Jacob has labored 14 years for Rachel and Leah, and he wants to go home. Now here is where the Blessing of the Abrahamic Covenant comes out. Out of Laban's own mouth came these words because

---

[112] Fruchtenbaum, *The Remnant of Israel*, 75.

of his association with Jacob: *I have learned by experience that the LORD has blessed me for your sake* (vs. 27). So Laban and Jacob work out an agreement for Jacob to earn flocks for himself. Jacob agreed to the arrangement and was very fair in his dealing with Laban over the next 6 years. However, now we have both the blessing and cursing working out.

The blessing was in Jacob's life because of the enlargement of his flocks, and now cursing came upon Laban because he had been cheating Jacob (31:7). As a result, Laban's flocks were now decreased. Now Laban and his sons grew angry with Jacob because of the decrease of Laban's flocks, which Jacob observed (31:1-2). Here, as long as Laban, the pagan, had a positive association with Jacob, a Jew, Laban was blessed. But when Laban's greedy heart arose, God cursed Laban's flocks and blessed Jacob's. Once again we see the clear outworking of the Abrahamic Covenant in blessing for Laban when he treated Jacob fairly, and then cursing for Laban in kind when he tried to reduce Jacob's flocks.

Joseph – Blessing
Genesis 39:1-6, 21-23; 41:38-44

In these passages, God blessed Joseph, not because of what happened to him at the hands of his brothers, but because there was to be a very severe famine in the entire region, including Canaan and Egypt, and probably beyond these borders. God used Joseph to preserve Israel as a people and also to protect them from being polluted by the Canaanites around them. A very real and present danger arose; Genesis 38 tells us of Judah's intermarriage with Shuah, a Canaanite woman. God removed Israel from the Land and kept them in Egypt to prevent them from sin and to bless them in Egypt as they grew in strength and numbers.

We learn from these Genesis passages that Joseph will serve as a blessing to three people in Egypt: Potiphar, the jailer, and Pharaoh. God ultimately blesses each one built on the foundation set in the Abrahamic Covenant, of blessing those who bless the Seed of Abraham.

First God *blessed the Egyptian's house for Joseph's sake* (39:5). Potiphar, who bought him in the slave market, was blessed as a pagan because of his positive attitude to Joseph. Second, when Joseph was thrown in prison by Potiphar on trumped up charges by Potiphar's wife, God once again blessed Joseph in the prison. The jailer gave his authority over to Joseph and the Scripture states that *that which he* [Joseph] *did, the LORD made it to prosper* (39:23). Joseph's administration of the prison was so effective, that the jailer did not even need to oversee his work. The third person to be blessed was Pharaoh, himself, for he made Joseph the second highest man in Egypt. God blessed Pharaoh for giving Joseph this high position; and, as a result, Egypt was enriched.

The outworking of the Abrahamic Covenant preserved Israel and provided a place for Israel to grow into a nation. So here you have the outworking of the Abrahamic Covenant in blessing Potiphar, the jailer, and Pharaoh because of their attitude toward an individual Jew who was used of God.

Hebrew Midwives – Blessing
Exodus 1:15-22

This may not be a blessing as it relates to Gentile midwives, for it appears that these two midwives, Shiphrah and Puash, were Hebrews and not Egyptian. Yet there is a blessing involved personally to them because they did not follow Pharaoh's orders to murder newly born Hebrew children. In verse 21, it states that *He made them houses.* It gives no further explanation, just that in some way, because of their defiance of Pharaoh's order and because they *feared God,* He blessed them by rewarding them for their faith by building them houses.

Rahab – Blessing
Joshua 6:17-27

In this passage, we have another incident of the blessing of God upon an individual because of her treatment of two Jewish spies directly, and Israel indirectly. Understand, this woman and the other Canaanites of Jericho were cursed for judgment (Genesis 15:13-16; 17:8; Exodus 3:17; 13:5; Deuteronomy 1:7-8). But God exhibited His grace to Rahab. Here is Rahab, who was not a woman of character; and yet, when confronted with the God of Israel, she was drawn to Him and expressed it in harboring two Jewish men who were spying on the city of Jericho. Because of her Faith displayed in her treatment of the spies, she and her family were the only ones spared in Jericho. She also appears in the line of Messiah as the wife of Salmon, the mother of Boaz who married Ruth (Matthew 1:5; Ruth 4:20-21; 1 Chronicles 2:11-12).

Rahab is mentioned in Hebrews 11 and is the only Gentile mentioned after Abraham in the Hall of Faith. Then look at James 2:21-25, where Rahab had the same kind of Faith that Abraham exhibited. She had Faith and backed up the reality of her Faith by displaying it before God and the Jewish people. Here was a Gentile woman whose Faith was put on the same plane as the Faith of Abraham (Genesis 15:6).

Because of her attitude towards the God of Israel directly, and the Jewish people indirectly, she was blessed. She knew nothing of the Abrahamic Covenant; she was unaware of the blessing and cursing aspect of the covenant. She was blessed and was married later to a man of Judah and entered the line of Messiah. The outworking of the Abrahamic Covenant is once again at work in the life of a pagan. It was said of her that *by Faith the harlot Rahab perished not with them that believed not, when she had received the spies with peace* (Hebrews 11:31). The outworking of the blessing of the Abrahamic Covenant went to an individual who was actually under the curse of God, being a Canaanite (Genesis 15:16-21), but managed to save the two Jewish spies. Rahab serves as a great example of a Gentile who blessed Israel and was in turn blessed of God.

Balaam – Cursing
Numbers 22:1-6, 25; 31:1-8, 16; Deuteronomy 23:4-5; Joshua 13:22, 24:9-10; Nehemiah 13:2; 2 Peter 2:15; Jude 11; Revelation 2:14

In the passages listed above, we see the outworking of cursing on the individual, Balaam. He was a pagan from Aram (Mesopotamia) in the town of Pethor on the Euphrates River.[113] According to Scripture (Joshua 13:22), he was a soothsayer. A soothsayer used divination to consult beings or things in an attempt to gain information about the future for the purpose of cursing.[114] Balaam studied about the LORD to become familiar with His person so that he could use the information to curse Israel. He was not a prophet of God; he was a pagan. An inscription about one of his prophecies was found on a temple wall near the area where Balaam came to Balak, king of Moab.[115]

---

[113] Ronald Youngblood, *Nelson's New Illustrated Bible Dictionary* (Nashville, TN: Thomas Nelson Publishers, 1995), 153.
[114] W. L. Liefeld, *The Zondervan Pictorial Encyclopedia of the Bible* (Grand Rapids: MI: Zondervan Publishing House, 1975), 2:146.
[115] B. G. Woods, "Prophecy of Balaam Found in Jordan." *Bible and Spade* 6 (Autumn 1977): 121-124; Timothy Ashley, *The New International Commentary on the Old Testament: Numbers* (Grand Rapids, MI: Erdmann Publishing, 1993), 437.

The New Testament speaks of Balaam as one *who loved the wages of unrighteousness* (2 Peter 2:15). His greed for riches caused him to counsel Balak (Numbers 31:16; Jude 11) to make Israel sin or make them stumble (Revelation 2:14) before God, so that God would judge them. His counsel to Balak was to send their women (the Midianites to send theirs) among Israel to seduce them so God could judge them. By his evil plan, he tried to curse them.

Balaam was paid his greedy financial reward. His counsel to Balak got Israel to sin, and God judged Israel in that 24,000 died as a result of the plague sent upon Israel.[116] However, the curse of God according to the Abrahamic Covenant was fulfilled in Balaam's death at the hands of Israeli swords (Numbers 31:8). Consequently, because of the Abrahamic Covenant and God's love for Israel, He turned Balaam's counsel (curse) into a curse on Balaam. Thus, again, the outworking of the Abrahamic Covenant continued in effect over 600 years after God had given the promise to Abram.

The New Testament writers use Balaam as a type. Peter, Jude, and John teach the Church about the *way of Balaam*, the *error of Balaam,* and the *doctrine of Balaam.* These counsels of Balaam become a warning to the Church to be very careful whom they allow to teach them. This principle has been largely ignored today by the Church for there are many "Balaams" in the Church today, for spiritual discernment is lacking even among the people in churches.

Jezebel – Cursing
1 Kings 11:1-8; 16:30-33; 18:13, 18-19; 22:51-53; 2 Kings 9:30-37

The background for Jezebel begins with Solomon and his marriages with pagan women, and his building temples for them in Jerusalem to accommodate their pagan worship. Solomon violated the law of Moses in Deuteronomy 17:17a which said:

Neither shall he multiply wives to himself, that his heart turn not away.

Solomon is responsible for sowing the seeds of idolatry that began to grow, bearing fruit in the days of Jehoshaphat, and growing in intensity. The next major point was the corruption of the worship of the LORD by

---

[116] J. J. Edwards, *The Zondervan Pictorial Encyclopedia of the Bible* (Grand Rapids, MI: Zondervan Publishing House, 1975), 1:454.

Jeroboam when he set up the corrupted form of true worship in the northern kingdom of Israel. Next, Omri, the wicked king of Israel, made a political marriage for his son Ahab by marrying him to Jezebel, the Zidonian, who was so wicked, corrupted, and ungodly that to me she was the female version of Satan; she was ruthless. Jezebel was a princess, the daughter of King Ethbaal of the Zidonians who served Baal.

Through this political marriage, Jezebel became the wife of Ahab, king of Israel. Then, in another political marriage involving good King Jehoshaphat, problems became compounded leading to the open entrance of Baalism and wickedness into Judah, the southern kingdom of Israel, through Jezebel's daughter Athaliah.

Jezebel was a pagan idol worshipper and not of Jewish ancestry; she was a Zidonian, a Gentile. She and Ahab gave themselves completely over to the worship of Baal and introduced it officially in Israel. Israel was already corrupted by the golden calf worship that Jeroboam the First had set up (1 Kings 12:25-33). What was left of the true worship of God was largely destroyed by this wicked woman.

The Scriptures are clear that **Jezebel** killed the Prophets of the LORD, and in their place she had 400 prophets of Baal that ate at her table. In other words, she was responsible for sponsoring them. She was the one who instigated the murder of Naboth so that her husband could have his vineyard (1 Kings 21:1-16). In 2 Kings, after Jehu had defeated the house of Omri (Ahab), he entered the city of Jezreel and commanded the eunuchs to throw Jezebel down. Her blood was sprinkled on the wall and on the horses, and he (Jehu) and his horsemen trod her underfoot. When they went to bury Jezebel, all that was left of her was her skull, the palms of her hands, and her feet. This was the fulfillment of the Prophet Elijah, who said, *In the portion of Jezreel shall dogs eat the flesh of Jezebel.*

Another connection to this was with Jehu killing Jezebel, which cancelled the political alliance between the Phoenicians (Zidonians) and Israel and may have also prompted the Phoenicians to attack Israel and Judah in the following years. With the marriage alliance broken, the way for war and slave trade extending to Jewish citizens had been opened up. The Phoenicians would later be judged for their part in the selling and exporting of Jewish slaves by other kingdoms such as the Philistines and the Edomites, to name two. We will deal with more of that when we get to the judgment of

Tyre and Zidon (Sidon) in the next chapter that deals with the judgment of nations that were anti-Jewish.

In summary, Jezebel cursed Israel and the true God of Israel, and she paid for it with her life. The horses of Jehu's men trampled her body, and the dogs of the city ate her flesh. She was one of the most evil women of Scripture, an idolater, a persecutor of those who believed in the LORD, and a persecutor of those that she did not like.

Jezebel valued Baal wholeheartedly and cursed the God of Israel and cursed Israel, God's covenant people. Even though Israel was already spiritually contaminated by the golden calf of Jeroboam, and she was cursed by God for her own hatred. Today the name Jezebel is not used by any godly parents in naming their daughters, just as no one uses the name Delilah.

Woman of Zarephath – Blessing
1 Kings 17:8-24

Elijah was sent to a woman of Zarephath which belongs to Zidon, the same nation that Jezebel was from. Here we had a complete turn of personalities and Faith. On one hand was Jezebel, a pagan whom God judged; on the other hand was the woman of Zarephath, perhaps a pagan woman who believed and was blessed of God.

While all Israel, along with King Ahab, was hunting everywhere for Elijah, God sent him to Zarephath, the same area that Jezebel was from, and provided for him there. The means was a poor widow woman who was beginning to prepare her last meal; she and her son were prepared to die afterward. Elijah asked this woman to step out on Faith and care for the prophet, with a promise from God that her *barrel of meal* and *cruse of oil* would not fail.

The poor widow was obedient and blessed the prophet, and God blessed the woman. Later, her son died; and she accused God and Elijah of using her son's death to remind her of her sin. Elijah took the child and prayed to the LORD to have his soul return again, and God answered his prayer. So the woman was blessed the second time because of her care for a Jewish prophet. Her testimony was, *Now by this I know that you are a man of God, and that the word of the LORD in your mouth is truth.* I believe her statement was a confession of Faith in the God of Israel. So a Gentile woman and her son were blessed because of her blessing a Jewish prophet.

Athaliah – Cursing
1 Kings 11:1-3; 2 Chronicles 21:6; 22:10-12; 23:16-17, 21

As you read through these passages, you will discover that God not only cursed Jezebel; He also cursed Athaliah, who was just like her. She was an ungodly, pagan idolatress, a vengeful, ruthless woman just like her mother. She, too, would curse God and Judah, the southern kingdom.

The foundation of this cursing is orchestrated by Jehoshaphat through a political alliance with Ahab, king of Israel, by the marriage of Jehoshaphat's son Jehoram to Ahab and Jezebel's daughter Athaliah. This act violated Deuteronomy 17:17. By genealogy, she would have been considered Jewish because her father was Jewish; but in every other aspect, she was a pagan, anti-Jewish woman that Satan used to try and destroy the house of David and to pollute Judah with idolatry.

Athaliah's husband Jehoram, the son of Jehoshaphat, was greatly influenced by the house of Ahab, as 2 Kings 8:18 and 2 Chronicles 21:6 state. He killed all six of his brothers, altering the line of succession to king. Later, after Jehoram died of a disease, Athaliah's son Ahaziah was made king. He was then killed by Jehu (2 Chronicles 22:8), after which Athaliah, herself, took the throne and had all the heirs of the throne of David also killed (2 Chronicles 22:10). This was a Satan-inspired attempt to destroy the Davidic Covenant, but God thwarted it.

Jehoshaphat's compromise with Ahab cost his family dearly, and it cost the house of David dearly as well as the southern kingdom of Judah because God would bring in judgment for the sins of Jehoram and Athaliah and their son Ahaziah. Edom rebelled, and God allowed the Philistines and Arabians to attack Judah (2 Chronicles 21:16-17; 22:1-3). 2 Chronicles 21:12-15 provides a picture of the sin that Athaliah and the house of Ahab brought on Judah, resulting in great sin against the LORD and violating the statutes and commands of God. This chain reaction of evil caused the judgments of God to come upon them.

Along came Jehoshabeath, the daughter of King Jehoram of Judah and wife of the godly high priest Jehoiada. She was also the sister of King Ahaziah, the subsequent king of Judah. Jehoshabeath hid her brother Ahaziah's son Joash, who was her nephew, from Athaliah, so that he was not killed. When he was eight, Joash was pronounced king; and Athaliah (who had been the Queen of Judah, the southern kingdom, up until that time) was taken and killed by sword outside the Temple (2 Kings 11:15-16).

To summarize, Athaliah cursed God and cursed the covenant people of God; and she attempted to kill all the seed of the house of David. God, in kind, caused her to be slain by the sword and her line to be dead, for none of her parents' family, who were of Israel, the northern kingdom, survived the rebellion and judgment of God by the hand of Jehu.

Athaliah was a pawn in the hands of Satan in his attempt to destroy the house of David. This was a serious attempt to thwart God and the Davidic Covenant, and thus destroy the royal Seed of David. God once again responded kind for kind, curse for curse; and another anti-Jewish person received God's judgment according to the Abrahamic Covenant.

Naaman – Blessing
2 Kings 5:1-19

Naaman was the captain of the army of Syria and not a friend of Israel, but he had a pressing emergency. He had leprosy. Now along came an Israeli slave girl, probably from the west side of the Jordan where Reuben, Gad, and half the tribe of Manasseh settled under Moses. Now the Faith of this girl was exceptional. In all of Jewish history, there had never been a Jewish person cleansed of leprosy, and yet this young girl said in 2 Kings 5:2:

If only my master would see the prophet who is in Samaria! He would cure him of his leprosy. (NIV)

Now Naaman was a proud man; to humble himself to the king of Israel would have been bad enough. When the prophet did not even greet him or pray to his God, he would have been further insulted. When the prophet's servant told Naaman to go wash in the Jordan, he became very angry and said there were rivers in Syria that were cleaner than this Jordan. He demanded to know why he couldn't just go to one of them. But one of his servants spoke to him and convinced him to do what the prophet asked, to dip himself seven times in the Jordan. Naaman did so, and he was cleansed. Notice the complete change in his belief and his attitude in the following verse as he stood before Elisha in 2 Kings 5:15:

...Now I know that there is no God in all the earth, but in Israel....

That was a declaration of his Faith in the God of Israel. Notice that Naaman wanted to take dirt with him from this land; he pledged not to offer burnt offerings and sacrifices unto any other god, but to the LORD only. This Gentile man expressed Faith and commitment to the LORD. Then he asked for pardon as he returned to his duties. When his king worshipped in the house of Rimmon, he leaned on Naaman's hand and Naaman had to bow before the god in Damascus: For this he asks if the LORD will pardon him. Here is a Gentile military man expressing Faith in the God of Israel, and the hand of God's blessing was upon him; he had been healed of leprosy. Because Naaman followed the words of God's prophet, he was healed and blessed by the God of Israel. If you bless Israel and the God of Israel you will be blessed by the God of Israel.

These last two are very good examples of the outworking of the blessings and cursings of God when individuals attempted to use and abuse or bless the chosen people. The last two examples are very clear pictures of anti-Jewish actions and God's clear response.

Haman – Cursing
Esther 3:1-6, 12-13; 5:13-14; 6:1, 6, 10; 7:9-10; 8:9-14; 9:16

Arnold G. Fruchtenbaum places the story of Haman as an example of the national outworking of the Abrahamic Covenant; however, it seems to me that it better fits into the overall picture of an individual being cursed. True enough, Haman's personal hatred of Jews is an example of how national anti-Semitism against the Jewish people was being set in motion by a national decree. Yet in this case, the cursing was predominantly the outworking of the Abrahamic Covenant on an individual, Haman.

Because of Haman's hatred of Mordecai the Jew, all the Jews were to be destroyed in the empire. Mordecai would not bow to Haman, and Haman was incensed. In the end, Mordecai was exalted above Haman, with Haman leading Mordecai through the streets of Shushan mounted on the king's horse and wearing the king's clothing and the king's crown. So Haman, who planned honor for himself, was forced to honor Mordecai the Jew instead. This is an example of turnabout, a curse for a curse.

Haman later wanted to hang Mordecai in a public display; but instead, because of his cursing of Israel, Haman was individually hung on his own gallows that he had prepared for Mordecai the Jew, another turnabout, a curse for a curse, kind for kind. We also see that the curse affected Haman's 10 sons who were also hung.

There were other anti-Semites in the empire, for the first law sealed by the king allowed them to massacre all the Jews, but the second law sealed by the king allowed the Jews to protect themselves. As a result, the Jews were empowered to defend themselves, and killed 75,000 anti-Semites in the empire. So there was a national aspect to the curse, but the point of the story of Purim in Esther is the curse upon Haman, the anti-Semite. Fruchtenbaum correctly states that "Haman sought to destroy the Jews by making anti-Semitism the official government policy."[117]

Because of Haman's hatred of Mordecai, he went before King Ahasuerus to destroy all the Jews in every province (123 of them) of the empire, men, women, and children and take their belongings as spoil (3:8, 12-15). Now Haman is identified as the son of Hammedatha the Agagite (3:1, 10). What is interesting is that the king of the Amalekites that the Prophet Samuel killed was King Agag of the Amalekites. As a national identity they were destroyed not to arise again as a people. However, it is strongly believed that Haman the Agagite was a direct descendent of King Agag, the Amalekite.[118] We will discuss the national outworking of the Abrahamic Covenant later, in chapter 10.

As you read through Esther you see the outworking of curses of the Abrahamic Covenant, curse for curse. It was still in force 1500 years after the giving of the Covenant to Abraham. Haman was humiliated, just as he planned to humiliate Mordecai and the Jews. Haman, who sought to have Mordecai killed, was himself killed with his 10 sons. The second law put fear in the hearts of the government officials and caused them to help the Jews protect themselves; in the process, approximately 75,000 were killed, including 500 even within the palace at Shushan. So instead of destroying the Jews, 75,000 anti-Semites in the kingdom died, curse for curse in kind.

Presidents Under Darius
Daniel 6:4-24 – Cursing

Here is an act of jealousy against Daniel the Jew by his peers, two presidents of what today is Iran. Daniel was the third president, a position of great power that he had been granted because Darius knew of Daniel and his great leadership for the Babylonians. It came about that some of the 120 princes in the kingdom wanted to get rid of Daniel by having him killed. They told King Darius that the other two presidents of the kingdom, the governors, princes, counselors, and captains had a desire: to proclaim a month where whoever prays to another god or man would be cast into a lions' den.

---

[117] Fruchtenbaum, *The Remnant of Israel*, 82.
[118] Max Seligsohn, *The Jewish Encyclopedia*, Isidore Singer, Editor (New York, NY: Funk & Wagnalls Company, 1904), 6:189.

Because of Daniel's stature before men, this was an aggressive act against Daniel, the Jew, personally. But, also, Daniel was a significant person before God. In Ezekiel 14:14, 20, God through Ezekiel puts him in the company of Noah and Job, who were both faithful men. Daniel was a man that purposed in his heart from his youth to worship and live for God alone.

The law, once sealed by Darius, was final and could not be changed; it had become the unalterable law of the Medes and Persians. Because Daniel prayed daily to his God, it appeared Daniel was doomed by his own faithfulness. Daniel was found guilty and was placed in the lions' den; but the next morning, Darius found Daniel alive and well with not a mark on him, for God shut the mouths of the lions and preserved Daniel.

Because Daniel, who was faithful to his God, had been cursed by several anti-Semites, Darius knew that he had been deceived, tricked into sealing the law. God, through Darius, carried out the curse of the Abrahamic Covenant, curse for curse and in kind. These men and their families were all cast into the lions' den, and they were killed by the lions, the same fate they had wished upon Daniel.

The next area that we are going to see is when Israel is cursed and/or their national existence is threatened, God will repay curse for curse. This we will see in the next main section.

Summary Points

- Pharaoh and Abimelech were **cursed** of God less than 25 years after the Abrahamic Covenant.

- Individually Laban experienced **both the blessing and cursing** of God in connection with Jacob the Jew about 200 years after the Abrahamic Covenant.

- Potiphar, Joseph's jailer, and Pharaoh were all **blessed** by their relationship with Joseph 200 years after the Abrahamic Covenant.

- Individually, Rahab was **blessed** by God 400 years after the Abrahamic Covenant.

- Individually, Balaam was **cursed** by God 600 years after the Abrahamic Covenant.

- Individually, Jezebel and Athaliah were **cursed** by God 1,150 years after the Abrahamic Covenant.
- Individually, the Presidents in Daniel's day cursed Daniel the Jew and were **cursed** by God 1,450 years after the Abrahamic Covenant.
- Individually, Haman was **cursed** by God 1,500 years after the Abrahamic Covenant.

Chapter 10
The Outworking of the Abrahamic Covenant Nationally

In this section we will shift our focus to nations who cursed or blessed Israel, and how this is related to the outworking of the Abrahamic Covenant.

Egypt – Cursing
Exodus 1:7-22; 12:1-36; 14:13-31

God in Genesis 12 promised Abram to multiply his seed and make a great nation of him. This God accomplished in the nation of Egypt. However, when the new king arose in Egypt, it was a new dynasty. From the time of Joseph to this new king, Egypt had been conquered by the Hyksos, who were also *Semitic* (descendants of Shem, son of Noah), like the Israelites; the Egyptians were Hamitic (descendants of Ham, the son of Noah). When the Egyptians finally defeated the Hyksos and controlled their own country, they looked at Jewish people, who were Semitic, and feared that they would side with a foreign people like the Hyksos against them. Consequently, the new king or dynasty undertook its first national, anti-Semitic action against the Jewish people 400 years after the Abrahamic Covenant was given (Genesis 15:13).

The new pharaoh's first approach was to enslave the Hebrew people (Exodus 1:7-14). With that done, he then instructed the midwives to the Hebrew women to kill all male children when they were born (Exodus 1:16). However, the midwives would not follow Pharaoh's orders, for they *feared God*. They made up a good story when questioned by Pharaoh as to why they could not comply with his command. So plan two was to have all male babies drowned in the Nile River (Exodus 1:22). The biblical account of Moses being saved in a basket arose as a result of the second command.

The first act by Pharaoh went against God, but the second went against the Abrahamic Covenant given to Abram. It set the curses of the covenant in motion. It would take 80 years for God to get His servant Moses ready to be the deliverer of Israel from Egypt; nevertheless, He implemented the curses upon Egypt.

When God began to work through Moses, all of Egypt was introduced to the God of Israel in a very real and clear way. God sent the plagues, which were directed at destroying Egypt, which God had blessed through Joseph centuries earlier when Egypt blessed Israel. God used the plagues to get Pharaoh's attention, but these plagues were also directed towards all the multiple gods of Egypt. It was a two-prong attack on Egypt for enslaving Israel, but also to attack the false belief system that Egypt had formed around their man-made gods.

God did not destroy all the Egyptian people, but gave them the opportunity to repent and believe in the God of Israel. His mercy did have some impact, for a mixed multitude did join with Israel in the Exodus (Exodus 12:38). Still, Pharaoh and the people did not learn very well. As God had promised Abraham 400 years before in Genesis 15:13-16, the Israelites went out with great substance and in fulfillment of that prophecy. The people of Egypt paid their freed Israelite slaves back wages by giving them their gold, silver, jewels, and raiment (clothing).

Thus, God judged Egypt using a two-phase approach. First, all the firstborn in Egypt were killed by God during Passover by the Angel of death. Second, the army of Pharaoh was destroyed completely in the Red Sea (Exodus 14:13-31) by drowning.

The outworking of the curses of the Abrahamic Covenant became a reality nationally to Egypt. That outworking or the curse, kind for kind, is seen in Pharaoh who wished to destroy all newborn Hebrew males. God, in the 10th plague, during the first night of Passover, reciprocated in kind. Now all the firstborn throughout the land of Egypt, except for in Goshen where the Israelites lived, were to receive the same curse. Any family, who in obedience to God's Word through Moses placed the blood of the Passover Lamb on the door posts and lintels of their homes, was exempted.

The Passover deliverance served as a picture for Israel of the coming Lamb of God (John 1:29, 36) who in 26 A.D. presented Himself to Israel as the Promised King, then because of His rejection He presented Himself as the Lamb four days before their annual Passover celebration. In 30 A.D.,

Jesus (Yeshua) presented Himself on the 10th of the 1st month of the year as the Lamb and then became the Passover sacrifice on the 14th day. He became the voluntary sacrifice for sin that had been pictured 1,400 years earlier at the first Passover (Exodus 12; Isaiah 50:1-6; 52:13-53:12; Matthew 21:4-11; Luke 19:28-40; John 12:12-19).

One other aspect that needs to been seen is that Pharaoh wanted to destroy all Jewish males by drowning. God's curse against Egypt was kind for kind, as the entire army that pursued Israel into the wilderness into the Red Sea was drowned by God, a curse for a curse. Egypt became the first anti-Semitic nation to be disciplined, punished, or destroyed by the wrath and anger of Israel's covenant-keeping God because of Egypt's national anti-Semitic attitude and actions against the God of Israel and His covenant people. The blessings and cursings of the Abrahamic Covenant were active 400 years after God gave it to Abram.

Amalekites – Cursing
Exodus 17:8-16; Numbers 14:43-45; 24:20; Deuteronomy 25:17-19; Judges 6:33; 7:12; 2 Samuel 15:1-3

The second example of national anti-Semitism is the cowardly attack on the lingering people at the rear of the procession out of Egypt by the Amalekites, who were descendants of Esau (Genesis 36:10-12). The Amalekites were related to Edom. Amalek was the grandson of Esau. As Moses led the Israelites out of Egypt, Israel fought to defend itself against the unprovoked attack of the Amalekites. Exodus 17:14 records God's curse against the Amalekites when He states, *I will utterly put out the remembrance of Amalek from under heaven*. The discipline and punishment to the Amalekites was not immediate; it was not until the time of King Saul that they were removed as a national identity because of their attitude and animosity towards Israel. The outworking of the curse of the Abrahamic Covenant was not forgotten, but was instead carried out about 300 years later.

We find in Numbers 14:43-45 that the Amalekites were part of the army that routed Israel after the rebellion of Kadesh-barnea. In Deuteronomy 25:17-19, Moses repeated the story of the attack of the Amalekites from the Exodus account and reminded the Israelites not to forget the Amalekites but to *blot out the remembrance of Amalek from under heaven*.

Amalekites also show up in the correlation of armies in Judges 6-8, when God uses Gideon to judge them and the Midianites. The next key passage comes when King Saul is commanded to destroy them, which he did; but his obedience was incomplete (1 Samuel 14:47; 15:1-35). The outworking of the curses of the Abrahamic Covenant again became a reality when the remembrance of Amalekites as a national identity was completely removed. However, it appears that a few individuals escaped, for Haman was an Agagite, a descendent from King Agag of the Amalekites (1 Samuel 15:20). He also met his cursing face to face with the Abrahamic Covenant as we have seen in the previous chapter: He was hung from the gallows he had prepared for the Jewish man Mordecai. So the cursing on the Amalekites remained active 400; 600; 1,000; and even 1,500 years after the giving of the Abrahamic Covenant to Abram.

Midian – Cursing
Numbers 22:4-7; 25:1-9; 31:1-19; Joshua 13:21; Judges 6-8

The Midianites go back to one of the four sons of Abraham's marriage to Keturah, whom he married after Sarah died (Genesis 25:2-4). Abraham sent his son Midian to the country of the east (Genesis 25:6). This area probably included the fringe areas of Moab and Edom. It would include parts of southern Syria and the western part of Arabia, with perhaps a portion of the northeastern Sinai.[119] Outside of the friendly relations that Moses had with Jethro, the Midianite, whose daughter Zipporah he married, Israel always had trouble with the Midianites. It would be my observation that the branch of the Midianites that Jethro was part of was a different branch of the Midianite family, because out of this branch were the Kenites (Midianites) who traveled with Moses to the land of Canaan. We will deal with the Kenites separately in the next section.

The Midianites were involved with Moab to curse Israel through Balaam, and it was also the Midianites who used their women, along with the Moabite women, to seduce Israeli men in sin (Numbers 25:1, 6). In Numbers 31, the Midianites were judged for their part in causing Israel to sin. Verses 7-8 state that all males were killed along with five kings of Midian and the false prophet Balaam. In Judges 6 through 8, because of Israel's sin against Him, God raised up Midian to plague Israel. Then we have the story of Gideon, whom God uses to judge the Midianites for provoking Israel to sin. (The

---

[119] Youngblood, *Nelson's New Illustrated Bible Dictionary*, 835.

Amalekites, whom we already covered, were confederated with the Midianites in Judges 6 through 8.)

The outworking of the Abrahamic Covenant continued against the Midianites because of their actions and attitudes toward Israel. After the Judges period, the Midianites never prospered and are only mentioned as points reflected in history in 1 Chronicles 1:46; Isaiah 9:4; 10:26, and 60:6; and Habakkuk 3:7. The Midianites ceased to be a problem to Israel because of their cursing of Israel and its outworking in the Abrahamic Covenant.

So in the case of the Midianites, the active cursing of the Abrahamic Covenant was present from 400 to 600 years after the Abrahamic Covenant was given.

Kenites/Rechabites – Cursing/Blessing
Genesis 15:19; Exodus 18:1; Numbers 24:21-22; Judges 1:16; 4:17-24; 2 Samuel 15:6; Jeremiah 35

The Kenites are somewhat of a confusing group of people. Genesis 15:19 mentions them as Canaanites whose land will be taken by Israel. Yet according to Exodus 18:1 and Judges 1:16, the Kenites were a sub-group of the larger group of Midianites that were connected to Jethro, Moses' father-in-law. Now we know that the Midianites came from Abraham's marriage to Keturah, which makes them a distinct group of people from the Kenites of Genesis 15:19. It appears that perhaps the Kenites moved from Canaan and became absorbed into the Midianites, becoming one people. This meant that the Kenites, who were Canaanites (Hamitic), and the Midianites, who were Semitic, intermarried and became one group. This I do not believe can be dogmatically proven, only assumed. That seems to be where the Hebrew Scriptures lead us.

So initially, the Kenites were under the curse of God because of being part of the Canaanites in Canaan that God was going to give to Abraham's descendants 400 years later. What transpires in Exodus is that Moses invites Jethro to come to Canaan with him. It appears that Jethro did not, but one (or more) of his sons did accept Moses' offer. They traveled with Israel and were observed by Balaam in Numbers 24:21-22, but were dwelling separately. According to the *Jewish Encyclopedia*, they settled in southern Judah and were absorbed eventually into the tribe of Judah, with a branch of them moving to the north within Israel.[120] Sisera was the commander of the forces against Israel who had a tent nail put through his head by a woman who was a Kenite. So these Kenites (Midianites) became allies with Israel and a friend to Israel contrary to the rest of the Midianites.

The Kenite friendship with Israel is expressed by King Saul when he tells the Kenites to separate themselves from the Amalekites so that they are not destroyed with them. Now this reflects the blessing aspect of the Abrahamic Covenant, as the Kenites in the Land dealt well with Israel. Originally, a people that were under a curse through intermarriage with the Midianites, they now receive the blessing of God under the Abrahamic Covenant because of their blessing and friendship with Israel and Jethro's connection with Moses.

Now there is one other connection to the Kenites. The Rechabites of Jeremiah 35 are a branch of the Kenites who lived in Israel. Jeremiah describes them as an example of faithfulness. Their father had his family make a covenant that they and their descendants would uphold their father's teachings. Through Jeremiah, God stated that the faithfulness of the Rechabites to their father was greater than the faithfulness of the Israelites to God, stating in Jeremiah 35:19 that *Rechab shall not want a man to stand before me* [God] *forever*.

So here we have the outworking of the blessing of the Abrahamic Covenant again towards the Kenites. The Kenites, who were originally under God's judgment, ended up receiving God's blessing because of their positive attitude and relationship to Israel and their wonderful example of faithfulness. Once again, the outworking of the Abrahamic Covenant continued to function.

So the Kenites were blessed by God because of their friendship with Israel. The blessing aspect of Genesis 12:3 was still active 400 to 1,400 years later, under Jeremiah's ministry.

---

[120] George A. Barton, *The Jewish Encyclopedia* (New York, NY: Funk & Wagnalls Co, 1904), 7:467.

Edom – Cursing
Genesis 25:21-23; Numbers 20:14-22; 2 Samuel 8:14; 1 Kings 11:14-18;
Psalm 83:1-8; Psalm 137:6-7; Lamentations 4:21-22; Isaiah 34:5-15; Jeremiah 30:16
(with 27:1-3); 49:7-22; Ezekiel 25:12-14; 35:1-15; Amos 1:6, 9, 11-12;
Obadiah 1-3, 8-14, 18

Esau was the father of the nation of Edom and one of the twin sons of Isaac (Genesis 25:19-26). Esau and his brother Jacob managed to live peaceably with each other, but there was an undercurrent of animosity on Esau's part; I believe that his attitude translated to the attitude and actions of Edom in biblical history. In Genesis 25:21-23, there is a prophecy given to Rebekah that Esau (Edom) the firstborn would serve the younger, Jacob (Israel), and that Jacob (Israel) would be stronger than Esau (Edom). The outworking of God's plan unfolded between the struggles of these two nations.

To understand the relationship between Edom and Israel, remember that Israel came from Jacob, and Edom came from Esau, the twin brother of Jacob. National hostility came out between Moses and Edom when he spoke of Israel (Jacob) as Edom's brother who wanted to pass through Edom, and they would not permit it. In fact, in Numbers 20:14, Moses mentions to Edom when asking permission to pass through, *your brother Israel*, referencing the brotherly relationship between the twins. So when God judges Edom, He judges them more severely because of their brotherly relationship and lack of brotherly compassion and concern towards Israel.

Later, in the Land, when Judah is being attacked by the Philistines and Arabs during the reign of Jehoram, around 845 B.C., Edom rejoiced when Israel lost and was persecuted by her enemies. In Obadiah verses 10-14, there are 6 points that Fruchtenbaum brings out to show why the judgment of God was so severe against Edom:

1. In verse 10 [Edom is] guilty of violence against Israel, which is looked upon by God as **violence of a brother** against brother, *"for the violence done to your brother Jacob, shame shall cover you and you shall be cut off forever."* [Remember] These were not merely brothers, these were twin brothers, and yet Esau's turning against Jacob, or Edom against Israel, is looked upon by God as violence of a brother against a brother, and that's why God says there will be two results: Edom will be shamed; Edom will be totally cut off, and that forever.

2. The second sin against Israel is having a **hostile attitude** in verse 11. *In the day that you stood on the other side, in the day that strangers carried away his substance, and foreigners entered into his gate and cast lots upon Jerusalem, even you were as one of them.* They are guilty of having an attitude of hostility against their brother nation. As the Philistines and the Arabs attacked the city and began spoiling it and sacking it, Edom stood back without coming to Israel's aid. And as the Arabs and the Philistines cast lots for Jerusalem and for her spoil, by standing back and waiting for her share, she's looked upon by God as being equally guilty. From God's viewpoint, He says *you were just like one of them.* Though they were not actively participating in the casting of lots for the spoil, they did not come to their aid and looked upon it with satisfaction. Therefore they were equally guilty. Their attitude went beyond hostility.

3. The third sin is given in verse 12: They **showed actual glee** over what was happening. *Look not you on the day of your brother, on the day of his disaster, and rejoice not over the children of Judah in the day of their destruction; neither speak proudly in the day of their distress.* The picture is they actually exercised glee, they were happy to see what was happening. They rejoiced on the day of Jerusalem's destruction; they spoke proudly in a day of Israel's distress.

4. Their fourth sin in verse 13 is they are **guilty of spoiling the city**, *Enter not into the gate of My people in the day of their calamity; yes, look not on their affliction in the day of their calamity, nor lay your hands on their substance in the day of their calamity.* After the Philistines and the Arabs were through taking what they wanted, Edom came in and began taking what was left. They entered the gates of Jerusalem; they were happy about the affliction and they laid hands on the substance that was left behind.

5. A fifth sin they were guilty of is in verse 14, *"stand you not in the crossway to cut off those of his that escape."* **As the Jews were escaping, since the army was defeated, as Jews were fleeing, trying to get across the Jordan River, the Edomites did not even permit Jewish escapees to make it.** They blocked the passageways that they needed to escape.

6. But then sixthly, it goes a step further, *"deliver not up those that remain in the day of distress."* The fleeing Jews they did capture, **they turned them over to the enemy**, the Philistines and the Arabs.[121]

After the fall of Jerusalem to the Babylonians, the Edomites moved into southern Judah. One reason was that the Nabateans (Arabs) had pushed them out of Edom, which was God's judgment on them for their hostile attitude and actions against Israel. Then around 100 B.C., John Hyrcanus of the Maccabees again conquered Edom and forced them to convert to Judaism, which again was a judgment on them for their cursing of Israel. This action by the Maccabees set the stage for Herod the Great, who was an Idumean (Edomite). Today there are no known descendants of Edom, and Jeremiah in his prophecy states that the land of Edom would be destroyed by God as Sodom and Gomorrah had been destroyed because as a brother to Israel they cursed Israel. During the Millennial Reign of Messiah, there will be no one living in what we today call southern Jordan (Edom) (Jeremiah 49:16-18; Ezekiel 25:12-14). The Prophets also speak of God's judgment against Edom for their perpetual hatred of Israel (Amos 1:11; Ezekiel 35:5).

Once again we have the outworking of the Abrahamic Covenant in the cursing of Edom because of her attitude and actions against the country of Esau's own brother, Israel. Obadiah in verses 15-16 states that because they drank (swallowed wine) on the Temple Mount, God says that Edom will be swallowed up by the nations in the Day of the LORD because of their actions: *…it shall be done unto you, your reward shall return upon your own head*. Cursing kind for kind, it further states in Obadiah 18 and Ezekiel 25:12-14 that Edom will ultimately be destroyed by Israel.

We have been following Genesis 12:3 in tracing the blessings and cursings to anyone who blesses or curses Israel. The complete destruction of Edom is the most severe of all the judgments, next to the Amalekites. So again their active cursing of God became evident from 450 – 1,150 years after the covenant was made with Abraham, and God remembered His covenant with Abraham and his Seed.

---

[121] Arnold G. Fruchtenbaum, *The Minor Prophets: Obadiah*. Transcribed notes of his class on Obadiah from Camp Shoshanah.

Moab – Cursing

Genesis 19:33-38; Deuteronomy 2:9; Judges 3:12-30; 2 Samuel 8:2; Isaiah 16; Jeremiah 30:16 (with 27:1-3); 48:1-47; Ezekiel 25:8-11; Amos 2:1-3; Zephaniah 2:5-10

Moabites are descendants of Lot through an incestuous relationship initiated by Lot's oldest daughter to make their father drunk and lay with him. She conceived and bore Moab (Genesis 19:33-38). According to Deuteronomy 2:9, God distinctly told Israel not to fight the Moabites, for He had given them the land that they dwelled in. In fact, there will be a kingdom of Moab in the Millennium (Jeremiah 49:47).

Moab was not generally friendly to Israel, even though they were national cousins. The first instance of conflict was when Israel camped on the border of their land and Moab felt threatened and joined with Midian. King Balak of Moab summoned Balaam to come and curse Israel. But Israel was still not to fight them, even with the sin that Moab helped to instigate, which caused Israel to fall into sin. As a result of the private counsel of Balaam, Israel attacked Midian; but Moab seems to have escaped that attack. In Judges 3, when Israel was weak, God used King Eglon of Moab to judge Israel for their sin. Israel was then was delivered by the second judge of Israel, Ehud, a Benjaminite. There was evidently a good period early on in David's reign, probably because of family connections through Ruth. Later, under the control of Israel, they were free for a short period before being subdued by Assyria, and then Babylon took Israel into captivity.

Jeremiah brings out the anti-Semitic attitudes of Moab in 49:27 where they skipped with joy over Israel and her difficulties. Fruchtenbaum makes the following statement on the anti-Semitic attitude of the Moabites:

> In verse 27, more to the point is Moab's anti-Semitism. *For was not Israel a derision unto you?* Were not Israel and the Jews someone to be poked fun at by the Moabites? The Moabites used the Jews for the same reason as many Gentiles have used them, as a [target] of mocking. The Moabites held the Jews in derision. Since the Moabites held the Jews in derision, under the principle of curse for curse in kind; the Moabites will be held in derision as well. Then God asks Moab a question, "Was he found among the thieves?" Or, "Was Israel caught in the very act of stealing that he was held in such high contempt by the Moabites?" Even though Israel was not guilty of stealing, when the Moabites made mention of the Jews, they

wagged their heads. They wagged their heads as a sign of contempt. This is something that the Moabites may have done, but many Gentiles ever since have done the same. The wagging of the heads against the Jews and holding them in derision and contempt was done by the Moabites and many Gentiles ever since.[122]

This act of Moab falls into the cursing aspect of the Abrahamic Covenant; and Moab, who, rejoiced at the demise of Israel, will have the same thing happen to them, cursings kind for kind. Two other authors speak to the same issue, although they do not use the word *anti-Semitism*:

> The specific way in which Moab "magnified itself" is that it made a laughingstock of Israel. The language is not unlike that of the Psalms of Lament, which complain of people treating Israel with contempt (Psalm 59:8; Lamentations 1:7; Jeremiah 20:7). Moab has treated Israel with contempt. This is the way in which Moab has violated Yahweh. Thus, sin against the "brother" here is indeed sin against God.[123]

> Here the prophet describes the mocking attitude (18:16) of Moab as, so far exempt from disaster, she gloated over the demise of her neighbor. Edom is denounced for the same attribute in Psalm 137:7. By the irony of judgment, Moab shall herself become a derision.[124]

Moab, in mocking Israel, was mocking God. The cursing of the Abrahamic Covenant again remained alive and active. If anyone mocked or cursed Israel, it was the same as cursing God; so His reprisals should be expected. Moab's punishment was not merely an "irony of judgment"; it was the deliberate outworking of the curse of Genesis 12:3, kind for kind. Mock Israel now and be mocked in the same way in turn. A nation will receive the curse of God in return for cursing Israel. Yet in the Millennium, there will be a kingdom called Moab (Jeremiah 48:47).

So the blessing and cursing was active in relationship to Moab from 450 to 1,350 years after the making of the Abrahamic Covenant.

---

[122] Arnold G. Fruchtenbaum, *The Book of Jeremiah*, Transcription from his class at Camp Shoshanah.
[123] Walter Brueggemann, *A Commentary on Jeremiah: Exile and Homecoming* (Grand Rapids, MI: Erdmann Publishing Co., 1998), 447.
[124] Douglas R. Jones, *The New Century Bible Commentary: Jeremiah* (Grand Rapids, MI: Erdmann Publishing Co., 1992), 505.

Ammon – Cursing
Genesis 19:33-38; Deuteronomy 2:19; Judges 10:7-12; 11:1-40; Jeremiah 30:16 (with 27:1-3); 49:1-6; Amos 1:13-15; Zephaniah 2:5-10

Ammonites were descendants of Lot through another incestuous relationship initiated by Lot's youngest daughter to make her father drunk, lay with him, and conceive. (In the vast isolation the two daughters experienced after the terrifying destruction of Sodom and Gomorrah, they may have thought that the whole world had been destroyed. They may have had the misguided notion that they needed to repopulate the earth; this was merely an assumption and not fact.) This time, the youngest daughter lay with her father Lot, and she conceived and bore Ammon (Genesis 19:33-38). In Deuteronomy 2:19, God distinctly told Israel they were not to fight Ammon; for He had given them the land that they dwelled in. In fact, there will be a kingdom of Ammon in the Millennium (Jeremiah 49:6).

Once again, a relative of Israel, Ammon in this case, attacked and suppressed Israel because of their (Israel's) sin. In Judges 11 is the story of Jephthah, who was called into action against the Ammonites to make war with them because they possessed the land of Gad. Jephthah gave a response with a history lesson to the Ammonites, showing their claims to the land of Gad as completely untrue.

The Ammonites also opposed Judah during Jehoiakim's reign (2 Kings 24:2), and they also helped to kill Gedaliah, the new governor appointed by Nebuchadnezzar. Gedaliah was protecting the remnant of the people of Israel not taken into captivity. The Ammonites sent Nethaniah, an Ishmaelite, to assassinate him (2 Kings 25:22-26). Ammon opposed Israel even after the return of Israel in Nehemiah 4:1-5 and during the Maccabean era in 1 Maccabees 5:6, 30-33. So there was a continuous negative attitude that produced actions against "family," and God judged them for it as He also judged Moab and Edom. To curse God through the Abrahamic Covenant by harming the Jewish people will unleash God's repayment, curse for curse.

The sin of Ammon was the confiscation of the land of Gad as if Gad (or Israel) had no heirs. If Israel had no heirs, then it was okay for Ammon to take the land; but the Israelite tribe of Gad did have heirs, and God judged the Ammonites for taking land that was not theirs to have. Feinberg states that the "land still belonged to them [Israel] and was to be inherited by their sons."[125] This ought to be a warning from history to all nations today in the twenty-first century as they relate to Israel. It should be a warning to the Islamic nations around Israel, to Egypt, Jordan, Lebanon, Syria, and Iran: This is Israel's Land, not theirs or Allah's.

The fact that Israel did not control their Land for 1,900 years after their dispersion until 1948 makes no difference to God. In light of His covenant with Abraham, the Land belongs to Israel by the direct command of God. (See Appendix 3.) He has always viewed them as a nation, whether in the Land or in the Diaspora. It should be a warning to Europe, who already has an anti-Semitic track record against Israel. It should be a warning to the United Nations as they continue anti-Semitic resolutions in their stance against Israel. Lastly, it should be a warning to the United States of America not to turn its back on Israel. This warning is to every administration in the White House. It would include Protestant churches that boycott Israel and support the Palestinian Authority, Hezbollah (in Lebanon), and Hamas (in the Gaza Strip).

Too many have been willingly deceived into opposing Israel and the Jewish people by the propaganda machine of radical Islam who would, if given the chance, just as soon slit the throats of these naïve Christians. Today we see ISIS, the Islam of Mohammed, killing Christians in the wake of destruction and death throughout the Middle East.

We as a nation could be standing at the crossroads today and, depending on our alliances with Israel, could place ourselves ripe for judgment for anti-Semitism ourselves. The Palestinian Christians are attacking Israel with Replacement Theology which I described early in this book and with the relatively new Palestinian Liberation Theology.

Again, you have the outworking of the Abrahamic Covenant nationally as it relates to Ammon from 450 to 1,800 years out from the giving of the blessing and cursing of the Abrahamic Covenant. Years may go by, and that seems such a long time; but what is 1,000 or 2,000 years in respect to an eternal God who is ever Present?

---

[125] Charles L. Feinberg, *Jeremiah: A Commentary* (Grand Rapids, MI: Zondervan Publishing House, 1982), 309.

Damascus – Cursing
2 Samuel 8:5-7; 2 Kings 16:9-18; Isaiah 7:1-8, 16; 8:4; 17:1; Jeremiah 49:23-27; Amos 1:3-5

Damascus was a city that was settled early in history. It appears it was the home town of Abraham's servant Eliezer (Genesis 15:2). Damascus did not play a role in the history of Israel until David conquered Damascus and had a garrison there for his soldiers (2 Samuel 8:5-6; 1 Chronicles 18:5-6). Later, under Solomon's reign, because of Solomon's sin, God raised up Rezon, who formed a dynasty that lasted 200 years in Damascus. Rezon gathered surrounding cities and united them to throw off Israeli control (1 Kings 11:23-25). The Bible says he abhorred Israel. After Israel was divided into northern and southern kingdoms, Syria (Damascus) became a constant source of conflict to the kings of Israel (the 10 northern tribes).

After Syria was conquered by Assyria, Damascus continued as an important city as the residence of Assyrian and Persian governors for five centuries. Alexander the Great made Damascus a provincial capital, and later Rome made it their seat of government. Later yet, the Muslim Umayyad is mentioned as being a ruler of Damascus from 661-750 A.D., showing that Damascus continued on as a hub of Islam, controlling Palestine for an extended period. Today Damascus is still the capital of Syria.[126] So the city of Damascus has been in existence since before the days Abraham.

God often used pagan countries as tools of judgment on Israel for its sins against the LORD. However, Damascus crossed a line related to the Davidic Covenant that God could not accept. Syria had made an agreement with its enemy Israel (the northern kingdom), to conspire with them to attack Judah (Jerusalem and the southern kingdom). They conspired to remove king Ahaz and the Davidic dynasty from the throne and replace them with a new dynasty. Damascus was anti-Semitic towards Israel in general. However, because of the Assyrian threat to their nation and Israel at this time, they wanted Judah to join the confederacy; but King Ahaz would not. So Israel and Syria planned to combine forces to attack Judah and remove the Davidic dynasty so that Judah, Israel, and Syria – who were normally enemies – could fight together against Assyria (Isaiah 7:1-2).

This was a serious offense of Syria (Damascus) against God and His covenant with David (2 Samuel 7:12-16; 1 Chronicles 17:10-14; Psalm 89:1-

---

[126] John B. Metzger, "Jerusalem and Islam," *Israel Messenger* (Summer, 2006), Jewish Awareness Ministries.

37). Damascus was not only guilty of anti-Semitism and worthy of the curse in Abrahamic Covenant, they were even more guilty of conspiring to dethrone the Davidic dynasty, a violation of the Davidic Covenant. The fate of Syria (Damascus) and Israel is recorded in Isaiah 7:16. Both will be conquered. Once again, the outworking of the cursing of the Abrahamic Covenant is evident in a nation opposing Judah (Israel), this time affecting Syria even 1,100 to 1,500 years after the covenant.

Philistines – Cursing
2 Samuel 8:1; Isaiah 14:28-31; Jeremiah 47:1-7; Ezekiel 25:15-17; Joel 3:4; Amos 1:6-8; Obadiah 19; Zephaniah 2:5-10

The Philistines were not indigenous people to Canaan. The Scriptures state that they were from Caphtor (Genesis 10:14), which has been generally identified with the island of Crete. Crete was also the home of the Cherethites, who had been associated with the Philistines. In 1 Samuel 30:14 as well as in Ezekiel 25:15-16, the Philistines are called Cherethites. They evidently came in two waves; one was an early colony that Abraham had dealings with in Genesis 20-21. The early wave seemed to be much more peaceful than the later wave. With the second wave, these people were warlike and very aggressive. They established five city-states in what we call Gaza today. These cities were Ashkelon, Ashdod, Ekron, Gath, and Gaza.

Contact between the Philistines and Israel began during the time of the Judges. The Philistines dominated the areas of Dan, Judah, Benjamin, and other tribal areas north in the Israeli cities of Megiddo and Beth Shean. Samson dealt with these same Philistines, and they were a thorn in the side of Israel during the period of the Judges, under the Prophet Samuel, and persisting under King Saul. The Philistines were subdued by David and Solomon and were intermittent problems in the time of Jehoshaphat (2 Chronicles 17:11). Jehoram, son of Jehoshaphat, suffered a serious raid by the Philistines (2 Chronicles 21:16-17). Uzziah attacked the Philistines (2 Chronicles 26:6-7); but during the reign of Ahaz (2 Chronicles 28:18), the Philistines raided the lowlands and southern Judah because of the sins of Ahaz. The Philistines were conquered by the Assyrians and then finally by the Babylonians and were deported as captives. From that point on, there is no mention of the Philistines.

The passages that reveal their anti-Semitism are Amos 1:6-8, Ezekiel 25:15-17, and Zephaniah 2:5-10. Hating Israel, the Philistines showed by actions a full contempt toward Israel, which by default goes against the LORD. Again, God made a covenant with Abraham to bless and curse those that bless or curse Israel. This example shows the patience of God before He carries out His judgment. God does not forget the anti-Semitic acts of nations. Once again I will reference Fruchtenbaum on God's ultimate judgment on the Philistines from the above three passages:

> So because *they sold Jews as slaves to Edom* in verses 7-8 [of Amos 1] comes the judgment. The city of Gaza in verse 7 is destined for destruction. In verse 8 he mentions three other Philistine cities: Ashdod, Ashkelon and Ekron. For Ashdod, the inhabitants will suffer; for Ashkelon, the king will suffer; for Ekron, the city will suffer until the remnant of the Philistines is destroyed. Now Philistia, the land of the Philistines, was comprised of five cities of which he mentions only four: Gaza, Ashdod, Ashkelon, and Ekron. The one missing is Gath, and the reason is that by this time Gath was already destroyed by King Uzziah in 2 Chronicles 26:6. So one of the Philistine cities is already gone; the other four will suffer destruction in accordance with this prophecy.[127]

In verses 15-17 [of Ezekiel 25], he now deals with Philistia, better known as the Philistines. In verse 15, he first of all tells us the **cause of the judgment**, *because the Philistines have dealt by revenge.* In doing so, they have done three things. **First**: They *have taken vengeance.* **Second**: They have done this *with despite of soul.* **Third**: They have chosen to *destroy with perpetual enmity.* Basically then, the Philistines are guilty of a continuous war against Israel, and this is the reason why judgment will come upon them. Parallel passages on this are to be found in Isaiah 14:28-31; Jeremiah 47:1-7; and Amos 1:6-8. In Ezekiel 25 verse 16, he deals with the judgment. He begins again with the word *Therefore*, meaning, because of the sinful attitude of the Philistines in verse 15, God is going to do the following. He is going to *stretch out My hand upon the Philistines*; and as with the Edomites, the stretching out of God's hand is to bring about a **total destruction**. In emphasizing this, Ezekiel says two things. **First**: *I will cut off the Cherethites.* This is another name for the Philistines, emphasizing where they originated. In Hebrew, this is a play [on] words. The Hebrew word for "to cut off" and the Hebrew word for "Cherethites" are similar in

---

[127] Arnold G. Fruchtenbaum, *The Minor Prophets: Amos*, Transcripts from class at Camp Shoshanah.

sound. In Hebrew it reads as follows: *Hichratiy et Keretim.* In English it would be something like: "I will cut off the cutters-off." **Second**: *I will destroy the remnant of the sea coast.* A parallel passage on this specific point is found in Zephaniah 2:5. After spelling out the judgment in verse 16, in verse 17 he shows that there will be two results. **First**, *I will execute great vengeance upon them with wrathful rebukes.* Once again this is in keeping with the principle of the Abrahamic Covenant. It is vengeance for vengeance, curse for curse in kind. **Second**, *they shall know that I am Jehovah when I shall lay My vengeance upon them.* Here the verse does not merely say that they will "know Jehovah," but rather they will know Him experientially because of His vengeance. As with Edom, there is no restoration promised to the Philistines.[128]

[In] the land of Philistia [Zephaniah 2:5-10], the Philistines did not have one national king like the others had, but the nation of the Philistines was a combination of five key cities known as the cities of the Pentapolis. Each city had its own king. Three of these cities were on the sea-coast running from north to south: Ashdod, Ashkelon, and Gaza. Working inland north to south, it was Ekron and Gath. In this passage he mentions four of the five Philistine cities: Gaza, Ashkelon, Ashdod, and Ekron. Only Gath is not mentioned in this account. As for Gaza, Gaza would be forsaken. As for Ashkelon in verse 4, [they would] become a desolation. Ashkelon – Hebrew meaning the *fruitful city,* will prove to be "fruitless." Ashdod – they will be driven away at noonday. Normally at noon the armies rest because it is the heat of the day; but in this case, in the noonday, [they] will be taken in the heat of battle. The name Ashdod means *fortress* or *fortress town,* and here he says "the fortress town will be no fortress." As for Ekron, [they] will be rooted up, and again he plays upon the meaning of "Ekron." Hebrew – Ekron is going to be rooted up. The judgment of God will be so severe that in verse 5, the Philistine population is going to totally disappear.[129]

The Philistines constantly harassed and oppressed Israel until they were subjugated by David. The Philistines were referred to in the Hebrew

---

[128] Arnold G. Fruchtenbaum, *The Book of Ezekiel*, Transcripts from classes at Camp Shoshanah.
[129] Arnold G. Fruchtenbaum, *The Minor Prophets: Zephaniah*, Transcripts from classes at Camp Shoshanah.

Scriptures more than any other nation.[130] Today, with all the problems with Palestinian Gaza, according to Obadiah 19, Israel will dwell in the plain of the Philistines.[131] While Gaza did come back under Israel, it was ceded back and currently exists as the possession of Hamas; but in the future, during the physical reign of Messiah, Gaza will belong to Israel.

The constant revengeful animosity against Israel is viewed according to the Abrahamic Covenant as a direct act against God Himself. So once again, the outworking of the Abraham Covenant was still working, and the anti-Semitism of the Philistines was rewarded by God with total destruction with no one left called a Philistine; they as individuals and as a nation ceased to exist. So the active cursing of God against the Philistines went from 900 to 1,400 years from the making of the Abrahamic Covenant. As animosity continues from the Palestinian Gaza strip up until today, God is again showing restraint.

Tyre – Cursing
Isaiah 23; Jeremiah 30:16 (with 27:1-3); Ezekiel 26:1-28:19; Joel 3:5-6; Amos 1:9-10

Tyre is a Phoenician city of Canaanite origin. Not much is said about this city until the time of David, who had a treaty with Hiram king of Tyre. Solomon continued the treaty and bought materials to build the Temple in Jerusalem. Tyre became a very wealthy city with sea-going trade routes throughout the Mediterranean. Tyre was friendly up through the time of Ahab and Jezebel. Jezebel's father, a Phoenician priest, usurped the throne of Tyre from the dynasty of Hiram. Jezebel, a very pagan woman, became a major problem for Israel and Judah. The coastal city of Tyre was finally conquered by Babylon. The city then moved to a small island off the coast and was still able to maintain its influence, though diminished. It regained its strength until Alexander the Great finally completely destroyed it.

What brought Tyre under the judgment of God? There were two separate things that caused God to curse the city. First, Tyre became the point of slave trade, and many of those slaves were Israelis who were captured by Ammon, Moab, Edom, and the Philistines and then sold to the Greeks (Joel 3:5-6). Because of the slave traffic of Jewish citizens, God said He would judge

---

[130] Charles L. Feinberg, *The Prophecy of Ezekiel: The Glory of the Lord* (Chicago, IL: Moody Press, 1969), 145.

[131] Jarl Waggoner, *Prophets For Our Time: An Exposition of Obadiah and Jonah* (Wipf & Stock Publishers, 2009), 41.

Tyre for its anti-Semitic actions. In Amos 1:9-10, God condemned them for not remembering their brotherly covenant that they had with the Jewish nation in the days of David (2 Samuel 5:11) and Solomon (1 Kings 5:1-12).

Because of the assassination of Queen Jezebel of Israel by Jehu, the political alliance between Tyre and Sidon was broken and they were no longer obligated to be friendly to Israel. However, that still does not explain their anti-Jewish attitude and actions toward Judah and their past relationship to David and Solomon. In Isaiah, Jeremiah, and Ezekiel, there are some lengthy passages dealing with Tyre's demise. Those passages speak of the pride and self-deification of its ruler in later years. That will bring us to the second point as to why God would judge Tyre. God speaks of the king of Tyre as a representative of a supernatural power. In Ezekiel 28:1-10, God speaks of the downfall of the king who deified himself and then addresses the power that was really behind him. That power behind him in verses 11-19 was a fallen *anointed cherub* who had covered the throne of God, He was *created perfect* until *iniquity was found* in him (Isaiah 14:12-15). His name was Lucifer, Son of the Morning. We know him today as the devil or Satan.

So God curses Tyre for their anti-Semitic actions against Israel and for self-deification. God remembers His covenant with Abraham: If anyone blesses Israel, God will bless him. But if anyone chooses to curse Israel, thereby cursing God, he will be cursed, judged by God. God judged all these nations so far because of the negative attitudes and actions against His people, Israel. God's covenant with Abraham was still active. Beware!!

Sidon – Cursing
Genesis 10:15; 49:13; Joshua 19:24-31; Judges 1:31; 1 Kings 16:31; 2 Kings 23:13; 1 Chronicles 1:13; Jeremiah 30:16 (with 27:1-3); Ezekiel 28:20-26

Biblically, the origin of Sidon goes back to Sidon, the first born son of Canaan (Genesis 10:15; 1 Chronicles 1:13) who was the son of Ham, the son of Noah. Geographically, Sidon was about 30 miles north of Tyre. Sidon was probably founded before Tyre and was the dominant city on the Mediterranean coast for centuries. Its location was near the tribal territories of Zebulun and Asher, but Israel never took it. In other words, Sidon was within the area called the Promised Land that Israel never took (Genesis 49:13; Joshua 19:24-31; Judges 1:31). Even though Tyre later became the dominant city, Tyre was at times called Sidon, or of the Zidonians (1 Kings 16:31).[132]

We find in the book of Judges that Israel lived among the Zidonians and usually served them. When the Kingdom split from King Rehoboam, the ten northern tribes of Israel controlled a large area, but as under David and Solomon, Israel never took that part of the Promised Land. Solomon in all his wisdom was so foolish as to build temples for his wives on the Mount of Corruption, which was southeast of the city walls across the valley. There he built temples to Ashtoreth, the abomination of the Zidonians, Chemosh the abomination of the Moabites, and for Milcon the abomination of the children of Ammon (2 Kings 23:13). Then Jeroboam set up a counterfeit religion of the golden calf in Bethel and Dan. Solomon's building temples for false gods and Jeroboam's counterfeit religion laid the foundations for adopting the Baal worship of the Zidonians. Later, Omri, king over the ten northern tribes, made a political marriage for his wicked son Ahab to a Zidonian princess by the name of Jezebel, daughter of Ethbaal, king of the Zidonians (Tyre). So Israel became infested with the worship of Baal and all other kinds of idolatry (1 Kings 16:30-33).

The two significant passages that reflect Sidon's impact on Israel (the ten northern tribes) are found in 1 Kings 16:31 and Ezekiel 28:20-24. The first passage in Kings relates to the spiritual impact that Sidon (the Canaanites) had on Israel, and the Ezekiel passage refers to their impact as *thorns* in the side of Israel. Sidon would fall under the curse of the Abrahamic Covenant in causing Israel to worship Baal through King Ahab's wife Jezebel. Israel was already predisposed to it, as mentioned above. The LORD, through Moses and Joshua, warned the people that the Canaanites would be a snare unto them (Deuteronomy 7:16; Joshua 23:13; Judges 2:3). So Sidon fell under the curse of the Abrahamic Covenant because they caused Israel to stumble and fall into gross idolatry. God used foreign empires like Assyria and Babylon to destroy their kingdoms.

Assyria – Cursing
Genesis 10:11, 22; 1 Chronicles 1:17; 5:25-26; 2 Chronicles 33:10-13; Isaiah 10:4-19, 24-34; 20:1-6; 36-37; Nahum 2:2

Asshur, the son of Shem according to Genesis 10:11, 22 and 1 Chronicles 1:17, is the one who founded Nineveh, which became the

---

[132] Youngblood, *Nelson's New Illustrated Bible Dictionary*, 1176-1177.

capital city of the future Assyrian empire. Assyria and Egypt were two of the most significant countries of early history, with Babylon always challenging Assyria for domination. Under the control of Nebuchadnezzar, Babylon destroyed Nineveh (the Assyrian Empire) so thoroughly that it never rose again. The destruction came in three steps as three key cities fell: Nineveh in 612 B.C., Haran in 610 B.C., and Carchemish in 605 B.C.

The timing of Assyria's first real impact on Samaria, the capital of the northern kingdom of Israel, was around 750 B.C., according to 2 Kings 15:19-20. Pul, the king of Assyria, came against the northern kingdom when Menahem ruled in Samaria. King Menahem paid Pul off, and he left Israel; but he took the tribes of Reuben, Gad, and half the tribe of Manasseh into captivity (1 Chronicles 5:25-26). These two-and-a-half tribes would have settled on the east side of the Jordan River in Deuteronomy 32:1-33. So around 750-740 B.C., Pul took two-and-a-half tribes into captivity; and then in 722, the rest of the northern kingdom of Israel fell and went into captivity to Assyria. At that point, King Ahaz of the southern kingdom of Israel (also known as the Kingdom of Judah) became a servant to Assyria.

In 701 B.C., the son of king Ahaz, Hezekiah, revolted against the words of the Prophet Isaiah to remain under tribute to Assyria and was punished by Sennacherib, king of Assyria. However, Sennacherib was unable to take Jerusalem. So from that point to the rise of Babylon, Assyria for the most part controlled the southern kingdom of Israel (Judah), but in a weakened position. Sometime in the later part of King Manasseh's reign in the southern kingdom of Judah, he was taken captive by the Assyrians and then later released (2 Chronicles 33:10-13).

God used other nations that were far more wicked and pagan than Israel to judge Israel. The Prophet Habakkuk later questioned how that could be so as it then related to Babylon (1:12-13). The Assyrians were a ruthless people, striking fear into the hearts of their enemies, as the following quote reveals:

> The Assyrians were merciless and savage people. The Assyrian army was ruthless and effective. Its cruelty included burning cities, burning children, impaling victims on stakes, beheading, and chopping off hands. These people were to be the instrument of God to judge Samaria and Jerusalem.[133]

---

[133] Ibid., 134.

This wicked empire that also would skin people alive made two fatal mistakes, both revolving around their pride. Assyria basically said at two different times, "We are great, and no one and no god can stop us. We have done it ourselves." Although Assyria was to be the tool in the hand of God to judge Israel for its sin, they viewed themselves as all-sufficient, the masters of their own lives. Once again we will see the outworking of the Abrahamic Covenant, this time on the nation of Assyria. The Assyrians flaunted themselves in the face of God, cursing the God of Israel, the God of the Abrahamic Covenant; and they would pay for their words and actions.

In Isaiah 10:5-11, God laid out His argument against Assyria. Assyria was aware that Israel had been given into their hands, but they made some judgments that were based on faulty knowledge. In verse 7, God zeroed in on the heart of Assyria, which was to *destroy and cut off nations*. Now in the following verses, the Assyrian king spilled their hand. In verse 8, the king of Assyria spoke of the kings that were conquered and claimed that he was the king of kings. In verse 9, he spoke of kings that had fallen, and he named six cities. Arpad fell in 740 B.C.; Calno and Hamath fell in 738 B.C.; Damascus fell in 732 B.C.; Samaria fell in 722 B.C.; and Carchemish fell in 717 B.C.

The Assyrian king mocked the gods of the nations and mocked the God of Israel and Judah. He was confused by the corrupted worship going on in Israel and did not understand that the God of apostate Israel was a corrupted form of their worship of the LORD, the only true God. So he compared the God of Israel with the gods of the other nations. He claimed the gods of the nations were not able to help them, and neither would the God of Judah be able to help Judah. These are very foolish words coming out of the mouth of a prideful nation. The Scriptures are correct when they say pride goes before a fall (Proverbs 16:18). In Isaiah 10:13, their pride is stated to their own demise:

> *For he says, by the strength of My hand I have done it, and by My wisdom; for I am prudent: and I have removed the bounds of the people, and have robbed their treasures, and I have put down the inhabitants like a valiant man.*

Their second foolish statement came during the attack on Jerusalem by Sennacherib in 701 B.C., found in 2 Kings 18-19. Rabshakeh, a captain of the Assyrian army, made the same mistake of issuing boastful statements against God while his forces surrounded Jerusalem, as pointed out in Isaiah 10. In other words, in both foolish statements, Israel's Assyrian enemies said that the God of Israel was impotent, powerless to help them. The morning after, the Angel of the LORD went through the Assyrian encampment leaving 185,000 dead Assyrian soldiers. Sennacherib had to retreat and go home, where he was assassinated (Isaiah 37:36-38).

The outworking of the blessings and cursings of the Abrahamic Covenant is sure and will be carried out in judgment against the perpetuators of the curse against the God of the Abrahamic Covenant.

One final point comes from Nahum the Prophet. In his prophecies, he addressed the fate of Assyria, who had plundered many nations including the ten northern tribes of Israel and had emptied those countries of their wealth. Assyria would have the same thing done to them. Notice in Nahum 2:2, 10 that the Assyrians are the *emptiers* of other nations (verse 2), and God will say of them that Assyria will now be *empty, and void, and waste: and the heart melted, and the knees* [smitten] *together, and much pain* [felt] *in all loins, and the faces of them all gather*[ing] *blackness*.

So as they emptied the nations and the cities of Judah, once again we see curse for curse. Assyria, who plundered or emptied Israel and 46 fortified cities of Judah, will now themselves be emptied of their wealth by God, curse for curse. Once again, the blessings and curses of the Abrahamic Covenant remain active in connection with Assyria 1,200 to 1,400 years after the giving of the covenant.

Babylon – Cursing
Genesis 10:8-10; 2 Kings 20:12-19; 24:31-25:9; 2 Chronicles 36; Isaiah 13:1-14:23; 21:1-10; 46:1-47:15; Jeremiah 25:12-14; 50:1-51:63; Revelation 18:1-24

According to Genesis 10:8-10, Nimrod, son of Cush, who was the son of Ham, was the principle force in founding Babel (Babylon) and other cities such as Erech, Accad, and Calneh in the land of Shinar. Genesis 11 speaks to the division of the people in the *plain of Shinar* to force them to spread out over the earth. Despite its long existence, Babylon did not play a role in Israel's history until the days of Hezekiah, when he entertained foreign visitors from Babylon (2 Kings 20:12).

Babylon did not actively come against Judah until the end of the reign of Josiah in 609 B.C. At that point, Babylon besieged Jerusalem and captured it in 606 B.C. That is when Daniel was taken to Babylon. It is at the revolt of Jehoiakim in 596 B.C. that Babylon came again and captured Jerusalem for the second time; in this deportation, Ezekiel the Prophet was taken to Babylon with the captives (2 Kings 24:1-5; 2 Chronicles 36:6-7). Finally,

King Zedekiah also revolted, and Babylon came the third time and destroyed the city of Jerusalem completely in 586 B.C. (2 Kings 24:17-25:9; 2 Chronicles 36:15-21).

Babylon was the heart of all of idolatry, for it all sprung from there to all the ends of the earth. Babylon, in the book of Revelation, is called Mystery, Babylon the Great, the Mother of Harlots, and Abominations of the Earth (Revelation 17:5). This is the legacy of Babylon; it was the source of all idolatry that spread throughout the world, and Babylon will be judged by God. In Jeremiah, chapters 50 through 51, we find that God will judge Babylon; and two judgments are in view. The first judgment came at the hands of the Medes and the Persians in 539 B.C. The second judgment will come at the end of the Great Tribulation period, with the utter and complete destruction. No one will live there again (Isaiah 13:19-22).

Why does God destroy Babylon so severely? In Jeremiah 50:7, one reason given is that Babylon tried to pass off their own sin and blame it on Israel, basically saying Israel had it coming to them:

> *We* [Babylon] *offend not, because they* [Judah] *have sinned against the LORD, the habitation of justice, even the LORD, the hope of their fathers.*

Fruchtenbaum makes an interesting observation concerning the words of Babylon as he relates it to history:

> Notice this verse carefully. People are persecuting the Jews and having persecuted the Jews, hated the Jews, killed the Jews, they then proceed to say that they are not guilty. They say, "We are not guilty. The Jews have brought it upon themselves by forgetting their God." Jews have been called Christ killers. This is a good example that Gentiles fulfill this verse when they try to cover up their own anti-Semitism by saying that the Jews killed the Messiah and therefore it is acceptable to persecute the Jews. This is a good example of fulfilling verse 7, but it is not of divine sanction, as these verses make clear. No one who persecutes the Jews can use Jewish unbelief as a reason for doing so. God will hold those who persecute the Jews responsible. This excuse will not be held in high esteem by God. The fact of Jewish unbelief never gives the Gentiles a free reign to persecute the Jews. I repeat, the fact of Jewish unbelief never gives the Gentiles a free reign to persecute the Jews. God will not

hold anyone guiltless who has animosity against His Jewish people.[134]

God will raise up peoples from the north to judge Babylon. The destruction of Babylon will be the work of God. The Babylonians may hold themselves guiltless for what they did to the Jews, but God will hold them guilty. They believed that the Jews had it coming to them because of their unbelief. Nevertheless, God will destroy Babylon for its own sins and save the Jews.

The Jews were once the prey of Babylon, but now Babylon will be the prey of God because of their own sin. Babylon has its own sinful track record because they have been one of the primary causes of worldwide idolatry. From them arose all the man-made gods, myths, and legends of gods that spread to Egypt, Greece, Rome, and many other places in the world. God will dig out the root and destroy it completely.

Babylon received the active cursing of God 1,300 to 1,500 years after the giving of the covenant, at the hands of the Medes and the Persians in 539 B.C. However, their complete destruction described in Jeremiah 50-51 has yet to be fulfilled, but God will destroy Babylon completely during the Tribulation. There will be no Babylon in the Messianic Kingdom; the outworking of the Abrahamic Covenant will still be in effect well over 4,000 years after God made the covenant with Abraham in Genesis 12. The Abrahamic Covenant was active in the days of Babylon the Great and is still active today, over 2,500 years later.

Summary Points on God's Judging the Nations Who Cursed Israel

In giving my summary points, let us review the points that God makes for the judgments against the nations and see if they fit into the present day events as they relate to Israel in the Land in the twenty-first century:

- Pharaoh and Abimelech, for attempting the potential destruction of Israel even before Isaac was born.

- Laban, for cheating and deceiving Jacob.

---

[134] Arnold G. Fruchtenbaum, *The Book of Isaiah*, Transcription from class at Camp Shoshanah.

- Balaam, for causing Israel to sin against their God and commit immorality.
- Jezebel, for promoting wholesale worship of Baal.
- Athaliah, for killing off the seed of David and for her idolatry.
- Presidents, who were jealous of Daniel.
- Haman, for his personal hatred, pride and jealousy and lack of humility.
- Edom, for perpetual hatred of Israel.
- Moab, for skipping for joy at the derision of Israel.
- Ammon, for rejoicing over Israel's calamity.
- Amalekites, for their unprovoked attack and hostilities on Israel when leaving Egypt.
- Midianites, for intentional actions and attitudes as adversaries of the Jewish people throughout the period of Judges.
- Philistines, for active hostilities by harassing and oppressing Israel from the time of the Judges though the time of King Uzziah.
- Syria, for hostilities and hatred against Israel and attempting to overthrow the House of David.
- Tyre and Sidon, for not upholding the brotherly covenant with Israel and for merchandising Jewish slaves in the Mediterranean world.
- Assyria, for their cruelty to Israel and for cursing the God of Judah.
- Babylon, for their cruelty to Judah and for blaming Israel for their sin as an escape mechanism to avoid their own sins.

Many of these points fit like a glove to the actions, hostilities, outright hatred of Israel, joy over Israel's difficulties we see in the news. It is not only the unsaved who join in with these offenses against God, Israel, and the Jewish people; today, many within Christendom, even Evangelical believers who once believed in the literal interpretation of the Bible, have partaken of the poisoned "Kool-Aid" of the enemies of Israel. If we understand the Jewishness of the Scriptures and the place of Israel in God's plan, we will not curse Israel and be used as a pawn in the anti-Semitic hatred and schemes of Satan.

We saw in the previous chapter the length of years that the Abrahamic Covenant has been active in the lives of individuals. In this chapter we saw the length of years the Abrahamic Covenant has been active in the lives of nations. God made the Covenant with Abraham in 2,000 B.C., and now we see all the nations that have been anti-Semitic or anti-Jewish from 2,000 B.C. to 500 B.C. His judgments against the nations range from 400 to 1,500 years since the covenant was made by God to Abraham. **The Covenant is still in force.** (See Table 5.)

God calls all these countries to judgment for their anti-Semitic attitudes and actions against Israel, but also notice the hundreds of years of God's grace to them before their judgment began.

Now one other point before we move on to the inter-testament period. God, in His grace, gives even anti-Semitic nations mercy in warning of judgment. If you look at the following passage in Jeremiah 27:1-3, we see once again the undeserved mercy and grace of God to pagan people and even to their anti-Semitism.

> *[1] In the beginning of the reign of Zedekiah the son of Josiah king of Judah came this word unto Jeremiah from the LORD, saying, [2] Thus says the LORD to me; Make you bonds and yokes and put them upon your neck, [3] And send them to the king of Edom, and to the king of Moab, and to the king of the Ammonites, and to the king of Tyrus [Tyre], and to the king of Zidon, by the hand of the messengers which come to Jerusalem unto Zedekiah king of Judah.*

All of these nations were to submit to and serve Nebuchadnezzar King of Babylon. In verse 7, we see that *all nations shall serve him and his son and his son's son*. If they chose not to serve Nebuchadnezzar, Jeremiah, who is speaking for the LORD, says in verse 8, *that nation will I punish*. That punishment is then given or described as follows, *with the sword, and with the famine and with pestilence, until I have consumed them by his* [Nebuchadnezzar's] *hand*.

Table 5. Summary of God's National Blessings and Cursings

Nation	# Yrs. after the Abrahamic Covenant	Bible Reference	Reason for God's Blessing or Cursing under the Abrahamic Covenant
Egypt	400	Moses states in Exodus 1:8-22	Cursed because of Egypt's slavery and brutality of Israel
Amalek	400 – 1500	Exodus 17:14; Deuteronomy 25:17-19	Cursed because of their enmity against Israel
Midian	400 – 600	Numbers 25; Judges 6	Cursed because they caused Israel to sin at the counsel of Balaam and during the period of Gideon, the Judge
Kenites	400 – 1400	Exodus 3:1; Judges 1:16; 4:17; Numbers 24:21-22; 1 Samuel 15:6; Jeremiah 35:7-10	Blessed of God because of their friendship with Israel.
Edom	450 – 1900	Amos 1:11	Cursed because of their perpetual hatred for Israel.
Moab	450 – 1350	Jeremiah 49:27	Cursed because they skipped with joy at the demise of Israel, mocked Israel, and wagged their heads at Israel.
Ammon	450 – 1800	Amos 1:13	Cursed because they ripped open pregnant Gadites in Gilead to inherit their land.
Damascus (Syria)	1100 – 1500	Amos 1:4	Cursed because of killing the citizens of Gad by use of threshing instruments and because they threatened to remove the Davidic dynasty from Israel.
Philistia	900 – 1400	Amos 1:6	Cursed because they carried away Israelis as captives and sold them to Edom as slaves.
Tyre & Sidon	1200 – 1600	Amos 1:9	Cursed because they traded Israeli citizens as slaves with the Philistines, Ammon, and Edom.
Assyria	1200 – 1400	Isaiah 36:18-20	Cursed because of Sennacherib's general Rabshakeh's cursing of the God of Israel.
Babylon	1300 – 1500	Jeremiah 50-51; Isaiah 13:9-22	Their pride and thirst for riches, their going beyond their God-given right to judge Judah, rejection of the God of Israel which was demonstrated to them through Daniel and his three friends. Rejection of Daniel's counsel (Daniel 4:27).

All of these nations that we have looked at in the chapter were going to be judged because of their anti-Semitism against the Jewish people (as well as their own personal sin of paganism). Even the people of Edom, who had perpetual hatred for Esau's twin brother, Israel (Jacob), were included for judgment. God's waiting gives them a door of opportunity to change and receive God's grace and mercy. However, most of them did not change. Even with all the possibility of receiving God's grace and mercy, they will not serve Nebuchadnezzar. Jeremiah then gives us the following outworking of the cursing of the Abrahamic Covenant from Genesis 12:3 in Jeremiah 30:16. Look at this verse carefully:

> *Therefore* **all they** [the anti-Semitic nations] **that devour you** [Israel] **shall be devoured**; *and all your adversaries, every one of them, shall go into captivity; and* **they that spoil you shall be a spoil,** *and* **all that prey upon you will I give for a prey**.

If they **devoured** Israel, they would be devoured by God through Nebuchadnezzar, King of Babylon. All those nations that **spoiled** Israel would in turn be spoiled by Babylon. All those nations that **preyed** on Israel would themselves become prey to Babylon. Also, notice that when God curses an individual or nation, He will curse **kind for kind**; and that is what you have clearly presented here in the book of Jeremiah.

Now the promises of God laid out in the verses above related to the anti-Semitic nations in and before Jeremiah's day. However, the principle of cursing and blessing from the Abrahamic Covenant does not pertain to just Jeremiah's day, but to OUR day as well. As I said before, anti-Semitic words, attitudes, and actions were taken very seriously by God, whether it was 300 years after God made the covenant with Abraham of 1,400 years after giving the covenant. Just as in Jeremiah's day, the Abrahamic Covenant given 4,000 years ago relates equally to individuals and nations in the twenty-first century. God remembers even when man brushes it aside and purposely rejects it. Even when man does not know anything about the Abrahamic Covenant, mankind is still responsible for it.

So look out, England, Germany, Spain, Russia, Poland, and Europe in general. Look out, Muslim world; the ultimate day of judgment for anti-Semitism against the Jewish people and Israel are fast approaching. Look out, Palestinian Christians and Muslims! Look out, France, as you seek to divide Israel from its Land. Look out America, because the Obama administration you voted into office has cursed Israel by approving in December 2016 a United Nations Security Council vote making it international law that Israel is guilty of possessing occupied land. We have now placed ourselves under the judgment of God. Look out, Evangelical Christians who do not believe in the Abrahamic Covenant or who neglect it. Look out, Protestant denominations that stand against Israel; your day of judgment is coming.

Chapter 11
The Outworking of the Abrahamic Covenant During the Inter-Testament Period

King Seleucus IV of Syria – Cursing
Daniel 8:9-14; 11:21-35; 12:11; 1 & 2 Maccabees; Matthew 24:15

In the third century B.C., in the period that is called the Inter-Testamental period or "the 400 Silent Years," there was a struggle between the Greek Ptolemies of Egypt and the Greek Syrian Seleucids of Syria. In that power struggle, Israel found herself caught in the middle between the two warring factions. Around 200 B.C., the Syrians finally took control under the leadership of Antiochus Epiphanes. He wanted to consolidate his power by forcing the Jewish people to Hellenize, meaning they were to cast off their Jewish culture and customs, their Scriptures, in short, everything that made them Jewish and accept Greek gods and culture.

Antiochus Epiphanes, in his fury against the Jewish people, polluted the temple by offering a pig on the altar and setting up a statue of Zeus. The Bible shows that a similar, shocking desecration of the rebuilt Temple will occur during the seven-year Tribulation that is yet to come. In fact, when the Jewish people of that future time see this occur, they are to flee to a place in Scripture referred to as the wilderness, to the mountains, to a place in Hebrew called Bozrah and in the Greek called Petra.

Antiochus was set on wiping out Judaism and the Jewish people. Like other anti-Semitic figures through history, he tried to force Jewish practices out of existence. Jewish people were not to circumcise their sons, observe the Sabbath, or read the Scriptures. Torah scrolls were destroyed, and Jewish people died if they resisted. This threat was not the destruction of all the Jews initially, but it was the destruction of everything that made them Jewish. Ultimately, if left unchecked, this campaign could have destroyed the Jewish people and prevented the coming of the Messiah.

We read in the Apocryphal[135] books of the Maccabees the type of man Antiochus was and his ruthlessness:

2 Maccabees 5:11-14

When these happenings were reported to the king, he thought that Judea was in revolt. Raging like a wild animal, he set out from Egypt and took Jerusalem by storm. He ordered his soldiers to cut down without mercy those whom they met and to slay those who took refuge in their houses. There was a massacre of young and old, a killing of women and children, a slaughter of virgins and infants. In the space of three days, eighty thousand were lost, forty thousand meeting a violent death, and the same number being sold into slavery.

2 Maccabees 6:1-11

Not long after this, the king sent an Athenian senator to force the Jews to abandon the customs of their ancestors and live no longer by the laws of God; also to profane the temple in Jerusalem and dedicate it to Olympian Zeus, and that on Mount Gerizim to Zeus the Hospitable, as the inhabitants of the place requested...They also brought into the temple things that were forbidden, so that the altar was covered with abominable offerings prohibited by the laws. A man could not keep the Sabbath or celebrate the traditional feasts, nor even admit that he was a Jew. At the suggestion of the citizens of Ptolemais, a decree was issued ordering the neighboring Greek cities to act in the same way against the Jews: oblige them to partake of the sacrifices, and put to death those who would not consent to adopt the customs of the Greeks. It was obvious, therefore, that disaster impended. Thus, two women who were arrested for having circumcised their children were publicly paraded about the city with their babies hanging at their breasts and then thrown down from the top of the city wall. Others, who had assembled in nearby caves to

---

[135] The Apocrypha consists of 14 (or some sources say more) books written between the last prophet Malachi and the writing of the four gospels, the period called the 400 Silent Years. These books were not accepted as Scripture in the Hebrew Bible by the Jewish religious leaders. They are not considered authoritative, but were valuable as simply literature. Here are two reasons why they were never accepted: (1) They have historical and geographical inaccuracies; (2) They teach doctrines which are false, confirming they are NOT inspired Scripture. Only the books of First and Second Maccabees have accurate historical information.

observe the Sabbath in secret, were betrayed to Philip and all burned to death.

In 171 B.C., in his crowning outrage, in his supreme atrocity, Antiochus erected a statue of Zeus in the Jewish Temple and sacrificed a pig on the altar in the Temple compound itself. Afterward, Greek Syrian soldiers would go from Jewish town to town and force a Jewish sympathizer to offer a pig on the town altar. On one occasion, they came to the village of Modin, which was located at the northern edge of the Shephelah (lowlands). In a surprise move, an old priest by the name of Mattathias Maccabee prevented the sacrifice from being made. The old priest killed the sympathizer who was a Jewish man from Modin who was assisting with the sacrifice, and then his five sons killed the Greek soldiers.

The Maccabees fled to the Judean hills and formed a guerrilla army. This triggered the uprising known as the Maccabean revolt. In the year 165 B.C., Judah Maccabee liberated Jerusalem from the Greeks and the Second Temple from its defilement. The Temple was then rededicated for worship with great public rejoicing that lasted for eight days. Judah Maccabee then declared that future celebrations of Hanukkah should last for eight days as well.

Antiochus Epiphanes cursed the God of Israel by cursing Israel in a very active way, opposing the Jewish way of life and their biblical practices. He removed their freedom to practice their religion, and they were forced to indulge in practices that were repulsive to them and went against their consciences. He overrode their Scriptures, the feasts, circumcision, as well as the Sabbath rest. The Syrian leader and his army were later completely thrown out of Israel. The outworking of the cursings of Genesis 12:3 was that Antiochus Epiphanes and his Greek Syrian armies were judged by the same God who used the Maccabees to oppose them and restore the Temple and biblical worship to the people of Israel.

Summary Points

- Antiochus Epiphanes was completely defeated by the guerrilla force of the Maccabees because of his anti-Semitic attitude and actions.

- Greek Syrian Seleucids – 1,800 years after the giving of the Abrahamic Covenant, the Abrahamic Covenant with God's blessings and cursings was still in force!

- Principle: So far in history, all who stand against Israel – whether individuals or individual nations – will suffer punishment from the hand of God, and all individuals who bless Israel will be blessed.

Chapter 12
The Outworking of the Abrahamic Covenant in the New Testament

Centurion of Capernaum – Blessing
Luke 7:2-10

Now we understand from history that Rome tolerated the Jewish people and all their peculiarities. The Roman soldiers did not like, and for the most part, did not want to be in this land with all these unique laws and a God that you could not see. On the other side of the coin, the Jewish people could not stand to have the Romans occupying their country. Thus, the feelings were mutual, and there was constant tension between the two nations. Yet here in this passage, we find a Roman centurion in Capernaum who was a lover of Israel. How unusual! That is the context of this passage.

In this passage, we will see the outworking of the blessing aspect of the Abrahamic Covenant to a Roman centurion. This man has a love for Israel, and he showed his love by building a synagogue for the Jewish people in Capernaum. He also understood authority, that when a person in authority makes a command, the command will be carried out. So he understood who Yeshua was and believed that He had the authority to heal his servant, just by His command.

Here we see the outworking of the blessing of the Abrahamic Covenant on a centurion because of his love and what he had done: Yeshua (Jesus) healed the centurion's servant without even entering his house.

Yeshua made the statement about this centurion, *I have not found so great Faith, no, not in Israel;* and that was said of a Roman centurion.

Syro-Phoenician Woman – Blessing
Matthew 15:21-28; Mark 7:24-30

Here we have an instance of a Gentile woman being blessed because of the promised blessings that will flow from the Abrahamic Covenant. In this passage, the Gentile woman comes to Yeshua (Jesus) and asks for a healing of her daughter on the basis of His Messianic Person, and He does not answer her, a Gentile Syro-Phoenician woman from the coasts of Tyre and Sidon (Lebanon today).

Then Yeshua says to her, *I am not sent but to the lost sheep of the house of Israel*. So she re-phrases her request on the basis of personal need and not on the basis of His Messiahship, for two reasons: first, because Yeshua was rejected as the Messiah in chapter 12 of Matthew, and second because He came to *the lost sheep of the house of Israel* and not to the Gentiles. So now she asks as a Gentile, on the basis of personal need.

Yeshua, wanting to make sure that this Gentile woman understood the issue, says, *It is not meet* [good] *to take the children's bread* [Israel's bread], *and to cast it to dogs* [Gentiles – puppies]. The Gentile woman answers Him by saying, *Truth, Lord: Yet the dogs eat of the crumbs which fall from their master's table*. Yeshua responds to her, calling her Faith great; then He heals her daughter. This woman had great insight into the difference between Jew and Gentile and her place as a Gentile. Because her attitude and understanding were positive to Israel, she was granted her request of her daughter's healing.

The Gentile woman in her second statement showed that she understood that Yeshua had come to the Jewish people. Yet the Gentiles receive of the promises that flow from the covenants with promised blessing to the Gentiles, as Genesis 12:1-3 states. Because she understood this, she was blessed by Yeshua with the healing of her daughter. The point is not the healing, but her Faith and her understanding of the covenantal outworkings, that the Gentiles will be blessed through these promises. She had blessed Israel by understanding her position as a Gentile in relationship to the Abrahamic Covenant. As the result of her positive attitude and Faith, God's blessings in turn flowed to her, blessings for blessings.

Centurion Cornelius – Blessing
Acts 10:22

The next example that the Scriptures give is of another centurion. Notice the biblical description of him that the Scriptures give. He was *a righteous man and one that fears God, and well reported of by all the nation of the Jews.* Look at verse 25. Even though it is biblically incorrect to bow and worship a man, which Peter immediately corrects, notice the heart of the Roman centurion, that he would humble himself and bow and worship a Jew.

The outworking of the blessings of the Abrahamic Covenant was not only to a Roman centurion – a Gentile – but through this Gentile in Acts 10; God opened the door of salvation to all Gentiles, which was inaugurated by Yeshua with the **Blood** of the New Covenant at the cross of Calvary. This is borne out in Acts 11 as Peter has to defend himself before other believing Jews; these Gentiles received the same outpouring of the Holy Spirit as they did themselves at Pentecost in Acts 2 (see 10:44; 11:15; 15:7-11).

What do these three New Testament examples show us? We see that God is eager to bless those who bless Israel in attitude and action. The Syro-Phoenician woman and both centurions are examples of this love and blessing of Israel, as demonstrated by the declaration of the Jewish people living around them.

It is obvious to see that the blessings promised in Genesis 12:3 are still at work 2,000 years after being given to Abraham. God is serious about what He says! Keep this thought in mind as I begin to answer the question at the beginning of this paper: Would foreign missions have been more blessed of God if all missions loved Israel and showed it by their attitude and actions in reaching out to the Jewish people within the countries where they serve?

Alexander the Coppersmith – Cursing
2 Timothy 4:14-16

In the second epistle to Timothy, his son in the Faith, Paul encouraged Timothy to continue to walk in the Faith. In this chapter, he also warned Timothy of a coming apostasy by those in the Church. In chapter 4, Paul mentioned Alexander the coppersmith (who may also have been one of the two men excommunicated by Paul in 1 Timothy 1:20). It is somewhat conjecture, but it appears that Alexander testified against Paul at his Roman trial. There is also an Alexander in Acts 19:33-34 who was a Hellenized Jew in Ephesus. We do not know for certain his exact identity, or if it was the same person Paul speaks of in 2 Timothy. What we do know is that Paul called down a curse on him for doing much evil.

Now if Alexander was a Greek and not Jewish, you also have Paul referencing the curse on Gentiles given in the Abrahamic Covenant of Genesis 12:3. Again, it is kind for kind as Paul states, *the Lord reward him according to his works*. If he was a Gentile believer who later apostatized, Paul is still calling on *the Lord to reward him according to his works*.

Summary Points

- 2,000 years ago God promised Abraham that those who bless him and his descendants would receive God's blessing. These three examples point this out very clearly.

- Centurion of Capernaum was blessed because of his love for Israel.

- Syro-Phoenician woman as a Gentile was blessed because she understood her place in relation to Israel.

- Centurion Cornelius was blessed because he feared the LORD and because he was also a lover of Israel.

- Alexander the coppersmith was cursed because he opposed Paul's work to spread the Gospel.

Chapter 13
The Outworking of the Abrahamic Covenant in Post-Biblical History

It will appear that I am very hard on the Church and countries of Europe in this chapter. I am dealing with the facts of Church history, and the historical facts of these countries are readily available. However, most people never bother to research it out before making judgments or decisions, especially when an issue relates to Israel.

What I have to say, you yourself can search out from documented authorities and resources. I am only dealing with the sin of the Church and countries as they relate to the blessings and cursings of the Abrahamic Covenant. I am not even touching the other sins of these churches and countries: their greed for power, wealth, and prestige and their spiritual abuses. I am not dealing with their evil plots, murders, thefts, manipulation of the population, their sinful pride, the sanctioning of immoral sins and so on. Our focus is on how Gentile countries, the Church, and Gentile peoples in general have treated the Jewish people.

The Church of Rome – Cursing
Matthew 13:31-32; Mark 4:30-33; Romans 16:17-18; 2 Corinthians 11:3-4; 2 Peter 2:1-3, 10-22; Jude; Revelation 2-3; 17:1-7

The organized body called the Church, including elements of the actual believing Church, has been the largest anti-Semitic organization on the planet! This will be demonstrated by four examples from "Christian" countries as well as the Islamic world in general. I will not attempt to repeat all of Church/Jewish history, so I will just give some general headings without lengthy explanations.

These examples are only a sampling of decade upon decade, century upon century, of anti-biblical, demonic, satanic, inhuman responses to the

Jewish people, totally contradicting the words of Jesus Himself to LOVE our enemies. Below is just a sampling of what the (Catholic and Orthodox) Church has done in the name of Jesus that Jesus NEVER condoned. These acts have been done to the Jewish people century after century after century:

Spiritualization of Scripture: Early Church councils began the move to take the Jewishness out of the Bible and replace it with Gentile spiritualization and allegorical interpretation based on the Church Father Origen. That pattern has only increased in speed and intensity as the centuries rolled on to this very day.

Economic Discrimination: Jewish people have been forbidden to enter trades, own real estate, or hold political office.

Removal of Civil Rights: Jewish people were forced to live in servitude to Christians.

Forced Conversions: Christians have given Jewish people the ultimatum: be baptized, tormented, or die by hanging, being burned at the stake, or by the edge of the sword.

Marriage Discrimination: Marriage between a Jew and a Christian has been considered adultery.

Pogroms: Unspeakable atrocities and demonic actions have been committed by people in riotous mobs who called themselves Christians, often with the sanction of the Orthodox and/or the Catholic Church.

Ghettos: There has been separation of the Jewish people from us (Christians), because they were supposedly not worthy to live among us (Christians), being forced by Christians to live in walled areas in cities and forced to live in designated areas in the countryside. Ghettos were first instituted in the Catholic country of Italy. The largest ghetto, called the "Pale of Settlement," was created in parts of Ukraine, western Russia, and Poland. From those horrors we get the term *beyond the Pale,* meaning something horrible beyond description.

Blood Libel Accusations: These have been utterly false claims that Jews were killing Christian children and using their blood in Passover. The results were Christian mobs descending on innocent Jewish communities, burning, raping, killing, stealing, and plundering Jews.

Host Desecration Accusation: This is the false accusation that Jewish people were stealing the Host, the wafer used in the Mass of the Catholic Church, to stab it so that they could inflict more pain on Jesus. Again, this false accusation has resulted in Christian mobs descending upon innocent Jewish communities, burning, raping, killing, stealing and plundering Jewish people.

The Black Plague Accusation: This accusation was used by Luther and others because Jewish people were not dying from the plague like the "Christian" public, so the Jews must have poisoned the springs and wells. We today know that the plague was passed on by rats in an unclean environment. The Jewish people kept kosher laws, thus were cleaner and habitually washed their hands before eating.

82 Banishments from Regions or Countries: Jews were banished from England, France, Portugal, Spain, and Germany or regions within those countries. No wonder you have the phrase "the wandering Jew."

Persecution: Inspired by Satan, persecutions in every way imaginable, in ways that are too inhuman to put into writing, have been carried out towards Jewish people

"Jews are greedy" Stereotyping: They are no greedier than anyone else. The welfare class in the U.S. shows the same trait of greed in wanting free money and benefits without having to work for it. Jewish people work for it. Jewish people often became wealthy, and it was not because of being greedy; it was because of one of the promises of blessing to the Jewish people in the Abrahamic Covenant.

"Jews are all wealthy" Stereotyping: No, there have always been poor Jewish people. Moses (Deuteronomy 15:11) and Jesus (Yeshua) (Matthew 26:11) both make this point. Ironically, it is the apostate church of the Middle Ages that taught the Jewish people how to make money in the banking industry. The Church used the Jewish people as money lenders since in the Medieval Church it was against the law for Christians to charge interest on loans to other Christians, so the Jews became wealthy and then were persecuted for doing so.

"Jews are clannish" Stereotyping: You would stick together, too, if you were persecuted for eighteen centuries by people who said they were Christians!

Beating and Murdering of Jews: Often, with the complete sanction of the Church, Jews were beaten or murdered; some of these attacks were unimaginable in horror, even unspeakable.

Destruction of Synagogues: These destructive actions were sanctioned by Christian leaders like Chrysostom and Luther as well as others. The Jewish people of Germany will never forget Kristallnacht, the night of November 10, 1938, when hundreds of synagogues were burned to the ground and thousands of Jewish shops looted or burned. What was their crime? They were Jews.

Destruction of Villages: The Crusaders of Europe and the Cassocks of Ukraine and the Pogroms[136] of Russia, to name only three examples, savagely slew thousands upon thousands of Jews while they also completely destroyed Jewish villages with the sanction of the Orthodox Christian Church and the Catholic Church.

Raping of Multitudes of Jewish Women: The Crusaders were guilty of rape.

Martyrdoms: Christian Zionists who believed that Israel still had a future – for example, Frances Kett in 1589 – were persecuted.

Confiscation of Jewish Property, such as land and buildings.

Forced Indoctrination of Children: Jewish children were forcibly taken from their homes and families, and were indoctrinated with Christianity.

---

[136] Pogroms: Organized massacres of a particular ethnic group, in particular that of Jews in Russia or Eastern Europe. Synonyms for pogrom include: massacre, slaughter, mass murder, annihilation, extermination, decimation, carnage, bloodbath, bloodletting, butchery, genocide, holocaust, purge, ethnic cleansing.

Church Father Augustine's "Witness People" Claim: That God let the Jewish people live on in misery instead of destroying them as a perpetual witness against them for their crime in killing Christ.

The Inquisition: Unspeakable, sadistic tormentors in Spain and South and Central America who used stretching racks, the iron maiden (torture device), and other hideous methods of torture and murder.

The Crusades in Europe and Palestine: More Jews were killed by armed assaults in Europe by the Crusaders than were killed in Palestine by the Crusaders as they went to "liberate the Holy Land."

Publication of Lies: *The Protocols of the Elders of Zion*: This lie-filled book originated in Orthodox Russia, and Henry Ford later financed it to be printed in America; he was also an anti-Semite. Radical Islam today promotes the same lie with the same book re-published in Arabic.

Hatred and Insults: Jews have been called Christ killers and have had their youth beaten up by mobs of "christian" youth. Why? Through the ages until today, Jewish people have been blamed for killing Christ. Even in America there used to be signs that said "no blacks or Jews." These examples can go on and on; they are legion.

Wearing of the Star of David: Jews had to wear a Star of David made of yellow cloth on their clothing to point them out and to keep them separate from the "Christian" population. This was forced on them by the Church at different points in history and by the Nazis of Germany.

Anti-Semitic Christian Literary Works: The purpose of these works was to spread the lies of the Church against the Jews to poison the minds and hearts of the laity.

Labeling Jews as Christ Killers: Christians have blamed the Jews for deicide, the Murder of Jesus, by applying their claim to all Jews from the Cross forward to today.

Death by Fire and Hanging: Jewish people have been burned at the stake as well as hanged.

Naming the Jewish People an Inferior Race: The Nazis made the attempt to remove them from off the planet, using terms like *vermin,* leading to the concept of extermination. This was also a bi-product of Darwin's Theory of Evolution which helped build the concept of the Aryan race as superior.

Allegorical Teaching: This technique has been applied and is still being applied to Scripture to make the Jews look bad and the Church look good.

Holocaust: The Nazis eventually attempted to murder all Jewish people and others by branding them as racially inferior, thus purging Europe of 12 million people.

Most Christians today have never heard of these things because this history is not taught in our Bible Colleges and Seminaries or in the churches. As a result, few are familiar with the many crimes and atrocities perpetrated upon Jewish people. Church history books do not mention the multiple centuries of crimes against the Jewish people by the Church. For anyone interested in learning more, here is a list of some books written by lovers of Israel that expose the anti-Semitism of the Church from the third century to today:

> Michael L. Brown, *Our Hands Are Stained With Blood* (Shippensburg, PA: Destiny Image, 1990).
>
> James Daane, *The Anatomy of Anti-Semitism and Other Essays on Religion and Race* (Grand Rapids, MI: Erdmann Publishing, 1965).
>
> Richard E. Gade, *A Historical Survey of Anti-Semitism* (Grand Rapids, MI: Baker Book House, 1981).
>
> William Heinrich, *In the Shame of Jesus* (Keller, TX: JHousePublishing, Purple Raiment Label, 2016) or see either Evidence of Truth Ministries or www.PromisesToIsrael.org
>
> William Heinrich, *Reality Denied: The Inconvenient Truth about the Palestinian-Israeli Conflict* (Witmer, PA: Evidence of Truth Ministries, 2008-2011).

Olivier J. Melnick, *They Have Conspired Against You: Responding to the New Anti-Semitism* (Huntington Beach, CA: JHousePublishing, Purple Raiment label, 2007).

In the next section of this book, we will see the outworking of the Abrahamic Covenant as it will relate to the Church in future prophecy. Suffice to say the Church has not been an example to the Jewish people of the love of Yeshua for His physical brethren.

The apostate church has cursed the Jew and in so doing has cursed God. The Church has in many ways become a reprobate organization of apostates who have corrupted the Gospel and the Word of God. Their punishment began with the Asian hordes that destroyed Rome, continued with the Muslim invasions and the Reformation (a positive judgment), and will be completed at the middle of the Tribulation (Revelation 17) by the hand of the Antichrist who will be worshipped. Antichrist will destroy the apostate church, for he will be presenting himself as god to be worshipped. So there is no confusion concerning the Church, the true body of Messiah – the Church – will be raptured out of this world before the Tribulation period. However, the apostate non-believers who call themselves Christians will go into the Tribulation. Under his one world religion, the Antichrist will destroy the apostate church. His desire is to be worshipped, so he dispenses with the apostate church.

The Church through History

The Church has felt the impact of God's response to anti-Semitism through judgments. Nevertheless, error has continued through history, resulting in persecution of Jewish people. In the previous pages, I have listed in detail the sin of the Church, but I only deal with its relationship to Jewish people and to Israel. The Church's bad behavior has caused the Almighty to judge the Church.

1. The Church was judged first at the hands of the hordes that invaded Rome in (476 A.D.), but the Church did not learn from that judgment.

2. The Church was judged a second time, this time at the hands of Islam, when Islam conquered North Africa, the Middle East, Turkey, southern Russia, and even parts of Europe, territory which was all Christian and was lost to Mohammed and his Islam. Sadly, the Church did not learn from that judgment either.

3. In a third instance, the Roman Catholic Church persecuted the remnants of biblical Faith (who were not without error) with the massacres of the Waldensians, Albigensians, and the Huguenots. These were the forerunners of the Reformation which the Church tried to silence.

4. Fourth, the Roman Catholic Church came under judgment by God at the Reformation, even though some Reformers, such as Martin Luther, were not consistent in their teachings related to the Jewish people. Overall, in the Reformation, the Jewish people were treated somewhat better, but often not much better than before.

5. Today, both apostate Christianity and biblical Christianity are being threatened by Islam.

6. Many of the churches of the Reformation today have once again come out against Israel in support of Israel's enemies. True biblical believers who are supporters of Israel are, sadly, in the minority within the churches of the Reformation.

7. Lastly, the Church will be judged finally and completely. The apostate church will be destroyed by the beast upon which it rides in Revelation 17 at the middle of the Tribulation, never to arise again.

Now as we move on to individual nations in post-biblical history, we have to understand that much of what happened in Spain, England, Germany, and Russia was a direct result of the twisted teaching of the Bible by various expressions of the Church. Roman Catholicism, Russian Orthodoxy, the apostatizing of the Church of England, and the entrance of secular humanist thought incubated pure hatred into the state Churches that polluted the minds and hearts of peoples of those countries. This is the baggage the Church has carried from its theological foundations of error, beginning in the second century, resulting in anti-Jewish words, actions, and Church philosophy for the centuries that have followed.

As we will see, the outworking of God was still there and working to discipline the Church over 2,500 years from the giving of the Abrahamic Covenant by means of the invading barbarian hordes coming from Asia and Eastern Europe. Two hundred years later, the Church also suffered God's judgment as a result of the invasion of Islam. A third time, the Church was purged, this time 3,500 years after the Abrahamic Covenant, by means of the

Protestant Reformation. The final judgment of the apostate church will occur in the Tribulation over 4,000 years removed from the giving of the Abrahamic Covenant.

God, regardless of time, keeps His eternal covenant with Abraham and his descendants. God showed great long-suffering, mercy, and patience while the Church in its various expressions has cursed God by cursing Israel; and God, because of the covenant He made with Abraham, has judged her and will judge her. He will reward blessings with blessings and cursings with cursings, just as He does with all groups and individuals.

Europe – Cursings and a Blessing

The east and western expressions of the Church, Roman Church in the West and the Orthodox Church in the East, set the tone against Jewish people starting in the second century. Their influence spread to Western Europe, Eastern Europe, and Russia. The injustice and unbiblical propaganda spewed out against the Jewish people by the historical Church will invoke the judgment of God. A payday is coming, and God will pour out His wrath in the Tribulation period as He judges the Gentile peoples, and especially Europe and Russia, for millennia of atrocities against God's chosen people, the Jewish people.

Remember what God said in the Abraham Covenant: If anyone or any nation curses Abraham and his descendants, God will curse them in return. Many in the Gentile Church have never studied the Scriptures from a Jewish perspective and have no clue what the Abrahamic Covenant means to them, but they are still accountable. They are more interested in their apostate, fallen Christianity, even though it has no resemblance to the heart of the God of Scripture nor to the spotless Bride of Jesus Christ. There are unfortunately so many examples of faithlessness on the part of the Church.

In **Spain,** thousands of Jewish people fell prey to the continuous recurring riots and massacres in the fourteenth and fifteenth centuries. In **Spain, Switzerland, Germany, and France,** thousands more were massacred because of the false accusation that the Jewish people were responsible for the Black Plague. That plague may have killed half the European population in the fourteenth century. **England** had the first recorded Blood Libel case, and that would spread over Europe in the centuries that followed. In the seventeenth century, Eastern European countries like **Poland** were deeply involved in the deaths of over 100,000

Jewish people by the Orthodox Church. **Ukraine** was not exempt from other atrocities. It has also been documented that the Cossacks of Poland between 1648 and 1658 destroyed over 700 communities of Jewish people along with 100,000 murdered in the name of Christ.

One source said the following, that the Greek Orthodox Cossacks of that period (in the 17th century) ravaged Jews with startling savagery, sawing them to pieces, flaying them alive, roasting them to death over slow fires – even slitting infants in half with their swords.

This is not all, thanks to Charles Darwin and his Theory of Evolution that began a movement called "Social Darwinism." He taught the survival of the fittest, which appealed to those with satanic hearts. The Aryans believed they were superior, carrying so-called pure bloodlines, while the Jewish people were inferior. This belief fell into place with Hitler's Final Solution, to kill all the Jewish people. Statements many centuries before by Martin Luther added gasoline to the anti-Semitic hatred that was already on fire in wicked hearts, helping to usher in the Holocaust of World War II.

Spain – Cursing

The Spaniards finally succeeded in taking control of their country from the Moors (Islam) in 1300 and conquered the last remnant of the Moors from Granada in 1492. Spain was a Roman Catholic country with a very large presence of Sephardic Jewish people (those who are mainly Spanish speaking and influenced by the Spanish culture) who had been living there since before the time of Christ. Remember that it was Paul's desire to go to Spain and preach the Gospel (Romans 15:24), and he did.

Under the Moors, Jewish culture expanded culturally, intellectually, and religiously under Muslim control. However, when the Moors were finally pushed out by Catholic Spain, many Jews were murdered in places like Toledo and other cities. The Roman Catholic Church re-exerted itself by pressuring King Ferdinand and Queen Isabella to persecute the Jews. Roman Church theological baggage brought along with it anti-Semitic words, actions, and policies within Spanish culture. Over the coming century, anti-Semitism rose sharply so that by 1492, the Jewish people were evicted from the country of Spain. As an example, let me give the following quotation:

> During the latter half of the 14th century, hostility towards the Jews spread through the Peninsula [of Spain], but the civic authorities furnished the Jews some protection, and usually the outrages were

summarily suppressed. Official protection, however, ultimately proved disastrous. On Ash Wednesday of 1391 an unreasoning Church dignitary, Ferrand Martinez, incited a riot in Seville, during which the Jewish quarter was burnt down. The governor at once arrested two of the ringleaders and, as a warning to other rioters, ordered them to be flogged. The severity of the governor infuriated the community, and when an opportunity came, in June, to assault the Jews with impunity, an orgy of bloodshed began. In Seville several thousand were butchered, other thousands were driven into baptism to escape death, and hundreds were sold as slaves to the Moors.

The riots spread like a plague, undoubtedly stimulated as much by the desire for plunder as by religious bigotry. In Cordoba, once the proudest center of Jewish life, the whole Jewish quarter was destroyed, and the 2,000 Jews who were slain were left in heaps in the streets. Toledo, with the largest Jewish population in Spain, was ravaged, probably on the 9th of Av, the anniversary of Jerusalem's downfall, and the brutality of the mobs gave the day a doubly tragic meaning. About 70 cities of Old Castile were thus devastated and a trail of broken homes and broken hearts was left in the wake of the bloody hooligans.

From Castile the fury spread to Aragon, where the well-meaning king, John I, was too weak to make his authority felt. One town learned quickly from another how to pillage and destroy. The fertile province of Valencia, the prosperous seaport of Barcelona, even the islands off the coast of Spain, were all swept by the ferocity of the persecutors. After 3 months the orgy ended, with thousands of Jewish lives snuffed out and tens of thousands of forced baptisms. Germany and Austria were paradise now in comparison with ensanguined Spain.[137]

What a sad state of affairs for the Jewish people in Spain! What a sad day for the name of Christ as it was also persecuted and tarnished by those Christians who perpetrated the vicious acts of anti-Semitic terrorism!

That anti-Semitism eventually became codified into what we know as the **Inquisition,** which was nothing more than sanctioned religious brutality,

---

[137] Abram Leon Sachar, *A History of the Jews* (New York, NY: Alfred A. Knopf, 1958), 206.

torture, slaughter, murder, and the butchering of Jewish people. It began in 1492 and was not legally abolished until 1992. In 1492, at the hands of King Ferdinand of Aragon and Queen Isabella of Castile, the Jews of Spain were evicted, perhaps as many as 300,000, by the General Edict on The Expulsion of the Jews from Spain. The Jewish people went to the countries that surrounded the Mediterranean Sea and to the New World.

God would provide a whole new land that would eventually be a safe haven for the Jewish people: the United States of America. Christopher Columbus was a Jew for whom wealthy Spanish Jews purchased three ships for him to discover the New World; it was a Jew who first saw land, and it was a Jew who first set foot in the New World.[138]

Spain had become very wealthy and powerful with its naval armada controlling the seas. In July 1588, the Spanish Armada sailed to conquer England. The English did not defeat them; instead, the LORD God of Israel that they had cursed defeated them with the sea itself, and Spain has never recovered from that loss, even until today. Spain also in time lost much of its holdings in the New World. So in 1588, God judged Spain for cursing Israel, the Jewish people.

Spain with its anti-Semitic attitude and actions suffered great losses. **First,** they lost a rich source of her scholars, doctors, and bankers: the Jewish people. **Second**, the Spanish economy began to crumble; and, **finally,** its source of strength, their navy, was destroyed by God because Spain cursed the Jewish people and the God of Israel Who had made the Abrahamic Covenant with their ancestor Abraham.

So in brief, Spain, because of anti-Semitism rooted in Roman Catholicism, was judged by God for cursing Abraham and his descendants. God's promises were once again found true as He rewarded national anti-Semitism with curses for curses in kind, just as He consistently had done with all other nations before them. The ramifications of the outworking of the Abrahamic Covenant were still active 3,500-3,600 years after the covenant was given to Abraham.

England – Blessing/Cursing

England's early history involved the expulsion of Jews from its shores in 1290 by King Edward I, who issued an edict expelling all Jews from

---

[138] Fruchtenbaum, *The Remnant of Israel*, 87-88.

England. The expulsion edict remained in force for the rest of the Middle Ages. The edict was not an isolated incident, but the culmination of over 200 years of increased persecution. It was not until 1657, under Oliver Cromwell, a believer in Christ, that Jews were permitted to return to England. So England had cursed Abraham and God by the English expulsion of the Jewish people in 1290 and would pay for that later.

England will provide the second point of the outworking of the blessings and cursings of the Abrahamic Covenant. It was said of England that the sun never set on the British Empire. Britain had been generally favorable to the Jews after the days of Oliver Cromwell. One of the interesting points of British history is that Prime Minister Benjamin Disraeli (December 21, 1804 – April 19, 1881), a Jewish believer in Messiah, gained for England two significant links in building their empire: India and the Suez Canal.

Later, in November, 1917, another committed believer in Christ named Arthur James Balfour (July 25, 1848 – March 19, 1930) became the Secretary of State of Foreign Affairs. He was also a committed believer in Israel having its own homeland because, biblically, he believed in the restoration of Israel. As a result, you have the following document, called the Balfour Declaration of 1917:

> His Majesty's government views with favor the establishment in Palestine of a national home for the Jewish people, and will use their best endeavors to facilitate the achievement of this object, it being clearly understood that nothing shall be done which may prejudice the civil and religious rights of existing non-Jewish communities in Palestine, or the rights and political status enjoyed by Jews in any other country.[139]

However, a few years later in 1922, the British government began to renege on its commitment to the Jewish people with the establishment of Trans-Jordan (the State of Jordan), a Palestinian State. Next, they restricted Jewish immigration to Palestine, as it was then known, before and during World War II, sealing the fate of hundreds of thousands, if not millions, of Jewish people trying to escape Nazi Europe and the Nazi murder machine. They also restricted Jewish settlers in Israel from arming themselves against Palestinian Muslim attacks, and made many other restrictions that I will not take the time here to mention.

---

[139] Heinrich, *In the Shame of Jesus: The Hidden Story of Church-Sponsored Anti-Semitism*, 165.

So the once mighty empire of Great Britain, like Spain, has been reduced to a few holdings. It is no longer a superpower; take note America! For now, the sun does set on the British Empire; this empire has fallen. Britain was initially blessed because of their favorable attitude and actions to the Jewish people, but Britain forgot Who made them great!

History will support the fact that Great Britain expelled the Jewish people from their shores and later restricted Jewish people from escaping Nazi Germany and restricted the Jewish people in Palestine from protecting themselves by arming. The blood of Jewish people lay at the feet of the British Empire, for hundreds of thousands were murdered because Britain did not keep its word. Also the Allied Command of World War II could have bombed the railways that led to the death camps of Hitler, but they did not try to disrupt the Nazi killing machine.

Thus, Great Britain was cursed of God and has never recovered from turning their back on Jewish people trying to escape Hitler, and even trying to prevent their escape. Should I say in reality they pulled an Edomite, Moabite, and Ammonite stunt in turning over Jews, not to slave trade, but to the gas chambers of Nazi Germany! The outworking of the blessings and cursings of the Abrahamic Covenant are just as real today as when God made the covenant with Abraham 4,000 years ago. God has a looooong memory!

England has and is paying the price for their anti-Semitism by not learning their historical lesson. They expelled the Jewish people who were an asset to their country and economy and now they have opened their doors to the Islam hordes. Refugees have flooded England and have not assimilated into English society, but have maintained Islamic beliefs and are now destroying what is left of England from within as they become a larger part of English society. Islam may even completely control England within the next 50 years. England is, and will be, spiritually a darkened country as the Gospel is continually eroded there. The Church of England is apostate and so is much of the population. There are more practicing Muslims in England than there are practicing Anglicans. England is doomed! England cursed Israel, and God has cursed England.

Germany – Cursing

In Germany unbridled emotions of hatred ran high against the Jewish people of their land as depravity of the hearts was poured out against the Jewish people. Below is a quotation from Abram Sachar:

Then massacres spread from one end of Europe to the other. Among the beautiful lakes of Switzerland and the fertile valley of the Rhein, in the cultured cities of Germany and the affluent cities of Austria, flame and sword devoured Jewish homes and cut down Jewish lives. Everywhere captured Jews were put on trial and tortured and confessions were forced from lips wrung with pain. 60 large communities were destroyed and 150 smaller ones. Property losses were staggering, but the toll of lives made these pale. In Strasburg, despite the protests of the council, 1,800 Jews were dragged out to the cemetery on the Sabbath and there burnt alive, after which their possessions were distributed. In Maylene 6,000 Jews perished; in Erfurt 3,000. And in the shadow of every visitation the Flagellant monks stood, in flowing robes, like ghouls, crying in one voice for penance and blood.[140]

The second example occurred several hundred years later in 1879 when a German author named Wilhelm Marr wrote a book called *The Victory of the Jews Over the Germans*. His fear-mongering book was so successful that in one year it had twelve reprintings. His major theme is captured in his statement: "The Jews so dominated Germany that one could hardly distinguish between commerce and crime." In his book he portrayed Jews as biologically inferior beings, anti-social, unable to be assimilated, because of a corruption of their blood. He warned Germans that Jews were conquering Germany and that Germans would become slaves to Jews.[141]

What can be said about Germany, the land of my ancestry? It has a long history of anti-Semitic attitudes and actions against the Jewish people going well back into the Middle Ages. They were not alone in this, for France was equally as anti-Semitic as Germany. The anti-Semitism of Germany was immense, and it formed the foundation within the German society for the Nazis to take over.

What else can be said about Germany and its cursing of the Jewish people? The Holocaust was just the culmination of a long history of it. The Nazis who put the Jewish people in walled ghettos like the Warsaw Ghetto would later, themselves, be walled apart from each other with the Berlin Wall. God curses in kind that nation that curses Him and His people.

---

[140] Sachar, *A History of the Jews*, 201.
[141] Arnold P. Abbott, *When in Doubt ... Blame a Jew* (Bloomington, IN: Arnold Abbott, 2004), 68.

The Nazis forced Jews to assist them in killing Jews in the death camps. Later, under the Soviet era, you have Germans killing Germans trying to escape the walls of Communism in Berlin. The Jewish people tried to hide from the Nazi pursuers; ever since the fall of Germany, the Nazis have hidden from Jewish pursuers to keep themselves from being brought to justice. God will curse kind for kind, and Germany is a perfect example of the outworking of the curses of the Abrahamic Covenant given to Abraham still being in effect 4,000 years later.

Will Germany be one of the nations with Gog and Magog that attack Israel in Ezekiel 38-39? Many believe so. In that military attack of Gog and Magog, God will not only destroy their armies on the mountains of Israel but will also destroy parts of those countries trying to attack Israel.

How do we know these are judgments from God? We can discern His response because He visits curse for curse in kind. This is His signature, so that all may come to see He is faithful to avenge the Jewish people. He is righteous, and He is just. Man will plan, but God disposes according to His promises.

France – Cursing

France has a long history of anti-Semitic words, actions, and events. There were four notable expulsions from France of the Jewish people. Philip Augustus in 1182 expelled them from Paris, Louis IX expelled them from all of France in 1264, Charles IV did so in 1306, and Charles VI repeated that in 1394.

The First Crusade led to nearly a century of accusations (such as the Blood Libel claim) against the Jews, many of whom were killed or attacked in France. Immediately after the coronation of Philip Augustus on March 14, 1181, the King ordered the Jews arrested on a Saturday, in all their synagogues, and despoiled of their money and their investments. In April 1182, he published an edict of expulsion, but accorded the Jews a delay of three months for the sale of their personal property.

The Jews of France suffered during the First Crusade (1096), when the Crusaders shut up the Jews of Rouen in a church and murdered them without distinction of age or sex, sparing only those who accepted baptism. According to a Hebrew document, the Jews throughout France were at that time in great fear, and wrote to their brothers in the Rhine countries making known to them their terror and asking them to fast and pray. In 1243, King

Louis IX ordered, at the urging of Pope Gregory IX, the burning in Paris of some 12,000 manuscript copies of the Talmud, a revered commentary on the Jewish Scriptures, and other Jewish books.

The story of the Dreyfus Affair in France (1894-1906) was very telling and gripped the heart of a young Jewish journalist by the name of Theodore Herzl. He watched the injustice done to Captain Dreyfus and the massive anti-Semitic rallies in the streets with mobs shouting "death to the Jews."

These citations are only a few of the many anti-Semitic words and actions of France as they interacted with the Jewish people in their midst. France today is only one of numerous European nations that were once great nations but have succumbed to the curse of the Abrahamic Covenant. France, who expelled the Jews and treated them poorly, was judged by God through various defeats, such as the French Revolution, World War I, and again in World War II by being diminished as a power and even being occupied by Nazi Germany for a time because of their history of anti-Semitism. Since the 1960s, France has opened their doors to a flood of Muslim immigrants; in 50 years or less, France may be an Islamic State like England and Germany. The judgment of God is in process.

France on September 15, 2015, presented a paper before the Security Council of the United Nations of which she is a member to have Israel give up Jerusalem to the Palestinians as their capital. The French measure fell one vote short of the nine-vote majority needed, so it was not adopted. The ramifications of this anti-Semitic act by France will only add to the hatred of people for the Jewish people and the Jewish nation of Israel.

Also, according to Caroline Glick, the web edition of *The Jerusalem Post* (October 20, 2015) stated that the French government pays millions of euros, dollars, and shekels to a Palestinian Non-Governmental Organizations Network whose stated goal is to destroy Israel, another clear indicator of France's continued anti-Semitism.

Portugal – Cursing

Portugal expelled the Jewish people from their borders in December 1496. They decreed that any Jew who did not convert to Christianity would be expelled. In 1504, there was a popular riot that ended in the death of 2,000 Jews. Like Spain, Portugal has an anti-Semitic history.

Summary of European Nations

All of these European countries mentioned here, as well as others, do not support the State of Israel today and believe that it is the biggest deterrent for peace in the Middle-East. They have drunk the Palestinian "Kool-Aid" and have esteemed Israel and the God of Israel lightly so that all remain under the curse of God.

Isn't it interesting that Israel, the Jewish people, have been abused and abused by these European nations, and it has not ended yet? When Israel refuses to give up the Land that God gave them the title deed to, these European nations still show themselves as anti-Semitic, anti-Israel, Jew haters.

I believe the Tribulation will be the final judgment on all these nations that curse the God of Israel, the LORD Himself, by cursing Israel.

Russia – Cursing

Russian history is replete with examples of horrendous atrocities against the Jewish people. Most of what has transpired came about with the approval of the Russian Orthodox Church and Catholic Poland. Stalin in the Communist era slaughtered thousands of Jewish people along with millions of his own people. The repression of the Jewish people and bias against the Jewish people from Czarist Russia or Communist Russia is long standing and cannot be debated. I am not going to repeat what other authors have already written. Check out the book list on page 47.

Here are just a few examples of Russian anti-Semitism over the years. Ivan the Terrible of Russia in 1563 commanded that all Jews in one city were to either receive Christian baptism or be drowned in a river that ran through the city. In 1648-49, one hundred thousand Jews were massacred and 700 Jewish communities were destroyed by the Cassocks in Eastern Orthodox Ukraine. Large numbers were also massacred in Roman Catholic Poland in 1655-56 and 1768-88. In the 1740s, several imperial Russian czars decreed that those who would not submit to Christian baptism were to be deported from the Russian Empire.

In the late 1700s, the Pale of Settlement was designated for the Jewish people to live in, in a restricted ghetto in what today is known as Western Russia, Ukraine, Lithuania, Belarus, and Poland. In this area, the pogroms of the seventeenth through nineteenth centuries were carried out against Jewish communities with all kinds of physical attacks. By the early 1900s, there were an estimated four million Jewish people in the Pale.

The concentration of Jews in the Pale made them easy targets for pogroms, anti-Jewish riots by the majority "Christian" population. These, along with the repressive May Laws often devastated whole communities. The May Laws were temporary laws put in place in 1882 which lasted for thirty years, not so temporary. These laws forbade the Jews to settle anew outside of towns and boroughs of the Pale except for existing Jewish agricultural colonies. These laws also forbade issuing mortgages and other deeds to Jews, which included banning the registration of Jews as lessees of real property situated outside of towns and boroughs and also banning the issuing to Jews of powers of attorney to manage and dispose of such real property.[142] It also stated that no business transactions could take place on Sundays and other principle Christian holy days.

Though pogroms were staged throughout the existence of the Pale, particularly devastating attacks occurred in 1881–1883 and 1903–1906, targeting hundreds of communities, killing thousands of Jews, and causing considerable property damage. It is from this area, the Pale, that many of the Jewish people fled in the late 1800s and the early years of the 1900s and came to America as well as began immigrating to Israel. Many of the Jewish people in New York City and surrounding areas came to escape the Russian and Polish pogroms.

Russia, in the twentieth century, became a very powerful nation; but they have lost some of their prestige. The Union of Soviet Socialistic States has unraveled; but according to Bible prophecy, they will come together again in the future. In fact, we may be glimpsing this now as Russia has been able to fill the gap in world leadership left by the United States during the rise of ISIS. I will cover more of this in the prophetic section.

Russia, whether it was "Christian" czarist Russia or Communist Russia, stands guilty of ***Poking God's Eye*** and will be judged. The outworking of the curses of the Abrahamic Covenant is at work as Russia continues to support all of Israel's enemies in the Islamic world, providing Iran, Iraq, Syria, and Egypt with technology and military supplies. This has been going on since the formation of the State of Israel. Russia has a history of treating its Jewish citizens poorly and Russia's leaders have been accomplices to the Muslim states who want to destroy Israel. Russian has a long history of anti-Semitism

---

[142] Sachar, *A History of the Jews*, 318.

going back to the 1500s and extending into the twenty-first century. Russia is ripe for God's judgment which we will see in the next chapter.

In this section on European and Russian anti-Semitism, we have focused on centuries of many acts of violence against the Jewish people. Even though I have not quoted them in this book, I would encourage you to check out several other books on European and Russian anti-Semitism as follows:

- *History of the Jews* by Professor H. Graetz, published by Jewish Publication Society in 1896 in five volumes.
- *Christian Anti-Semitism; A History of Hate* by William Nicholls, published by Jason Aronson in 1995.
- *A Historical Survey of Anti-Semitism* by Richard E. Gade, published by Baker Book House in 1981.

Muslim States – Cursing

Since the beginning of the Jewish State in 1948, the Muslim nations of Syria, Iraq, Jordan, Egypt, and Lebanon have been challenging Israel for its very existence. We understand that Ezekiel 37 is still taking place as Jewish people worldwide have returned to Israel, to the home of their fathers, to the Land that God promised to them through Abraham.

Even before Israel became a State again, anti-Jewish attitudes began to flourish in the Land beginning in 1919 with armed rebellions and attacks on Jewish people living in the Land. This anti-Jewish activity was initiated by the Mufti of Jerusalem, Haj Amin al-Husseini.

In discussing the Muslim response to the Jewish people, notice I am exchanging the word *anti-Semitic* for a more accurate term: anti-Jewish. It technically is not correct to use the word *anti-Semitism* within the Middle East conflict, for most all of the Middle East is made up of Semites, meaning they are descendants of Shem, son of Noah. To be precise, their bias is based on an anti-Jewish attitude, and these attitudes and actions are coming from **Semites and non-Semites** who would be descendants of Ham and Japthah, sons of Noah. Their Islamic hatred is religious hatred at its core. Let me list just some of the Islamic incursions upon Israel since 1919:

- 1919 to today – Armed attacks against the Jewish people have continued and have intensified with the addition of the PLO in

1967 with their twisted anti-Jewish propaganda war and increased violence against unarmed Jewish citizens.

- 1919-1921 – The Mufti of Jerusalem riots called for attacks using rhetoric laced with hatred and lies about the Jewish people.
- 1948-49 – Muslim nations attacked Israel.
- 1967 – Israel was attacked by Egypt, Jordan and Syria – called the 6-Day War.
- 1973 – Israel was attacked again – called the Yom Kippur War.
- 1980 – Israel attacked Lebanon because of all the cross-border attacks by the Hezbollah, which is a terrorist organization headquartered in Lebanon.
- 1990 – During the First Intifada, riots, suicide bombers, and armed attacks were incited against citizens of Israel.
- 2000 – During the Second Intifada, riots, suicide bombers, and armed attacks were again incited against citizens of Israel.
- 2014 – Israel attacked Gaza after over 4,000 rockets were shot at them by the Hamas terrorist group headquartered in Gaza.
- 2015 – Because of the failed leadership of the Obama administration in the U.S., and with the support of the Democratic minority in both houses of the U.S. Congress, Iran is poised to develop a nuclear bomb, and Israel is in their sites.

Israel's very existence is again at stake, and God would judge these Islamic States for their hatred, which is first based in the religion of Islam and second in their own national interests. I will quote Fruchtenbaum as he shows the outworking of the curses of the Abrahamic Covenant:

> [Here is the disposition for the] four Arab states of Syria, Iraq, Jordan, and Egypt, all of which combined their armed forces in 1967 with the avowed purpose of destroying Israel. Nasser, the leader of Egypt, vowed that the Jews would be driven into the Mediterranean Sea and forced to swim to Europe. King Hussein of Jordan swore to move his border so as to encompass all of what he called "occupied Palestine." After four days of the Six Day War, however, it was not the Jews but the Egyptians who were doing the swimming as they fled across the Suez Canal from the Israeli forces. As for King Hussein, after three days, his border was indeed moved, but in the

opposite direction. The Arabs cursed the Jewish State with war and were defeated by war.[143]

The outworking of the Abrahamic Covenant came through again as the Jewish people were threatened and cursed, and God provided for them. We will look at the Muslim states again in the Prophetic Future section of this book. There are some interesting, miraculous stories that can only be explained by saying that God fought for Israel as part of His continuing faithfulness to the Abrahamic Covenant.

Summary Points

You may say that I am hard on the Catholic and Orthodox Churches and the individual states within Europe and Russia. In response, I say I am; because the heart of anti-Jewish words, actions, and beliefs has been centered in Europe for the last 1,500 years. Anti-Semitism and anti-Jewish sentiments and policies have been entrenched in the Muslim world for 1,300 years, but the Jewish people faired reasonably better in the Muslim world than in Europe or Russia, except for the last 100 years, beginning in 1919.

Understand the Abrahamic Covenant and also understand that this is not a game that God is playing; He is very serious about it, and He will – He has to because of His integrity – judge these anti-Jewish nations for speaking and acting against Him as they attack Jewish people on all levels.

In reading through Moses and the Prophets, you cannot help but grasp the seriousness of God and His promised cursing of those that curse Him by cursing His people Israel. This book is only trying to capture the essence of God's heart toward the Jewish people and warn those that go against Him by going against Israel.

Here is a summary of God's cursings in kind for those organizations and states who have harmed His people Israel:

- The Roman Catholic Church has been and is being cursed for over 1,500 years of its anti-Jewish speech, actions, and laws and for its role as an adversary to Jewish people.
- Spain was and is being cursed as a result of its eviction of Jews from Spain (1300 through 1492) and the sadistic acts of the Inquisition even into South and Central America. God has

---

[143] Fruchtenbaum, *The Remnant of Israel*, 89.

judged Spain by its being downsized and losing a significant degree of its former worldwide influence.

- England has been and is still being cursed because of their complete bungling of their leadership position from 1922 through World War II and their restricting Jewish immigrants who desired to get out of Europe by holding them in internment camps on Cyprus. Today England is no long a dominant world power.

- France has been and is still being cursed for their handling of the Dreyfus Affair and their failures throughout the centuries to bless Jewish people and not curse them. France has fallen as a world power just as England and Spain did.

- Portugal has been and is still being cursed for following the lead of Spain.

- Russia has been and is still being cursed for centuries of anti-Jewish words and actions against God and His people, the Jewish people. This is manifested by the fall of the USSR beginning with the Berlin Wall being torn down, economic woes, and loss of power, even though it will emerge again, according to Bible prophecy.

- Muslim states have been and are still being cursed because of their acts for 1,300 years, and especially the last 100 years, as they curse the God of Israel. They will pay for it as God judges them.

Chapter 14
The Outworking of the Abrahamic Covenant in Prophecy

United States of America – Blessings and ???

Now we come to the United States of America, a safe haven for Jewish people for over 300 years. Not all Americans have treated the Jewish people correctly. Today, there is a growing anti-Jewish attitude among many. In America, we used to have segregation – places Jewish people and blacks could not attend or organizations that they could not participate in. However, overall, Jewish people were free from the tyranny of the anti-Jewish attitudes and actions of Western and Eastern Europe, Russia, and the Muslim world. Yet there have been twists and turns in American policy towards the Jews.

The U.S. did not at first endorse a Jewish State. Many Jewish people that immigrated early to Israel were from Russia, and they set up Kibbutzim (socialist agricultural communities); in response, the American State Department did not want President Truman to vote yes for statehood in 1948. Yet, because of some previous Jewish contacts, Truman was eventually persuaded to vote yes for Israel in the United Nations. We have been a very close ally with Israel since then.

The United States has one of the largest Christian Zionist organizations of any country in the world, and America in general loves Israel. Unfortunately, the seeds of anti-Jewish attitudes are growing within liberal Protestant denominations who advocate boycotting Israel. They have fallen prey to the propaganda machine of the Palestinians and the Liberal (now calling themselves Progressive) Socialist anti-Semitic press in the U.S. Even Evangelicals and conservatives are beginning to turn their backs on Israel in favor of the Palestinians.

In recent years, under the Obama administration (2009-2017), our government has been more anti-Semitic than most Americans realize. I will deal with this more shortly.

I have grown up hearing if we ever stop being a blessing to Israel, we are in trouble. Well, we are already in deep trouble, and we only have a few redeeming qualities left. One of them is that we still do support Israel at this writing. However, that support is fading. On December 23, 2016, the Obama administration abstained on a critical vote in the UN Security Council on resolution 2334 against Israel. We did not stand with Israel. God drew a line in the sand 4,000 years ago with the Abrahamic Covenant and the two provisions that relate directly to Gentiles, which are the blessings and cursings of Genesis 12:3. The United States just crossed that line by abandoning our ally Israel, inviting God to judge us.

So what will become of the U.S. as a nation? We have been blessed like no other nation on the earth (except for Israel) because of our blessing of the Jewish people and of Israel. Unfortunately, the wind has recently changed in America. Today, our loyalty to Israel hangs in the balance. As our elected administrations come and go, will we continue to support the Jewish people and Israel; or will we abandon them and incur the curses of God?

Many of us are apprehensive about our future, in general, and our future relationship to Israel, for we understand that we have not been a true friend of Israel in our recent policies in the Middle East; our government has even turned its back on Christians around the world in distress! Unless there is a major change in national policy, we will go the way of all nations before us.

Even though we support Israel and have been a safe haven for Jewish people, all is not well. Since the days of President Bush, Senior (1989-1993), we have been pushing Israel to give up land for peace, the Two-State Plan. As has been seen in history, the Muslims are not interested in a just peace. Their concept of peace is to rid the Middle East of the presence of Israel. If they wanted peace, they have had two huge opportunities to achieve it:

- First, from 1948-67, Jordan controlled the area called the West Bank. They had a 19-year window to establish a Palestinian State and did absolutely nothing.

- Second, Ehud Barak, the Prime Minister of Israel, under pressure from Bill Clinton (1993-2001), President of the United States, offered Yasser Arafat, the head of the PLO, everything he wanted except east Jerusalem; Arafat turned it down and began Intifada #2 against Israel.

These two instances should send huge signals to both Israel and the United States as to the inner motivation of the Palestinian Muslims. Their interest is not in a Two-State solution, but in a world without the State of Israel. Yet, the push for the Two-State solution continued through the Clinton administration (1992-2000) and Bush administration (2001-2009) into the Obama administration (2009-2017). I would encourage that you read chapter 6 in John McTernan and Bill Koenig's book[144] *Israel, the Blessing or the Curse?* Each time that United States presidents have tried to push the supposed land-for-peace deals, America has suffered from God's warning to us:

- He sent the "perfect storm" to New England (October 1991) because of the Madrid Conference in Spain. The purpose of that "peace" conference was to establish a Palestinian State.
- He sent Hurricane Andrew into Florida (August 1992) after the Madrid Conference moved to Washington, D.C.
- In January 1994, President Clinton met with Assad of Syria in Geneva, and a massive 6.9 earthquake rocked California.
- As Yasser Arafat engaged in a speaking tour in the United States in March/April 1994, the mid-section of America was devastated by tornados and flooding.
- The horrifying event of the Twin Tower and Pentagon bombing of 9-11 provided a wake-up call as America experienced the first major attack on its citizens on the U.S. mainland.
- Hurricane Katrina hit New Orleans and the Gulf Coast states in the U.S. in August 2005 because we pushed Israel to give up Gaza to the PLO.

The list can go on and on. America has been walking the fence, supporting Israel, and yet trying to appease the Muslims with the Two-State Plan because of our dependence on Middle East oil. God for the last 20+ years has been warning the United States of its error of turning our backs on Israel, and we as a country have turned blind eyes to our consequences

---

[144] John McTernan and Bill Koenig, *Israel: the Blessing or the Curse?* (Higginsville, MO: Hearthstone Publishing, 2001).

and deaf ears to His Word. For excellent reading on this topic, get the book *The Israel Solution: A One State Plan* by Caroline Glick.[145] This well-researched book sheds light on why Israel is not to give up land for peace and why the One-State Plan is the only real viable future path.

Now let me deal briefly with the Jekyll-and-Hyde face of Obama as it relates to the antagonism he has displayed towards Israel, Christians, and the Constitution of the United States of America. Five observations stand out, and I realize these are only visible as the tip of the Obama iceberg:

- Obama is against the Constitution of the United States.
- Obama is against the Christian Faith specifically.
- Obama is against the Nation of Israel.
- Obama is pro-Muslim.

It has become very apparent that Obama has cursed Israel. It is sobering to realize that God placed us as a nation under the authority of such an anti-Semitic and anti-Christian leader. As a nation, we stand to receive the curse of the Abrahamic Covenant unless there is a complete repentance and reversal on our part nationally.

If you are a careful student of prophecy, you will discover that the Bible says absolutely nothing about the United States in the End Times. Nothing! Prophetically, we know two things; first, America is nowhere mentioned in the prophecies of the Bible. So there is no help there. Second, in the study of Ezekiel, we discover a very concerning verse in 38:13.

In Ezekiel 38:13, two places are mentioned that will protest the attack on Israel: Saudi-Arabia (Sheba and Dedan) and Tarshish (most likely Spain) along with its young lions or nations that came from them, which would be South and Central America. If Tarshish is the Tarshish of England, which it is most likely not, then the young lions would be America, Canada, Australia, and New Zealand. But notice, these nations only protest and they do nothing else. So if America is involved in the protest, it will do nothing to help Israel. Then we have the question why, but the answer is not known. We can only guess if we are involved at all; and, if so, why we do not defend Israel but only protest the attack.

---

[145] Carline B. Click, *The Israeli Solution: A One-State Plan for Peace in the Middle East* (New York, NY: Crown Publishing Group, division of Random House, 2014).

At that point in time, we will have become of low national consequence on the world's stage:

- We are committing economic suicide by spending ourselves into $20 trillion dollars of debt. Our actual debt level is much greater, taking into account our future. We have placed approximately $60 trillion dollars of debt upon the shoulders of our sons and daughters, grandchildren, and great-grandchildren.

- We have become morally like Sodom and Gomorrah. We have jumped off the moral cliff with the June 2016 ruling by our Supreme Court as they have now redefined marriage. We now have made immoral sins legal, including pornography in all its forms on paper and digitally on the internet. Pornography has become big business while it eats the moral fiber out of our society.

- Religiously, the Church is in spiritual chaos, unbiblical teachings reign from her pulpits, and apathy and indifference reign in the pews.

- Ethically, truth is relative; right has been come wrong, and wrong has become right. Our country is adrift on the humanistic sea of thought without any anchor.

What can explain the absence of the United States from End Times prophecies? Perhaps the above bullets points may help. Will we have been destroyed? Total destruction is not probable in the immediate future. Beyond that, God may choose to pour out His wrath, anger, and fury on our sinful nation in time. On the hopeful side, He is very patient and restrains Himself, allowing for repentance and a return to Him and His ways.

Have we as a nation become uninvolved in world affairs because we no longer have the power to do anything about it or lack the desire to do so? Certainly our waning influence and growing debt have down-sized our ability to be effective on the world stage in defense of Israel.

Have we become immersed to the point of oblivion into anti-Semitic attitudes being pushed by Socialistic Liberal Left political leaders, our news media, the entertainment industry, and institutions for higher learning? As these strong forces have grown in dominance in our culture, are we going along to get along? If so, we have cursed God and Israel, even if not intentionally, at least by letting our guard down or by neglect.

With the 2016 election of Trump, his inauguration in January of 2017, and the generally pro-Israel makeup of his administration; there is some hope in the air. But we are witnessing chaos, lawlessness, and what approaches anarchy within our society. Many people no longer have a biblical conscience, or a national constitutional conscience; they are instead purely humanistic, socialistic, revealing a blatantly unethical response in the street as well as in the House and Senate of Congress. Trump seems to be a very strong supporter of Israel; however, can he turn the country around? If not, Israel eventually will be abandoned. On May 14, 2018, the day after the 70th year celebration of Israel's becoming a State, President Trump moved the U.S. Embassy from Tel Aviv to Jerusalem, the capital of the State of Israel. That was a something that needed to be done decades ago.

All realms of corrupted society are today sadly falling into place. The presidential election of 2016 will go down in history as an example of the widespread corruption and divisions that have affected the United States at the highest levels in shocking and disappointing ways. Will we as a nation turn a corner with the new Republican administration, or will we fall from the weight of our many sins? Our leaders never point to the moral and spiritual decay of the human heart in America; and this failure to do so is tragic. Will future leaders in America turn us around? One thing I can confidently say is that if we do not turn to God and repent as a nation of our sins, we will have only delayed God's judgment temporarily.

The UN vote against Israel in December of 2016, with the United States abstention under the Obama administration has sealed our judgment before God. The die is cast; Israel is now in International violation according to the United States, the UN and the EU because of our abstention. That decision down the road will have longer-term drastic effects, putting additional pressures on Israel.

Back to our subject at hand, we simply do not know the answer as to why the U.S.A. is not mentioned as being involved in helping Israel in the prophecies of Ezekiel 38; we do know we are being faced with an accumulation of the consequences of years of our own unaddressed national sins.

During our history, we have been a blessing to Israel; and we as a nation have been greatly blessed. The question is: What will the United States do in the future? Will we continue to be a blessing to Israel, or will we become like the nations before us and curse Israel and go into decline or even disappear?

We are moving in a negative direction. There are some signs. The Liberal (Progressive) news media are obviously biased against Israel and are taking the side of the enemies of Israel. The apostate Protestant churches have been boycotting Israel and instead supporting Israel's enemies: the Palestinian Authority, Hezbollah, and Hamas. We have even come to the low point of having a U.S. president who is not a friend to Israel, who has scorned her and scolded her leaders in a denigrating way.

Lastly, and so very, very importantly, it must not be missed: We have a nation that is rapidly becoming biblically and scripturally illiterate in the Scriptures in general; thus, we do not have a biblical understanding of Israel. Biblical ignorance lays down the foundation for anti-Semitism. Bible illiteracy allows theological error to run rampant. How sad is it that "We the people" have no biblical foundation for the support of Israel! These indicators do not bode well for the United States in the future.

To give examples of why I believe America will become uninvolved or stop actively supporting the enemies of Israel, let me refer to the 2016 political landscape. Israel has been reduced to a pawn in a political race to be used to get votes and is no longer being treated as a serious ally. Will isolationists prevail, abandoning Israel if she is attacked?

Corruption and division threaten our political process, and many worry that such an internal conflict destabilizes the United States. Some have embraced corruption as the best road ahead because it is a known force. Others embrace the anti-government movement to defeat corruption, accepting inexperience in a new set of political outsiders as the price for defeating lies and having a fresh start. Either way forward seems problematic to most.

Those who love Israel worry that even the once stalwart defenders of Israel have fallen into disarray and confusion, just at a time when our commitment as a nation may be called into play. How will our leaders respond?

My gut feeling as I observe the moral, spiritual, and political landscape of America in 2016 is that "We the People" must speak out again. Our voices are an ingredient that needs to be incorporated into the national fabric. The answer is not a conservative, godly President, as no one person can be our salvation as a nation; but our Faith in God can intervene. If "We the People" decide we are sick of being morally, spiritually, and politically bankrupt, a spiritual revival can spread across the length and breadth of this country, to every city, town, and community. Otherwise, America's days are numbered!

What does the Bible say about the future of Islam and of Russia? Let us look to Scripture for what we may expect God to do.

Islam and Russia – Cursing
Ezekiel 38-39

Here I would like to again identify the difference between two terms: *Arab* and *Muslim* (or Islam). *Arab* is a term for descendants of Ishmael, an ethnic group of people who largely live in the Saudi Peninsula. The term *Muslim* or *Islam* identifies a religion that has currently conquered other countries by force in North Africa, Iran, Turkey, and the countries of southern Russia. These terms are not to be used interchangeably.

We see from history that Islam has treated Israel poorly over the years. Yet their treatment of the Jewish people was generally better than that of "Christian" Europe, until the twentieth century. As a religion that controls many nations, Islam will come under God's judgment just as other religious organizations have been judged. This is what the text of Ezekiel 38-39 is all about.

While Islam will also be judged because of their animosity toward Israel, for cursing Israel and the God of Israel, our attention here is directed toward the shocking prophecy in Ezekiel 38-39 of the downfall of Islam as a false religion and the humiliation of their god, "allah," before the God of Israel.

The nations mentioned in Ezekiel 38:2-3 are not Semitic, but are descended from Japheth. These people came from the area that we today call Turkey, who migrated and became the nations of southern Russia, Russia itself, and Germany; these are all descendants of Japheth and not Shem. God is clear about two things regarding His judgment against this group. First, He will *put hooks in their jaws* (38:4) and bring them upon the mountains of Israel (38:8; 39:2); and, second, His purpose will be to glorify His Name before all the nations of the world (38:23; 39:7).

Look at the exact wording that the LORD uses, and notice as well the first personal, singular pronouns that the LORD uses:

Ezekiel

$^{38:23}$ *Thus will* **I** *magnify* **Myself***, and sanctify* **Myself***; and* **I will** *be known in the eyes of* **many nations,** *and they shall know that* **I** *am the LORD.*

$^{39:7}$ *So will* **I** *make* **My** *holy Name known* **in the midst of My people Israel***; and I will not let them pollute* **My** *holy Name any more: and* **the heathen** *shall know that* **I am the LORD, the Holy One in Israel***.*

Two things will become obvious to both the nations (all the Gentile nations, meaning all the world with the exception of Israel) and to Israel. That includes everyone. Both the Gentile world and the Jewish world will know that the God of Israel is LORD. The Gentiles and the Jewish people in the Land will become aware of the supernatural outpouring of God on the armies of this Islamic coalition.

Chapter 39 of Ezekiel describes what God will do. He will draw these armies to the mountains of Israel, and there He will smite them by means of an earthquake, with confusion in the armies that will cause them to kill each other, by pestilence, by raining down great hailstones upon them, by fire, and by brimstone (38:21-22; 39:2-6). God states that all this is being done by Him supernaturally to sanctify His Name before many nations (39:23).

Notice God's purpose is to sanctify His Name and make known before many nations that He is God alone! He further states in 39:7 that He will make his *holy Name known in the midst of My people Israel*. Israel will wake up the next day and say, "The God of our Fathers did not die in the Holocaust! He is alive, and He fought the battle for us." This will be the beginning of the Jewish people searching the Scriptures to know their God.

Most Jewish people in Israel today are secular and not religious. God also states in Ezekiel 39:7 that *the heathen shall know that I am the LORD, the Holy One in Israel*. There will be no guesswork being done. The Islamic nations will wake up that next day and see for the first time that the God of Israel is God and that Allah is just another false man-made god inspired by satanic visions in the mind of a seventh-century Arab. This revelation may be the beginning of the greatest revival to the God of Israel that has ever been known in the Muslim world. These judgments will not only fall on Islamic countries, but also on Russia as well. Ezekiel 39:2-7 states this in the "I wills." Don't miss that!

Now look at Ezekiel 39:6. Not only will God destroy the armies on the Mountains of Israel, He will also send down fire from heaven on the land of Magog (the land of Russia), even unto the isles of the sea. The other nations around them that join Gog from the land of Magog will also suffer the consequences. So you will have complete destruction of the armies, but you will also have massive destruction of the countries that they represent. Now all these nations will know that He is God, the God of Israel, He is God alone. I believe that not only will Russia (as Gog, the leader of the confederated area of Magog) be judged for its cursing of God's people at this time, but Islam as well will begin to suffer the judgment of the God of Israel for their cursing of Israel in both modern and ancient history. That judgment will not be completed until the end of the Tribulation.

The Apostate Church – Cursing
Revelation 18

We covered the judgment of the Church in the previous section. With the Rapture of the Body of Messiah from the earth before the Tribulation, the earthly church will lose all elements of the believing Church. The Bride will be whisked away. The church on earth in the Tribulation period will now be 100 percent apostate. It will be full to capacity in corruption, pride, and arrogance, overflowing in its cesspool of sin. That apostate church will ride the back of the Beast of Revelation, the Antichrist, to the midpoint of the Tribulation; and then the Antichrist will destroy the apostate church and command that he be worshipped as God.

We briefly reviewed how the apostate church through the ages has cursed God, cursed Abraham, and cursed the seed of Abraham for 18-plus centuries. Understanding how God has dealt with other nations when they cursed Israel; we must come to the conclusion that judgment must come, and indeed it will come. It will come at the hands of the Antichrist in his bid to be worshipped by the world and his final attempt to destroy all Jews from the face of the planet.

If God could destroy the apostate church during the Tribulation, how can we be sure that He will spare His people Israel, who have in large part continued on in unbelief? The purpose of the Tribulation is to purge Israel of their rebels and to judge the Gentile nations with these seven years to bring Israel to the place where they will embrace Messiah Yeshua at the end of the Tribulation. This fact God repeats time and time again in the Prophets. Just as we can be sure that God will destroy the enemies of Israel, we can be sure that God will spare His people Israel based on the promises of the Abrahamic Covenant. As reinforcement for God's faithfulness to Israel, God states that there is one way that His covenants with Israel could be broken and be made invalid, and that is found in Jeremiah 31:35-37:

> *35 Thus says the LORD which gives the sun for a light by day, and the ordinances of the moon and of the stars for a light by night, which divided the sea when the waves thereof roar; That LORD of host is His Name: 36 If those ordinances depart from before Me, says the LORD, then the seed of Israel also shall cease from being a nation before Me forever. 37 Thus says the LORD; If heaven above can be measured, and the foundations of the earth searched out beneath, I will also cast off all the seed of Israel for all that they have done, says the LORD.*

God gives only two possible options for backing out of His covenant with Israel. In verse 36, He allows that if anyone can cause the sun, moon, and stars to depart from Him, then He will break His Covenant with Israel. Now you understand if that could be done, it would also mean the destruction of life on this planet. Also understand that not even Satan has that kind of power. No earthling is capable, and no created messenger, either angelic or fallen demonic being, has that kind of power. The thought is an absurdity.

Then He gives a second option in verse 37 for how He could be convinced to cast off His promises to the seed of Abraham. If anyone can measure the heavens above and search out the foundations of the earth beneath, then and only then will He cast off Israel. Even Hubble, with all the pictures it has taken, has not found the end of the universe created by God. The easiest part to measure is the earth we stand on, and we have not begun to search out the foundations of the earth.

What God is saying in Jeremiah to egotistical man – who is just dust, chaff of the earth – is that it is impossible for any of these things to be done. So the possibility of God breaking the Abrahamic Covenant is an absurdity. The reality of God's cursings and blessings is unshakeable. End of discussion!!

Armageddon – Cursing
Joel 3:1-8; Revelation 16:13-16; 19:11-15; Zechariah 12 & 14

Satan, through the Antichrist, will make his bid. Since not even he has the power to remove the sun, moon, and stars or measure the heavens and discover the foundations of the earth, he has only one thing that could be possible. His plan is to destroy all the Jews so that Messiah will have no seed of Abraham to rule over, and in so doing thwart God's plan, defeat God, and save his own fate from the Lake of Fire forever.

Armageddon will be Satan's last attempt to catch God asleep at the wheel, but God *never sleeps or slumbers*. He is fully engaged, as the Prophets reveal.

Have you ever considered why God revealed His Word progressively? Lucifer, when he sinned, became Satan according to Ezekiel 28:12. He was given by God a full sum of wisdom, so he is wise in his now-twisted mind. Satan has been reacting to God's revelation and never instigating new unknown responses. He has been at a complete disadvantage with the revelation of God trying to figure out God's next move. The Bible tells us that Satan will ultimately fail, but he will succeed in destroying two-thirds of the Jewish people (Zechariah 13:8). He will not be able to complete the job, for Messiah will return to Bozrah (Petra) upon Israel's confession of Faith in Him, Messiah Yeshua, as their God. Messiah will kill the Antichrist and his armies, and Satan will be thrown into Hell.

If you're Jewish and reading this, beware. Holocaust II is coming. Believers in Messiah, if you are reading this, be aware; now is the time to reach out in love to your Jewish friends, family, and acquaintances and thoughtfully share with them the wonderful news of God's grace for them in Messiah. If you are part of Church missions, take notice. Be sure to include outreach to Jewish people wherever you go, sharing with them God's Good News.

The Armageddon campaign against Israel will fail, as the Prophets foretold; and Messiah will reign on the throne of David in Jerusalem for 1,000 years, fulfilling the Abrahamic Covenant, Land Covenant, Davidic Covenant, and the New Covenant.

Egypt – Cursing
Ezekiel 46:2-28; Jeremiah 45:2-28; Ezekiel 29:1-32:32

Much has already been said about the cursing of Egypt because of Egypt's anti-Semitic attitudes and actions over time. The final cursing of Egypt will come in the Millennium. At the beginning of the Millennium, Egypt will be exiled from its land for 40 years; no one will live there. After that, they will be regathered from all the nations of the earth and settled in their land once again; but after that, Egypt will be the least of all the nations.

So Egypt will pay dearly for their anti-Semitism. Only Edom and Babylon will fare worse. Their lands will be a complete waste, and there will be no nation in the Millennium called Babylon or Edom. Their lands will be uninhabitable. So in the end, all God's cursings will play out and end; only the blessing of His Presence will remain forever.

Summary Points of Current Nations

What does the future hold for individuals and nations who continue to bless or curse God? It is no secret that all will be treated in kind, according to God's covenant with Abraham. This is a summary of how the Bible says future blessings and cursings will play out:

- **The United States: Cursings or Blessings?** The God of Israel has blessed the United States of America, but will that continue? Hearts must seek God's Word and embrace and support His enduring love of the Jewish people if blessings are to continue to be poured out on "We the People." Also, a national revival is needed with believers and a massive turning to Christ by the unsaved public.

- **Our Leaders:** What will be the legacy of our leaders? If they have opposed Israel and aided her enemies, they will suffer God's curses, kind for kind. They will be held accountable.

- **Russia and Islam: Cursings.** What awaits Russia and Islam? Ezekiel 38-39 tells the story of God's unmistakably miraculous judgment of Gog and Magog, and how God will use it to prove He is God. Jewish hearts will begin to open up to their Messiah Yeshua, and many Muslims will turn to Christ in Faith.

- **The Apostate Church: Cursings.** Revelation 18 shows a picture of cursing for the apostate church during the Tribulation period. Just as it has long tried to remove the Jewish people from their midst and have caused them harm, the apostate church will be destroyed in return.

- **Armageddon: Cursings.** Revelation 19:11-20 describes God's judgment of anti-Jewish nations who, incited by Satan, attempt one last time to wipe out the Jewish people. They will fail and be cursed with destruction, kind for kind.

- **Egypt: Additional Cursings.** According to Scripture, Egypt's curses towards Israel will be returned to them once more during the beginning of the Millennium, when they will be temporarily removed from their land and then be permanently reduced in importance.

Chapter 15
Summary of Curses

In summary, let's pull all this together. The blessings and cursings of God go to those who bless or curse Abraham. By Abraham, we mean Israel, all Jewish descendants of Abraham. God will bless all those who bless Abraham and his descendants. On the other side of the coin, those who curse Abraham (Israel – all Jewish descendants) will receive God's curses, kind for kind.

Notice the blessings and cursings of the Abrahamic Covenant do not apply to the seed of Abraham but instead to all Gentiles as to whether they bless or curse Israel. It all has to do with how the Gentiles treat Israel.

In the blessings and cursings concerning individuals, we looked at **nine** biblical examples of how Gentiles treated the Jewish people; the blessings are apparent, and the cursings are quite obvious. So God begins with dealing with individuals in the outworking of the Abrahamic Covenant in Genesis 12:3 and God continues to do so today.

We also saw that the outcome of the Abrahamic Covenant is sure, whether it takes 300 years; or 1,000 years; 2,000 years; or even 4,000 years. God's covenant with Abraham is just as real today as it was in the day of Abraham. So if you harbor anti-Israel or anti-Jewish tendencies in your thoughts, actions, words, deeds, or theologies, it may be time to re-evaluate your position biblically. The same applies to individuals and nations. If you choose to continue down your anti-Jewish road, understand that you are choosing God's cursing on you and your descendants!

Now from a biblical context, what does the cursing of Israel look like? Here is a bullet-point summary showing the heart motive or actions committed by an individual or nation. This subject could be and needs to be greatly developed. The first observation is that if anything threatens God's plan for Israel or the survival of the Jewish people, God's response is immediate. Now beyond that, let us take a look. What types of behavior and what attitudes provoked God's cursings?

- Laban **cheated** and **deceived** Jacob. His inward attitude was focused on personal greed and gain.

- Egypt perpetuated **unprovoked cruelty** and **slavery** towards the Jewish people, causing the death of male infants and drowning of infants.

- The Amalekites perpetrated an **unprovoked attack on Israel** as Israel was leaving Egypt, revealing an inward animosity and hatred, probably originating from Esau (Edom). This was a cowardly attack against the weak and vulnerable.

- Edom **harbored an inward, perpetual hatred** of a brother **expressed outwardly in antagonism and persecution towards their brother Israel**.

- Moab **harbored an unprovoked fear of Israel**, calling on Balaam to curse Israel and sending their Moabite women among the men of Israel to tempt them to sin.

- Balaam **caused Israel to sin**; he was a stumbling block because of his lust for wealth at Israel's expense.

- Ammon **rejoiced over Israel's calamity**.

- Midianites **attacked Israel with no provocation**.

- Jezebel conducted wholesale worship of Baal and slew God's Prophets; she was a **perverted egotist** and **promoter of idolatry**.

- Athaliah was a carbon copy of her mother, **killing of the seed of David** to try and **cut off his line** and engaging in and promoting idolatry.

- The two other co-presidents of Medo-Persia were **jealous** of Daniel and tried to have him killed.

- Haman **harbored personal hatred, pride, and jealousy** towards Mordecai; tried to have all the Jews in his country killed; and lacked humility.

- Moab was judged for their **contempt for Israel** and also for their pride.

- Syria attacked Israel and **desired to remove the Davidic dynasty**.

- Assyria persecuted the Jewish people cruelly and **blasphemed their God**.

- Babylon mistreated Israel during their period of captivity and was also **riddled with pride and the desire to get wealth**.

- Philistines **desired to conquer Israel** and **put Jewish people in servitude**.

- Tyre and Sidon **violated a brotherly covenant** (with David and Solomon) and engaged in wholesale slavery of Jewish people.

- Antiochus Epiphanes **provoked widespread anti-Semitism** against Israel and desecrated the Temple in Jerusalem.

Heart motivation, whether it consists of viewing Israel lightly, as unimportant, or as insignificant or instead consists of actively and aggressively coming against Israel, God views it as anti-Semitic and anti-God. Behind these words and actions of individuals and nations were power grabs, land grabs, suppression of Israel, and outright hatred and murder. In God's view, cursing Israel even included political alliances against Israel and bad-mouthing Israel.

Next, we looked at examples where God cursed nations that dealt improperly with the seed of Abraham by punishing them. We looked at **thirteen** biblical examples of the outworking on a national level. These are examples of anti-Semitism coming from the hands of the surrounding nations as described in the text of the Hebrew Scriptures. We saw a clear pattern that God is following in relationship to the outworking of Genesis 12:3.

We discovered that when individuals curse Israel, they individually will be cursed; if they individually bless Israel they will, in turn, be individually blessed by the covenant-keeping God of Israel. The same pattern applies to nations. If a nation curses Israel, that nation as a whole is judged. However, if a nation blesses Israel, then as a whole they will be blessed.

This principle is clearly seen in the words of Yeshua in the Olivet Discourse regarding the end of the Tribulation. In Matthew 25:31-46, Yeshua is referencing Joel 3:11-16 (Revelation 14:17-20; 16:12-16) as it speaks of the interval period of 75 days between the end of the Tribulation and the beginning of the Millennium (Daniel 12:4-13). Here is Matthew 25:31-46 in its entirety:

³¹ When the Son of man shall come in His glory, and all the holy angels with Him, then shall He sit upon the throne of His glory: ³² And before Him shall be gathered all nations: and He shall separate them one from another, as a shepherd divides his sheep from the goats: ³³ And He shall set the sheep on his right hand, but the goats on the left.

³⁴ Then shall the King say unto them on His right hand, Come, you blessed of my Father, inherit the kingdom prepared for you from the foundation of the world:³⁵ For I was hungry, and you gave Me meat [food]: *I was thirsty, and you gave Me drink: I was a stranger, and you took Me in: ³⁶ Naked, and you clothed Me: I was sick, and you visited Me: I was in prison, and you came unto Me.*

³⁷ Then shall the righteous answer Him, saying, Lord, when did we see You hungry, and feed You? or thirsty, and give You drink? ³⁸ When did we see You a stranger, and take You in? or naked, and clothe You? ³⁹ Or when did we see You sick, or in prison, and come unto You?

⁴⁰ And the King shall answer and say unto them, Verily I say unto you, Inasmuch as you have done it unto one of the least of these My brethren, you have done it unto Me.

⁴¹ Then shall He say also unto them on the left hand, Depart from Me, you cursed, into everlasting fire, prepared for the devil and his angels: ⁴² For I was hungry, and you gave Me no meat [food]: *I was thirsty, and you gave Me no drink: ⁴³ I was a stranger, and you took Me not in: naked, and you clothed Me not: sick, and in prison, and you visited Me not.*

⁴⁴ Then shall they also answer Him, saying, Lord, when did we see You hungry, or thirsty, or a stranger, or naked, or sick, or in prison, and did not minister unto You?

⁴⁵ Then shall He answer them, saying, Verily I say unto you, Inasmuch as you did it not to one of the least of these, you did it not to Me. ⁴⁶ And these shall go away into everlasting punishment: but the righteous into life eternal.

Throughout this book, I have pointed out what the Scriptures declare concerning the blessings or cursings that apply to Gentile individuals and nations. Look at these additional passages with me for further insight.

In Joel 3, God declared His judgment on the peoples for trying to annihilate the Jewish people and selling survivors very cheaply as slaves. God commands in verses 11-12 to *assemble yourselves, and come, all you heathen ... and come up to the valley of Jehoshaphat for there* **will I sit to judge** *all the heathen round about.* Now look at the parallel passage in Matthew 25 and see who sits and judges and why:

- Verse 31 states that it is Yeshua who sits on His throne, *the throne of His glory.* So the one who sits to judge is the Jewish Messiah who in the Tanakh (Hebrew Scriptures) is identified as the LORD.

- Verse 32 and following state that He will judge. Don't miss this: He will judge the nations on how they treated the Jewish people in the Tribulation. He will divide the Gentile people and Gentile nations into sheep and goat nations. Those who were pro-Israel in their dealing with the Jewish people during the 70th Week of Daniel will be set on His right hand. The goat nations that were anti-Jewish will be removed from the earth and will not enter the Kingdom, but the sheep will enter the Kingdom.

- God reciprocates in kind. The goat nations sold the Jewish people as slaves, and now they will be the slaves of the Jewish people. According to Zechariah 13:7, two-thirds of the Jewish people will die (be slaughtered) in the Tribulation (Holocaust II). Now according to Revelation 14:17-20, the Gentiles responsible will also be slaughtered. God will judge kind for kind.

- God's wrath will be poured out on the nations as the book of Revelation declares. God's judgment of the Gentiles will be for the centuries of Anti-Jewish attitudes, actions, and words of all the nations, not just during the Tribulation period.

The point made is that Jesus Christ, Yeshua the Messiah, will be judging the Gentiles on their treatment of His physical brothers and sisters, the Jewish people. Notice in Matthew 25:35-36, 42-43 how personal He makes it:

- You have given Him food when He was hungry.
- You have given Him water to drink when He was thirsty.
- You took Him in when He was a stranger.

- You clothed Him when He was naked.
- You visited Him when He was in prison and when He was sick.

These are pro-Jewish people who treated the physical brothers of Yeshua with love. Jesus (Yeshua) draws an equivalent between them being loving and caring for His physical Jewish brothers and sisters as being the same as loving and caring for Him! Now on the other side in verses 42-43, for those who did not display the compassion and caring discussed in the bullet points above, it is counted as if they denied compassion and caring to Him. Those who neglect to come to the aid of Yeshua's physical brothers will not be going to the Kingdom but shall, instead, be removed from the earth.

This is not just a principle for the end of the Tribulation. This principle began in Genesis 12:3 with the blessings and cursings of the Abrahamic Covenant and has continued throughout history for 4,000 years. Woe unto them that disregard Israel and mistreat Israel, for they will have to stand before the Creator of the universe for their attitudes, actions, and words toward the Jewish people, the physical brothers and sisters of Messiah, whether they were believers in Him or not!

Next we saw three examples from the New Testament: two from the Gospels and the other from the book of Acts. Two different individual Roman centurions blessed Israel, and they were in turn blessed by the covenant-keeping God of Israel. A Gentile woman with Faith in God's goodness and power received a blessing because of the witness of her confidence in God.

In post-biblical history we saw six examples where God has cursed Gentile nations and national religious bodies who adamantly showed anti-Semitic attitudes and actions towards the very people God made an eternal covenant with. He has and will curse nations if they curse the chosen people of God, Israel. One of these groups that received curses was the very group that called themselves "Christians," the "Church." All are treated under the same principle of Genesis 12:3.

Lastly, we looked at the outworkings of the Abrahamic Covenant of Genesis 12:3 in relationship to the blessings and cursings in the prophetic future. We see a pattern being laid out by God which has not changed since the Abrahamic Covenant was given over 4,000 years ago. In all those years which have passed since then, the Abrahamic Covenant is still very active, alive, and current today, and will continue to be until the end of time.

Contemplate what God has said and what God has done to both individuals and nations that bless or curse His people, both past, present and future. God has carried out the blessings and cursings of the Abrahamic Covenant in a consistent manner since its inception. He means business!

Keep that in mind as we move to the next chapter and contemplate God's attitude towards fundamental, conservative, and conservative Evangelical missions in this country as well as around the world. Does it matter to Him if any are anti-Jewish as they take Gospel of the Messiah around the globe? Do we go to the Jewish people first, as God's Word instructs us in Romans 1:16? Or do we ignore God's people Israel, the Jewish people?

Chapter 16
The Outworking of the Abrahamic Covenant in Missions

Now I wish to deal with a subject that is ignored or at best neglected. Why doesn't the believing body of Messiah present the Gospel of Messiah to the Jewish people worldwide as churches, missionaries, and mission agencies go to all areas of the globe? Would God bless our labors for Him abundantly more if we carried out the pattern of Romans 1:16, presenting the Gospel to the Jew first wherever we go?

We as Bible believers and our fundamental, conservative mission agencies have obeyed most of the priorities for biblical missions as laid out before us in the Scriptures. We have the following criteria in our favor:

1. We are largely dispensational in our approach to the Scriptures.
2. We interpret Scripture literally.
3. Our spiritual gifting as believers enables our missionaries to carry out the Great Commission. (But there is also a Great Omission in our understanding of the Great Commission.)
4. We are people who are willing to leave the comfort of our own cultural setting and go to different cultural peoples.

But in all our going out to share the Gospel in the last 100 years, we have ignored, neglected, and by-passed as unimportant or insignificant the Jewish people scattered around the world. The same missionaries are going around the world and yet purposely withholding the Gospel of Messiah from Jewish people.

In our going through Scripture, it becomes very evident that God has a genuine, eternal love for His firstborn, Israel, in the Abrahamic, Land, Davidic, and New Covenants. Now you can use allegorically-inducted interpretation and try to do an end run around God and His Word, but that is a futile exercise of unbelief. Those who follow Covenant/Replacement Theology may try that end-run around reaching out to God's people Israel, but I also find the same thing with conservative, fundamental Bible and Baptist Churches, and other fundamental denominational churches. This is at odds with what the Bible teaches. God loves Israel and you can track that from Genesis 12 through Revelation. We have looked at clear statements from God, Himself, in His Word.

The passage at the center of this discussion is Romans 1:16, which churches and mission agencies do all kinds of religious gymnastics to ignore. However, we cannot dismiss the thrust of God's love for Israel in the writings of Paul. It is interesting that we pride ourselves on interpreting the Scriptures literally and yet here we do not use the literal method of understanding Paul's heart as well as God's heart for the Jewish people. Let us first look at Romans 1:16:

> *For I am not ashamed of the gospel of Messiah: for it is the power of God unto salvation to everyone that believeth; to the Jew first, and also to the Greek* [Gentiles].

We need to examine this verse. I checked 20-plus different commentaries on Romans that I have in my possession and discovered the following. Most of them give a very superficial treatment of this verse while a few of them only say that this was a historical procedure followed by Paul and was only applicable to his own personal ministry. It is viewed as not being applicable or a working principle for believers today to follow; mind you, this belief is very prevalent among Bible believing, fundamental, conservative and dispensational pastors as well as among missionaries and mission agencies!

I was surprised that even dispensational writers hold that position, that we no longer need to reach out to Jewish people with the Gospel. I believe that interpretation is biased, and a clear example of not *rightly dividing the Word of Truth* as this passage is approached. The bias is evident even among dispensationalists, who see God as primarily working with Gentiles in this age because the Jewish people and nation have rejected Jesus as Messiah and LORD. They fail to see the big picture that God has and is putting together in His Word from a Jewish background. They miss the overarching themes that God has placed in the Scripture beginning with Moses, even though these themes span all through His Word.

Who is preeminent in the Scriptures: God or man? You know the answer to that, for His nature, or His person, is preeminent as He progressively revealed His Person, plan, and themes in Scripture. He is the object of Faith, and Israel is His tool in presenting His personal revelation of Himself and the salvation that He has provided. But in the name of scholarship, we have never recovered completely from 18 centuries of Replacement Theology. Instead, we have allowed a subtle form of anti-Jewish bias against Israel to continue. This bias has blinded us to God's themes that frame a picture of His grace and mercy; we have missed them. Here is the rest of the frame for the beautiful picture that God is painting:

- The frame of God's picture is the overarching theme of **Israel** throughout all of Scripture.

- God shares His overarching theme of the **Covenants to Israel** throughout all of Scripture.

- God's overarching theme of the **Seed** throughout all of Scripture is the redemptive cord of the coming of the Messiah to Israel and the world.

Based on these overarching themes presented by God, Himself, and His immediate tool, Israel, and His secondary tool, the Bride of Messiah, let us look again at Romans 1:16.

Romans 1:16

First, let us key in on the words *for it is the power of God unto salvation to everyone that believeth; to the Jew first, and also to the Greek*. Is the *power of God* to save just a historical statement? Is it just applicable in Paul's day? Is this *power of God* not applicable in our day? Absurd you say! I agree that is absurd.

The *power of God* to save *the Jew first* was not just in Paul's day, but it is applicable in our day as well. You cannot have it both ways. If the *power of God* is always to save those that believed in Paul's day *to the Jew first and also to the Greek* [Gentile] then it is still the *power of God unto salvation to everyone that believeth* today. Do not miss the obvious point: If *it* [was] *the power of God unto salvation* in Paul's day, *it is* still *the power of God to salvation* today *to the Jew first and also to the Greek*.

Second, look at Paul's mission procedure; everywhere he traveled as the apostle to the Gentiles he went to the *Jew first*, to the synagogues (Acts 13:5,

14;14:1; 16:12-13; 17:1, 10, 17; 18:4; 19:8; 28:17). Remember that he was not sent to the Jews; that was Peter's title. If it was Paul's procedure to preach the Gospel in his day to save the Gentiles and the Jew by the *power of God*, it is still the *power of God* to save today, *to the Jew first and also to the Greek*. Nothing has changed.

Third, let us look at a series of questions to make us think biblically:

- If we say that we are Dispensationalists and believe in interpreting the Scripture literally, then why do we try to pull rank on God and change the emphasis of God?

- Why do we divert the meaning of the text? God spoke through Paul using the literal plain sense of Scripture. Don't you believe in the literal plain sense of Scripture?

- Why do we interpret and change the meaning, the plain sense of Scriptures, as our Replacement/Covenant brothers do in both the Hebrew Scriptures and the New Testament?

- Let me ask you a heart question, a rough question. Now lay this book down and take some time and think through history. Here is the question: Have we ever really escaped the anti-Jewish bias of the Church that has been passed down to us from the second century? Do we join those who believe the Jewish people deserve scorn and hatred because they rejected Jesus as the Messiah and had Him crucified? Have we been blinded by the subtle anti-Semitism that we have unknowingly inherited from the Church that through the ages has been against the Jewish people? Have we missed picking up this long-running error of Christian theology on our radar screens?

Our Bible colleges and seminaries do not teach Church history from the anti-Semitic stance of the Church. They teach only the doctrinal issues of the Church but DO NOT teach the anti-Semitism of the Replacement Theology that is clearly traced through the Church to our present day!

So the conclusion is that the residual effect of 1,900 years has never been corrected by the Church. We as fundamentalists today are left with the outworking of RT in our relationship with Jewish people. I challenge you who are missionaries and heads of mission agencies to look at all of the impact that Church history has had on the fundamental, conservative, and Evangelical churches of today and our response to Jewish people.

Fourth, in Romans 2:8-11, Paul uses the statement *to the Jew first and also to the Greek* concerning judgment and blessing. Before I go further, let's look at the passage from Romans:

⁸ But unto them that are contentious and do not obey the truth, but obey unrighteousness, indignation and wrath, ⁹ Tribulation and anguish, upon every soul of man that does evil, of **the Jew first and also of the Gentile***. ¹⁰ But glory, honor, and peace, to every man that works* [for] *good,* **to the Jew first and also to the Gentile:** *¹¹ For there is no respect of persons with God.*

God always judges sin, whether it is Jewish sin or Gentile sin, and God always will bless when His Word is obeyed, to the *Jew first and also the Greek*. We must be consistent. If God's proscribed method for the evangelization of the *Jew first* is not applicable in Romans 1:16 today, neither is God's judgment or blessing applicable to the *Jew first and also to the Greek* [Gentile] today if it is only, as many say, an historical application.

Let's face it: God is not biased, but He is faithful. He has an eternal Covenant with Israel, the Jewish people, for they are His firstborn son (Exodus 4:22-23; Hosea 11:1); He loves them. No one wants to go and deny that truth in their teaching, so we circumvent it by interpreting it biblically in Romans 2:9-10 and then being inconsistent in Romans 1:16, saying that was just an historical reference but not true today.

Fifth, Paul dedicates three chapters in the book of Romans[146] to showing God's continuing care for Israel. He showed that God has not set Israel aside; He has not abandoned Israel. If we say we believe what Paul taught about God's love for the Jewish people in Romans chapters 9 through 11, why isn't *the power of God unto salvation … to the Jew first and also to the Greek* taught and practiced by churches and mission agencies around the world today? When was the last time pastors and missions agencies made a thorough study of Romans 9-11? There is not space in this book to do a complete study on Romans 9-11, but let us look at a couple of verses in Romans 11 starting with verse 11:

---

[146] Here are two books that deal specifically with Romans 9-11. Steven A. Kreloff, *God's Plan For Israel: A Study of Romans 9-11* (Neptune, NJ: Loizeaux Brothers, 1995) – ISBN 0-87213-468-7; Richard Freeman, *The Heart of the Apostle: A Commentary on Romans 9-11* (New York, NY: Chosen People Ministries, 2007) – ISBN 1-59872-809-5.

> *I* [Paul] *say then, Have they* [God's people Israel] *stumbled that they should fall? God forbid: but rather through their fall salvation is come unto the Gentiles, for to provoke them to jealousy.*

Don't skip that verse: Read it again! If you will, consider this question: How did you as a Gentile receive salvation? It was because the Jewish people stumbled and rejected their Messiah. If the Jewish people had not rejected Him, where would your salvation come from? It would be non-existent! The Blood of Christ the Jewish Messiah had to be shed on the cross to open the door of salvation to Jew and Gentile alike.

Notice Paul's clear conclusions at the end of the verse: We Gentiles are to *provoke* the Jewish people *to jealousy*. Yet today in missions, we ignore Jewish people. We send missionaries all over the earth to many places where Jewish people live; and instead of provoking them to jealousy by our Faith in the God of Israel, we purposely withhold the Gospel to Jesus' physical brothers and sisters. Is this not anti-Semitism at its worst? On what grounds can we justify withholding the Gospel of Messiah from the very people that gave us the blessing of the Gospel? Because they stumbled, God opened the door to us Gentiles to be saved without becoming Jewish. Please go back to that verse and read it again and contemplate what Paul has said to us Gentiles.

Now also go to Romans 11:21 and contemplate the picture that Paul is painting against our own spiritual smugness. This verse is dealing with discipline. Let me use a very simple example to help us understand this verse. If God took His son Israel to the woodshed, He will also take believers to His woodshed for discipline. Now read this verse (from a larger section of verses 16-29 on this subject):

> *For if God spared not the natural branches* [Jewish people], *take heed lest he also spare not you* [the Gentile members of the bride of Messiah].

Reform theologians (and many dispensational, Evangelical, conservative Christians theoretically) want to cast Israel aside; yet, as always, there is a believing remnant of Israel. This believing remnant of Israel is part of a visible group of people called the Body of Christ, the Church. In many respects, they are more unfaithful than unfaithful Israel. So if God is not a respecter of persons and is completely finished with Israel and has broken off the *natural branches* and *grafted* in the *wild olive branch*, consider the following correlation. Could God also break off the wild olive branches, the unfaithful believing Gentiles, in discipline? Is God's salvation conditional, or not?

Think about it. Look around at the so-called Church of Christ, the Catholic Church, Eastern Orthodox, Russian Orthodox, liberal and apostate Protestants. The believing remnant of His body is very small compared to all who call themselves Christian. Much of today's Church is like the Laodicean Church of Revelation 3, lukewarm at best. Read Romans 11:16-29 and understand Paul's argument, and understand that today even the believing remnant of the (Gentile) Church is arrogant, prideful, boastful, and selfish. Take your blinders off and look at God's Word as He wrote it. After you have studied the Scriptures searching for God's heart for the Jewish people, then also take a good look at the two books listed in footnote #140 on Romans 9-11 (see page 255).

We the Church, the Body of Messiah, tend to be an egotistical bunch that completely ignores our roots, the Jewish background of the Scriptures, and think that everything revolves around us, the Bride of Messiah. The Bible is a Jewish book immersed, enveloped in Jewish culture and customs and written from a Jewish theological viewpoint by Jewish men. Consider your Bible:

- The Hebrew Scriptures (Old Testament) are Jewish.

- The Gospels are Old Testament theologically, for Yeshua (Jesus) lived and ministered under the Law; the Gospels are Jewish.

- Acts 1-9 completely deals with the Jewish Church; chapters 10-26 are mixed between a Jewish and Gentile audience.

- In Romans, Paul put a very strong emphasis on the Hebrew Scriptures as he developed his tremendous treatise of theology. He quoted or referenced at less 120 times the Hebrew Scriptures as He laid out the doctrines of the Church.

- In Corinthians, Paul taught them about the Feasts of Israel.

- In Galatians, Paul's strong emphasis is on the Hebrew Scriptures and his argument against Gentiles adhering to the Jewish Law.

- The books of Hebrews, James, 1 and 2 Peter, and Jude were written to the Jewish Church.

- In Revelation, there is nothing new between chapters 6-19. Everything else had already been written about in Moses and the Prophets.

As you hold your Bible in your hands, understand it was written by Jewish people. Please contemplate the ramifications of this. Also understand that the regeneration of the Holy Spirit that we enjoy is the outworking of the New Covenant, a Jewish Covenant (Jeremiah 31:31-34; Ezekiel 36:26-27; Joel 2:28), which is the blessing aspect of Genesis 12:3c; *and in you shall all families of the earth be blessed.*

Without the New Covenant and the One who was Jewish Who initiated it, your sins and mine would still be on our heads and we would never be able to go to heaven. That is a sobering thought; yet some are so immersed in a Greek/Western perspective of the Scriptures that they want to make Jesus a Gentile with blondish hair and blue eyes. He was not and is not!

What I am saying is that the New Covenant and the spiritual blessings (Ephesians 1:3) that we enjoy are Jewish; if Yeshua had not initiated it, there would be no New Testament. There would be no Great Commission to preach and teach, baptizing them in the name of the Father, the Son, and the Holy Spirit. Now where does that leave us?

Paul will again say in Romans 15:27 that you and I are *partakers* of their (Jewish) spiritual things, making us debtors to Jewish people, to show the love of Messiah to them physically. Look with me at the verse:

It has pleased them verily; and their debtors they are. For if the Gentiles have been made partakers of their spiritual things, their duty is also to minister unto them in carnal [physical] *things.*

Paul the Apostle to the Gentiles states that Gentiles are first of all *partakers* with their Jewish brothers in Messiah in the *spiritual blessing* in Christ. Those spiritual blessings came from Abraham in the Covenant. That is the meaning of *in him shall all the families of the earth be blessed.* That promise was initiated by the **Blood** of the New Covenant, a Jewish covenant. Do you realize what was involved in your salvation, which is through the **Blood** of the New Covenant?[147]

Three Examples of the "Great Omission"

Now I want to introduce a subject that most Church and mission leaders have turned their back on. Based on the blessings and cursings and the outworking of the Abrahamic Covenant, how does God relate to the Body of

---

[147] Metzger, *Israel's Only Hope: The New Covenant.*

Messiah when we purposely withhold the Gospel of Messiah from Jewish people when we are in their midst?

Let me relate the **first** case in point. This short story was given to me by Rev. Ken Symes, then director of Jewish Awareness Ministries, when he related the words of fundamental Baptist mission directors that he was interacting with. When he asked about Baptist mission agencies being involved in Jewish evangelism around the world, they replied, "You cannot build churches with Jews."

That is an anti-Semitic statement to the core; it is actively cursing the Jewish people from ever hearing the Gospel of their own Messiah! It is interesting that years ago, when I was in Washington Bible College, we had a course on evangelism. One part of it was on evangelism in general, and the second part was largely on Jewish Evangelism. The college had a good biblical understanding and heart to reach the Jewish people for Messiah as they reached the Gentiles for Christ. That is not done today!

Let me share one other personal story as a **second** case in point. I was representing Jewish missions at a Bible college mission conference and I began speaking to a fellow representative from a mission in Bolivia, South America. I asked him if there were Jewish people in Bolivia, and he said there were. I asked him if the mission has an outreach to the Jewish people there; he said no, they did not. I then asked him if anyone in that mission in Bolivia was even equipped to witness to Jewish people, and he said no. My response was, "Are they [Jewish people] not Bolivians also?" Why is it we send missionaries around the globe and then ignore Jewish people in our midst? What is even more alarming was that he knew the presence of Jewish people in that country.

The **third** case in point comes from someone I am very close to and respect for his years of faithful service to the LORD. His heart was immersed in reaching a very difficult people group for Christ. However, in a lengthy conversation with him, he stated that every missionary believes and promotes his or her own ministry and believes the people that he ministers to are all important. They believe that everyone should focus on their particular people group to reach them. He claimed that I did the same with thing with Jewish missions; he said that I promote it as the only ministry to be supported and prayed for.

Now I understand in principle what he is saying, because that is what has been done historically in most protestant missions. Missionaries ministering in Africa, for example, support their mission agency in that country or region as does every other mission agency. He was promoting the idea that this is what I do in Jewish ministry. I had to answer, "That is not how I promote missions."

Jewish missions are special beyond all other missions because we are dealing with the covenant people of God who are the source for everything we believe today. We are debtors to them for the Scriptures, the Messiah, and our salvation through Messiah, the **Blood** of the New Covenant. In short, everything that we have in our Faith, all the spiritual blessing that Paul referenced in Ephesians 1:3, is ours because of God's covenant relationship with Israel. The Jewish people are the **focus of the Scriptures**, the **focus of the covenants**, the **focus of our salvation**. More importantly, **they are God's focus throughout the Scriptures**.

God's people Israel are the special tool of God to bring forth the reality of His promise to Abraham that *in you* [Abraham] *shall all the families of the earth be blessed*. That is why Paul said we are to bring the Gospel message *to the Jew first and also to the Greek*. We are dealing with a unique people.

My thrust in missions is, if God calls you to Europe, South America, Africa, or Russia, remember as you go ministering to those peoples that among them are Jewish people who equally need to be reached for Messiah. Instead, in reality, Jewish people are consistently ignored by mission agencies and personally by missionaries, to our own shame. If God calls you to reach Germans for Christ, God will inevitably put Jewish people in your path to be ministered to as well.

So I believe that my friend was biblically incorrect and had missed the whole point of the heart of God to reach the world for Himself. Never, never, never forget to minister to Jewish people, His chosen, Yeshua's physical brothers and sisters. Know your God's heart!

These three observations reflect a much larger problem in missions in general and mission agencies in particular. I believe that missions in general have largely bypassed ministry to the Jewish people because it is difficult and the response is relatively small. Americans want numbers to send back home to supporting churches; but contrary to popular belief, God is not interested in numbers. He is interested in obedience to His Word.

I do firmly believe that the fundamental and conservative mission agencies are esteeming the Jewish people lightly. In other words, they are cursing Israel by not reaching out to Jewish people wherever they are all over the world. I do understand that we are not going to experience the wrath of God as the Bride of Messiah; all of God's wrath was poured out on Messiah on the cross of Calvary. But remember Revelation, chapters 2 through 3 and the judgment, or should I say discipline, that Yeshua said He would bring against five of those churches, each represented by a Jewish menorah? Look what He says:

Revelation 2:5 – Church of Ephesus:

Or else I will come unto you quickly, and will remove your candlestick out of His place, except you repent.

Revelation 2:16 – Church of Pergamos:

Repent; or else I will come unto you quickly, and fight against them with the sword of My mouth.

Revelation 2:21-23 – Church of Thyatira:

^{21} And I gave her space to repent of her fornication; and she repented not. ^{22} Behold, I will cast her into a bed, and them that commit adultery with her into great tribulation, except they repent of their deeds. ^{23} And I will kill her children with death; and all the churches shall know that I am He which searches the reins and hearts: and I will give unto every one of you according to your works.

Revelation 3:3 – Church of Sardis:

Remember therefore how you have received and heard, and hold fast, and repent. If therefore you shall not watch, I will come on you as a thief, and you shall not know what hour I will come upon you.

Revelation 3:19 – Church of Laodicea:

As many as I love, I rebuke and chasten: be zealous therefore, and repent.

Those five verses in Revelation are dealing with Yeshua's discipline and judgment on local churches. He can and does use discipline on individual believers and local churches, and He can also discipline our mission agencies. What will missionaries and mission agencies say to Christ at the Bema Seat – the reward seat – when we stand before a Jewish Messiah, a Jewish Judge, to have our works judged by Him? Will He ask, "Did you love my physical brothers and sisters in the flesh? Did you make a point to share the Gospel with them, or did you ignore them?"

Why do missionaries and agencies degrade the importance of witnessing to the Jewish people? It is a historical fact about missions when they went to the unreached around the world in the 1800s; many of the denominational missions of those days, the Anglican, Presbyterian, Lutheran and many other independent mission agencies, all had ministries to reach Jewish people for Messiah Yeshua. God blessed missions around the world as each Protestant denomination ministered to Jewish people, and thousands of Jewish people came to Faith in Jesus Christ as their Messiah. It is estimated that there were over 250,000 Jewish believers in Europe before the beginning of World War II. What has happened that our outreach to them has stopped? What derailed the mind and heart of missions from reaching out to the Jewish people?

Is it possible that the LORD will rebuke you, your mission, or your mission agency? Have we been faithful to reach the Jewish people, who have been ignored since World War II? I cannot answer that question. However, I have begun to understand the heart of God for His people after studying the cursings and blessings of the Abrahamic Covenant through biblical history and post-biblical history. I am acutely aware and fearful of how God could rebuke or chasten His Bride for not loving His physical descendants, the Jewish people.

But is it possible that due to our purposeful neglect of Jewish people, the fruits of our labor in missions are in general low, only 30 fold? Now we know that God loves us, and He will discipline His children. Why would we even put ourselves in that position to be disciplined or chastened by Him when we know where God's heart is? If we followed God's procedure to go *to the Jew first and also to the Greek,* is it possible that our laborers would bring in a harvest of 60 or 100 fold around the world from the masses of unsaved Catholics, Hindus, Muslims, Buddhists, Animists, secularists and others?

Looking around at churches in the northeast, southeast, and west of our country, where I have spoken primarily, I have observed several things. **First**, I understand that all churches have problems with getting their people to witness and lead others to Christ, let alone getting them to reach out to other ethnic groups from their own. We will send our monies to support missions in Europe, Africa, Asia, South and North America, but we most often do not witness to the peoples in our own neighborhoods who have come from those countries where we support missionaries. Do we support missionaries in general to soothe our consciences, because we do not witness ourselves?

Then we come to the Jewish people. I come into churches that do not support or even pray for even one missionary to Jewish people, while at the same time they may pridefully display pictures of missionaries they support around the world and the flags from their host countries, yet with no sign of missions to the Jews. How many churches and mission agencies pray for the salvation of Jewish people and *pray for the peace of Jerusalem: they shall prosper that love thee* (Psalm 122:6)?

I know of one large church in Pennsylvania that is very big on worldwide missions with a very large mission's budget. I understand that their yearly mission's budget is one million dollars, yet they will only support one missionary to the Jewish people. They have no outreach (to my knowledge) to the Jewish community in their city, yet they boast of multiple missionaries with many ethnic groups around the world. Why are Jewish people ignored? One Jewish believer who in the past tried to draw the attention of that church to Jewish missions has said sarcastically, they have a "token mission presence to the Jew." Why is that so? If we were to bless Israel in our missions outreach, wouldn't God also give greater blessing to our total mission endeavor because we placed Jewish people first as instructed by God?

Do not miss what God has said in Genesis 12:3. Just because we are the Bride of Messiah does not mean that God cannot bless our endeavors in local missions and foreign missions beyond our goals of seeing even more Gentiles come to Faith. Are we satisfied we have made a concerted effort to reach His people, the Jewish people? We can expect that the apostate church, along with the Roman Catholic Church, Orthodox Churches, and World Council of Churches and any other unrepentant groups who harm the Jewish people will receive the curse of God. God has promised in Genesis 12:3 to destroy any such persecutors during the Tribulation because they have inflicted unrighteous judgments on Israel in the name of Jesus Christ!

One final observation to show just how Israel, the Jewish People, the seed of Abraham, have blessed us and the world. First, spiritually, they have given us Gentiles the Written Word of God so that we could know God and learn of His love for us and His plan of redemption for those who will believe. They have given us the Messiah, our Savior, who died and shed His **Blood**, the **Blood** of the New Covenant, on the cross for our sins and rose again. Sit down and contemplate what Paul says in Romans 15:26-27 to us as Gentile members of the Body of Messiah:

> *^{26} For it has pleased them of Macedonia and Achaia to make a certain contribution for the poor saints which are at Jerusalem. ^{27} It has pleased them verily; and their debtors they are. For if the Gentiles have been made partakers of their spiritual things, their duty is also to minister unto them in carnal things.*

Gentiles in Macedonia and Achaia benefited spiritually because of the Jewish people. Today, we as Gentile believers have benefited spiritually; we have been grafted into the vine (Romans 11:17), into Abraham by means of the New Covenant, a Jewish covenant which is part of the Abrahamic Covenant. We do have a great indebtedness to the Jewish people for what they have given to us. Now Paul says we are to bless them back in the love of Messiah, and do it in a physical way (as well as spiritual). Will we accept this, or are we going to conveniently say that blessing the Jewish people is just a historical reference with no relevance for today?

Israel is an exceptional nation. Think about what they have experienced and yet still thrive despite being exiled from their country and their many times of being persecuted and attacked. They survived the Assyrian, Babylonian and Roman expulsions from the Land that had been visited on them by God because of their disobedience. They have survived 83 major expulsions at the hands of "christian" European nations and have experienced the following:

- public humiliations
- forced conversions
- being murdered, hanged, and tortured
- the rape of their women
- communities burned and pillaged; being burned alive
- forced to wear the Star of David, forced to wear horned hats
- the destruction of their synagogues
- the burning of Talmud and religious books

- attacks by mobs, having their villages destroyed and possessions taken, having children taken from them to be raised as Christians
- the Inquisition and its hideous satanic torture
- Judaism outlawed, land confiscated, and being thrown out of trades or guilds
- the onslaught of the Crusades, pogroms
- being wrongly accused of Blood Libel, Host Desecration, and of causing the Black Plague
- Being drowned and burned at the stake

Why did the Jewish people experience all these persecutions? Because they were Jews, and the "christian" church deemed them worthy of these atrocities for "killing Christ" (even though we are all guilty of His death because of our sins). Others, such as Hitler, fanned the flames of anti-Semitism with outrageous claims against them and fervor to annihilate Jews from the face of the earth. Here are some Satan-inspired words of lunatic Adolf Hitler:

> Providence has ordained that I should be the greatest liberator of humanity. I am freeing man from ... a false vision called conscience and morality. The 10 Commandments have lost their validity. Conscience is a Jewish invention, it is a blemish. The heaviest blow which struck humanity was Christianity. Bolshevism is Christianity's illegitimate child. Both are the inventions of the Jew. The struggle for world domination is between me and the Jews, all else is meaningless....[148]

This man was demon indwelt, and his person and actions form a type of the anti-Christ to come in the future. I found an interesting statement concerning the reason behind men like Hitler:

> The devil hates the Bible and he hates the Christ of the Bible. He therefore hates the nation that gave to the world these precious things. Wicked men hate the Bible and the Christ of the Bible,

---

[148] Hermann Rauschning, *Hitler Speaks* (Whitefish, MT: Kessinger Publishing, 2010). Reprint of the 1939 original.

therefore Satan finds them willing instruments through which to carry out his purpose in attempting to destroy the Jews.[149]

It is equally disheartening to see Christians, as well as Christian and secular institutions and nations, who are pawns in the hands of Satan to afflict the Jewish People. Mankind in his hatred and rage at the Jew is willingly ignorant of God, for it is God who has "hedged the Jew in with promises and covenant,"[150] and He has sworn by Himself that Israel will abide forever!

Yet, despite facing staggering attempts to unleash harm upon the Jewish people, the Jew still survives and even flourishes in amazing ways. Let me give you a series of quotes from others as to the uniqueness of the Jewish people. In the following quotations, read slowly the words of various wise men of history. Most of these quotes were secured from a website[151] and I have found them also independent of that site. Look at the first one, by Mark Twain:

> If the statistics are right, the Jews constitute but one percent of the human race [now less than half of a percent]. It suggests a nebulous dim puff of star-dust lost in the blaze of the Milky Way.
>
> Properly the Jew ought hardly to be heard of; but he is heard of, has always been heard of. He is as prominent on the planet as any other people, and his commercial importance is extravagantly out of proportion to the smallness of his bulk. His contributions to the world's list of great names in literature, science, art, music, finance, medicine, and abstruse learning are also way out of proportion to the weakness of his numbers.
>
> He has made a marvelous fight in this world, in all the ages; and has done it with his hands tied behind him. He could be vain of himself, and be excused for it. The Egyptian, the Babylonian, and the Persians rose, filled the planet with sound and splendor, then faded to

---

[149] Louis T. Talbot, *Three Reasons Why the Gentile Nations Are Attempting to Destroy the Jewish People and Three Reasons Why They Can Not Succeed* (Los Angeles, CA: Jewish Department of the Bible Institute of Los Angeles, Daniel Rose, n.d.), 12.

[150] Talbot, *Three Reasons Why the Gentile Nations Are Attempting to Destroy the Jewish People and Three Reasons Why They Can Not Succeed*, 13.

[151] www.SimpleToRemember.com/jewish/blog/mark-twain-and-the-jews/ Then click on link called "The Mystery of the Jews" at the bottom of the website.

dream-stuff and passed away; the Greek and the Roman followed, and made a vast noise, and they are gone; other peoples have sprung up and held their torch high for a time, but it burned out, and they sit in twilight now, or have vanished.

The Jew saw them all, beat them all, and is now what he always was, exhibiting no decadence, no infirmities of age, no weakening of his parts, no slowing of his energies, no dulling of his alert and aggressive mind. All things are mortal but the Jew; all other forces pass, but he remains. What is the secret of his immortality?[152]

To partially answer Mark Twain's question, their longevity has been sustained by God's promises and covenants with Abraham, Isaac, and Jacob and to their descendants. God's oath, His integrity and character, is at stake; and He will not relent on His Word, His Oath. In addition, the Jewish people, themselves, have unknowingly vindicated the truth of the Bible by living out all the prophecies and their fulfillments to this very hour. Now look at a few other quotations.

Paul Johnson – Author of *A History of the Jews*[153]

It is almost beyond our capacity to imagine how the world would have fared if they [the Jews] had never emerged. Certainly the World without the Jews would have been a radically different place. Humanity might have eventually stumbled upon all the Jewish insights, but we cannot be sure. To them we owe the idea of equality before the law, sanctity of life, dignity of the human person, social responsibility, peace as an idea and many other items which constitute the basic furniture of the human mind. Without it the world might have been a much emptier place.

John Adams – U.S. President (1797-1801)

The Hebrews, the Jews[,] have contributed more to civilized man than any other nation.... They are the most glorious nation that ever inhabited this Earth. The Romans and their empire were but a bubble in comparison to the Jews. They have given religion to [three-quarters] of the globe and have influenced the affairs of mankind more and more happily than any other nation ancient or

---

[152] Mark Twain, *Concerning the Jews* (Harper's Magazine, September 1899).
[153] Paul Johnson, *A History of the Jews* (NY: Harper Perennial, 1988).

modern. (From a letter to F. A. Van der Kemp [Feb. 16, 1808] Pennsylvania Historical Society)

Winston Churchill – British Prime Minister (1940-1945 & 1951-1955)

Some people like the Jews and some do not, but no thoughtful man can deny the fact that they are beyond any question the most formidable race that has ever appeared in the world.[154]

Natan Sharansky – a Russian Politician & Human Rights Activist, said the following before a Russian Communist court prior to his sentencing, speaking of the yearning of Jews to return to their homeland:

For 2000 years, the Jewish people, my people[,] have been dispersed all over the world and still each year Jews have stubbornly, and apparently, without reason said to each other "'L' Shana Ha' Bah B' Yerushalayim," next year in Jerusalem and today when I am further than ever from my dream and from my people and when many difficult years of prison camps lie ahead of me, I say to my wife and my people, "'L' Shana Ha' Bah B' Yerushalayim," next year in Jerusalem.

Thomas Cahill – Author of *The Gift of the Jews*[155]

Without the Jews we would see the world through different eyes, hear with different ears, even feel with different feelings and we would set a different course for our lives.

J. M. Robert – Author of *The New History of the World*[156]

No other people have produced a greater historical impact from such comparatively insignificant origins and resources.

---

[154] Excerpt from Winston S. Churchill, "Zionism versus Bolshevism. A Struggle for the Soul of the Jewish People, *Illustrated Sunday Herald* (Feb. 8, 1920), p. 5. See the full article at http://www.fpp.co.uk/bookchapters/WSC/WSCwrote1920.html, last accessed at Focal Point Publications on 10/9/2018.

[155] Thomas Cahill, *The Gifts of the Jews: How a Tribe of Desert Nomads Changed the Way Everyone Thinks and Feels* (The Hinges of History series), (NY: Anchor Books, 1999).

[156] J. M. Roberts, *The New History of the World*, (Oxford: Oxford University Press, 2014).

Sir Thomas Newton – Bishop of Bristol (1761-1782)

> The Preservation of the Jews is really one of the most single and illustrious acts of divine providence. What, but a super-natural power could have preserved them in such a manner as no other nation has been preserved and no less remarkable is the destruction of their enemies. Let it serve as a warning to all those who at any time or occasion are raising a clamor or persecution against them.[157]

Leon Tolstoy – Russian Writer (1852-1910)[158]

> What is the Jew? What kind of unique creature is this? Whom all the rulers of all the nations of the world have disgraced, expelled, destroyed, persecuted, burned and drowned and who, despite the anger and fury of their oppressors continues to live and to flourish. The Jew is the symbol of eternity. He is the one who following the faithfulness of his ancestors has for so long had guarded the prophetic message and transmitted it to all mankind. A people such as this can never disappear.

David Lloyd George – British Prime Minister (1916-1922), lived 1863-1945

> Of all the extreme fanaticism which plays havoc in man's nature[,] [t]here is not one as irrational as anti-Semitism.[159]

So what is the answer to the Jewish presence, to the Jewish mystery as to why they are so gifted? "The achievements of the Jewish people are founded upon God's supernatural calling of the Jewish people to be a light to the nations."[160] It is also the fulfillment of Genesis 12:3c where God said to Abraham, *in you shall all the families of the earth be blessed* and that is both spiritual in providing redemption for those who believe in the human race. Whether the human race believes or not in Jesus Christ, or hates the Jew, we and they are blessed physically by the giftedness of His people.

---

[157] Anonymous, "9 Great Quotes About Jews by Non-Jews," www.aish.com, p. 1.

[158] Count Leo Tolstoy, "What is a Jew?" an excerpt or possibly a summary of an article or essay penned by him in 1891 in St. Petersburg, Russia.

[159] David Lloyd George stated this in 1923.

[160] Jim Melnick, *Jewish Giftedness and World Redemption: The Calling of Israel* (Baltimore, MD: Lederer Books, 2017), Foreword by Mitch Glaser.

May I also commend to you Jim Melnick's new book *Jewish Giftedness and World Redemption: The Calling of Israel?*[161] He uncovers why the Jewish people filter to the top when freedom is in their possession.

One further note from David Jeremiah, pastor of Shadow Mountain Community Church Of El Cajon, CA:

> Considering all that the Jews have endured, there is no human explanation for their continued existence. No other people in the world have been driven from their homeland, have maintained their identity through eighteen-plus centuries of exile, and then have re-emerged as an intact nation.
>
> The Bible makes it clear why the Jews have endured despite these centuries of hardship. They are God's special people, chosen for a specific purpose.[162]

Too many times, the historic Church has been the enemy of the Jewish people, showing them the Church's depravity instead of God's love. The Church is off balance; and it largely has been negative to neutral, with very little positive biblical input into the lives of the Jewish people. Yet the Jewish people continue to give so much to benefit us physically. Look at the list of Jewish benefits and benefactors that we have received with little or no thanks from the **historic "christian" church:**

1. Hyman Salomon, a Jewish banker from Philadelphia, helped to finance the American Revolution. Without him, we might still be flying the Union Jack.[163]

2. Albert Einstein brought many discoveries to us as a physicist; for example, in 1921 he received the Nobel Prize in Physics.

3. Jonas Salk created the first Polio vaccine in 1955.

4. Albert Sabin developed the oral vaccine for Polio (1957-59). He also developed vaccines for encephalitis (sleeping sickness), sand-fly fever and dengue fever during his tour of duty in the U.S. Army during WWII.

---

[161] Melnick, *Jewish Giftedness and World Redemption: The Calling of Israel.*
[162] David Jeremiah, *Is This The End?* (Nashville, TN: W Publishing Group, 2016), 151.
[163] David Allen Lewis, *The Forgotten Patriot: The Story of Haym Salomon* (ISBN 10: 9657155258 / ISBN 13: 9789657155257, 2007).

5. Selman Waksman discovered Streptomycin and coined the word *antibiotic* (1951).

6. Gabriel Lipmann discovered color photography (1908).

7. Baruch Blumberg discovered the origin and spread of infectious diseases (1976).

8. G. Edelman discovered the chemical structure of antibodies (1972).

9. Briton Epstein identified the first cancer virus (1964).

10. Maria Meyer discovered the structure of atomic nuclei (1963).

11. Julius Mayer discovered the Law of Thermodynamics (1841).

12. Sigmund Freud became the Father of Psychotherapy (1890s).

13. Christopher Columbus, arguably a Spanish Jew, discovered the Americas (1492).

14. Benjamin Disraeli served as Prime Minister of Great Britain (1874-1880).

15. Isaac Singer invented an affordable sewing machine 1850).

16. Levi Strauss became the largest manufacturer of denim jeans (1873).

17. Joseph Pulitzer established the Pulitzer Prize for achievements in journalism, literature, music, and art (1917).

18. Milton Berle (1908-2002), Dinah Shore (1916-1994), Jack Benny (Benjamin Kubelsky – 1894-1974), Groucho (1890-1977) and Harpo (1888-1964) of the Marx Brothers, Phil Silvers (1911-1985), the Fonz (TV's Happy Days), Curly (1903-1952), Larry (1902-1975) and Moe (1897-1975) of the Three Stooges, Jerry Lewis (1926-2017), Paul Newman (1925-2008), Tony Randall (1920-2004), Joan Rivers (1933-2014), Danny Kaye (1911-1987), Don Rickles (1926-2017) – all American Jewish entertainers who made us laugh.

19. Wolfgang Mozart (1756-1791), Felix Mendelssohn (1809-1847), Benny Goodman (1909-1986), Bob Dylan (b. 1941), and George Gershwin (1898-1937) are a few of many acclaimed Jewish musicians.

20. Maurice Levy invented lipstick (1915).
21. Lazlo Biro invented the ballpoint pen (1938).
22. J. Robert Oppenheimer invented the Atomic Bomb (1945).
23. Edwin Herbert Land invented instant photography (Polaroid Camera) (1947).
24. Denis Gabor invented holography (1948).
25. Peter Carl Goldmark invented long playing records (1948).
26. Robert Adler invented the television remote control (1950).
27. Edward Teller invented the thermonuclear bomb (1952).
28. Paul M. Zoll invented the defibrillator and cardiac pacemaker (1952).
29. Charles Ginsburg invented the videotape (1950s).
30. Gordon Gould invented the laser (1958).
31. Stanley N. Cohen invented genetic engineering (1973).
32. Abraham Stern invented the adding machine (1887).
33. Charles Adler invented the traffic light (1920s).
34. Leo Sternbach invented Valium (1956).
35. Emile Berliner invented the microphone (1977).
36. Benno Strauss invented stainless steel (1931).
37. Abraham Levis invented hot dog buns.
38. Joe Friedman invented flexi-straws.
39. Emilio Segro won a Noble Prize for his part in the discovery of anti-protons (1959).
40. James Franck and Gustav Hertz discovered laws governing the impact of electrons on the atom (1925).
41. Alan Greenspan served as former Federal Reserve Chairman.
42. Alan King (b. 1933) hosted CNN, king of talk shows.
43. Michael S. Brown and Joseph L. Goldstein made discoveries concerning the regulation of cholesterol metabolism (1985).

44. Menachem Begin – Camp David Agreement with Egypt (1978).

45. Charles Krauthammer (1950-2018) was a contributor on Fox News.

46. Sandy Koufax (b. 1935) was a famous Dodgers baseball pitcher.

The Jewish population of the world is one-fifth of 1 percent of the world's population, yet they hold about 25 percent of all Noble Prizes. When Jewish people have enjoyed freedom, they totally out-produce any other people group on the planet. It is not because they have more intelligence; it is because of the Abrahamic Covenant and the promise of God to make them a blessing to the world, whether they are believing or unbelieving Jewish people in Messiah Yeshua.

Yes, a few Jewish people have done harm, such as Karl Marx who in 1848 published his *Communist Manifesto*. Today, George Soros (Schwartz Gyorgy) is another key figure behind so much of the Liberal (also known as Progressive) agenda of making the U.S.A. Socialist. Here are two corrupted Jewish men, but there are so many more who have contributed to all people on earth. These people and their accomplishments can be found very easily on the internet.

Beware of Satan and his goal, to annihilate the Jewish people from the planet. He cannot defeat God; he cannot destroy the earth, but he strives to destroy the Jewish people. Satan is the evil heart behind all the Hamans and Hitlers and the Antichrist who will be responsible for Holocaust II (the Tribulation period, the 70 Weeks of Daniel, the Time of Jacob's Trouble).

Although God is sovereign, and we know He will prevail to bring the Jewish people back to Himself, Satan works overtime to defeat that plan. On one hand, Satan works in the plans, goals, and agendas of Christians and deceives them into ignoring the Jewish people. On the other hand, Satan works through the unsaved to incite them to destroy the Jewish people. If he can destroy the Jewish people, he can thwart the plan of God in the future Millennium. Understand, we are not just fighting against the flesh but against the god of this world system, even as it relates to Jewish people.

God's Foundation – His Truth Stands

You have read by this time and worked through the two parts of this book: the first focusing on the importance of correct theology based on

God's Word, and the second focusing on the disastrous results of entertaining and acting on the error of anti-Semitic theology.

God's Word Is Truth!

Yeshua declared that He, Himself, would build His Church, and the gates of hell – all those many error-filled paths to destruction – would not prevail (Matthew 16:18). Just as a builder starts with a firm foundation, God started His building project of the Church with a strong foundation that has caused the Church to endure through many struggles to this day. The foundation has been laid, and it is Jesus Christ, with the Apostles and Prophets building upon that foundation. God's foundation was off to a great start.

Now the same thing is true in theology, for theology is the foundation that sets the godly, biblical direction and course for interpretation of God's Word that will either breed Truth or Error. What I have attempted to show in the two parts of this book is that while the theology of the early Church began on the perfect foundation of Christ with the Apostles and Prophets, it took a wrong turn early on, creating a faulty theological structure called anti-Semitism which was expressed in theology.

How Does Error Start?

Why are we concerned with ERROR within the Church? Doesn't all theology suffer from human bias? All systems of theology have a bias! That bias is either taking God's Truth as Truth without man tarnishing it with personal human input, or man in his imperfection and finite reasoning powers supplanting God's Truth with Error.

Sadly, in attending to many matters of lesser significance, many theologians have missed the big picture of Bible truth as it relates to Israel and the Abrahamic Covenant. God's people Israel and the Church are distinct, and both have received God's unmerited favor, and both have a future in God's plan. The Church comprised of Jewish and Gentile believers has been the focus of the Church Age, as the Bible prophecies have foretold. In the Millennial Kingdom, the Jewish people will return to God and be restored.

Three Waves of Anti-Semitic Theology

Anti-Semitism has long been integrated into the Church; it was laid down by those who adhered to: (1) Replacement Theology, (2) Amillennial Theology, and (3) Covenant Theology.

Replacement Theology began in the second century with the hatred of the Jews. Like many today, the early Church Fathers forgot about the sinfulness of all mankind and accused the Jews, in particular, of killing Christ. The first half of this book shows how this false teaching against the Jewish people began and how it is extra-biblical – having no foundation in the Word of God. In fact, on the contrary, the Word of God states God's unconditional, eternal love for the Jewish people. Yeshua (Jesus) declared that He was laying His life down; it was not being taken from Him. He was the willing sacrifice for the sin of all.

Amillennial Theology was developed in the fifth century by Augustine. It is the false teaching that the End Times prophesied in the Bible have already been fulfilled. It teaches that Yeshua/Jesus has returned in a figurative way, and that we are now living in the Millennial Kingdom. Building on the errors of Replacement Theology, the idea took hold that God was done with the Jewish people; they were condemned, and the Church supposedly took their place in God's heart.

However, Amillennial Theology is not biblical either. The Bible clearly teaches that Yeshua (Jesus Christ) will return to fulfill to His people Israel all that God promised to Abraham and the Jewish people, Abraham's descendants. His people Israel will come to recognize and accept Him, and He will build His Kingdom physically on earth in Jerusalem. It will be a glorious kingdom, and not the broken world we see and live in now. God is not finished with the Jewish people; He has not yet done all that He said He will do.

Covenant Theology is the third wave of error, denying that God's covenant to the Jewish people is still in force, teaching that the Jewish people have been scorned by God and have no future. Its adherents teach that the Jewish people do not have a title deed to the Land of Israel.

Dispensational Theology: Going Back to God's Word

Dispensational Theology returns to God's Word as the source for our understanding of His perspective, rather than our own. It takes the Word of God literally and takes into account the overall Word of God as progressively revealed to His people. It focuses on what God has said and done, and how He has interacted with Jewish people from within their own culture, even coming to earth as a Jewish man, reaching out to the Jewish people, and having Jewish men write the Old and New Testaments.

In this book, I have shared with you the teachings from this perspective related to the Abrahamic Covenant in the past, the present, and the future.

Dispensational Theology teaches that God is working out the Abrahamic Covenant, and part of that is the physical, literal return of His people – the Jewish people – to the Land of Israel. He will accomplish this whether we approve of His plan or not, just as He makes the stars to shine in the sky without our approval. A time of great testing, called the Great Tribulation, or Jacob's Trouble, is coming; and those who assist the Jewish people will be blessed greatly. The biggest blessing we can share with Jewish people is the Good News of Yeshua ha Mashiach, Jesus the Christ. Those who believe in Jesus will not suffer the Great Tribulation, but will be raptured out of this world and will be worshipping Him in glory.

Anti-Semitism is rebellion against God's people Israel and against God, Himself; it is like a cancer. Beginning in the second century and intensifying, anti-Semitism has encroached time and time again throughout Church history against the Jewish people. It climbed within the world system to the atrocities of the Holocaust, a regional manifestation of wickedness and death. It has climbed to a global phenomenon in which many, even within the Church, deny that Israel has the right to the Land or any relevance to the God they worship.

The Accuracy, Certainty, and Continuity of God's Blessings and Cursings

The second part of this book provides many examples of how God has remembered His covenant with Abraham down through the ages and even today, visiting blessings and curses on individuals, nations, and organizations that have tried to harm the Jewish people, whom He calls the apple of His eye. Strong evidence points to God's fingerprint on His judgments in kind. Those individuals and nations who have treated the Jewish people lightly, tried to harm them, or tried to defeat or wipe them out have in time reaped what they sowed. Indeed, any who continue down the path of anti-Semitism will also reap what they have sown.

God's Words and His covenants cannot be removed, suppressed, or cancelled by man. The Church has attacked God's covenants, in particular the Abrahamic Covenant with its blessings and curses which are directed specifically towards the Gentiles. All non-Jews will be rewarded or punished according to their relationship with God's covenant people Israel. God's Word CANNOT be broken or cancelled out by man.

Are you building on God's foundation? God is God; man is man. Look at the following verses from 1 Corinthians 3:11-15:

> *^{11} For other foundation can no man lay than that is laid, which is Jesus Christ. ^{12} Now if any man build upon this foundation gold, silver, precious stones, wood, hay, stubble, ^{13} Every man's work shall be made manifest: for the day shall declare it, because it shall be revealed by fire; and the fire shall try every man's work of what sort it is. ^{14} If any man's work abide which he has built thereupon, he shall receive a reward. ^{15} If any man's work shall be burned, he shall suffer loss: but he himself shall be saved yet so as by fire.*

Whether or not we acknowledge it, the Scriptures, beginning to end, emphasize God's relationship to His people Israel. We as Gentiles became partakers in God's grace according to God's pleasure, as a result of the **Blood** of the Lamb, as did Jewish people who believed in Him. The End Time prophecies, about a third of Scripture, that have not yet been fulfilled deal with God's future for His people Israel. Much is yet to unfold.

In the second part of the book, I provided many historical examples of God's blessings to Gentiles for blessing Jewish people and God's curses for cursing God's people Israel. Theology has determined the fate of individuals and nations throughout history. Remember, the Jewish people have an everlasting covenant that God made by Himself and did not let Abraham participate in; it was unilateral. Jewish people have stood at the graves of all the Hamans, Jezebels and Hitlers throughout history as well as standing at the graves of many once-powerful nations who have been greatly diminished or no longer exist today. Jewish people live on because of God's covenant. So every believer in Christ should contemplate 1 Corinthians 3:11-15 as to how he or she is building on His foundation.

Are We Condemned for Past Wrongs?

Suppose we have failed to love God's people, the descendants of Abraham, Isaac and Jacob? Are we condemned? First, let me assure you, true believers cannot lose their salvation! Your salvation is secure in Christ, just as the Jewish nation, whether dispersed or in the Land, is secure in its future with God because of the Abrahamic Covenant. Our salvation is an everlasting, unconditional covenant made valid through the blood of the Second Person of the Godhead, Jesus Christ. Just as we did nothing to deserve this unconditional, unmerited favor, God's people Israel benefit from God's promises in Genesis 15.[164]

The day IS coming when Jesus Christ, a Jewish Judge and Creator of the universe, will evaluate our labor for Him at His Bema Seat (rewards seat for all true believers in Him). Then, but hopefully before we see Him, we will realize that theology throughout the Church Age has Poked the Eye of Jesus Christ, a Jew who is God incarnate. God's people Israel are His physical brothers and sisters, and what we have done, or not done, to them in love will be rewarded or punished (by the removal of our rewards), as the Bible makes clear.

So in your salvation, you can rejoice in a covenant-keeping God, but you may lose your rewards as you stand before the Bema Seat of Christ (2 Corinthians 5:9-10), the same Person who made the Abrahamic Covenant and secured your Salvation in His **Blood**, the **Blood** of the New Covenant.[165]

Despite past ignorance of His Word, blindness due to false teachings, or immersion in a culture of anti-Semitism, God is slow to anger and quick to forgive. Now is a good time to search His Word with an open mind, asking Him to reveal His heart for His people Israel. We can choose to turn from provoking Him, embrace His plan for the Jewish people, and reach out in love to them with the Gospel message of the death, burial, and resurrection of their Messiah. They deserve to know how much the Father loves them!

Conclusion

In this book we have traced the blessings and cursings that God promised to give to individuals or nations that blessed or cursed Israel. Moses laid out the standard that God gave in Genesis 12:3. This pattern resurfaces periodically throughout the biblical text and should not be ignored by individuals or nations. The pattern continues throughout the post-biblical period, and Israel has stood at the graves of individuals and nations who have tried to destroy her as God has measured out His judgment.

We recognize that future prophecy on the nations reflects God's unwavering promises to bless or curse those that bless or curse Abraham

---

[164] John B. Metzger, *Discovering the Mystery of the Unity of God* (San Antonio, TX: Ariel Ministries, 2010).

[165] Metzger, *Israel's Only Hope: The New Covenant.*

(Israel). We as believers need to take God seriously, take note of His *"I will"* statements, and recognize that God will protect Israel against all odds.

Reform Replacement theologians have placed themselves in a precarious position in cursing the God they say they worship when they curse Israel and reinterpret God's Word to fit their theological biases. We must instead take God's Word as He wrote it! How can anyone say, "I love God" and then deprecate God's people, the Jewish people, even if they are in a present state of unbelief? Israel was in a state of unbelief when God judged the following individuals, nations, or organizations that cursed Israel: Egypt, Assyria, Babylon, Haman, Antiochus Epiphanes, Rome, the Catholic Church, Germany, and Russia.

A final thought: Where will the United States finally stand in God's chronicle of history? More importantly, what will be the rebuke from our Master if we disregard His physical brothers and sisters, Israel? Let us fervently pray for Israel and the Jewish people and that our nation will be found blessing them instead of cursing them. As individuals, let us open our minds to God's Word and seek His blessings as we reach out in love to God's people, Israel, with the richest blessing of all, the Gospel message.

Appendix One
Palestinian Liberation Theology
(PLT)

Whenever we look at the conflict in the Middle East between Israel and the Palestinians, we need to realize that there are two sides to every story. To understand the issues, we need to take an honest look at the best facts at hand, and not flinch from them. We also need to understand that two opposing sides will inevitably see the same situation very differently; that is to be understood. I want to assure you that I understand that neither Israel nor the Christian Palestinian movement is saintly; I do not want to argue that. What I do want to address is what the Bible says about the relationship of Israel to the Land, and how that relates to the ongoing Palestinian refugee crisis.

I read a book entitled *Israeli Peace, Palestinian Justice: Liberation Theology and the Peace Process*[166] which is pro-Palestinian Christian. The author, Thomas Are, speaks of the atrocities of Israel against Palestinians. I have taken the position that the documented stories of abuse by Israel's military are actual and disturbing.

I am not going to repeat Are's examples, just as I have not repeated the hideous unspeakable crimes done against Jewish people throughout the ages by the Christian Church. However, we must not turn a blind eye and deaf ear to actions done by either side! This book was written in the mid-nineties, and even more violence has taken place since then. I cannot disagree with facts reported, if they are truthful and accurate, but I do completely disagree with how these facts get interpreted. My concern is to view the facts in a biblical context, to discern how today's events relate to the blessings and cursings of the Abrahamic Covenant.

---

[166] Thomas L. Are, *Israeli Peace, Palestinian Justice: Liberation Theology and the Peace Process* (Atlanta, GA: Clarity Press, 1994).

What is the basis of the conflict between Christian Palestinians and the State of Israel? Is this a new conflict, or does it have deeper roots? What does the Bible say regarding this conflict and its resolution?

Why are Israel and the Palestinians enemies? Jewish people tend not to trust Christian Palestinians because of living through 1,900 years of anti-Semitism coming from the Christian Church in general. Add to that long-standing distrust the last 100 years of mostly radical Islamic terrorism against Israel. In response, Israel has often responded harshly or with suspicion towards Palestinians, whether Muslim or Christian.

Zionism, of course, creates further conflict between the Palestinians and Israel. Whose Land is it? Today Zionism continues as a movement of Jewish people who want to go home to the Land of their forefathers. It also involves true believers in Messiah, who want to help and encourage Jewish people and be genuine friends to them.

On a religious level, Palestinian Christians believe in Replacement Theology and consequently do not believe that Israel has a legal right to the Land. The answer is not only complex; it is impossible, and it will never be solved on a human level.

The conflict between Palestinians and the Jewish people is, of course, political as well. Jewish and Muslim immigrants started coming to the Land at about the same time, and both claim rights to the Land. Immigration to Israel of many Jewish people from Europe and the Islamic countries in the 1940s, '50s and '60s were completely absorbed into the Israeli society so that today there are NO Jewish refugee centers anywhere in the world. In the Islamic world, Palestinian refugee camps that appeared during the 1948 war for Israeli Independence have lingered on for decades and even grown larger. The Palestinians were crowded into refugee camps by uncaring Islamic nations and peoples, making solutions to the current problems even more complicated. Those challenging Israel's right to exist use the refugees as pawns to gain international sympathy.

Palestinian leaders continue to force the issue of resettlement of the Palestinian refugees; yet it is telling that they provide little help to them despite generous international aid. Many deceitful tactics are used to make Israel appear to be an aggressor and to tip the international community against Israel. As a result of terrorism against Israel that literally plays against unarmed Israeli citizens, Israel has had to take a stand to protect their own citizens from violent aggression and the State of Israel against attacks from many sides.

Israel knows all too well the position of being a minority in a foreign Land, and ceding land, giving up defensive positions, or allowing a huge influx of hostile immigrants all add up to pressure to eliminate Israel as a sovereign nation. Nineteen centuries of anti-Semitism is again pushing its ugly head to the forefront with the purpose to destroy and displace the Jewish people from the Land that God gave to them, the Land where their forefathers lived.

I want to share with you an article by Shelley Neese from FrontPageMagazine.com that is helpful in understanding the heart of Christian Palestinians as they relate to Israel and Israel's purpose and place in the heart and plan of God. First, we need to understand several points. These are important to grasp because there are numerous things reported about Israel that are disturbing to the mind and heart of a Zionist.

First, God is faithful and righteous. We know that God's commands are clear as to how we treat our fellow man, whether as an enemy or a friend. Israel has the written Word of God, and therefore has a moral high ground and is accountable to God for their actions, perhaps more than any other people group. However, we also know that the Nation of Israel is an unregenerate, unbelieving secular state.

Israel has been walking in disobedience to their Scriptures for over two-and-a-half millennia. Although God divorced Israel, the Prophets clearly state that she will be regenerated. This will occur in the future, when they place their Faith in the Messiah, confessing their sin against Messiah, the second Person of the God-head. At that time, He will come and destroy the armies of the Antichrist and establish the throne of David in Jerusalem and rule over the world, with faithful Israel at His side.

Even though we as Bible-believing Christians support and embrace Israel today, we also must recognize that Israel is an unregenerate people, and that applies to all peoples whether Jew or Gentile who have not yet come to Faith. However, whatever honorable or dishonorable deeds Israel undertakes, nothing can remove the fact that they are the covenant people of God. It does not matter whether they are faithful or unfaithful to God; the blessings and cursings of the Abrahamic Covenant still hold, and all Gentiles will be judged by God as to whether they bless Israel or curse Israel. That biblical fact cannot be altered because the Abrahamic Covenant is an unconditional covenant of God recorded in the very Word of God:

Genesis 12:1-3:

^{1} Now the LORD had said unto Abram, Get you out of your country, and from your kindred, and from your father's house, unto a land that I will show you. ^{2} And **I will** *make of you a great nation, and* **I will** *bless you, and make your name great; and you shall be a blessing; ^{3} And* **I will** *bless them that bless you and curse him that curses you: and in you shall all families of the earth be blessed.*

Second, the Bible is clear about ownership of the Land of Israel. There is a term carelessly thrown around, that term being the word *occupation*. It is a term that is biblically illegitimate, and the Christians who use it are mostly Replacement, Amillennial, Covenant theologians, and secular supporters of the Palestinian cause. Other naïve Christians also support it, out of a sense of compassion, but without any understanding of what the Bible says about the Land of Israel. They have absolutely no theological background of the Abrahamic and Land covenants that God made with Israel and the events in Israel today that directly relate to them.

Let me pose a question. As has been presented throughout this book, God gave to Abraham, Isaac, Jacob, and all their descendants the title deed to the Land of Israel; it is theirs by covenant and divine right. *So how can they be occupiers concerning a Land that already is theirs?* Yes, they had lost the privilege of possessing the Land because of sin and disobedience, but nowhere – and I mean nowhere – has God ever removed it and given it to some other group of people. Palestinian Replacement Theology conveniently ignores the Promises of God made to Israel. There are NO biblical promises made to Palestinians, even though they hopelessly try to invent them.

Third, the Church has not replaced Israel. In Palestinian propaganda you will often hear the words of Jesus being used completely out of their biblical context. You hear them speak of the *Good News to the poor and liberty to the oppressed* (Isaiah 61:1). Here are a couple of points to clarify the intent of Scripture and the intent of Palestinian (Replacement) Theology. The phrase above is taken out of context. First, the Good News or Gospel preached by Jesus was the Good News of the Kingdom that He was presenting to Israel in His First Coming. He was not sending this message to a future, newly-created ethnic group called Palestinians. The context of *the poor* and *liberty to the oppressed* was what Messiah would do for Israel if He was embraced by Israel at His First Coming, which would have been a fulfillment of the Prophets. It was one of the many signs that He gave to have Israel acknowledge Him as their Messiah.

When Jesus (Yeshua) uttered these words in the synagogue (Luke 4:17-18), he specifically said that His reading of the passage was the fulfillment of the passage. The context of those words belongs to Jewish people, the Nation of Israel, and NOT Palestinian Christians (or Muslims). But if you believe in Replacement Theology, you can jerk Scripture from its context and spiritualize it to someone else (by arbitrary replacement of one for the other).

Because many Evangelical Christians in the United States are biblically illiterate, they do not have the ability to discern truth from error. Without discernment of what God is saying in Scripture, they have taken the words of Jesus and the Prophets and misappropriated, misapplied, and twisted the Scriptures to fit their Replacement Theology bias.

Fourth, be aware of unbiblical Liberation Theology. As we read the following article, also understand that Palestinian Christians have combined Replacement Theology with Liberation Theology to come up with even a greater twisting of Scripture to fit the bias and context of Palestinians. Liberation Theology is a socialistic, Marxist philosophy merged with Christianity that says that poverty and social injustice can be overcome through progressive social policies. Problems emerge when unbiblical principles are used to address human problems. One example would be a human attempt to help individuals who are homosexual by re-writing the definition of marriage and gender. While many causes are humanly popular, they may not be biblical.

Liberation Theology first appeared in the Roman Catholic Church in South America in the 1980s. It was then and still is Marxist and unbiblical and an abuse of Scripture to fit the poor and to liberate the downtrodden. It has been called Christian Marxism.

Palestinian Liberation Theology (PLT) attempts to turn the Bible upside-down to impose a humanistic bias to the biblical text. What the Palestinians have done is further tweak Liberation Theology to fit the specific context of the Palestinians, without any biblical basis. This is another attempt by Satan to destroy the Jewish people. Remember, when a person reinterprets the Scriptures to suit his or her own desires, that is an attempt to be an authority over God, the same prideful attitude that caused Satan to rebel against God. That did not work out well for Satan!

Please read the following article by Shelley Neese, used by permission, on the position of the Palestine Liberation Organization [PLO][167] on why they believe the Land of Israel belongs to them. Shelley pinpoints the devious abuses of Scripture that result from changing the original intent of God, Himself. Be biblically discerning.

FrontPageMagazine.com | Friday, April 20, 2007

by Shelley Neese

[Bold - Emphasis mine]

Replacement Theology – the belief that the Christian Church replaced Israel in God's plan – has found a new home in the work of the *Sabeel Center* – the Jerusalem-based ecumenical organization for Palestinian Christians. After experiencing decades of decline and total rejection by many denominations, Replacement Theology has resurfaced in the form of Palestinian Liberation Theology (PLT) – a theological movement pushed by *Sabeel*. **PLT rejects the eternalness of God's promises to the Jewish people based on a dangerous manipulation of scripture. PLT's goal is to radically reinterpret the Bible to make it more relevant to Palestinians and less partial to Jews**. PLT grew out of the Liberation Theology movement popularized in Latin America in the 1970s and 80s, a faddy form of Christian socialism where Replacement Theology met Marxism. They emphasized oppression of the poor and encouraged political activism to abolish perpetual class struggle. The rich were against God by way of their wealth, and the poor were privileged by way of their poverty. **The Bible was reduced to nothing more than stories about the poor and the persecuted**.

The heyday of Liberation Theology was its inception. With the fall of the Soviet Union and the failure of Marxist revolutionary movements in Latin America, Liberation Theology lost most of its justification and influence. **The premise did appeal to Palestinians, because of its favor for the underdog and its potential to de-Zionize the Old Testament**.

---

[167] The PLO was founded in June 1964 by Yasser Arafat for the purpose of "liberating" the Land that belongs to Israel, meaning to take it over, through armed conflict. They push themselves off as the sole legitimate representative of the Palestinian people to the world. The PLO constitution calls for the eradication (destruction) of the Jewish State.

It's no secret that Israel's founding ignited a theological crisis in the Palestinian Christian community. The Abrahamic covenants and Old Testament prophecies justified Israel's national rebirth. According to Naim Ateek, founder of the *Sabeel Center*, the Torah [first five books of the Bible] was seen as a "Zionist text" and became "repugnant" to Palestinians. **Palestinian Christians needed a new theology that would in Ateek's words "liberate God from the Old Testament."**

Ateek revived Liberation Theology and related it to the Israeli-Palestinian situation. He switched focus from liberating the economically poor to the politically oppressed. As stated by *Sabeel*, the purpose of PLT was to theologically "address the day to day reality of Palestinians who have been living under an occupation that destroyed homes, confiscated lands, killed and jailed children, and closed institutions." The *Sabeel Center* has been used to develop and implement this theology.

A central tenet of PLT is that the Bible cannot be taken literally. It needs continuous interpretation to ensure every passage matches PLT's notion of God. Anything considered violent, racist, chauvinistic, or unjust is discarded. This means most of the Torah, including Joshua, Judges, 1 and 2 Samuel, and 1 and 2 Kings are thrown out. In fact, according to Ateek, only the prophetic books of the Old Testament are accepted as Scripture for they alone present a "truly mature vision of God."

Replacement Theology teaches that the Church superseded Jews as the benefactor of God's covenants. PLT goes one step further saying that the Jews never had a place of favor in the first place. In some cases, they erase Israel from the Bible altogether. Many Palestinian Churches that teach PLT have changed the Psalms by removing every reference to "Israel" and "Zion."

Palestinians are also inserted into Biblical narratives in the place of Israel. The narratives are read metaphorically where Israel assumes the role of oppressor. For example, in the story of David and Goliath, the powerless and humble David represents the Palestinians who bring down the bloodthirsty Goliath, represented by Israel. The centerpiece of PLT is the story of Exodus, where Palestinians are the Hebrew Egyptians bound in slavery, and Israel is the obstinate Pharaoh who refuses to grant them freedom and a state of their own. "If the Exodus is the story of any people," writes Mitri Raheb (one of the most vocal PLT theologians), "it is actually the story of us Palestinians."

> **PLT's agenda is to nullify the whole concept of closeness, thereby voiding all land promises that justify Israel's rebirth.** According to Raheb, God did kind acts for many peoples so Jews were not exceptional. Raheb points to Amos 9:7 ["True, I brought Israel up from the land of Egypt, but also the Philistines from Caphtor and the Arameans from Kir"] to argue the Jews were not the only people to whom God showed kindness. **As for God's promise to "plant them in this land [Israel] with all my heart and soul," Ateek says Jewish and Christian Zionists need to move beyond their primitive notion of a nationalistic God to a more universal God.** Indeed, Israel's right to exist is something Ateek has never accepted. During a Jerusalem interfaith dialogue with Jewish leaders in 2005, **Ateek said that if Israel had the right to exist it should have been created somewhere else.**
>
> From Ateek's perspective, the Israeli occupation is the root of all evil. He makes no apology for Palestinian terrorism or its contribution toward the plight of Palestinian Christians. There is no recognition that Hamas, the Palestinian Islamist government, is a far greater threat to Palestinian Christians than Zionism.
>
> **Ateek presents PLT as a theology based on justice, but he redefines godly justice to fit a sociopolitical context. The result is more narrow than ever before, as God is only on the side of Palestinians.** *Sabeel* says "Christ is not in the tanks and jet fighters, fighting on the side of the oppressors... God is in the city of Gaza, in the Jenin camp and in the old city of Nablus, Ramallah, and Bethlehem."
>
> Sabeel enjoys the active support of many of the mainline liberal denominations (i.e., PC USA and the United Church of Christ). These church groups ignore the danger of *Sabeel's* theology. But PLT is not just an ill-informed misguided teaching. **It is a dangerous propaganda tool cleverly wielded by *Sabeel* to undermine Israel's right to the land. All the while, this anti-Semitic, politically-driven theology void of the Gospel hides behind a façade of peace, justice, and love.** As Jesus Christ warned His followers, "Beware of false prophets who come to you in sheep's clothing, but inwardly are ravenous wolves."

Let us examine the theological error and arrogance against God that Palestinian Liberation Theology is perpetrating upon a naïve and liberal Christian audience who gullibly drinks it down without any biblical discernment.

First, as I say many times as I teach the Scriptures, God is the author of Scripture and language and is perfectly capable of speaking for Himself. He does not need the "dust" of the earth to reinterpret or apply new meanings to the Scripture against what He has written. God calls men who do this *false prophets,* and God does not speak kindly or act kindly toward them.

Again, if a person intellectually researches the historical facts of the situation in Israel, they will clearly recognize that Israel is NOT the aggressor in the Palestinian-Israeli conflict. Palestinian radical Muslims are the aggressors, who have purposely put the Palestinian Christians in the middle of their hatred for Israel. Now let us look at some of the statements of the PLT leadership from the above quote from Shelley Neese's article and apply some discernment regarding the theological wrong turns that have been made:

> According to Naim Ateek, founder of the Sabeel Center, the Torah was seen as a "Zionist text" and became "repugnant" to Palestinians. Palestinian Christians needed a new theology that would in Ateek's words "liberate God from the Old Testament."

Look at what is being said because the Torah (the compilation of the Books of Moses) is Jewish; it is repugnant to Palestinians. Also notice it is Naim Ateek's desire to remove the God of the Hebrew Scriptures and insert a different god for the Palestinians – sounds like Jeroboam implementing the Golden Calf apostasy (1 Kings 12:25-33) all over again.

> A central tenet of PLT is that the Bible cannot be taken literally. It needs continuous [re]interpretation to ensure every passage matches PLT's notion of God.

Note these two sentences reflect an anti-God bias. Does God's Word that He wrote now need to have man's bias to make it applicable to the Palestinians? This is a complete departure from God to suit one's own bias and sounds very much like the stance of a false prophet of the Old Testament, or the apostates that the Apostles warned about in the New Testament.

> Anything considered violent, racist (showing favor to the Jewish people), chauvinistic, or unjust [in the Bible] is discarded. This means most of the Torah [Books of Moses, the Pentateuch], including Joshua, Judges, 1 and 2 Samuel, and 1 and 2 Kings are thrown out. These books are the history of Jewish people in the Land called Israel.

This sounds like what the Samaritans did when Israel returned from Babylon; the Samaritans were attempting to make the Scriptures applicable to themselves and their corrupted form of worship in their Temple on Mt. Gerizim by eliminating the distinctions between those who worshipped God in Jerusalem and those who worshipped on Mt. Gerizim. Isn't it interesting how history repeats itself and most Evangelical Christians cannot see through it because of their own biblical illiteracy?

> Replacement Theology teaches that the Church superseded Jews as the benefactor of God's covenants. PLT goes one step further, saying that the Jews never had a place of favor in the first place.
>
> In some cases, they [Christian Palestinian theologians] erase Israel from the Bible altogether. Many Palestinian Churches that teach PLT have changed the Psalms by removing every reference to "Israel" and "Zion."

This is a complete denial of the Abrahamic Covenant, the Land Covenant, the Davidic Covenant and the New Covenant given specifically to Israel by God in clear and unquestionable language. Again sounds just like the Samaritans who removed all references of Jerusalem in the Samaritan Pentateuch and replaced it with Mt. Gerizim. Solomon made an interesting observation in Ecclesiastes 1:9b; 12:7-8 concerning these would-be revisionists:

And there is no new thing under the sun.

Then shall the dust [man] return to the earth as it was: and the spirit shall return to God Who gave it. Vanity of vanities, says the preacher; all is vanity.

> Palestinians are also inserted into biblical narratives in the place of Israel. The narratives are read metaphorically where Israel assumes the role of oppressor. For example, in the story of David and Goliath, the powerless and humble David represents the Palestinians who bring down the bloodthirsty Goliath, represented by Israel. The centerpiece of PLT is the story of Exodus, where Palestinians are the Hebrew Egyptians bound in slavery, and Israel is the obstinate Pharaoh who refuses to grant them freedom and a State of their own. "If the Exodus is the story of any people," writes Mitri Raheb (one of the most vocal PLT theologians), "it is actually the story of us Palestinians."

Notice the Bible is not taken literally, but metaphorically, where Israel is falsely cast as the oppressor. In their turned-about interpretation, David represents the Palestinians and Israel is the Pharaoh of the Exodus that would not let the Palestinians have freedom and have their own state. When the Bible is twisted like a pretzel, it becomes a complete distortion of the Word of God into human biases that are the opposite of God's heart and clearly expressed language.

> PLT's agenda is to nullify the whole concept of the (personal) closeness of God [to Israel], thereby voiding all land promises that justify Israel's rebirth.

Ateek presents PLT as a theology based on justice, but he redefines godly justice to fit a socio-political context. The result is more narrow than ever before, as God is only on the side of Palestinians. Their religious views nullify and violate all the Land promises to Israel, for to them, God is only on the side of the Palestinians. When you nullify and violate the Written Word of God, you are in complete rebellion against God, His Word, and His Christ. God knew that in the future there would be men like this, so He referenced Israel's ownership of the Land over 200 times in the Hebrew text. (See Appendix Three.)

> As for God's promise to *plant them in this land* [Israel] *with all* [His] *heart and soul,* Ateek says Jewish and Christian Zionists need to move beyond their primitive notion of a nationalistic God to a more universal God.

In reality, they are on the wrong track. It is not an issue of a nationalistic God; God is the God of all Creation. The issue is that God made five covenants with national Israel and none with a Gentile ethnic group. Of what value is God to anyone if He does not keep His promises to Abraham, Isaac, Jacob and all of their descendants? They themselves who speak of God as not being nationalistic throw up a smokescreen; for they, themselves, want a god that is nationalistic!! They want a Palestinian god who is their nationalistic god.

> From Ateek's perspective, the Israeli occupation is the root of all evil.

This is a slap in the face of God; God will respond in kind to Ateek's deceived, wicked heart. These anti-Jewish attitudes, actions, and deeds are part of the same belief system shared by Adolph Hitler, the Nazis, and Haman. God had it right in Genesis 6:5; 8:21b; Job 5:7; and Jeremiah 17:9:

And God saw that the wickedness of man was great in the earth, and that every imagination of the thoughts of his heart was on the evil continually. (Genesis 6:5)

...And the LORD said in His heart, I will not again curse the ground any more for man's sake; for the imagination of man's heart is evil from his youth....(Genesis 8:2)

Yet man is born unto trouble, as the sparks fly upward. (Job 5:7)

The heart is deceitful above all things, and desperately wicked: who can know it? (Jeremiah 17:9)

Palestinian Theology adherents have blindly missed the very heart of God by their own unbiblical Palestinian bias. By opposing God's people Israel, they place themselves in rebellion against God, the God they say that they worship, and His Written Word.

> Ateek presents PLT as a theology based on justice, but he redefines godly justice to fit a sociopolitical context.

Justice will come only through a holy, righteous God who keeps His Word, not by elevating their bias over the Written Word of God. Ateek is a false prophet who speaks against the very character of God revealed in the Hebrew Scriptures.

In this next quotation is the vision statement by the PLT. Read it with discernment. The structure of this statement is very deceptive, so beware. We all believe in justice and peace, but on whose terms – man's or God's?

Vision

> Sabeel affirms its commitment to make the gospel **relevant ecumenically** and spiritually in the lives of the local indigenous Church. Our Faith teaches that following in the footsteps of Christ **means** standing for the oppressed, working for justice, and seeking peace-building opportunities, and it challenges us to empower local Christians. Since a strong civil society and a healthy community are the best supports for a vulnerable population, Sabeel strives to empower the Palestinian community as a whole and to develop the internal strengths needed for participation in building a better world for all, ...
>
> Only by working for a just and durable peace can we provide a sense of security and create ample opportunities for growth and prosperity in an atmosphere void of

> violence and strife. Although remaining political and organizational obstacles hinder the full implementation of programs, Sabeel continues to develop creative means to surmount these challenges. We seek both to be a refuge for dialogue and to pursue ways of finding answers to ongoing theological questions about the sanctity of life, justice, and peace.[168]

To follow in the footsteps of Christ means to believe in Him as our Savior from sin and to present the Gospel of Jesus Christ to the world. That is the death, burial, and resurrection of Jesus Christ, who regenerates our hearts, gives us His Holy Spirit and removes all our sins. The Gospel is not standing for the oppressed, working for justice, and seeking peace-building. These secondary things are fine IF they conform to the untwisted, un-reinterpreted Written Word of God, but their vision is a counterfeit of true justice and peace.

Go back again and read the promises of the covenants. If Ateek and the Sabeel Center are representing the true God with their teachings, then Palestinian Christians who follow them are guilty of breaking God's Word, even though they are not aware of it. I am not God, but from mere human observation I would doubt their spiritual status with God as being saved from sin. What is clearly seen is that their god is a liar and a deceiver, for his word is false when compared to the Bible.

One further thought that you need to know: The people called the Palestinians did not excess as a people group until 1948, or more precisely 1967, when all this Palestinian propaganda started with the PLO under Yasser Arafat.

There were no Palestinian people in Israel during the Ottoman Turk Empire, no Palestinian people in existence during the rise of Islam (seventh century), no Palestinian people in the Byzantine period of history, nor in Roman, Greek, Media/Persian, Babylonian and Assyrian, or Canaanite periods.

The Palestinians are a new people group that has been created and manufactured by Palestinian Islamic radicals and Replacement Theology Palestinian Christians because of their hatred of Jewish people. Palestinian Islamic radicals have used the Palestinian Muslims and Christians as

---

[168] Located on many websites. One listing of the above is on the website of a Presbyterian Church in Montgomery, AL. Last accessed November 18, 2016, at http://immanuelpcusa.org/CommunityOutreach.aspx under their Global Ministries.

propaganda tools against God, against the establishment of the State of Israel, and against Jesus Christ who is the author and originator of the Abrahamic Covenant. The vast majority of these "Palestinians" are immigrants to Israel in the last 120 years from all over the Middle East, North Africa, Turkey, and various other Muslim lands and speak as many as 70 languages.[169] While both the Muslim residents and Jewish residents of the Land are largely immigrants, Jewish people have the biblical title deed to the Land, and the others that are there do not.

In summary, anyone who reinterprets Scripture for their own purposes is heading for severe judgment and punishment from the Almighty hand of God in the Tribulation period. If they are believers and are raptured with the believing Church, they will suffer a great loss of rewards at the Bema Seat of Christ, a Jewish Judge.

---

[169] Joan Peters, *From Time Immemorial: The Origins of the Arab-Jewish Conflict Over Palestine* (New York, NY: Harper & Row, 1984).

Appendix Two
Biblical References to the
Abrahamic Covenant in Scripture

The Abrahamic Covenant is central to all the other covenants given to Israel. The Abrahamic Covenant is unconditional and has a total of 14 provisions, but I am only focusing on the promise to Israel and references to the Land that God would give to them when they are mentioned together.

Below are listed many of the verses in the Scriptures that relate to the Abrahamic Covenant and the promise of the Land to be inherited by Abraham's descendants through Jacob. These two covenants, the Abrahamic and the Land aspect of that covenant (which is developed into the Land Covenant of Deuteronomy 29-30), are inseparably linked and interwoven together; they simply cannot be separated.

In the passages that follow, the words bolded express the "I will" of God to give the Jewish people the Land.

The Old Testament (116)

Genesis 12:1-3, 7

> *¹ Now the LORD had said unto Abram, Get you out of your country, and from your kindred, and from your father's house, unto a land that I will show you. ² And* **I will** *make of you a great nation, and* **I will** *bless you, and make your name great; and you shall be a blessing; ³ And* **I will** *bless them that bless you and curse him that curses you: and in you shall all families of the earth be blessed.*
>
> *⁷ And the LORD appeared unto Abram, and said, Unto your seed* **will I give this Land***: and there built he an altar unto the LORD, who appeared unto him.*

Genesis 26:3

> **Sojourn in this Land**, *and I will be with you* [Isaac], *and will bless you; for unto you, and unto your seed,* **I will give all these countries**, *and I will perform the oath which I swore unto Abraham your father;*

Genesis 28:13

> *And, behold, the LORD stood above it, and said* [to Jacob], *I am the LORD God of Abraham your father, and the God of Isaac:* **the Land whereon you lay, to you will I give it, and to your seed.**

Genesis 31:42

> *Except the* **God of my father**, *the* **God of Abraham, and the fear of Isaac**, *had been with me* [Jacob], *surely you* [Laban] *would have sent me away now empty. God has seen my affliction and the labor of my hands, and rebuked you yesterday.*

Genesis 32:9

> *And Jacob said,* **O God of my father Abraham, and God of my father Isaac**, *the LORD which said unto me, Return unto* **your country**, *and to* **your kindred**, *and I will deal well with you.*

Genesis 35:12

> *And the* **Land which I gave Abraham and Isaac, to you** [Jacob]**, I will give it** *and to* **your seed after you will I give the Land.**

Genesis 48:15, 21

> [15] *And he* [Jacob] *blessed Joseph, and said, God,* **before whom my fathers Abraham and Isaac did walk**, *the God which fed me all my life long unto this day.*

> [21] *And Israel* [Jacob] *said unto Joseph, behold, I die: but God shall be with you, and bring you again* **unto the Land of your fathers**.

Genesis 50:24-25

> [24] *And Joseph said unto his brethren, I die: and* **God will surely visit you, and bring you out of this land unto the Land which He swore to Abraham, to Isaac, and to Jacob**. [25] *And Joseph took an oath of the children of Israel, saying, God will surely visit you, and you shall carry up my bones from hence.*

Exodus 3:8, 17

> [8] *And I am come down to deliver them out of the hand of the Egyptians, and to bring them up out of that land* **unto a good Land and a large, unto a Land flowing with milk and honey;** *unto the place of the Canaanites, and the Hittites, and the Amorites, and the Perizzites, and the Hivites, and the Jebusites.*
>
> [17] *And I have said, I will bring you up out of the affliction of Egypt unto the Land of the Canaanites, and the Hittites, and the Amorites, and the Perizzites, and the Hivites, and the Jebusites,* **unto a Land flowing with milk and honey.**

Exodus 4:5

> *That they may believe that the LORD God of their fathers,* **the God of Abraham, and the God of Isaac, and the God of Jacob**, *hath appeared unto you.*

Exodus 6:3-4, 8

> [3] *And* **I appeared unto Abraham, unto Isaac, and unto Jacob,** *by the name of God Almighty, but by My name Jehovah was I not known to them.* [4] *And* **I have also established My covenant with them, to give them the Land of Canaan, the Land of their pilgrimage, wherein they were strangers.**
>
> [8] **I will bring you to the land which I swore to give to Abraham, Isaac, and Jacob,** *and* **I will give it to you for a possession; I am the Lord.** (New American Standard Bible)

Exodus 13:5, 11

> [5] *And it shall be* **when the LORD shall bring you into the Land of the Canaanites,** *and the Hittites, and the Amorites, and the Hivites, and the Jebusites,* **which He swore unto your fathers to give you,** *a* **land flowing with milk and honey,** *that you shall keep this service in this month.*
>
> [11] *And it shall be when the* **LORD** *shall bring you into the Land of the Canaanites,* *as* **He swore unto you and to your fathers, and shall give it you.**

Exodus 32:13

> *Remember* **Abraham, Isaac, and Israel,** *Your servants to whom You swore by Your own self, and said unto them,* **I will multiply your**

seed as the stars of heaven, *and* all this Land that I have spoken of will I give unto your seed. *And* they shall inherit it forever.

Exodus 33:1

And the LORD said unto Moses, the people which you have brought up out of the Land of Egypt, **unto the Land which I swore unto Abraham, to Isaac, and to Jacob, saying, Unto your seed will I give it.**

Leviticus 26:42

Then will I remember **My [God's own] covenant with Jacob,** *and also* **My covenant with Isaac,** *and also* **My covenant with Abraham** *will I remember; and* **I will remember the Land.**

Deuteronomy 1:8, 20-21, 35

[8] *Behold,* **I have set the Land before you: go in and possess the Land which the LORD swore unto your fathers, Abraham, Isaac, and Jacob, to give unto them and to their seed after them.**

[20] *And I said unto you, You are come unto the mountain of the Amorites, which the LORD our God does give unto us.* [21] *Behold,* **the LORD your God has set the Land before you: go up and possess it. As the LORD God of your fathers has said unto you**; *fear not, neither be discouraged.*

[35] *Surely there shall not one of these men of this evil generation see that good Land,* **which I swore to give unto your fathers.**

Deuteronomy 2:29

(As the children of Esau which dwell in Seir, and the Moabites which dwell in Ar, did unto me;) until I shall pass over Jordan **into the Land which the LORD our God giveth [is giving to] us.**

Deuteronomy 3:20

Until the LORD has given rest unto your brethren, as well as unto you, and **until they also possess the Land which the LORD your God has given them beyond Jordan**: *and then you shall return every man unto his possession, which I have given you.*

Deuteronomy 4:1, 31, 37-40

[1] *Now therefore hearken* [listen], *O Israel, unto the statutes and unto the judgments, which I teach you, for to do them, that you may live,*

and **go in and possess the Land which the LORD God of your fathers gives you.**

³¹ For the LORD your God is a merciful God; He will not forsake you, neither destroy you, nor forget **the covenant of your fathers which He swore unto them.**

³⁷ **And because He loved your fathers, therefore He chose their seed after them,** *and brought you out in His sight with His mighty power out of Egypt;* *³⁸* **To drive out nations from before you greater and mightier than you are, to bring you in, to give you their Land for an inheritance, as it is this day.** *³⁹ Know therefore this day, and consider it in your heart, that the LORD He is God in heaven above, and upon the earth beneath: there is none else. ⁴⁰ You shall keep therefore His statutes, and His commandments, which I command you this day, that it may go well with you, and with your children after you, and* **that you may prolong your days upon the earth, which the LORD your God gives you, forever.**

Deuteronomy 5:16

Honor your father and your mother as the LORD your God has commanded you; **that your days may be prolonged, and that it may go well with you, in the Land which the LORD your God gives you.**

Deuteronomy 6:3, 10, 18, 23

³ Hear therefore, O Israel, and observe to do it; that it may be well with you and that you may increase mightily, **as the LORD God of your fathers has promised you,** *in the Land that flows with milk and honey.*

¹⁰ And it shall be, **when the LORD your God shall have brought you into the Land which He swore unto your fathers, to Abraham, to Isaac, and to Jacob, to give you great and goodly cities, which you did not build,**

¹⁸ And you shall do that which is right and good in the sight of the LORD, that it may be well with you, and **that you may go in and possess the good Land which the LORD swore unto your fathers.**

²³ And He brought us out from there that He might bring us in, **to give us the Land which He swore unto our fathers.**

Deuteronomy 7:8, 12-13

⁸ But because the LORD loved you and because **He would keep the oath which He had sworn unto your fathers**, *the LORD has brought you out with a mighty hand, and redeemed you out of the house of bondage, from the hand of Pharaoh king of Egypt.*

¹² Wherefore it shall come to pass, if you hearken [listen] *to these judgments, and keep, and do them, that the LORD your God shall keep unto you the covenant and the mercy which He swore unto your fathers. ¹³ And He will love you, and* **bless you**, *and* **multiply you; he will also bless the fruit of your womb, and the fruit of your land, your corn, and your wine, and your oil, the increase of your kine [herd], and the flocks of your sheep, in the Land which He swore unto your fathers to give you.**

Deuteronomy 8:1, 18

¹ All the commandments which I command you this day shall you observe to do, that you may live, and multiply, and **go in and possess the Land which the LORD swore unto your fathers.**

¹⁸ But you shall remember the LORD your God: for it is He that gives you power to get wealth, that He may establish His covenant **which He swore unto your fathers**, *as it is this day.*

Deuteronomy 9:5

Not for your righteousness, or for the uprightness of your heart, do you go to possess their Land: but for the wickedness of these nations the LORD your God will drive them out from before you, and **that He may perform the word which the LORD swore unto your fathers, Abraham, Isaac, and Jacob.**

Deuteronomy 10:11, 15, 22

¹¹ And the LORD said unto me, Arise, take your journey before the people, that they may **go in and possess the Land, which I swore unto their fathers to give unto them.**

¹⁵ Only the LORD had a delight in thy fathers to love them, and **He chose their seed after them, even you above all people**, *as it is this day.*

²² Your fathers went down into Egypt with 70 persons, and **now the LORD your God has made you as the stars of heaven for multitude.**

Deuteronomy 11:9-11, 21

⁹ and that you may **prolong your days in the Land, which the LORD swore unto your fathers to give unto them and to their seed, a Land that flows with milk and honey.** *¹⁰ For the Land,* **where you go in to possess it,** *is not as the land of Egypt, from where you came out, where you sowed your seed, and watered it with your foot, as a garden of herbs:* *¹¹* **But the Land, where you go to possess it, is a Land of hills and valleys, and drinking water of the rain of heaven.**

²¹ That your days may be multiplied and the days of our children, **in the land which the LORD swore unto your fathers to give them,** *as the days of heaven upon the earth.*

Deuteronomy 12:1, 9

¹ These are the statutes and judgments, which you shall observe to do **in the Land, which the LORD God of your fathers gives you to possess it, all the days that you live upon the earth.**

⁹ For you are not as yet come to the rest and to the inheritance, **which the LORD your God will give you.**

Deuteronomy 13:17

And there shall cling nothing of the cursed thing to your hand: that the LORD may turn from the fierceness of His anger, and show you mercy, and **have compassion upon you, and multiply you, as He has sworn unto your fathers.**

Deuteronomy 19:8

And if the LORD your God enlarges your coast, **as He has sworn unto your fathers, and gives you all the Land which He promised to give unto your fathers –**

Deuteronomy 26:3, 7-9, 15

³ And you shall go unto the priest that shall be in those days, and say unto him, I profess this day unto the LORD your God, **that I have come unto the country which the LORD swore unto our fathers for to give us.**

⁷ And when we cried unto the LORD God of our fathers, the LORD heard our voice, and looked on our affliction, and our labor, and our oppression: ⁸ And the LORD brought us forth out of Egypt with a mighty hand, and with an outstretched arm, and with great terribleness, and with signs, and with wonders. ^{9} **And He has brought us into this place, and has given us this Land, even a Land that flows with milk and honey.**

^{15} *Look down from your holy habitation, from heaven, and* **bless your people Israel, and the Land which you have given us, as you swore unto our fathers, a Land that flows with milk and honey.**

Deuteronomy 27:3

And you shall write upon them all the words of this law, when you are passed over, that you may **go in unto the Land which the LORD your God gives you, a Land that flows with milk and honey; as the LORD God of your fathers has promised you.**

Deuteronomy 28:11

And the LORD shall make you plenteous in goods, in the fruit of your body, and in the fruit of your cattle, and in the fruit of your ground, **in the Land which the LORD swore unto your fathers to give you.**

Deuteronomy 29:13

That He may establish you today for a people unto Himself, and that He may be unto you a God, as He has said unto you, and **as He has sworn unto your fathers, Abraham, to Isaac, and to Jacob.**

Deuteronomy 30:5, 20

^{5} *And the* **LORD your God will bring you into the Land which your fathers possessed, and you shall possess it; and He will do you good, and multiply you above your fathers.**

^{20} *That you may love the LORD your God, and that you may obey His voice, and that you may cleave unto Him: for He is your life, and the length of your days:* **that you may dwell in the Land which the LORD swore unto your fathers, to Abraham, to Isaac, and to Jacob, to give them.**

Deuteronomy 31:7, 20-21, 23

^{7} *And Moses called unto Joshua, and said unto him in the sight of all Israel, Be strong and of a good courage: for you must go with this people* **unto the Land which the LORD has sworn unto their fathers to give them; and you shall cause them to inherit it.**

²⁰ For when I shall have brought them **into the Land which I swore unto their fathers, that flows with milk and honey***; and they shall have eaten and filled themselves, and waxen fat; then will they turn unto other gods, and serve them, and provoke me, and break My covenant. ²¹ And it shall come to pass, when many evils and troubles fall on them, that this song shall testify against them as a witness; for it shall not be forgotten out of the mouths of their seed: for I know their imagination which they go about even now* **before I have brought them into the Land which I swore.**

²³ And he gave Joshua the son of Nun a charge, and said, Be strong and of a good courage: for you shall bring the children of Israel **into the Land which I swore unto them***: and I will be with you.*

Deuteronomy 34:4

And the LORD said unto him, **This is the Land which I swore unto Abraham, unto Isaac, and unto Jacob, saying, I will give it unto your seed***: I have caused you to see it with your eyes, but you shall not go over there.*

Joshua 1:6, 11, 13

⁶ Be strong and of a good courage: for unto this people shall you divide for an inheritance the Land, **which I swore unto their fathers to give them.**

¹¹ Pass through the host, and command the people, saying, Prepare you victuals, for within three days you shall pass over this Jordan, **to go in to possess the Land, which the LORD your God is giving you to possess it.**

¹³ Remember the word, which Moses the servant of the LORD commanded you, saying, **The LORD your God has given you rest, and has given you this Land.**

Joshua 2:9, 24

⁹ And she said unto the men, **I know that the LORD has given you the Land** *and that your terror has fallen upon us and that all the inhabitants of the Land faint because of you.*

²⁴ And they said unto Joshua, **Truly the LORD has delivered into your hands all the Land***; for even all the inhabitants of the country do faint because of us.*

Joshua 5:6

For the children of Israel walked forty years in the wilderness, till all the people that were men of war, which came out of Egypt, were consumed [perished], *because they obeyed not the voice of the LORD:* **unto whom the LORD swore that He would not show them the Land, which the LORD swore unto their fathers that He would give us, a Land that flows with milk and honey.**

Joshua 18:3

And Joshua said unto the children of Israel, **How long are you slack to go to possess the Land, which the LORD God of your fathers has given you?**

Joshua 21:43-44

[43] *And* **the LORD gave unto Israel all the Land which He swore to give unto their fathers; and they possessed it,** *and dwelled there.* [44] *And the LORD gave them rest round about,* **according to all that He swore unto their fathers:** *and there stood not a man of all their enemies before them; the LORD delivered all their enemies into their hand.*

Joshua 24:2-3

[2] *And Joshua said unto all the people, Thus says the LORD God of Israel, your fathers dwelled on the other side of the flood in old time, even Terah, the father of Abraham, and the father of Nachor: and they served other gods.* [3] *And* **I took your father Abraham from the other side of the flood, and led him through all the Land of Canaan,** *and multiplied his seed, and gave him Isaac.*

1 Kings 18:36

And it came to pass at the time of the offering of the evening sacrifice, that Elijah the prophet came near, and said, **LORD God of Abraham, Isaac, and of Israel, let it be known this day that You are God in Israel,** *and that I am Your servant, and that I have done all these things at Your word.*

2 Kings 13:23

And the LORD was gracious unto them [Israel], *and had compassion on them, and had respect unto them,* **because of His covenant with Abraham, Isaac, and Jacob,** *and would not destroy them, neither did He cast them from His presence as yet.*

1 Chronicles 16:16-17

¹⁶ Even of **the covenant which He made with Abraham, and of His oath unto Isaac;** *¹⁷ And* **hath confirmed the same to Jacob for a law, and to Israel for an everlasting covenant.**

1 Chronicles 29:18

O LORD **God of Abraham, Isaac, and of Israel**, *our fathers, keep this forever in the imagination of the thoughts of the heart of Your people, and prepare their heart unto You.*

2 Chronicles 20:7

Are not You our God, who did drive out the inhabitants of this land before Your people Israel, and **gave it to the seed of Abraham Your friend forever?**

2 Chronicles 30:6

So the posts went with the letters from the king and his princes throughout all Israel and Judah, and according to the commandment of the king, saying, You children of Israel, **turn again unto the LORD God of Abraham, Isaac, and Israel, and He will return to the remnant of you**, *that are escaped out of the hand of the kings of Assyria.*

Nehemiah 9:7-8

⁷ You are the LORD the God, **who did choose Abram,** *and brought him forth out of Ur of the Chaldees, and* **gave him the name of Abraham;** *⁸ And found his heart faithful before You, and* **made a covenant with him to give the Land of the Canaanites**, *the Hittites, and Amorites, and the Perizzites, and the Jebusites, and the Girgashites,* **to give it to his seed, and has performed Your words; for You are righteous.**

Psalms 47:9

The princes of the people are gathered together, even **the people of the God of Abraham**: *for the shields of the earth belong unto God: He is greatly exalted.*

Psalm 105:6, 9-10, 42, 44

⁶ O **you seed of Abraham** *His servant, you* **children of Jacob His chosen!**

⁹ Which **covenant He made with Abraham**, *and* **His oath unto Isaac;** *¹⁰ And* **confirmed the same unto Jacob for a law**, *and* **to Israel for an everlasting covenant**:

⁴² For **He remembered His holy promise, and Abraham His servant.**

⁴⁴ And **gave them the lands of the heathen**: *and they inherited the labor of the people;*

Isaiah 29:22-23

²² Therefore thus says the **LORD who redeemed Abraham, concerning the house of Jacob,** *Jacob shall not now be ashamed; neither shall his face now wax pale. ²³ But when he sees his children, the work of My hands, in the midst of him they shall sanctify My name, and sanctify the Holy One of Jacob, and shall fear the God of Israel.*

Isaiah 41:8

But you, **Israel, are My servant, Jacob whom I have chosen, the seed of Abraham My friend.**

Isaiah 51:2

Look unto Abraham your father, *and unto Sarah that bore you:* **for I called him alone**, *and blessed him, and increased him.*

Jeremiah 7:7

Then will **I cause you to dwell in this place, in the Land that I gave to your fathers, forever and ever.**

Jeremiah 11:5

That **I may perform the oath which I have sworn unto your fathers, to give them a land flowing with milk and honey, as it is this day**. *Then I answered and said, So be it, O LORD.*

Jeremiah 16:15

But, the LORD lives, that brought up the children of Israel from the land of the north, and from all the lands where He had driven them: and **I will bring them again into their Land that I gave unto their fathers.**

Jeremiah 25:5

They said, Turn again now everyone from his evil way, and from the evil of your doing, and dwell **in the Land that the LORD has given unto you and to your fathers forever and ever**.

Jeremiah 32:22

And has **given them this Land, which You did swear to their fathers to give them, a Land flowing with milk and honey**.

Jeremiah 33:25-26

[25] *Thus said the LORD; If My covenant be not with day and night, and if I have not appointed the ordinances of heaven and earth;* [26] *Then will I cast away the seed of Jacob, and David My servant, so that I will not take any of his seed to be rulers over the seed of* **Abraham, Isaac, and Jacob***: for I will cause their captivity to return, and have mercy on them.*

Ezekiel 33:23-25

[23] *Then the word of the LORD came unto me, saying,* [24] *Son of man, they that inhabit those wastes of the land of Israel speak, saying,* **Abraham was one, and he inherited the Land***: but we are many;* **the Land is given us for inheritance**. [25] *Therefore say unto them, Thus says the Lord GOD; You eat* [meat] *with the blood, and lift up your eyes toward your idols, and shed blood: and shall you possess the Land?*

Ezekiel 36:28

And **you shall dwell in the Land that I gave to your fathers***; and you shall be my people, and I will be your God.*

Ezekiel 37:1-28

Because of the length of this passage, please read it from your Bible.

Micah 7:20

You will perform the **truth to Jacob***, and the* **mercy to Abraham, which you have sworn unto our fathers from the days of old.**

The New Testament (73)

Matthew 1:1-2, 17

¹ The book of the generation of Jesus Christ, the son of David, the **son of Abraham**. *² Abraham begat Isaac; and Isaac begat Jacob; and Jacob begat Judah and his brethren;* [*Begat* means he generated his children.]

¹⁷ **So all the generations from Abraham to David are fourteen generations**; *and from David until the carrying away into Babylon are fourteen generations; and from the carrying away into Babylon unto Messiah are fourteen generations.*

Matthew 3:9

And do not think to say within yourselves, **We have Abraham for our father**: *for I say unto you, that God is able of these stones to raise up children unto Abraham.*

Matthew 8:11

And I say unto you, that many shall come from the east and west, **and shall sit down with Abraham, and Isaac, and Jacob**, *in the kingdom of heaven.*

Matthew 22:32

I am the God of Abraham, and the God of Isaac, and the God of Jacob. *God is not the God of the dead, but of the living.*

Mark 12:26

And as touching the dead, that they rise: have you not read in the book of Moses, how in the bush God spoke unto him, saying, **I am the God of Abraham, and the God of Isaac, and the God of Jacob**.

Luke 1:55, 72-73

⁵⁵ As He **spoke to our fathers, to Abraham, and to his seed forever**.

⁷² To perform the **mercy promised to our fathers**, *and to remember His holy covenant;* *⁷³ The* **oath which He swore to our father Abraham**.

Luke 3:8, 23-24

> ^{8} *Bring forth therefore fruits worthy of repentance, and do not begin to say within yourselves,* **We have Abraham for our father**: *for I say unto you, that God is able of these stones to raise up children unto Abraham.*
>
> ^{23} *And Jesus Himself began to be about thirty years of age, being (as was supposed) the son of Joseph, which was the son of Heli,* ^{24} *which was the son of Matthat, which was the son of Levi, which was the son of Melchi, which was the son of Janna, which was the son of Joseph,*

Luke 13:28

> *There shall be weeping and gnashing of teeth,* **when you shall see Abraham, and Isaac and Jacob**, *and all the prophets, in the kingdom of God, and you yourselves thrown out.*

Luke 16:22-31

> ^{22} *And it came to pass, that the beggar died, and was carried by the angels into* **Abraham's bosom**: *the rich man also died, and was buried:* ^{23} *And in hell he lifted up his eyes being in torment, and seeing Abraham afar off, and Lazarus in his bosom.* ^{24} *And he cried and said,* **Father Abraham**, *have mercy on me, and send Lazarus, that he may dip the tip of his finger in water, and cool my tongue; for I am tormented in this flame.* ^{25} *But Abraham said, Son, remember that you in your lifetime received your good things, and likewise Lazarus evil things: but now he is comforted, and you are tormented.* ^{26} *And beside all this, between us and you there is a great gulf fixed: so that they which would pass from there to you cannot: neither can they pass to us, that would* [want to] *come from there.* ^{27} *Then he said, I pray you therefore, father, that you would send him to my father's house:* ^{28} *For I have five brethren; that he may testify unto them, lest they also come into this place of torment.* ^{29} *Abraham said unto him, they have Moses and the prophets; let them hear them.* ^{30} *And he said, No,* **father Abraham**: *but if one went unto them from the dead, they will repent.* ^{31} *And he said unto him, If they will not hear Moses and the prophets, neither will they be persuaded, though one rose from the dead.*

Luke 19:9

> *And Jesus said unto him, This day has salvation come to this house, forasmuch as* [because] *he also is a* **son of Abraham**.

Luke 20:37

Now that the dead are raised, even Moses showed at the bush, **when he called the Lord the God of Abraham, and the God of Isaac, and the God of Jacob.**

John 8:33, 37, 39-40, 52-53, 56-58

³³ They answered him, **We are Abraham's seed**, *and were never in bondage to any man: how do you say, You shall be made free?*

³⁷ **I know that you are Abraham's seed**; *but you seek to kill me, because my word has no place in you.*

³⁹ They answered and said unto him, **Abraham is our father**. *Jesus said unto them,* **If you were Abraham's children, you would do the works of Abraham.** *⁴⁰ But now you seek to kill me, a man that has told you the truth, which I have heard of God: Abraham did not do this.*

⁵² Then said the Jews unto him, Now we know that You have a devil. **Abraham** *is dead, and the prophets; and You say, if a man keep My saying, he shall never taste of death. ⁵³ Are you greater than* **our father Abraham**, *who is dead? And the prophets are dead: whom do You make Yourself* [out to be]*?*

⁵⁶ **Your father Abraham rejoiced to see My day**: *and he saw it, and was glad. ⁵⁷ Then the Jews said unto him, You are not yet fifty years old, and You have seen Abraham? ⁵⁸ Jesus said unto them, Verily, verily, I say unto you,* **Before Abraham was, I AM**.

Acts 3:13, 25

¹³ The **God of Abraham, and of Isaac, and of Jacob, the God of our fathers**, *has glorified His Son Jesus; whom you delivered up, and denied Him in the presence of Pilate, when he was determined to let Him go.*

²⁵ You are the children of the prophets, of **the covenant which God made with our fathers, saying unto Abraham**, *and in your seed shall all the kindreds of the earth be blessed.*

Acts 7:2, 7, 16-17, 32

² And he said, Men, brethren, and fathers, listen; the God of glory appeared unto our **father Abraham**, *when he was in Mesopotamia, before he dwelled in Haran.*

⁷ And the nation to whom they shall be in bondage I will judge, said God" **and after that shall they come forth, and serve Me in this place.**

¹⁶ And were carried over into Sychem, and laid in the sepulcher that Abraham bought for a sum of money of the sons of Emmor the father of Sychem. ¹⁷ But when the time of the promise drew near, **which God had sworn to Abraham,** *the people grew and multiplied in Egypt,*

³² Saying, **I am the God of your fathers, the God of Abraham, and the God of Isaac, and the God of Jacob.** *Then Moses trembled, and dared not look.*

Acts 13:26

Men and brethren, **children of the stock of Abraham,** *and whosoever among you fears God, to you is the word of this salvation sent.*

Romans 4:1-3, 9, 12-13, 16

¹ What shall we say then that **Abraham our father**, *as pertaining to the flesh, has found? ² For if Abraham were justified by works, he has whereof to glory* [he would have something to boast about]; *but not before God. ³ For what do the scriptures say? Abraham believed God, and it was counted unto him for righteousness.*

⁹ Does this blessedness come then upon the circumcision [Jewish people] *only, or upon the uncircumcision* [non-Jewish people] *also? For* **we say that Faith was reckoned to Abraham for righteousness.**

¹² And the father of circumcision to them who are not of the circumcision only, but who also walk in the steps of that Faith of **our father Abraham**, *which he had being yet uncircumcised. ¹³ For the promise, that he should be the heir of the world, was not to Abraham, or to his seed, through the law, but through the righteousness of Faith.*

¹⁶ Therefore it is of Faith, that it might be by grace; **to the end [that] the promise might be sure to all the seed**; *not to that only which is of the law, but to that also which is of the Faith of Abraham; who is the father of us all,*

Romans 9:7

Neither, because they are **the seed of Abraham**, *are they all children:* **but, in Isaac shall your seed by called [named].**

Romans 11:1

I say then, has God cast away His people? God forbid. For I also am an Israelite, of the **seed of Abraham**, *of the tribe of Benjamin.*

2 Corinthians 11:22

Are they Hebrews? So am I. Are they Israelites? So am I. Are they the **seed of Abraham**? *So am I.*

Galatians 3:6-9, 14, 16, 18, 29

[6] **Even as Abraham believed God**, *and it was accounted to him for righteousness.* [7] *Know you therefore that they which are of Faith, the same are the children of Abraham.* [8] *And the Scriptures, foreseeing that God would justify the heathen through Faith,* **preached before the gospel unto Abraham, saying, In you shall all nations be blessed.** [9] *So then they which be of* [those who have] *Faith are blessed with faithful Abraham.*

[14] *That the* **blessing of Abraham might come on the Gentiles through Jesus Christ**; *that we might receive the promise of the Spirit through Faith.*

[16] **Now to Abraham and his seed were the promises made.** *He said not, and to seeds, as of many; but as of one, and to Your seed, which is Messiah.*

[18] *For if the inheritance is of the law it is no more of promise:* **but God gave it to Abraham by promise.**

[29] *And if you are Messiah's, then* **you are Abraham's seed, and heirs according to the promise.**

Galatians 4:22

For it is written, that **Abraham had two sons**, *the one by a bondmaid, the other by a freewoman.*

Hebrews 2:16

For in truth He took not on Him the nature of angels; **but He took on Him the seed of Abraham.**

Hebrews 6:13

For when God made promise to Abraham, because he could swear by no greater He swore by Himself.

Hebrews 7:1-2, 4-6, 9

^{1} For this Melchisedec, king of Salem, priest of the most high God, who met Abraham returning from the slaughter of the kings, and blessed him; ^{2} **To whom also Abraham gave a tenth part of all;** *first being by interpretation King of righteousness, and after that also King of Salem, which is King of peace.*

^{4} Now consider how great this man was, unto whom even the **patriarch Abraham gave the tenth of the spoils.** *^{5} And verily they are of the sons of Levi who receive the office of the priesthood, have a commandment to take tithes of the people according to the law, that is, of their brethren,* **though they come out of the loins of Abraham;** *^{6} But He whose descent is not counted from them received tithes of Abraham, and blessed him that had the promises.*

^{9} And as I may so say, Levi also, who received tithes, **paid tithes in Abraham.**

Hebrews 11:8, 17

^{8} **By Faith Abraham,** *when he was called to go out into a place which he should after receive for an inheritance, obeyed; and he went out, not knowing where he went.*

^{17} **By Faith Abraham,** *when he was tried, offered up Isaac: and he that had received the promises offered up his only begotten son,*

James 2:21, 23

^{21} Was not **Abraham our father** *justified by works, when he had offered Isaac his son upon the altar?*

^{23} And the Scripture was fulfilled which said, **Abraham believed God,** *and it was imputed unto him for righteousness: and he was called the Friend of God.*

Appendix Three
References to the Land of Israel
Belonging to God and Israel

In the passages quoted below, the references to the Land of Israel belonging to Israel and God are so clear that it should not be questioned; however, that is not the case. Covenant Reform and Replacement Theology instead give credence to their theological position that God has cast Israel aside and that now the Church has assumed all the blessings and covenants of God.

Here are the passages that God gave to Abraham, Isaac, and Jacob and to their descendants that point in only one direction: The promise of the Land was given to the Patriarchs personally and to their seed. The Jewish people are their seed; the Land belongs to them as well, as a people and as a nation as the Scriptures clearly state.

The Abrahamic Covenant and the Land are inseparably linked and interwoven together. I believe you will notice that as you go through this appendix. Read these passages carefully and observe what God has said. Remember God is the author of language and He is perfectly capable of speaking for Himself without the interference of scholars who are well over two millennia removed from Moses, the Prophets, and the Psalms.

Please notice that I am following the Jewish division of the Hebrew Scripture: the Law, the Prophets and the Writings. Next, there are basically three areas that the Land passages refer to:

- Promise of the Land to Abraham, Isaac, and Jacob and to their seed.
- Passages that deal with the loss or the privilege of living in the Land because of sin.

- Passages that deal with Israel's regathering to the Land in the future so that God can fulfill His personal promise to Abraham, Isaac, and Jacob as well as to the believing remnant of Israel, whether it is Israel past, present, or Israel future.

In the passages quoted below are over 252 quotations from the Hebrew Scriptures referring to the Land belonging to God, who gave it to Israel. As you read through these verses, also notice the personal pronouns that God uses in reference to the Land being His Land, My Land. The ownership of the Land has never been transferred to the Church; you can search in vain through the Scriptures, but it simply is not there. Even more so, the Land has never been transferred to Islam or the Palestinians. Look what the LORD says through the Prophet Zechariah concerning Jerusalem:

And in that day will I make Jerusalem a burdensome stone for all people: all that burden themselves with it shall be cut in pieces, though all the people of the earth be gathered together against it (Zechariah 12:3).

Today the world hates Israel and wants to partition or divide the Land which God calls *My Land* in Joel 3:2. So *beware,* those who reject God's Word – those without discernment in the United States, Europe, and the United Nations. That name "United Nations" is a misnomer; there is nothing "united" about this organization expect for an evil outlook. On an interesting note, I learned when in Israel that the United Nations headquarters there sits on a mountain called "The Mount of Evil Counsel." What an appropriate name! Beware! God will judge those who are trying to bring about a Two-State solution.

The Torah – The Law – The Books of Moses (106)

Genesis 12:1, 7

¹ Now the LORD had said unto Abram, Get you out of your country, and from your kindred, and from your father's house, **unto a land that I will show you***.*

⁷ And the LORD appeared unto Abram, and said, **Unto your seed will I give this Land***: and there he built an altar unto the LORD, who appeared unto him.*

Genesis 13:14-17

^{14} And the LORD said unto Abram, after Lot was separated from him, Lift up now your eyes, and look from the place where you are northward, and southward, and eastward, and westward: ^{15} **For all the Land which you see, to you will I give it,** *and* **to your seed forever.** *^{16} And I will make your seed as the dust of the earth: so that if a man can number the dust of the earth, then shall your seed also be numbered.* ^{17} **Arise, walk through the Land in the length of it and in the breadth of it; for I will give it unto you.**

Genesis 15:7, 18-21

^{7} And He said unto him [Abraham], *I am the LORD that brought you out of UR of the Chaldees,* **to give you this Land to inherit it.**

^{18} In the same day the LORD made a covenant with Abram, saying, **Unto your seed have I given this Land,** *from the river Egypt unto the great river, the river Euphrates:* ^{19} *The Kenites, and the Kenizzites, and the Kadmonites,* ^{20} *And the Hittites, and the Perizzites, and the Rephaims,* ^{21} *And the Amorites, and the Canaanites, and the Girgashites, and the Jebusites.*

Genesis 17:8

And I will establish **My covenant between Me and you** *and* **your seed after you, the Land wherein you are a stranger,** *all the Land of Canaan,* **for an everlasting possession;** *and I will be their God.*

Genesis 24:7

The **LORD God of heaven,** *which took me from my father's house, and from the land of my kindred, and which spoke unto me, and* **that swore unto me,** *saying* **Unto your seed will I give this Land;** *He shall send His angel before you, and you shall take a wife unto my son from there.*

Genesis 26:2-4

^{2} And the LORD appeared unto him [Isaac], *and said, Do not go down into Egypt; dwell in the Land which I shall tell you of: ^{3}* **Sojourn in this Land,** *and I will be with you, and will bless you; for unto you, and unto your seed,* **I will give all these countries,** *and I will perform the oath which I swore unto Abraham your father; ^{4} And I will make your seed to multiply as the stars of heaven, and will give unto your seed all these countries; and in your seed shall all the nations of the earth be blessed.*

Genesis 28:13, 15

¹³ And, behold, the LORD stood above it, and said [to Jacob], *I am the LORD God of Abraham your father, and the God of Isaac:* **the Land whereon you lay, to you will I give it, and to your seed**.

¹⁵ And, behold, the LORD stood above it, and said, I am the LORD God of Abraham your father, and the God of Isaac: **the Land whereon you lay, to you will I give it, and to your seed**.

Genesis 35:12

And **the Land which I gave Abraham and Isaac, to you I will give it**, **and to your seed after you will I give the Land**.

Genesis 48:21

And Israel said unto Joseph, Behold, I die: but God shall be with you, and **bring you again unto the Land of your fathers**.

Genesis 50:24

And Joseph said unto his brethren, I die: and God will surely visit you, and bring you out of this land unto **the Land which He swore to Abraham**, **to Isaac, and to Jacob**.

Exodus 2:23-25

²³ and it came to pass in process of time that the king of Egypt died: and the children of Israel sighed by reason of the bondage, and they cried, and their cry came up unto God by reason of the bondage. ²⁴ And God heard their groaning, and **God remembered His covenant with Abraham, with Isaac, and with Jacob**. *²⁵ And God looked upon the children of Israel, and God had respect unto them.*

Exodus 3:8, 17

⁸ And I am come down to deliver them out of the hand of the Egyptians, and to bring them up out of that land unto **a good Land and a large, unto a Land flowing with milk and honey**; *unto the place of the Canaanites, and the Hittites, and the Amorites, and the Perizzites, and the Hivites, and the Jebusites.*

¹⁷ And I have said, I will bring you up out of the affliction of Egypt **unto the Land of the Canaanites**, *and the Hittites, and the Amorites, and the Perizzites, and the Hivites, and the Jebusites, unto* **a Land flowing with milk and honey**.

Exodus 6:4, 8

⁴ And I have also established My covenant with them, **to give them the Land of Canaan,** *the Land of their pilgrimage, wherein they were strangers.*

⁸ And I will bring you in unto **the Land,** *concerning the* **which I did swear [which I swore] to give to Abraham, to Isaac, and to Jacob;** *and* **I will give it [to] you for a heritage***: I am the LORD.*

Exodus 13:5, 11

⁵ And it shall be when the LORD shall bring you into the **Land of the Canaanites,** *and the Hittites, and the Amorites, and the Hivites, and the Jebusites,* **which He swore unto your fathers to give you, a Land flowing with milk and honey,** *that you shall keep this service in this month.*

¹¹ And it shall be when the **LORD shall bring you into the Land of the Canaanites,** *as* **He swore unto you and to your fathers, and shall give it [to] you.**

Exodus 15:17

You shall bring them in and **plant them** *in the mountain of Your inheritance,* **in the place,** *O LORD,* **which You have made for You to dwell in,** *in the Sanctuary, O Lord, which Your hands have established.*

Exodus 20:12

Honor your father and your mother: that your days may be long **upon the Land which the LORD your God gives you.**

Exodus 23:23, 33

²³ For **Mine Angel shall go before you, and bring you in unto the Amorites, and the Hittites, and the Perizzites, and the Canaanites, the Hivites, and the Jebusites:** *and I will cut them off.*

³³ They [Canaanites] shall not dwell in **your Land,** *lest they make you sin against Me: for if you serve their gods, it will surely be a snare unto you.*

Exodus 32:13

Remember Abraham, Isaac, and Israel, Your servants to whom You swore by Your own self, and said unto them, I will multiply your seed as the stars of heaven, and **all this Land that I have spoken of will I give unto your seed, and they shall inherit it forever.**

Exodus 33:1-3

> *¹ And the LORD said unto Moses, Depart, and go up from here, you and the people which you have brought up out of the land of Egypt,* **unto the Land which I swore unto Abraham, to Isaac, and to Jacob, saying, Unto your seed will I give it***: ² And I will send an angel before you; and I will drive out the Canaanite, the Amorite, and the Hittite, and the Perizzite, the Hivite, and the Jebusite:* **³ Unto a Land flowing with milk and honey***: for I will not go up in the midst of you; for you are a stiff-necked people; lest I consume you in the way.*

Leviticus 20:24

> *But I have said unto you,* **You shall inherit their Land***, and* **I will give it unto you to possess it***, a* **Land that flows with milk and honey***: I am the LORD your God, which has separated you from other people.*

Leviticus 23:10

> *Speak unto the children of Israel, and say unto them,* **When you have come into the Land which I give unto you***, and shall reap the harvest thereof, then you shall bring a sheaf of the first fruits of your harvest unto the priest:*

Leviticus 25:2, 18, 23-24, 38

> *² Speak unto the children of Israel, and say unto them,* **When you come into the Land which I give you***, then shall the Land keep a Sabbath unto the LORD.*
>
> *¹⁸ Wherefore you shall do My statutes, and keep My judgments, and do them; and* **you shall dwell in the Land in safety.**
>
> *²³ The Land shall not be sold forever:* **for the Land is Mine***; for you are strangers and sojourners with me. ²⁴ And in all the Land of your possession you shall grant a redemption for the Land.*
>
> *³⁸ I am the LORD your God, which brought you forth out of the land of Egypt,* **to give you the Land of Canaan***, and to be your God.*

Leviticus 26:6, 33, 41-42

⁶ And **I will give peace in the Land**, *and you shall lie down, and none shall make you afraid: and I will rid evil beasts* **out of the Land**, **neither shall the sword go through your Land**.

³³ And I will scatter you among the heathen, and will draw out a sword after you: **and your Land shall be desolate**, *and your cities waste.*

⁴¹ And that I also have walked contrary unto them, and have brought them into the land of their enemies; if then their uncircumcised hearts be humbled, and they then accept of the punishment of their iniquity: ⁴² Then will I remember **My covenant with Jacob**, *and also* **My covenant with Isaac**, *and also* **My covenant with Abraham** *will I remember; and* **I will remember the Land**.

Numbers 11:12

Have I conceived all this people? Have I begotten them, that You should say unto Me, carry them in Your bosom, as a nursing father bears the sucking child, **unto the Land which You swore unto their fathers**?

Numbers 14:8-9, 23

⁸ If the LORD delight in us, **then He will bring us into this Land, and give it [to] us;** **a Land which flows with milk and honey**. *⁹ Only do not rebel against the LORD, neither fear the people of the Land; for they are bread for us: their defense is departed from them, and the LORD is with us: fear them not.*

²³ Surely **they shall not see the Land which I swore unto their fathers**, *neither shall any of them that provoked Me see it.*

Numbers 15:2, 18

² Speak unto the children of Israel, and say unto them, **When you have come into the Land of your habitations, which I give unto you**,

¹⁸ Speak unto the children of Israel, and say unto them, **When you come into the Land whither I bring you**.

Numbers 20:12

And the LORD spoke unto Moses and Aaron, Because you believed Me not, to sanctify Me in the eyes of the children of Israel, **therefore**

you shall not bring this congregation into the Land which I have given them.

Numbers 27:12

And the LORD said unto Moses, Get up into this Mount Abarim, and **see the Land which I have given unto the children of Israel.**

Numbers 32:11

Surely **none of the men** *that came up out of Egypt, from twenty years old and upward,* **shall see the Land which I swore unto Abraham, unto Isaac, and unto Jacob;** *because they have not wholly followed me:*

Numbers 33:53

And you shall dispossess the inhabitants of the Land, and dwell therein: **for I have given you the Land to possess it.**

Numbers 34:13

And Moses commanded the children of Israel, saying, **This is the Land which you shall inherit by lot***, which the LORD commanded to give unto the nine tribes, and to the half tribe:*

Deuteronomy 5:16

Honor your father and your mother, as the LORD your God hath commanded you; that your days may be prolonged, and that it may go well with you, **in the Land which the LORD your God gives you.**

Deuteronomy 6:3, 10, 18, 23

[3] *Hear therefore, O Israel, and observe to do it; that it may be well with you, and that you may increase mightily,* **as the LORD God of your fathers has promised you, in the Land that flows with milk and honey.**

[10] *And it shall be,* **when the LORD your God shall have brought you into the Land which He swore unto your fathers, to Abraham, to Isaac, and to Jacob, to give you great and goodly cities, which you did not build,**

[18] *And you shall do that which is right and good in the sight of the LORD: that it may be well with you, and* **that you may go in and possess the good land which the LORD swore unto your fathers.**

²³ And he brought us out from there, that He might bring us in, to **give us the Land which He swore unto our fathers***.*

Deuteronomy 7:1, 8, 12-13

¹ When the LORD your **God shall bring you into the Land** *whither you go to possess it, and has cast out many nations before you, the Hittites, and the Girgashites, and the Amorites, and the Canaanites, and the Perizzites, and the Hivites, and the Jebusites, seven nations greater and mightier than you.*

⁸ But because the LORD loved you, and because He would keep the oath which He had sworn unto your fathers, the LORD has brought you out with a mighty hand , and redeemed you out of the house of bondmen, from the hand of Pharaoh king of Egypt.

¹² Wherefore it shall come to pass, if you listen to these judgments, and keep and do them, that the **LORD your God shall keep unto you the covenant** *and the mercy which he* **swore unto your fathers***. ¹³ And He will love you, and bless you, and multiply you: He will also bless the fruit of your womb, and the fruit of your land, your corn, and your wine, and your oil, the increase of your kine* [herd]*, and the flocks of your sheep,* **in the Land which He swore unto your fathers to give you***.*

Deuteronomy 8:1, 18

¹ All the commandments which I command you this day shall you observe to do, that you may live, and multiply, and **go in and possess the Land which the LORD swore unto your fathers***.*

¹⁸ But you shall remember the LORD your God: for it is He that gives you power to get wealth, that **He may establish His covenant which He swore unto your fathers***, as it is this day.*

Deuteronomy 9:5

Not for your righteousness, or for the uprightness of your heart, do you go to possess their land but for the wickedness of these nations the LORD your God does drive them out from before you, and **that He may perform the word which the LORD swore unto your fathers, Abraham, Isaac, and Jacob.**

Deuteronomy 11:9, 21, 31

⁹ And that you may prolong your days **in the Land, which the LORD swore unto your fathers to give unto them and to their seed,** *a Land that flows with milk and honey.*

²¹ That your days may be multiplied, and the days of your children, **in the Land which the LORD swore unto your fathers to give them**, *as the days of heaven upon the earth.*

³¹ For you shall pass over Jordan **to go in to possess the Land which the LORD your God gives you, and you shall possess it,** *and dwell therein.*

Deuteronomy 12:10

But when you go over Jordan, and **dwell in the land which the LORD your God gives you to inherit,** *and when He gives you rest from all your enemies round about, so that you dwell in safety:*

Deuteronomy 15:7

If there be among you a poor man of one of your brothers **within any of your gates in your Land which the LORD your God gives you,** *you shall not harden your heart, nor shut your hand from your poor brother:*

Deuteronomy 16:20

That which is altogether just shall you follow, that you may live, and **inherit the Land which the LORD your God gives you.**

Deuteronomy 17:14

When you are come unto the Land which the LORD your God gives you, and shall possess it, and shall dwell there, *and shall say, I will set a king over me, like as all the nations that are about me.*

Deuteronomy 18:9

When you have come into the Land which the LORD your God gives you, *you shall not learn to do after the abominations of those nations.*

Deuteronomy 19:1-2, 8

¹ When the LORD your God has cut off the nations, **whose Land the LORD your God gives you***, and you succeed them, and dwell in their cities, and in their houses;* *² You shall separate three cities for you in the midst of your Land,* **which the LORD your God gives you to possess it.**

⁸ And if the LORD your God enlarge your coast, **as He has sworn unto your fathers, and give you all the Land which He promised to give unto your fathers.**

Deuteronomy 25:19

Therefore it shall be, when the LORD your God has given you rest from all your enemies round about, **in the Land which the LORD your God gives you for an inheritance to possess it***, that you shall blot out the remembrance of Amalek from under heaven; you shall not forget it.*

Deuteronomy 26:3, 9, 15

³ And you shall go unto the priest that shall be in those days, and say unto him, I profess this day unto the LORD your God, that I have come unto the country **which the LORD swore unto our fathers for to give us.**

⁹ And He hath brought us into this place, and **hath given us this Land, even a Land that flows with milk and honey.**

¹⁵ Look down from Your holy habitation, from heaven, and bless Your people Israel, and **the Land which You have given us, as You swore unto our fathers, a Land that flows with milk and honey.**

Deuteronomy 27:2-3

² And it shall be on the day when you shall pass over Jordan **unto the Land which the LORD your God gives you** *that you shall set you up great stones, and plaster them with plaster:* *³ And you shall write upon them all the words of this law, when you are passed over, that* **you may go in unto the Land that flows with milk and honey; as the LORD God of your fathers has promised you.**

Deuteronomy 28:8, 11, 21, 24, 33, 42, 51-53, 63

⁸ *The LORD shall command the blessing upon you in your storehouses, and in all that you set your hand unto; and* **He shall bless you in the Land which the LORD your God gives you.**

¹¹ *And the LORD shall make you plenteous in goods, in the fruit of your body, and in the fruit of your cattle, and in the fruit of your ground,* **in the Land which the LORD swore unto your fathers to give you.** [Blessing for obedience to the Law]

²¹ *The LORD shall make the pestilence cleave* [cling] *unto you, until He has consumed you from* **off the Land**, *where you go to possess it.* [Cursing for disobedience to the Law]

²⁴ *The LORD shall* **make the rain of your Land powder and dust**: *from heaven shall it come down upon you, until you are destroyed.* [Cursing for disobedience to the Law]

³³ *The fruit of your Land, and all your labors, a nation which you know not* [shall] *eat up; and you shall be only oppressed and crushed always.* [Cursing for disobedience to the Law]

⁴² *All your* **trees and fruit of your Land shall the locust consume** [Cursing for disobedience to the Law]

⁵¹ *And he shall eat the fruit of your cattle, and the* **fruit of your Land**, *until you are destroyed: which also shall not leave you either corn, wine, or oil, or the increase of your kine* [herd], *or flocks of your sheep, until He has destroyed you.* ⁵² *And He shall besiege you in all your gates, until your high and fenced walls come down, in which you trusted,* **throughout all your Land**: *and* **He shall besiege you in all your gates throughout all your Land, which the LORD your God has given you.** ⁵³ *And you shall eat the fruit of your own body, the flesh of your sons and of your daughters,* **which the LORD your God has given you**, *in the siege, and in the straightness, by which your enemies shall distress you.* [Cursing for disobedience to the Law]

⁶³ *And it shall come to pass, that as the LORD rejoiced over you to do you good, and to multiply you; so the LORD will rejoice over you to destroy you, and bring you to naught; and* **you shall be plucked from off the Land where you go to possess it**. [Cursing for disobedience to the Law]

Deuteronomy 30:3-5

³ That then the LORD your God will turn your captivity, and have compassion upon you, and **will return and gather you from all the nations**, *where the LORD your God has scattered you. ⁴ If any of you are driven out unto the outermost parts of heaven, from there* **will the LORD your God gather you**, *and* **from there will He fetch you**. *⁵ And the LORD your God will bring you* **into the Land which your fathers possessed, and you shall possess it**; *and He will do you good, and multiply you above your fathers.*

Deuteronomy 30:18, 20

¹⁸ I denounce unto you this day, that you shall surely perish, and that **you shall not prolong your days upon the Land, where you** [are] **passing over Jordan to go to possess it.**

²⁰ That you may love the LORD your God, and that you may obey His voice, and that you may cleave [cling] *unto Him: for He is your life, and the length of your days:* **that you may dwell in the Land which the LORD swore unto your fathers, to Abraham, to Isaac, and to Jacob, to give them.**

Deuteronomy 31:20-21, 23

²⁰ **For when I shall have brought them into the Land which I swore unto their fathers**, *that flows with milk and honey; and they shall have eaten and filled themselves, and waxed fat; then will they turn unto other gods, and serve them, and provoke Me, and break My covenant. ²¹ And it shall come to pass, when many evils and troubles fall upon them, that this song shall testify against them as a witness; for it shall not be forgotten out of the mouths of their seed: for I know their imagination which they go about* **even now before I have brought them into the Land which I swore.**

²³ And he gave Joshua the son of Nun a charge, and said, Be strong and of a good courage: for you shall bring the children of Israel **into the Land which I swore unto them**: *and I will be with you.*

Deuteronomy 34:4

And the LORD said unto him [Moses], **this is the Land which I swore unto Abraham, unto Isaac, and unto Jacob**, *saying,* **I will give it unto your seed**; *I have caused you to see it with your eyes, but you shall not go over there.*

In reading these verses, have you noticed the repeated promise of God to Israel, the promises made to Abraham, Isaac, and Jacob? From the time of Abraham to the end of the exodus from Egypt, the promise of God is laid out time and time again.

Did you also notice that the promise and ownership of the Land in the Abrahamic Covenant is unconditional? God stated it by swearing by His Name; His promise cannot be altered. However, did you notice that the possession of the Land was contingent on their obedience to the Laws of Moses? Notice what I did not say; I did not say the ownership of the Land. The ownership is God's, who gave it to Israel. So Israel's possession of the Land is conditional, based on their obedience to the Laws of Moses.

The eternal promise of the Land is a promise of God in the Abrahamic Covenant, but the possession of the Land is based on Israel's obedience to the Mosaic Law. Moses' statements in Deuteronomy chapters 28 through 32 also give us a prophetic panorama of the history of Israel in and outside the Land. Moses says that Israel will return to the Land and God will, in the future, circumcise their heart to love the LORD their God with all their heart and with all their soul.

We today are living in the Last Days before the coming of the LORD. What you and I are seeing today is in complete agreement with Moses and the Prophets, as Israel is being regathered in unbelief at this point into the Land of Israel. The Land today does not and has never been owned by Christians or Muslims; it is God's Land, and He has given it to Abraham, Isaac, and Jacob and to their descendants.

What we will see primarily in the Prophets is in complete agreement with Moses. The Land is God's. He is jealous for His Land and will judge the peoples and nations that curse Israel and that attempt to "partition" His Land, the Land that He has given by covenant to Israel.

The Prophets (125)

Joshua 1:2, 15

> ² *Moses My servant is dead; now therefore arise, go over this Jordan, you, and all this people,* **unto the Land which I do give to them**, *even to the Children of Israel.*
>
> ¹⁵ *Until the LORD has given your brothers rest, as He has given you, and* **they also have possessed the Land which the LORD your God gives them:** *then you shall return unto the Land of your*

possession, and enjoy it, which Moses the LORD's servant gave you on this side of Jordan toward the sun rising.

Joshua 5:6

For the children of Israel walked forty years in the wilderness, till all the people that were men of war, which came out of Egypt, were consumed, because they obeyed not the voice of the LORD unto whom the LORD swore that He would not show them the Land, **which the LORD swore unto their fathers that He would give us, a Land that flows with milk and honey.**

Joshua 23:13-16

[13] Know for a certainty that the LORD your God will no more drive out any of these nations from before you; but they shall be snares and traps unto you, and scourges in your sides, and thorns in your eyes, **until you perish from off this good Land which the LORD your God has given you.** *[14] And, behold, this day I am going the way of all the earth: and you know in all your hearts and in all your souls, that not one thing has failed of all the good things which the LORD your God spoke concerning you; and have come to pass unto you, and not one thing has failed thereof. [15] Therefore it shall come to pass, that as all good things are come upon you which the LORD your God promised you; so shall the LORD bring upon you all evil things, until He has destroyed you from* **off this good Land which the LORD your God has given you.** *[16] When you have transgressed the covenant of the LORD your God, which He commanded you, and have gone and served other gods, and bowed yourselves to them; then shall the anger of the LORD be kindled against you, and* **you shall perish quickly from off the good land which He has given unto you.**

1 Kings 8:40

That they may fear You all the days that they live **in the Land which You gave unto our fathers.**

1 Kings 9:7

Then will **I cut off Israel out of the Land which I have given them**; *and this house, which I have hallowed for My Name, will I cast out of My sight; and Israel shall be a proverb and a byword among all people:*

2 Kings 14:15-16

[15] For the LORD shall smite Israel, as a reed is shaken in the water, and **He shall root up Israel out of this good land, which He gave to their fathers**, *and shall scatter them beyond the river, because*

they have made their groves, provoking the LORD to anger. ⁱ⁶ *And He shall give Israel up because of the sins of Jeroboam, who did sin, and who made Israel to sin.*

2 Kings 17:23

Until the LORD removed Israel out of His sight, as He had said by all His servants the prophets. **So was Israel carried away out of their own Land** *to Assyria unto this day.*

2 Kings 21:8-9

⁸ **Neither will I make the feet of Israel move any more out of the Land which I gave their fathers**; *only if they will observe to do according to all that I have commanded them, and according to all the law that My servant Moses commanded them.* ⁹ *But they did not listen: and Manasseh seduced them to do more evil than the nations did whom the LORD destroyed before the children of Israel.*

2 Kings 25:21

And the king of Babylon smote them, and slew them at Riblah in the land of Hamath. So **Judah was carried away out of their Land**.

Isaiah 8:8

And he [Assyria] shall pass through Judah, he shall overflow and go over, he shall reach even to the neck: and the stretching out of his wings shall fill the breadth of **your Land, O Immanuel**.

Isaiah 11:10-12

¹⁰ *And in that day there shall be a root of Jesse, which shall stand for an Ensign of the people, to it shall the Gentiles seek: and His rest shall be glorious.* ¹¹ *And it shall come to pass in that day, that the Lord shall set His hand again the* **second time to recover the remnant of His people**, *which shall be left, from Assyria, and from Egypt, and from Pathros, and from Cush, and from Elam, and from Shinar, and from Hamath, and from the islands of the sea.* ¹² *And he shall set up an Ensign for the nations, and shall* **assemble the outcasts of Israel, and gather together the dispersed of Judah from the four corners of the earth**.

Isaiah 14:1

For the LORD will have mercy on Jacob, and **will yet choose Israel, and set them in their own Land**: *and the strangers shall be joined with them, and they shall cleave* [cling] *to the house of Jacob.*

Isaiah 62:4

You shall no more be termed Forsaken; **neither shall your Land any more be termed Desolate**: *but you shall be called Hephzibah, and* **your Land Beulah**: *for the LORD delights in you, and* **your Land shall be married.**

Jeremiah 3:2, 9

² Lift up your eyes unto the high places, and see where you have not been lien with [violated]. *In the ways* [by the roads] *have you sat for them, as the Arabian in the wilderness; and* **you have polluted the Land with your whoredoms and with your wickedness**

⁹ And it came to pass through the lightness of her whoredom, that she **defiled the Land, and committed adultery with stones and with stocks**.

Jeremiah 16:15

But, the LORD lives, that brought up the children of Israel from the land of the north, and from all the lands where He had driven them: and **I will bring them again into their Land that I gave unto their fathers.**

Jeremiah 16:18

And first I will recompense their iniquity and their sin double; because they have defiled **My Land**, *they have filled My inheritance with the carcasses of their detestable and abominable things.*

Jeremiah 17:4

And you, even yourself, **shall discontinue from your heritage [the Land] that I gave you**; *And I will cause you to serve your enemies in the land which you know not: for you have kindled a fire in My anger, which shall burn forever.*

Jeremiah 22:12

But he [Jehoahaz renamed Shallum by Pharaoh-nechoh] *shall die in the place where they have led him captive, and shall see* **this Land no more**.

Jeremiah 22:26-27

²⁶ And I will cast you [Jehoiachin or Coniah] *out, and your mother that bore you,* **into another country where you were not born**; *and there you shall die. ²⁷ But to* **the land where they desire to return, they shall not return there**.

Jeremiah 23:8

But, the LORD lives, which brought up and which led the seed of the house of Israel out of the north country, and from all countries where I had driven them; and **they shall dwell in their own Land.**

Jeremiah 24:5-6, 10

⁵ Thus says the LORD, the God of Israel; Like these good figs, so will I acknowledge them that are carried away captive of Judah, whom I have **sent out of this place** *into the land of the Chaldeans for their good. ⁶ For I will set My eyes upon them for good, and* **I will bring them again to this Land**: *and I will build them, and not pull them down; and I will plant them, and not pluck them up.*

¹⁰ And I will send the sword, the famine, and the pestilence, among them, till they are consumed [perish] **from off the land that I gave unto them and to their fathers.**

Jeremiah 25:5

They said, Turn again now everyone from his evil way, and from the evil of your doings, **and dwell in the Land that the LORD has given unto you and to your fathers forever and ever:**

Jeremiah 27:10-11

¹⁰ For they prophesy a lie unto you, **to remove you far from your Land**; *and that I should drive you out, and you should perish. ¹¹ But the nations that bring their neck under the yoke of the king of Babylon, and serve him,* **those will I let remain still in their own land, says the LORD,** *and they shall till it, and dwell therein.*

Jeremiah 29:10, 14

¹⁰ For thus says the LORD, That after seventy years are accomplished at Babylon I will visit you, and perform My good word toward you, **in causing you to return to this place.**

¹⁴ And I will be found of you, says the LORD: and I will turn away your captivity, and I will gather you from all the nations and from all the places where I have driven you, says the LORD: and **I will bring you again into the place from where I caused you to be carried away captive.**

Jeremiah 30:3, 10-11

³ For, lo, the days come, says the LORD, that I will bring again the captivity of My people Israel and Judah, says the LORD: and **I will cause them to return to the Land that I gave to their fathers, and they shall possess it.**

10 Therefore fear not, O My servant Jacob, says the LORD; neither be dismayed, O Israel: for, lo, I will save you from afar, and your seed from the land of their captivity; and **Jacob shall return, and shall be in rest, and be quiet, and none shall make him afraid.**
11 For I am with you, says the LORD, to save you: though I make a full end of all nations where I have scattered you, yet will I not make a full end of you: but I will correct you in measure, and will not leave you altogether unpunished.

Jeremiah 31:7-8

7 For thus says the LORD; Sing with gladness for Jacob, and shout among the chief of the nations: publish you, praise you, and say, O LORD, **save Thy people, the remnant of Israel.** *8 Behold,* **I will bring them from the north country**, *and gather them from the coasts of the earth, and with them the blind and the lame, the woman with child and her that travails with child together:* **a great company shall return there.**

Jeremiah 32:37, 41

37 Behold, **I will gather them out of all countries**, *where I have driven them in My anger, and in My fury, and in great wrath; and* **I will bring them again unto this place**, *and I will cause them to dwell safely.*

41 Yea, I will rejoice over them to do them good, and **I will plant them in this Land** *assuredly with My whole heart and with My whole soul.*

Jeremiah 33:14-17

14 Behold the days come, says the LORD, that I will perform that good thing which **I have promised unto the house of Israel and to the house of Judah.** *15 In those days and at that time, will I cause the Branch of righteousness to grow up unto David; and He shall execute judgment and righteousness* **in the Land.** *16* **In those days shall Judah be saved, and Jerusalem shall dwell safely**: *and this is the name wherewith she* [Jerusalem] *shall be called, The LORD our righteousness. 17 For thus says the LORD;* **David shall never want a man to sit upon the throne of the house of Israel.**

Jeremiah 35:15

I have sent also unto you all my servants the prophets, rising up early and sending them, saying Return now every man from his evil way, and amend your doings, and do not go after other gods to serve them, and **you shall dwell in the Land which I have given to you** and to your fathers: *but you have not inclined your ear, nor hearkened* [listened] *unto me.*

Jeremiah 52:27

And the king of Babylon smote them, and put them to death in Riblah in the land of Hamath. Thus Judah was carried away captive **out of his own Land.**

Ezekiel 11:17

Therefore say, thus says the Lord GOD; I will even gather you from the people, and assemble you out of the countries where you have been scattered, and **I will give you the Land of Israel.**

Ezekiel 28:25

Thus says the Lord GOD; When I shall have gathered the house of Israel from the people among whom they are scattered, and shall be sanctified in them in the sight of the heathen, **then shall they dwell in their Land that I have given to My servant Jacob.**

Ezekiel 20:33-38

^{33} As I live, says the Lord GOD, surely with a mighty hand, and with a stretched out arm, and with fury poured out, will I rule over you: ^{34} And I will bring you out from the people, and will gather you out of the countries wherein you are scattered, with a mighty hand, and with a stretched out arm, and with fury poured out. ^{35} And I will bring you into the wilderness of the people, and there will I plead with you face to face. ^{36} Like as I pleaded with your fathers in the wilderness of the land of Egypt, so will I plead with you, says the Lord GOD. ^{37} And I will cause you to pass under the rod, and I will bring you into the bond of the covenant; ^{38} And I will purge out from among you the rebels, and them that transgress against Me: I will bring them forth out of the country where they sojourn, and they [the rebels] *shall not enter in the* **Land of Israel**: *and you shall know that I am the LORD.*

Ezekiel 34:11-16

^{11} For thus says the Lord GOD; Behold, I even I, will both search My sheep, and seek them out. ^{12} As a shepherd seeks out his flock in the day that he is among his sheep that are scattered; so will I seek out My sheep, and will deliver them out of all places where they have been scattered in the cloudy and dark day: ^{13} And I will bring them out from the people, and gather them from the countries, and **will bring them to their own Land,** *and* **feed them upon the mountains of Israel** *by the rivers, and in all the inhabited places of the country. ^{14} I will feed them in a good pasture, and upon the high*

mountains of Israel shall their fold be: they shall they lie in a good fold, and in a fat pasture shall they **feed upon the mountains of Israel**. *⁵ I will feed My flock, and I will cause them to lie down, says the Lord GOD,* ¹⁶ *I will seek that which was lost, and bring again that which was driven away and will bind up that which was broken, and will strengthen that which was sick: but I will destroy the fat and the strong; I will feed them with judgment.*

Ezekiel 36:12, 17-24, 28

¹² *Yea,* **I will cause men to walk upon you** [the Land], **even My people Israel**; *and* **they shall possess you**, *and* **you shall be their inheritance**, *and you shall no more henceforth* [from now on] *bereave them of men.*

¹⁷ *Son of man,* **when the house of Israel dwelled in their own Land**, *they defiled it by their own way and by their doings; their way was before Me as the uncleanness of a removed woman.* ¹⁸ *Therefore I poured My fury upon them for the* **blood that they had shed upon the Land**, *and for their idols with which they had polluted it:* ¹⁹ *And I scattered them among the heathen, and they were dispersed through the countries: according to their way and according to their doing I judged them.* ²⁰ *And when they entered unto the heathen, where they went, they profaned My holy Name, when they said to them, These are the people of the LORD and are gone forth* **out of His Land**. ²¹ *But I had pity for My holy Name, which the house of Israel had profaned among the heathen, where they went.* ²² *Therefore say unto the house of Israel, Thus says the Lord GOD; I do not do this for your sakes, O house of Israel, but for My holy Name's sake, which you have profaned among the heathen where you went.* ²³ *And I will sanctify My great Name, which was profaned among the heathen, which you have profaned in the midst of them; and the heathen shall know that I am the LORD, says the Lord GOD, when I shall be sanctified in you before their eyes.* ²⁴ *For I will take you from among the nations, and gather you out of all countries, and will bring you into* **your own Land**.

²⁸ *And you shall* **dwell in the Land that I gave to your fathers**; *and you shall be My people, and I will be your God.*

Ezekiel 37:11-14, 21-22, 25

¹¹ *Then he said unto me, Son of man, these bones are the whole house of Israel: behold, they say, our bones are dried, and our hope is lost: we are cut off for our parts.* ¹² *Therefore prophesy and say unto them, Thus says the Lord GOD; Behold, O My people, I will open your graves, and cause you to come up out of your graves, and* **bring you into the Land of Israel**. ¹³ *And you shall know that I am*

the LORD, when I have opened your graves, O My people, and brought you up out of your graves, ^{14} *And shall put My spirit in you and you shall live, and* **I shall place you in your own Land**: *then you shall know that I the LORD have spoken it, and performed it, says the LORD.*

^{21} *And say unto them, Thus says the Lord God; Behold, I will take the children of Israel from among the heathen where they have gone, and will gather them on every side,* **and bring them into their own Land**. ^{22} *And I will make them one nation in the land upon the mountains of Israel;*

^{25} *And* **they shall dwell in the Land that I have given unto Jacob My servant**, *where your fathers have dwelt; and* **they shall dwell therein even they**, *and* **their children**, *and* **their children's children forever**: *and My servant David shall be their prince forever.*

Ezekiel 38:16, 18-19

^{16} *And you shall come up against My people of Israel, as a cloud to cover the land; it shall be in the latter days, and I will bring you* **against My Land**, *that the heathen may know me, when I shall be sanctified in you, O Gog, before their eyes.*

^{18} *And it shall come to pass at the same time when Gog shall come* **against the Land of Israel**, *says the Lord God, that My fury shall come up in My face.* ^{19} *For in My jealousy and in the fire of My wrath I have spoken, Surely in that day there shall be a great shaking in* **the Land of Israel**.

Ezekiel 39:28

Then shall they know that I am the LORD their God, which caused them to be led into captivity among the heathen: **but I have gathered them unto their own Land**, *and have left none of them any more there.*

Hosea 1:10-11

^{10} *Yet the number of the children of Israel shall be as the sand of the sea, which cannot be measured nor numbered; and it shall come to pass, that* **in the place** [the Land] *where it was said unto them, You are not My people,* **there it shall be said** *unto them, You are the sons of the living God.* ^{11} *Then shall the children of Judah and the children of Israel be* **gathered together**, *and appoint themselves one head, and they shall come up out of the land; for great shall be the day of Jezreel.*

Hosea 3:4-5

> [4] *For the children of Israel shall abide many days without a king, and without a prince, and without a sacrifice, and without an image, and without an ephod, and without teraphim:* [5] **Afterward shall the children of Israel return**, *and seek the LORD their God, and David their king; and shall fear the LORD and His goodness* **in the latter days**.

Hosea 9:3

> *They shall not dwell* **in the LORD's Land**; *but Ephraim shall return to Egypt, and they shall eat unclean things in Assyria.*

Joel 1:6

> *For a nation has come up upon* **My Land**, *strong, and without number, whose teeth are the teeth of a lion, and he has the cheek teeth of a great lion.*

Joel 2:18

> *Then will the LORD be jealous for* **His Land** *and pity His people.*

Joel 3:2

> *I will also gather all nations, and will bring them down into the valley of Jehoshaphat, and will plead with them there for* **My people** *and for* **My heritage Israel**, *whom they have scattered among the nations, and* **parted My Land**.

Amos 7:17

> *Therefore thus says the LORD; Your wife shall be a harlot in the city, and your sons and your daughters shall fall by the sword, and your land shall be divided by line; and you shall die in a polluted land: and Israel shall surely go into captivity forth of* **His Land**.

Amos 9:15

> *And I* [the LORD] *will plant them* [Israel – Jewish people] *upon* **their Land**, *and they shall no more be pulled up out of* **their Land** *which* **I have given them**, *says the LORD your God.*

Obadiah 17

> *But upon* **mount Zion** *shall be deliverance, and* **there shall be holiness***; and the* **house of Jacob shall possess their possessions.**

Micah 4:1-2, 6-7

¹ But in the last days, it shall come to pass, that the mountain of the house of the LORD shall be established in the top of the mountains, and it shall be exalted above the hills; and people shall flow unto it. ² And many nations shall come, and say, Come, **and let us go up to the mountain of the LORD,** *and* **to the house of the God of Jacob;** *and He will teach us of His ways, and we will walk in His paths: for the law shall go forth of Zion, and the word of the LORD from Jerusalem.*

⁶ In that day, says the LORD, will I assemble her that [is] halted, and **I will gather her that is driven out,** *and her that I have afflicted; ⁷ And I will make her that halted a remnant, and her that was cast far off a strong nation:* **and the LORD shall reign over them in Mount Zion from that time on, even forever.**

Micah 7:20

Thou will perform the truth to Jacob, and the mercy to Abraham, which you have sworn unto our fathers from the days of old.

Haggai 2:9

The glory of this later house shall be greater than of the former, says the LORD of hosts: and **in this place will I give peace,** *says the LORD of hosts.*

Zephaniah 1:17-18

¹⁷ I will bring distress upon men that they shall walk like blind men, because they have sinned against the LORD: and their blood shall be poured out as dust, and their flesh as the dung. ¹⁸ Neither their silver nor their gold shall be able to deliver them in the day of the LORD's wrath; but **the whole Land shall be devoured by the fire of His jealousy:** *for He shall make even a speedy riddance of all them that dwell in the land.*

Zephaniah 3:14-20

¹⁴ Sing, O daughter of Zion; shout, O Israel; be glad and rejoice with all your heart, **O daughter of Jerusalem.** *¹⁵ The LORD has taken away your judgments, He has cast out your enemy:* **the King of Israel, even the LORD, is in the midst of you:** *you shall not see evil anymore. ¹⁶ In that day it shall be said to Jerusalem, Fear not: and to Zion, Let not your hands be slack. ¹⁷ The* **LORD your God in the midst of you** *is mighty; He will save, He will rejoice over you with joy; He will rest in His love, He will joy over you with singing. ¹⁸ I will gather them that are sorrowful for the solemn assembly, who* *are of you, to whom the reproach of it was burden.* ¹⁹ *Behold, at that time I will undo all that afflict you: and I will save her lame, and gather her that was driven out; and I will get them praise and fame in every land where they have been put to shame.* ²⁰ **At that time will I bring you again, even in the time that I gather you: for I will make you a name and a praise among all people of the earth, when I turn back your captivity before your eyes, says the LORD.**

Zechariah 1:14, 18-21

¹⁴ *So the angel that communed with me said unto me, Cry, saying, Thus says the LORD of hosts;* **I am jealous for Jerusalem and for Zion with great jealousy.**

¹⁸ *Then I lifted up my eyes, and saw, and behold four horns.* ¹⁹ *And I said unto the angel that talked with me, what are these? And He answered me, These are the horns which have scattered Judah, Israel, and Jerusalem.* ²⁰ *And the LORD showed me four carpenters.* ²¹ *Then I said, What do these come to do? And He spoke, saying, These are the horns which have scattered Judah, so that no man lifted up his head: but these have come to fray* [terrify] *them,* **to cast out the horns of the Gentiles, which lifted up their horn over the Land of Judah to scatter it.**

Zechariah 2:10-12

¹⁰ *Sing and rejoice, O daughter of Zion: for, lo, I come, and* **I will dwell in the midst of you,** *says the LORD.* ¹¹ *And many nations shall be joined to the LORD in that day, and shall be My people: and* **I will dwell in the midst of you,** *and you shall know that the LORD of hosts has sent Me unto you.* ¹² *And the* **LORD shall inherit Judah his portion in the holy Land,** *and shall* **choose Jerusalem again.**

Zechariah 3:9

For behold the stone that I have laid before Joshua; upon one stone shall be seven eyes: behold, I will engrave the graving thereof, says the LORD of hosts, and **I will remove the iniquity of that Land in one day.**

Zechariah 8:2-3, 8

² *Thus says the LORD of hosts;* **I was jealous for Zion with great jealousy,** *and* **I was jealous for her with great fury.** ³ *Thus says the LORD;* **I have returned unto Zion, and will dwell in the midst of Jerusalem:** *and Jerusalem shall be called a city of truth; and the mountain of the LORD of hosts the holy mountain.*

⁸ And **I will bring them,** *and* **they shall dwell in the midst of Jerusalem:** *and* **they shall be My people, and I will be their God,** *in truth and in righteousness.*

Zechariah 9:16

And the LORD their God shall save them in that day as the flock of His people: for they shall be as the stones of a crown, **lifted up as an ensign upon His Land.**

Zechariah 10:6

And I will strengthen the house of Judah, and I will save the house of Joseph, and **I will bring them again to place them**; *for I have mercy upon them: and they shall be as though I had not cast them off: for I am the LORD their God, and will hear them.*

Zechariah 12:9-10

⁹ And it shall come to pass in that day that **I will seek to destroy all the nations that come against Jerusalem.** *¹⁰ And* **I will pour upon the house of David,** *and* **upon the inhabitants of Jerusalem**, *the spirit of grace and of supplications: and they shall look upon Me whom they have pierced, and they shall mourn for Him, as one mourns for his only son, and shall be in bitterness for Him, as one that is in bitterness for his firstborn.*

The Writings – (21)

1 Chronicles 16:15-17

¹⁵ Be mindful always of His covenant; the word which He commanded to a thousand generations; *¹⁶ Even of the* **Covenant which He made with Abraham, and of His oath unto Isaac;** *¹⁷* **And had confirmed the same to Jacob for a law, and to Israel for an everlasting covenant.**

2 Chronicles 6:25, 31

²⁵ Then hear from the heavens, and forgive the sin of your people Israel, and **bring them again unto the Land which You gave to them and to their fathers.**

³¹ That they may fear you, to walk in your ways, **so long as they live in the Land which you gave unto our fathers.**

2 Chronicles 7:20

Then will I pluck them up by the roots out of **My Land which I have given them**; *and this house, which I have sanctified for My Name, will I cast out of My sight, and will make it to be a proverb and a byword among all nations.*

2 Chronicles 20:7

Are You not our God, who did drive out the inhabitants of **this Land** *before Your people Israel, and* **gave it to the seed of Abraham Your friend forever**?

2 Chronicles 33:8

And I will not again remove the foot of Israel **from the Land which I have appointed for your fathers**, *if only they will observe to do all that I have commanded them according to all the law, the statutes, and the ordinances given through Moses* (New American Standard Bible).

Nehemiah 9:8, 15, 23, 36

⁸ And found his heart faithful before You, and **made a covenant with him to give the Land of the Canaanites, the Hittites, and Amorites, and the Perizzites, and the Jebusites, and the Girgashites, to give it to his seed**, *and has performed your words; for you are righteous.*

¹⁵ And gave them bread from heaven for their hunger, and brought forth water for them out of the rock for their thirst, and promised them that they should go **in to possess the Land which You had sworn to give them.**

²³ Their children You also multiplied as the stars of heaven, **and brought them into the Land**, *concerning which You had* **promised to their fathers**, *that they* **should go in to possess it.**

³⁶ Behold, we are servants this day, and **for the Land that You gave unto our fathers** *to eat the fruit thereof and the good thereof, behold, we are servants in it.*

Psalms 72:8-11

⁸ He shall have **dominion also from sea to sea**, *and* **from the river unto the ends of the earth**. *⁹ They that dwell in the wilderness shall bow before Him; and His enemies shall lick the dust. ¹⁰The kings of*

Tarshish and of the isles shall bring presents: the kings of Sheba and Seba shall offer gifts. ¹¹ *Yea,* **all kings shall fall down before Him: all nations shall serve Him.**

Psalms 105:6-11

⁶ *O you seed of Abraham His servant, you children of Jacob His chosen.* ⁷ *He is the LORD our God: His judgments are in all the earth.* ⁸ *He has* **remembered His covenant** *forever, the word which He commanded to a thousand generations.* ⁹ *Which* **covenant He made with Abraham,** *and* **His oath unto Isaac;** ¹⁰ *And* **confirmed the same unto Jacob for a law,** *and* **to Israel for an everlasting covenant.** ¹¹ *Saying,* **Unto you will I give the Land of Canaan,** *the lot of your inheritance:*

Appendix Four
A Failure of the Reformation

> The following article entitled "A Failure of the Reformation" written by Dr. Any Woods was taken from the November/December 2017 issue of *Lamplighter Magazine*, and the text is reprinted here in its entirety by permission.

When the story of the Protestant Reformation is told, the subject must be approached with candor and intellectual honesty. The great contributions of the Protestant Reformers to the Christian faith notwithstanding, the Protestant Reformation really represented a mixed bag. As much as the Reformers are idolized today, their revolution can only be described as partial, at best.

One of the greatest contributions of the Protestant Reformation to Christianity involves the restoration of a lost method of biblical interpretation. While the Protestant Reformers selectively applied this method to some of the Bible, the complete revolution would have to await subsequent generations, who took the Reformers' method of interpretation and applied it to the totality of God's Word. The purpose of this article is to tell this other side of the story.

Scriptural Interpretation in the Early Church

Concerning Old Testament prophecy, even a casual perusal of the New Testament demonstrates that its biblical characters and writers interpreted these prophecies in a literal sense (Matthew 1:18–25; 21:12–13; John 12:12–15; Romans 11:25–27, etc.). Thus, it is not surprising to discover that Christianity's second generation after the apostolic age also followed a literal approach when interpreting Bible prophecy.

In fact, what rose to prominence in early church history was the school at Syrian Antioch, which interpreted prophetic subjects in a literal manner. Accordingly, they taught that the kingdom of God would not materialize upon the earth until the King, Jesus Christ, first returns physically.

While this perspective is called Premillennialism today, it was known as *Chiliasm* then. This word, *Chiliasm*, comes from the Greek word, *chilia*, meaning "thousand" and is taken from the thousand year duration of Christ's kingdom (usually referred to as the Millennium) which is referred to six times in Revelation 20:1–10.

The school at Antioch exercised such great influence over early Christianity, that virtually all of its most influential leaders were noted *Chiliasts*. In fact, in that day, one's embracement of *Chiliasm* was viewed as a test to determine one's orthodoxy.

Note the words of respected Church Father Justin Martyr (A.D. 100–160) in his *Dialogue with Trypho*: "But I and every other completely orthodox Christian feel certain that there will be a resurrection of the flesh, followed by a thousand years in the rebuilt, embellished and enlarged city of Jerusalem as was announced by the Prophets Ezekiel, Isaiah, and the others."

With such a well-entrenched belief within earliest Christianity concerning a literal interpretation of prophecy and a yet future earthly kingdom of Christ, when did the Christian world begin to shift on this vital issue of interpretation?

The Triumph of Spiritualization

The dominance of the Antioch school was soon eclipsed by the influence of a competing school located in North Africa in the city of Alexandria, Egypt.

The Alexandrian school introduced allegorization as a method for interpreting Scripture, especially Bible prophecy. Allegorization (or spiritualization) involves using the literal meaning of the biblical text only as a vehicle for introducing a higher spiritual meaning, which is only clear to the one doing the allegorizing.

For example, Philo (25 B.C.–A.D. 50), an influential allegorizer, who lived during the time of Christ, saw the four rivers depicted in Genesis 2:10–14 (the Pishon, Gihon, Euphrates and Tigris) as not just four literal rivers in the Garden of Eden but also representing four parts of the human soul!

What caused the Christian Church to progressively reject the traditional, literal approach as espoused by Antioch and instead embrace the allegorical method as outlined by Alexandria? At the risk of oversimplification, there were likely a multiplicity of factors involved.

First, the allegorical approach met the need for immediate relevance and application in Christian preaching and teaching. When the text is allegorized, it can be used to meet virtually any emotional, spiritual or psychological need in the listener or reader.

Second, the allegorical method became increasingly more tenable as Bible interpreters became susceptible to merging human philosophy into the process of biblical interpretation.

Third, a related influence was that Alexandria, Egypt, was a hotbed for Gnostic dualism, which taught that while the spiritual world was inherently good, the physical world was evil. And since they believed that the physical world is inherently evil, Gnostic philosophers reasoned that the various biblical prophecies relating to a physical kingdom on earth were obviously not meant to be taken literally and that they therefore must be spiritualized.

A fourth factor leading the Church to embrace the allegorical method of interpretation was the decline in Jewish believers within the Church's ranks. By the time Paul wrote his epistle to the Romans, the Gentile Christians were in such numerical ascendancy over their Jewish counterparts that Paul had to instruct these Gentile believers not to be arrogant on account of Israel's apparent spiritual hardening (Romans 11:13,17–21).

Given the Jewish familiarity with not only the content but also with a proper understanding of [the] Hebrew Bible, or the Old Testament, it is doubtful that the Church would have ever embraced the allegorical method of interpretation espoused by the Alexandrian school had the Jews retained their majority status within the Church. However, the Gentile Christians, coming out of pagan backgrounds, were not so similarly educated. Thus, they were vulnerable to the suggestion that the Old Testament could be spiritualized, allegorized and consequently marginalized.

Fifth, Constantine's *Edict of Milan* (A.D. 313), which granted religious toleration to Christianity within the Roman Empire, also played a significant role in the Church's embracement of the allegorical method of interpretation. With the stroke of a pen, Christianity went from a persecuted status within Rome to a protected and even elevated status.

Such an abrupt transition from persecution to tolerance and even elevation convinced many within the Church that the kingdom of God had now come. This newfound belief caused them to allegorize many of the terrestrial kingdom promises related to national Israel into present spiritual kingdom realities.

This convergence of factors led to the ascendancy of the Alexandrian method of interpretation within Christendom.

Prominent Allegorizers

Several prominent allegorical interpreters arose out of the Alexandrian school. One such interpreter was Origen (A.D. 185– 254). But the most influential allegorizer was Augustine (A.D. 354–430). His book, *The City of God*, was the first major written systematization and exposition of Amillennialism in church history, and it is perhaps also the most influential book in church history. This work, more than any other, cast an allegorical spell over the Church which, as will be explained later, took Christendom well over a millennium to crawl out from under.

The City of God wildly allegorized the biblical passages dealing with the future earthly reign of Christ. For example, the *"first resurrection"* (Revelation 20:4–6) was reinterpreted to refer to spiritual regeneration rather than a future, physical, bodily resurrection. He also taught that the binding of Satan merely "means his being more unable to seduce the Church." Concerning the future thousand year reign of Christ along with His saints (Revelation 20:4), Augustine asserted that "the Church even now is the kingdom of Christ, and the kingdom of heaven. Accordingly, even now His saints reign with Him."

By 450 A.D. the Alexandrian method of interpretation had become so entrenched that the Church began to view the earlier *Chiliasm* as the product of the less enlightened and less intelligent. In fact, *Chiliasm* itself began to be viewed as a mere fable rather than the product of a careful study of the biblical text.

The Dark Ages

The ascendency of the Alexandrian school plummeted the Church into a time often referred to as the Middle Ages or even "The Dark Ages." During this era, the study of end time prophecy was rendered all but obsolete. This era dominated church history for well over a millennium. It lasted all the way from the 4th to the 16th Century.

During this era, only one church existed within Christendom, which was the Roman Catholic Church. Because of the dominance of the allegorical method of interpretation, only the clergy were deemed as qualified to read and allegorically interpret Scripture. Such a sharp clergy-laity distinction had the net effect of removing the Bible from the common man.

This problem was further compounded by the widespread illiteracy among the population, which made the Bible all the more inaccessible to the masses. To make matters worse, even up to the time of Luther, the Roman Catholic Mass continued to be read and conducted in Latin, although Latin was an unknown language to most people in Luther's time. Thus, although many regularly went to Mass, they were unable to understand what was being communicated.

Such biblical illiteracy made the people vulnerable to spiritual deception and manipulation. The sale of indulgences was common throughout the era. The people did not have access to the Scripture to ascertain if Purgatory was even a biblical concept. Thus, the Church authorities routinely told them that they could purchase deceased relatives out of Purgatory by paying the right monetary sum to the Church. In fact, Johann Tetzel, a friar during the time of Martin Luther, infamously quipped, "When the coin in the coffer rings, the soul from Purgatory springs."

The practice of the sale of indulgences was condoned by both the Church, as well as the existing political authorities, since they served as a convenient source of fund raising necessary to subsidize the Church's various building projects, such as the refurbishment of Saint Peter's Basilica in Rome.

In addition, due to the inaccessibility to the Scripture, God's future promises to the Jewish people were not available to serve as a natural defense or bulwark against the anti–Semitism of the day. Thus, rampant hatred of the Jews continued unabated and unchallenged. Due to these pitiful conditions, the Church was in dire need of theological rescue.

The Return to Literal Interpretation

The Protestant Reformation became the tool that God used to redirect the Church back to the solid foundation of His eternal Word. The Protestant Reformers rescued the Church from the Alexandrian allegorical method of interpretation through an application of a literal method of interpretation to selective areas of Scripture.

For example, William Tyndale (A.D. 1494–1536) asserted, "The Scripture hath but one sense, which is the literal sense." Luther also wrote that the Scriptures "are to be retained in their simplest meaning ever possible, and to be understood in their grammatical and literal sense unless the context plainly forbids." Calvin wrote in the preface of his commentary on Romans, "It is the first business of an interpreter to let the author say what he does say, instead of attributing to him what we think he ought to say."

Because of their adherence to literal interpretation, both Calvin and Luther condemned the allegorical method of interpretation. Luther denounced the allegorical approach to Scripture in strong words. He said: "Allegories are empty speculations and as it were the scum of Holy Scripture." "Origen's allegories are not worth so much dirt." "To allegorize is to juggle the Scripture." "Allegorizing may degenerate into a mere monkey game." "Allegories are awkward, absurd, inventive, obsolete, loose rags."

Calvin similarly rejected allegorical interpretations. He called them "frivolous games" and accused Origen and other allegorists of "torturing Scripture, in every possible sense, from the true sense."

The Reformers also did not want to see the biblical ignorance of the common man exploited for financial purposes, as had been the case with the sale of indulgences. Consequently, the Reformers laid stress on the idea that the people no longer had to go through an intermediary, such as a priest in order to receive and understand God's Word. They need not do so since they were already priests themselves (Revelation 1:6).

This notion, often called "the priesthood of all believers" also meant that the Scripture had to be both accessible and understandable to the clergy and laity alike. This new theological emphasis explains why prominent Reformers, like Tyndale and Luther, set out to translate the Scriptures into languages beyond simply Latin (as Jerome had accomplished in the 4th Century with his Latin Vulgate) and into the languages of the common man of their own day.

The privilege inherent in "the priesthood of all believers" theological construct also meant that literacy was necessary so that the common man could both read and understand the Bible. Thus, the Reformation introduced great advances in public education for the purpose of erasing illiteracy.

The Reformers' Selective Literalness

Although the Reformers were literal in their approach to Protology (the doctrine of Beginnings), Christology (the doctrine of Christ), Soteriology (the doctrine of Salvation), and Bibliology (the doctrine of the Scripture), other doctrines, such as Ecclesiology (the doctrine of the Church) and Eschatology (the doctrine of the End) were treated in an entirely different [manner]. Despite their emphasis upon literally interpreting some aspects of Scripture, Luther and Calvin did not go far enough in applying a literal interpretation to all areas of divine truth.

In fact, Calvin seems to have ignored much of God's prophetic Word. Despite having written commentaries on almost every book of the New Testament, Calvin failed to write a commentary on the Book of Revelation. When Calvin did pay attention to prophetic texts, he seemed preoccupied with employing the Alexandrian and Augustinian method of interpretation, and he held in contempt those who rejected his allegorical approach.

The Reformers' retention of the allegorical method of interpretation in the area of biblical Eschatology is also evident in the way they took the prophecies aimed at a future Babylon and the Antichrist and redirected them so as to make it seem as if these prophecies were instead speaking of the Roman Catholic Church. Such an interpretation was advanced at the expense of the literal sense of these passages.

Because the Reformers spiritualized prophecy, they rejected Premillennialism as being "Jewish opinions." They maintained the Amillennial view which the Roman Catholic Church had adopted from Augustine.

The Reformers Selective Reforms

Despite the Reformers' doctrinal progress in select areas, it is simply a matter of historical naïveté to assume that they made a clean break with Roman Catholicism back in the 16th Century. On the contrary, as Roman Catholics themselves who had even initially sought to remain within the Catholic Church, they dragged many vestiges of Roman Catholicism with them into their infant and newly developing Reformed Theology.

In addition to the retention of Augustinian Amillennialism, there were other Roman Catholic holdovers as well. One was the practice of infant baptism. Luther considered infant baptism a sacrament and therefore a means of grace. Still another holdover related to the doctrine of Consubstantiation, which appears to be only a slight modification of the doctrine of Transubstantiation.

Yet another carryover related to the Roman Catholic Church's view that it was the sole representative of the kingdom of God upon the earth. This Romanist failure to distinguish between the Church and God's earthly kingdom program for Israel carried over into Calvin's Geneva [his headquarters in Switzerland, a center for Reform Theology]. There, Calvin sought to reconstruct a society through the imposition of the Mosaic Law. This social experiment resulted in dire societal consequences.

Finally, it must be pointed out that some of the vitriolic anti-Semitism of the Middle Ages also found its way into the Reformation movement. After all, it was the respected and revered church reformer Martin Luther who, late in his life and frustrated at the Jews' unwillingness to receive Christ on the basis of faith alone, wrote a scathing tract against the Jewish people entitled, *On the Jews and Their Lies*. This tract contains numerous anti-Semitic rants.

Although some claim that Luther's level of anti-Semitic vitriol is not found in the work of John Calvin, such a claim is without merit. For example, note how Calvin's correction of distinguished Jewish scholar Rabbi Barbinel in Calvin's commentary on Daniel 2:44 laid bare the true intentions of the Reformer's heart toward the Jewish people: "But here he [the rabbi] not only betrays his ignorance, but his utter stupidity, since God so blinded the whole people that they were like restive dogs…I have never found common sense in any Jew."

Reasons for the Reformers' Inconsistency

With these aforementioned Catholic hangovers remaining, we might ask why did the Protestant Reformers not also reform the Church in these other areas as well?

Several possibilities can be given. Perhaps they were fatigued. They had already sacrificed greatly, and in some cases ultimately, in order to achieve what they did. To require them to take on any more beyond their monumental achievements would have been unrealistic, to say the least.

Also, these other doctrinal areas involving such things as Bible prophecy were not their focus. Their primary battle with the Roman Catholic hierarchy was over the issue of salvation. Any other theological subject matter was simply outside their narrow purview.

Consistent Literal Interpretation

Dispensationalists should be credited for completing the interpretive revolution begun by the Protestant Reformers. The Reformers deserve credit through the employment of the right methodology, a literal interpretation, to some of the Bible. Yet, as has been demonstrated, Reformed Theology continued to allow much allegorization of the Scripture, especially as it related to Ecclesiology and Eschatology.

Dispensationalism, on the other hand, as it came into its own roughly two centuries after the Reformation, took the Reformation method of interpretation and applied this same method to the totality of Scripture.

When such a consistent application of literalism is followed (taking into account figures of speech when they are textually conspicuous), what rapidly re-merges is Premillennialism, or the very *Chiliasm* initially espoused by the Antioch school of interpretation that dominated the life of the Church for its first two centuries.

Just as the Reformers demonstrated that literalism was the essential prerequisite necessary to restore the five "*solas*" to Christendom, Dispensationalists demonstrated that literalism was also an essential prerequisite necessary to restore to Christendom both Premillennialism and pre-Tribulationalism (the belief that the rapture will occur before the future Tribulation).

What makes Dispensationalism unique as a theological system is not merely its emphasis upon a literal, grammatical, historical method of interpretation. Many theological systems, such as Reformed Theology, selectively incorporate this method. Rather, Dispensationalism remains unique in its insistence in *consistently* applying the literal method of interpretation to the totality of biblical revelation. This approach causes the interpreter to recognize that Israel and the Church are unique.

Literalism's Restoration of Important Doctrines

When it is understood that God has separate programs for Israel and the Church, such theology acts as a natural deterrent against the Church from claiming Israel's earthly promises through the allegorical method of interpretation. Such a belief prevents the Church from seeing itself as the reigning New Israel. And it keeps the Church from misapplying Israel's Law of Moses to itself, as was done in Calvin's Geneva.

The Israel-Church distinction also helps the Church to see that God is not finished with Israel but rather has a special end time plan for her that will play out nationally. Comprehending this future for Israel acts as a restraint necessary to curb Anti-Semitic impulses among the Gentile-dominated Church in the present. The Israel-Church distinction also assists the Church in understanding that she will not be in Israel's Tribulation period. Thus, the Israel-Church distinction furnishes the proper foundation for embracing a Pre-Tribulation rapture.

Although none of these concepts were retrieved by the Protestant Reformers and although none are found in today's Reformed Theology, we still owe the Reformers a debt of gratitude since they introduced the correct literal interpretive methodology.

Giving Thanks

As we celebrate the five-hundred-year anniversary of Martin Luther nailing the ninety-five theses to the cathedral door in Wittenberg, Germany, let us rejoice in the fact that this event was used by God to trigger what is now known as the Protestant Reformation. However, at the same time, let us not idolize the Reformers based upon the faulty assumption that the Reformation instantaneously cured all the ecclesiastical ills introduced by the Alexandrian, Augustinian allegorical method of interpretation of the 4th Century.

The Reformation did introduce doctrinal progress. But perhaps more importantly, it also furnished the seed of literal interpretation that would be used by subsequent generations to restore doctrinal wholeness and health to Christ's Church.

Dr. Andy Woods

Dr. Andy Woods is a native of California, where he attended college and earned a law degree. In 1998 he shifted gears and started making the transition from law to theology when he decided to enter seminary.

He ultimately earned a doctorate degree in biblical exposition from Dallas Theological Seminary. He currently serves as pastor of Sugar Land Bible Church in the Houston area while serving as president of Chafer Theological Seminary in Albuquerque, New Mexico. He is a prolific writer and a much sought after conference speaker.

Appendix Five
Answer Key to Quiz on Pages 4-6

1. True
2. Jewish
3. Hebrew
4. Jewish
5. C – Hebrew
6. Jewish people
7. Passover
8. Feast of First Fruits
9. Pentecost
10. Jewish people
11. Israel
12. Jewish people
13. B
14. Israel – The Jewish people
15. By Faith in the then known will of God.
16. D
17. B, C, D, E
18. A, C
19. By Faith in the known will of God.
20. Yes

www.ingramcontent.com/pod-product-compliance
Lightning Source LLC
Chambersburg PA
CBHW051033160426
43193CB00010B/929